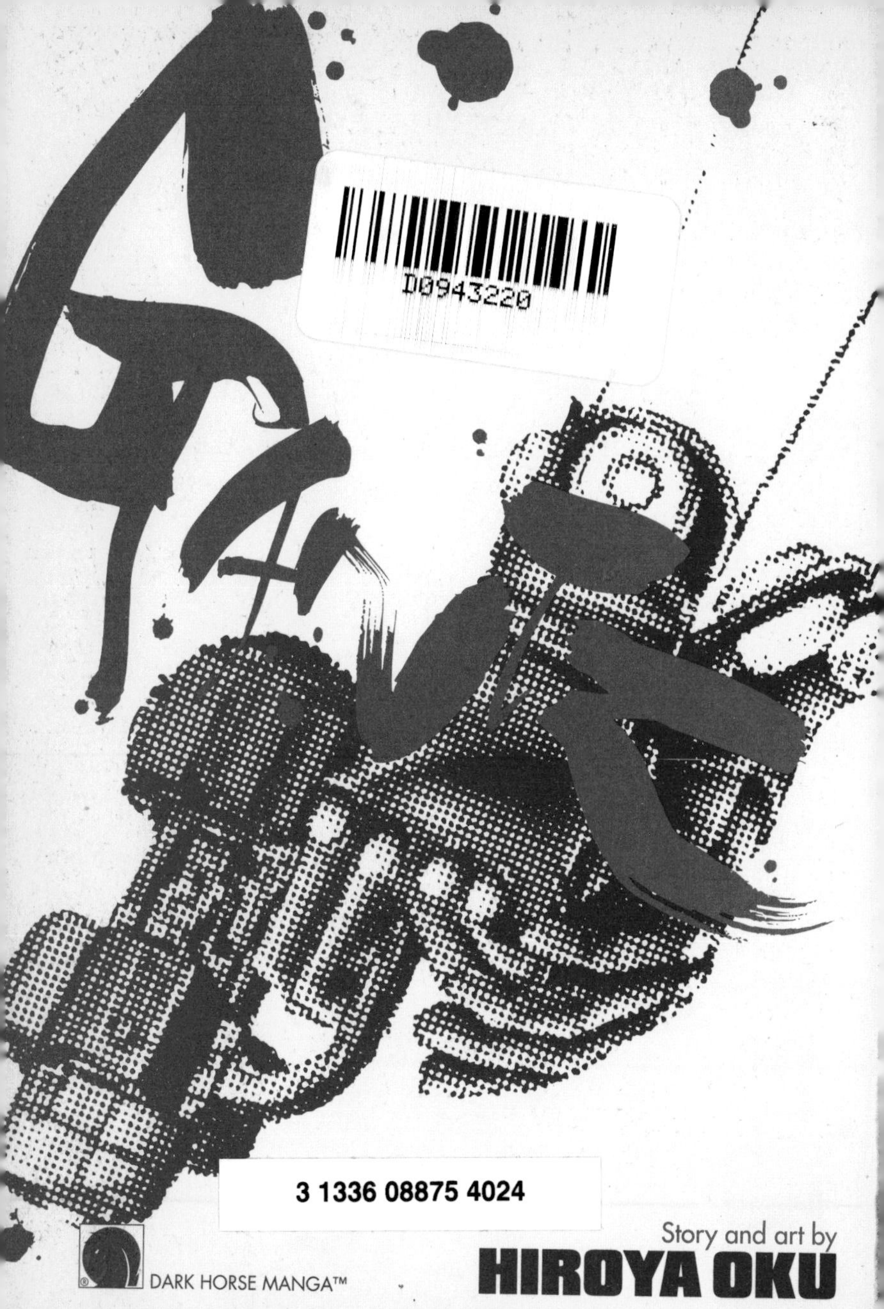

Story and art by

HIROYA OKU

DARK HORSE MANGA™

CONTENTS

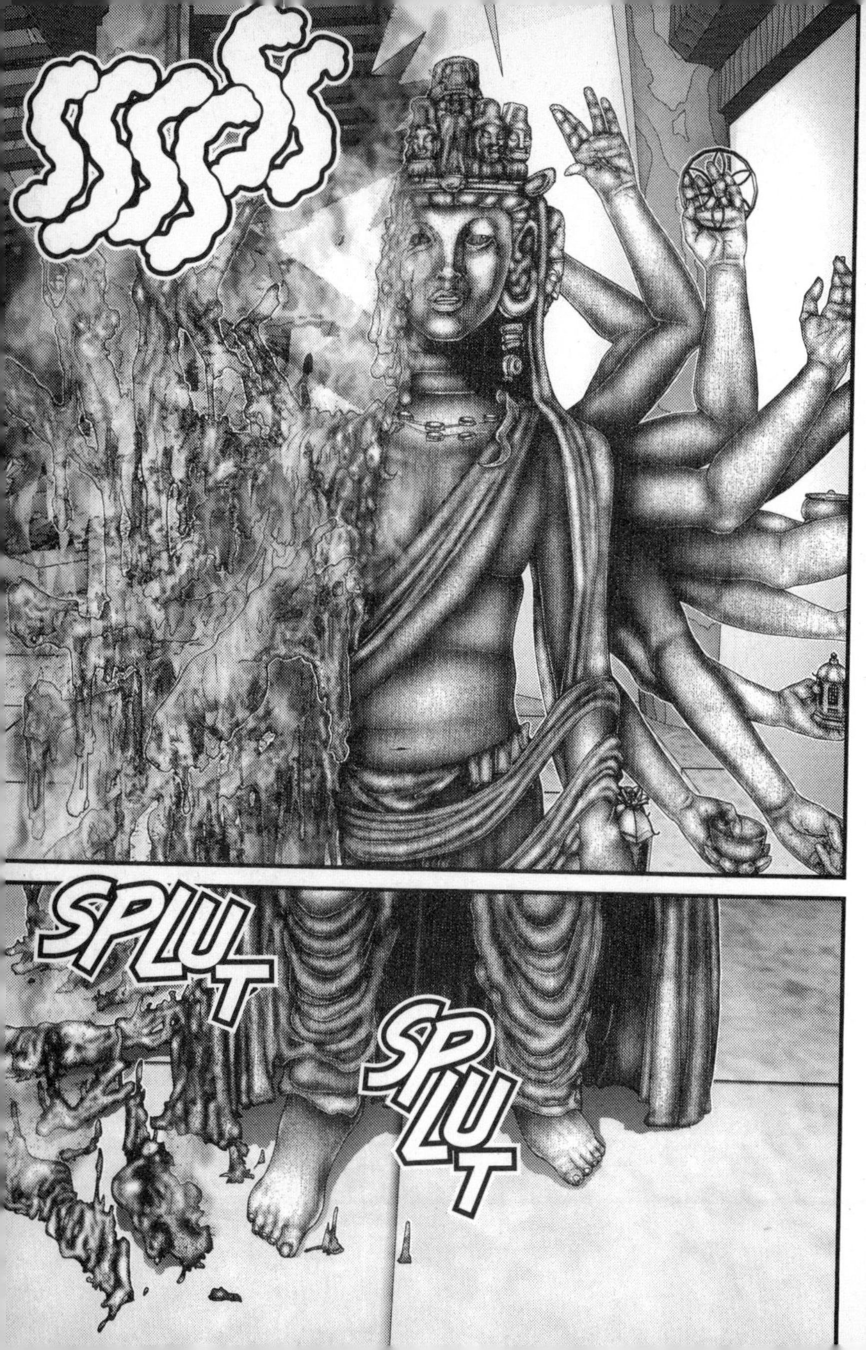
SSSSS
SPLUT
SPLUT

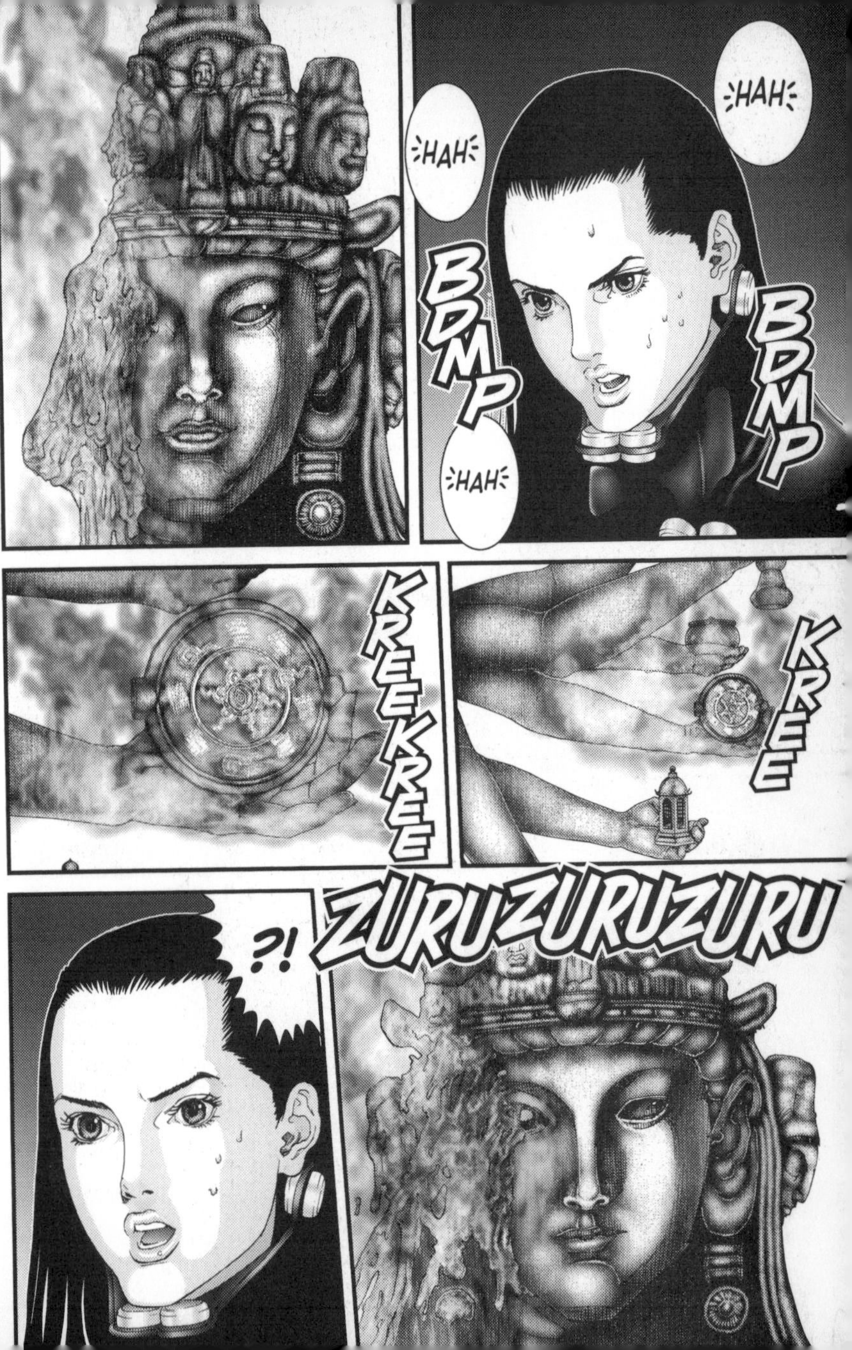
HAH
HAH
BDMP
BDMP
HAH
KREE
KREEKREE
ZURUZURUZURU
?!

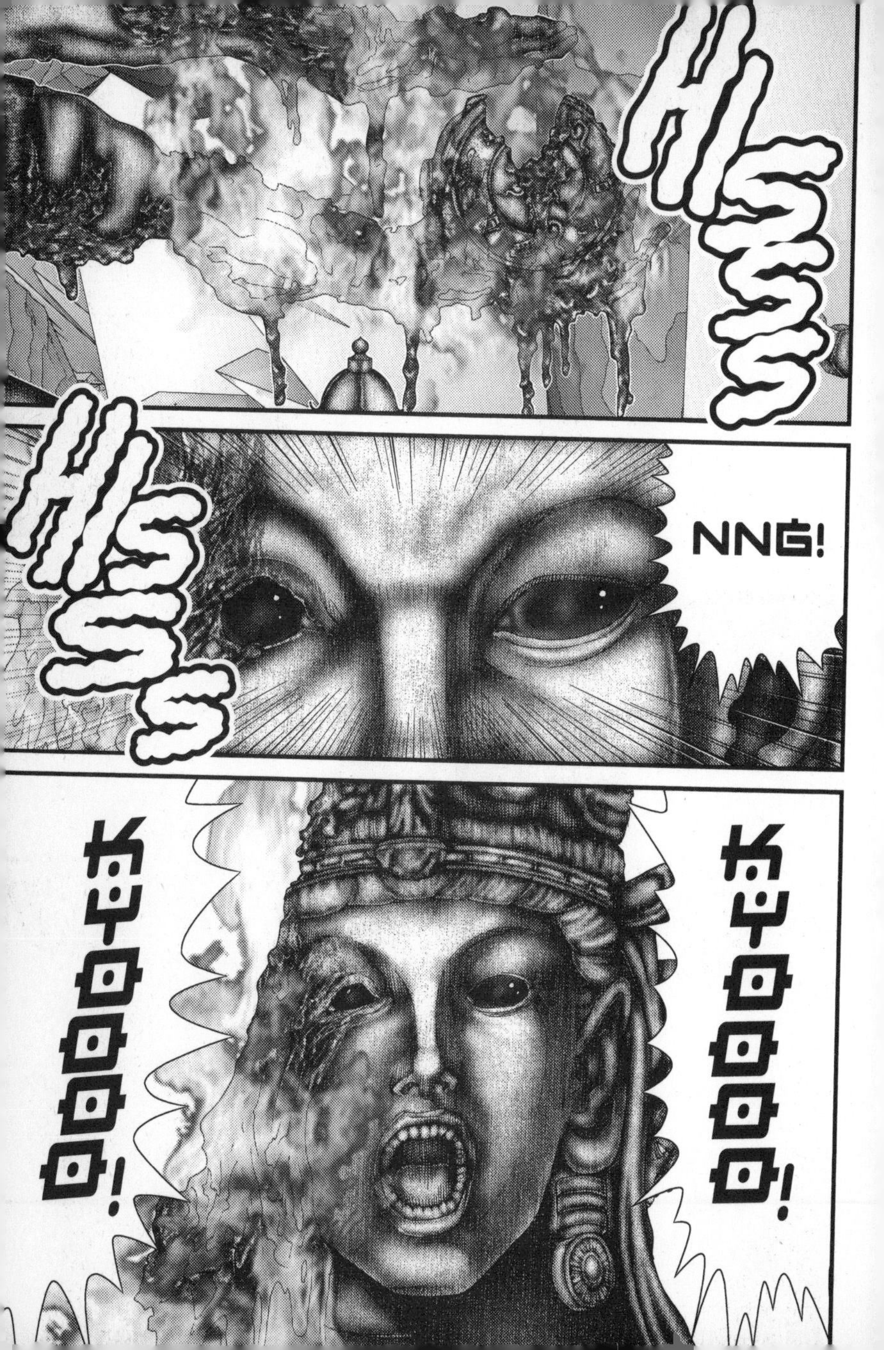
HISSSS
NNG!
HISSSS
KYOOOOOO!
KYOOOOOO!

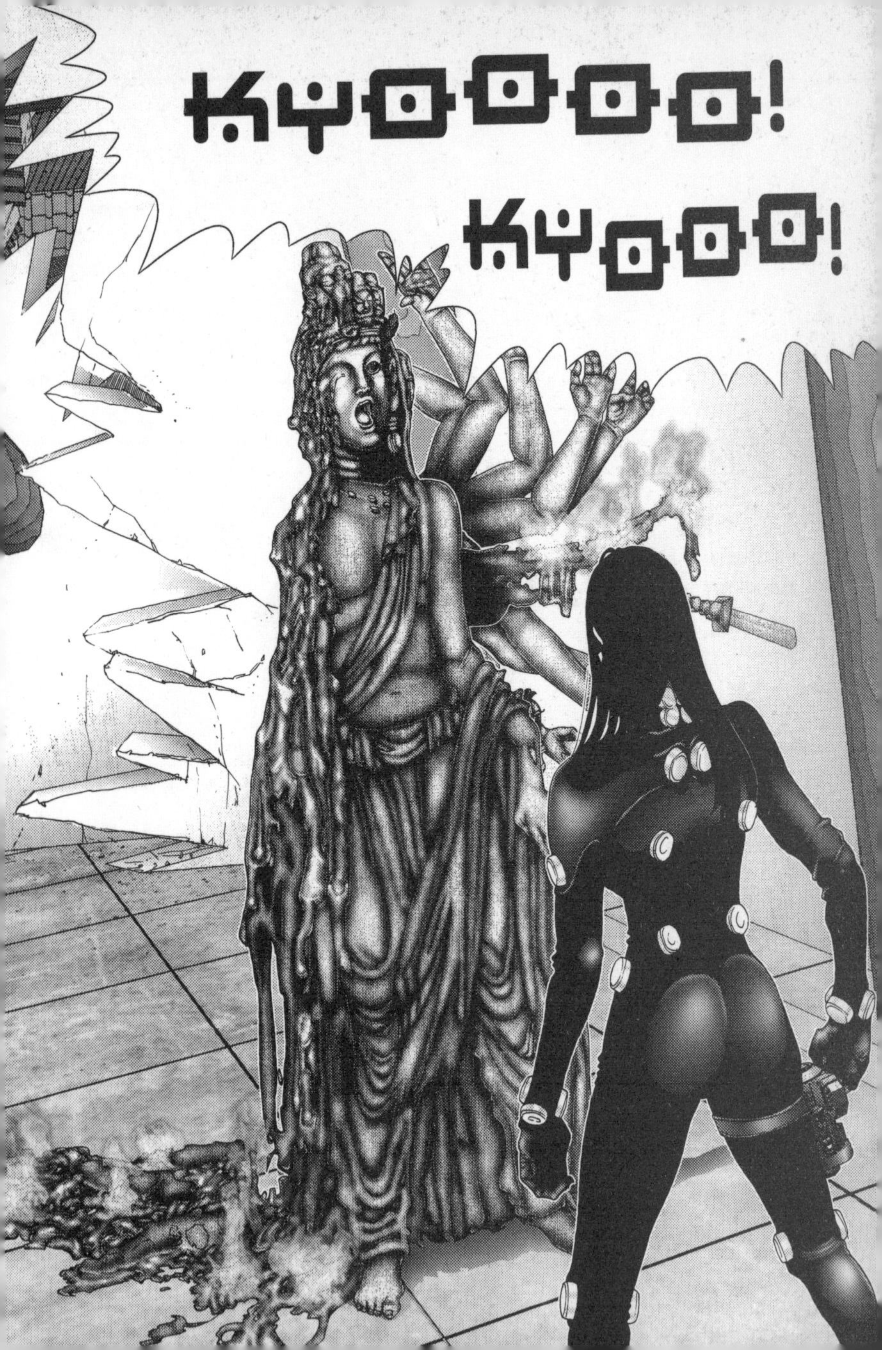
KYOOOOO!
KYOOOO!

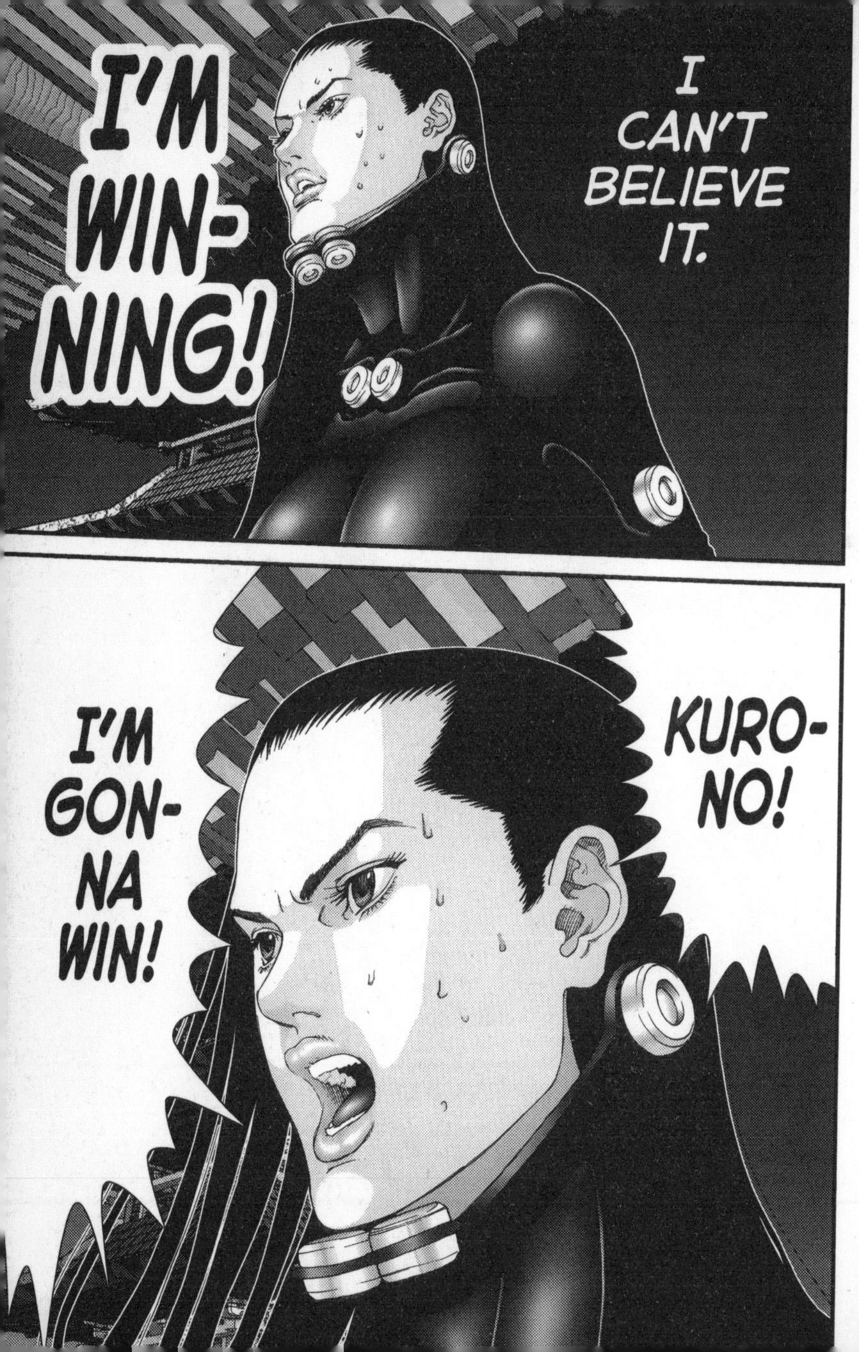
I CAN'T BELIEVE IT.
I'M WIN-NING!
KURO-NO!
I'M GON-NA WIN!

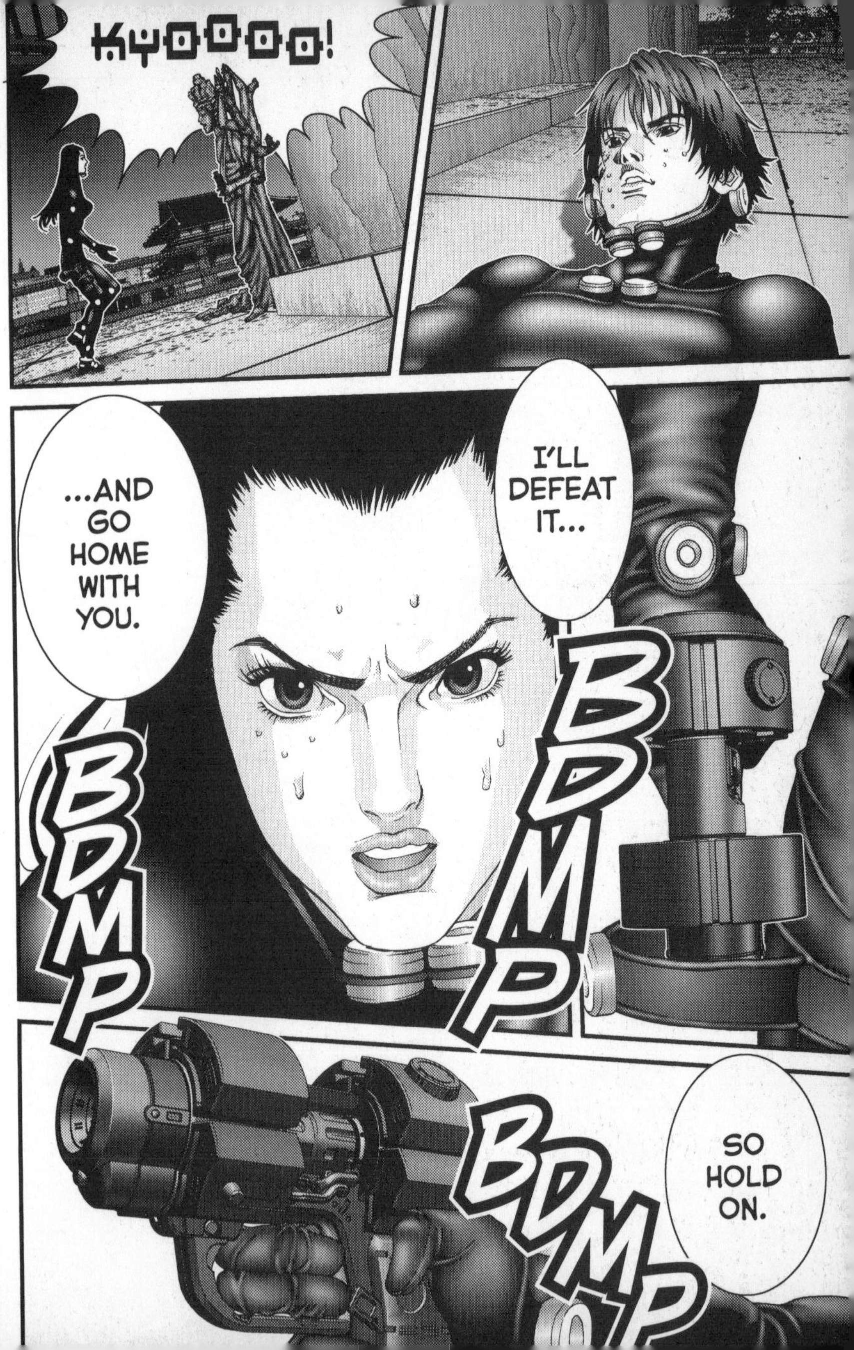
KYOOOOO!
I'LL DEFEAT IT...
...AND GO HOME WITH YOU.
BDMP
BDMP
SO HOLD ON.
BDMP

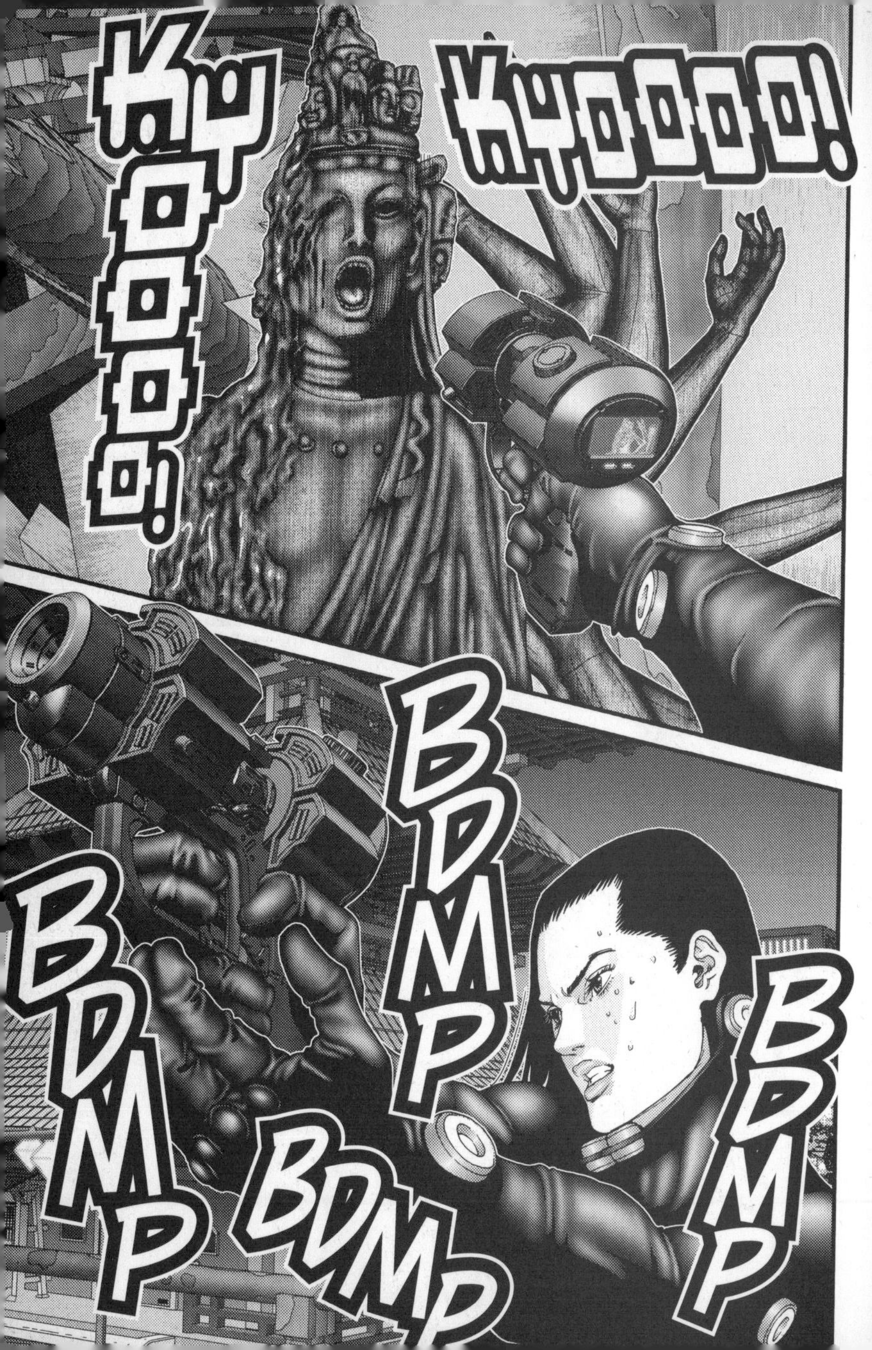
KYOOOOO!
KYOOOOOOO!
BDMP
BDMP
BDMP
BDMP

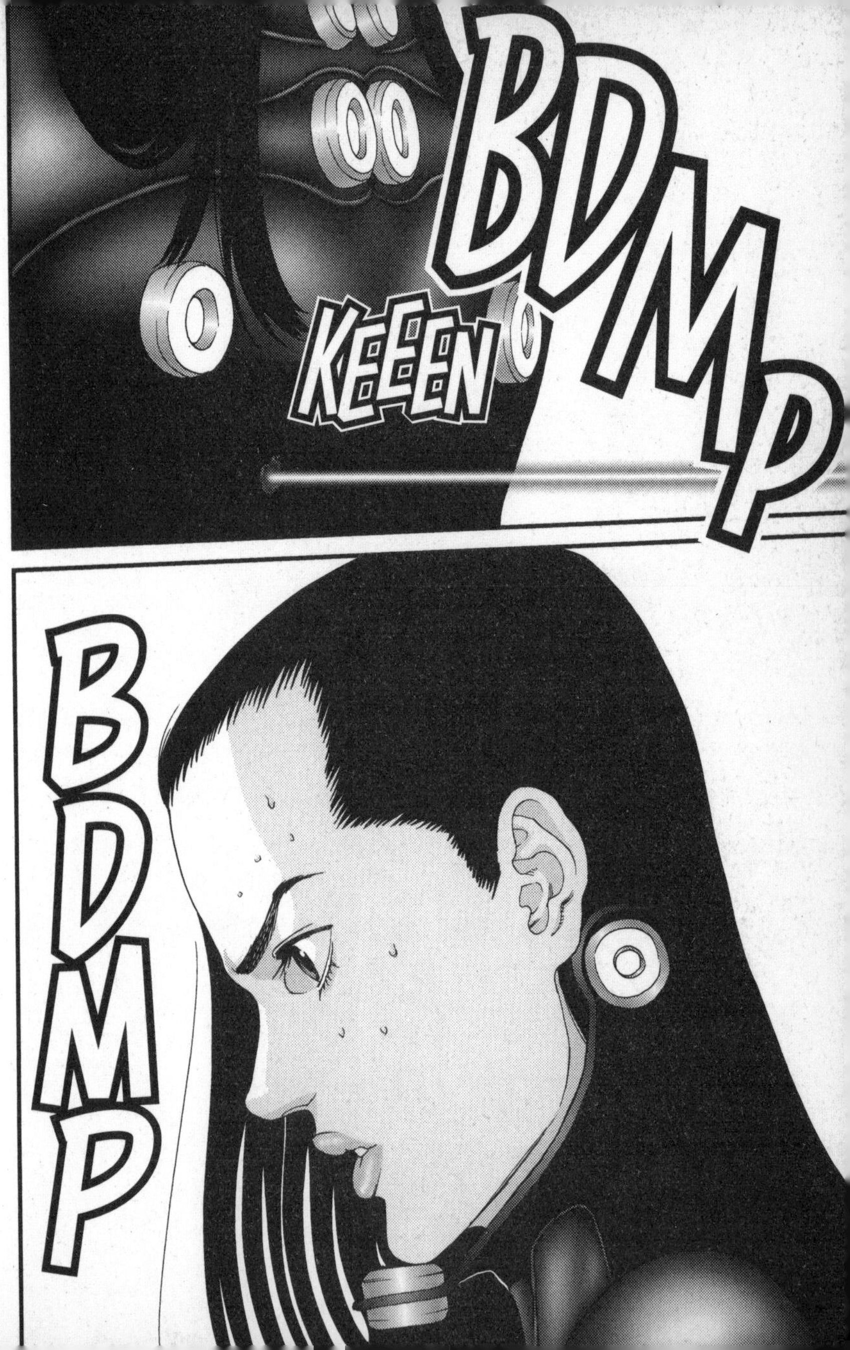

BDMP
KEEEN
BDMP

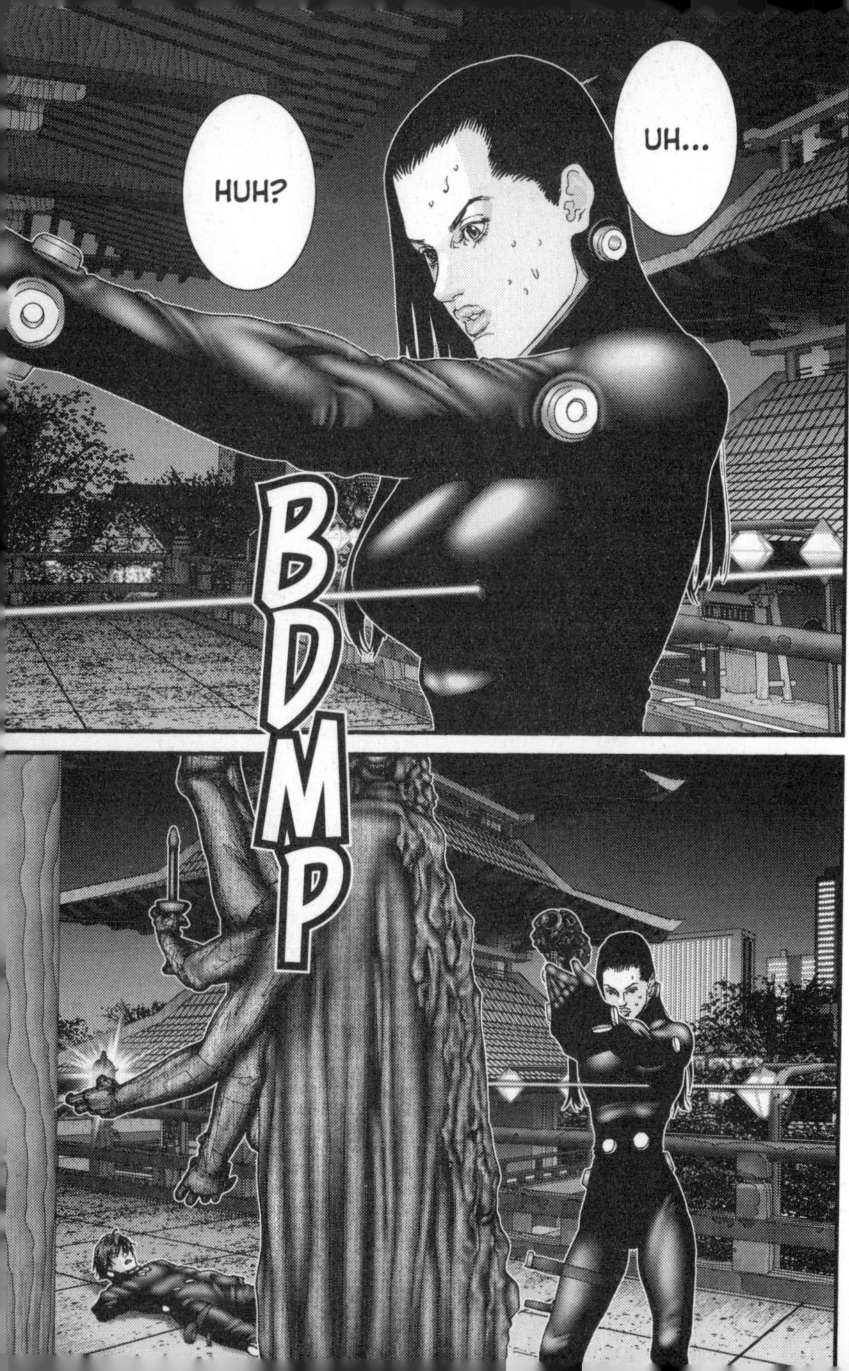

UH...
HUH?
BDMP

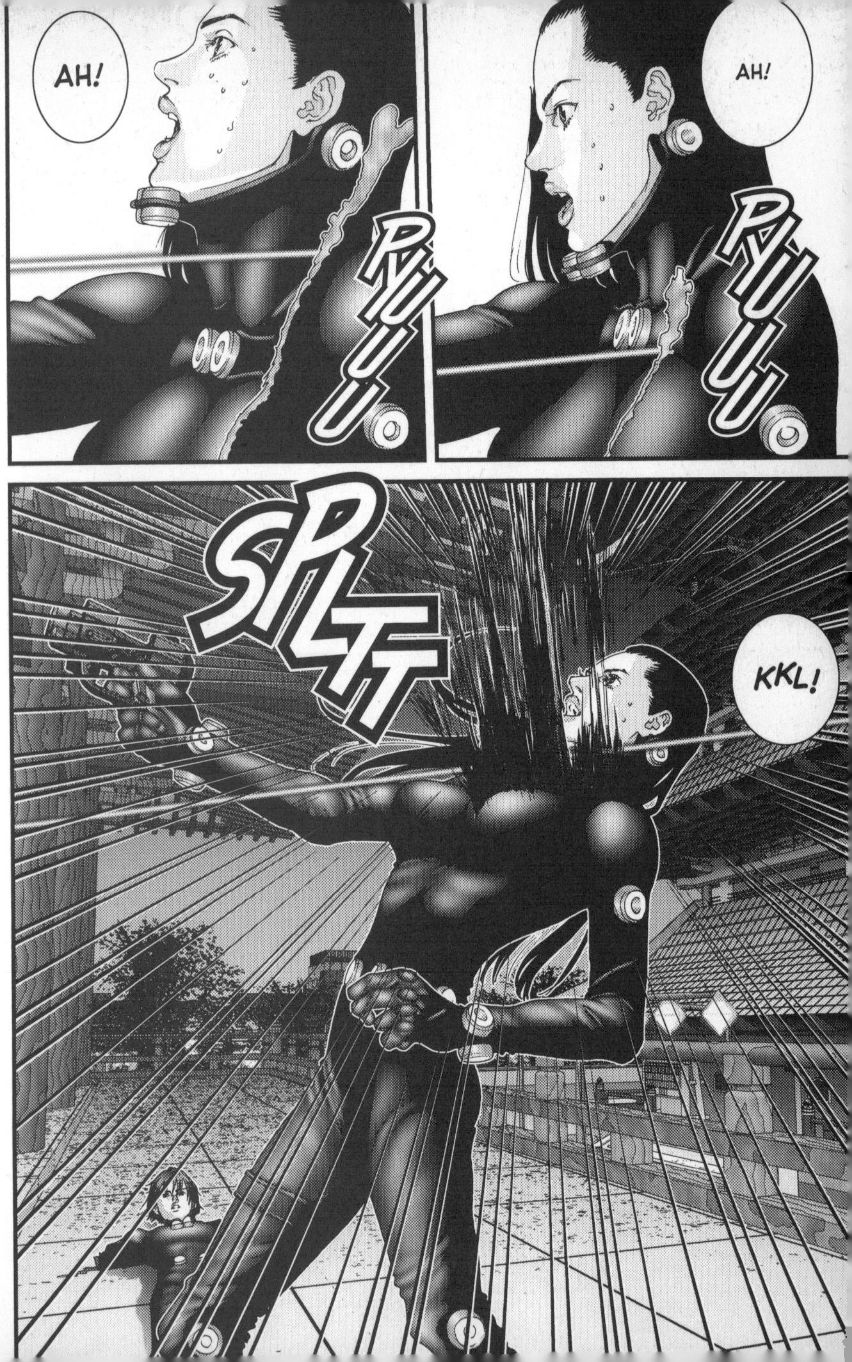
AH!
PYUUUU
AH!
PYUUUU
SPLTT
KKL!

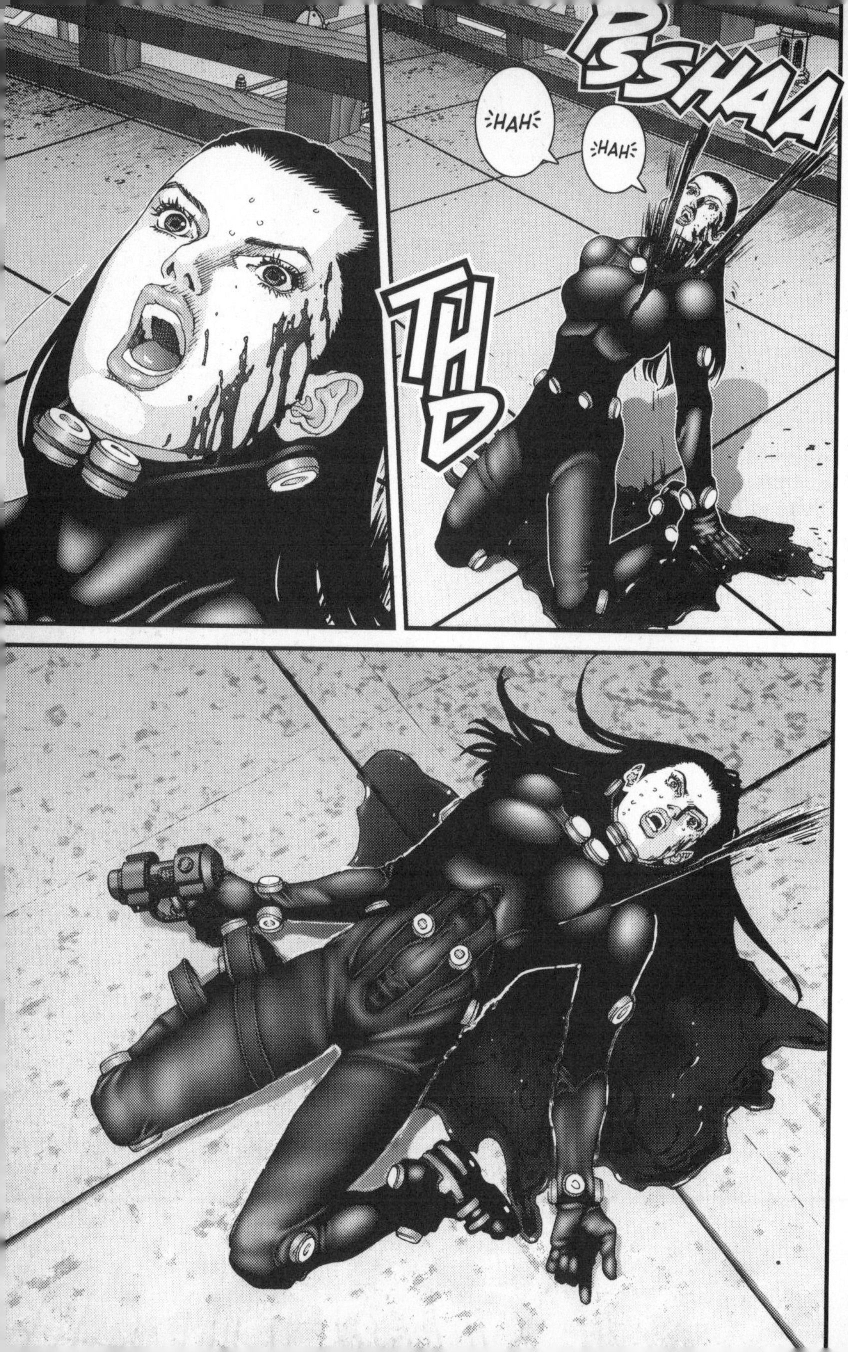
PSSHAA
HAH
HAH
THD

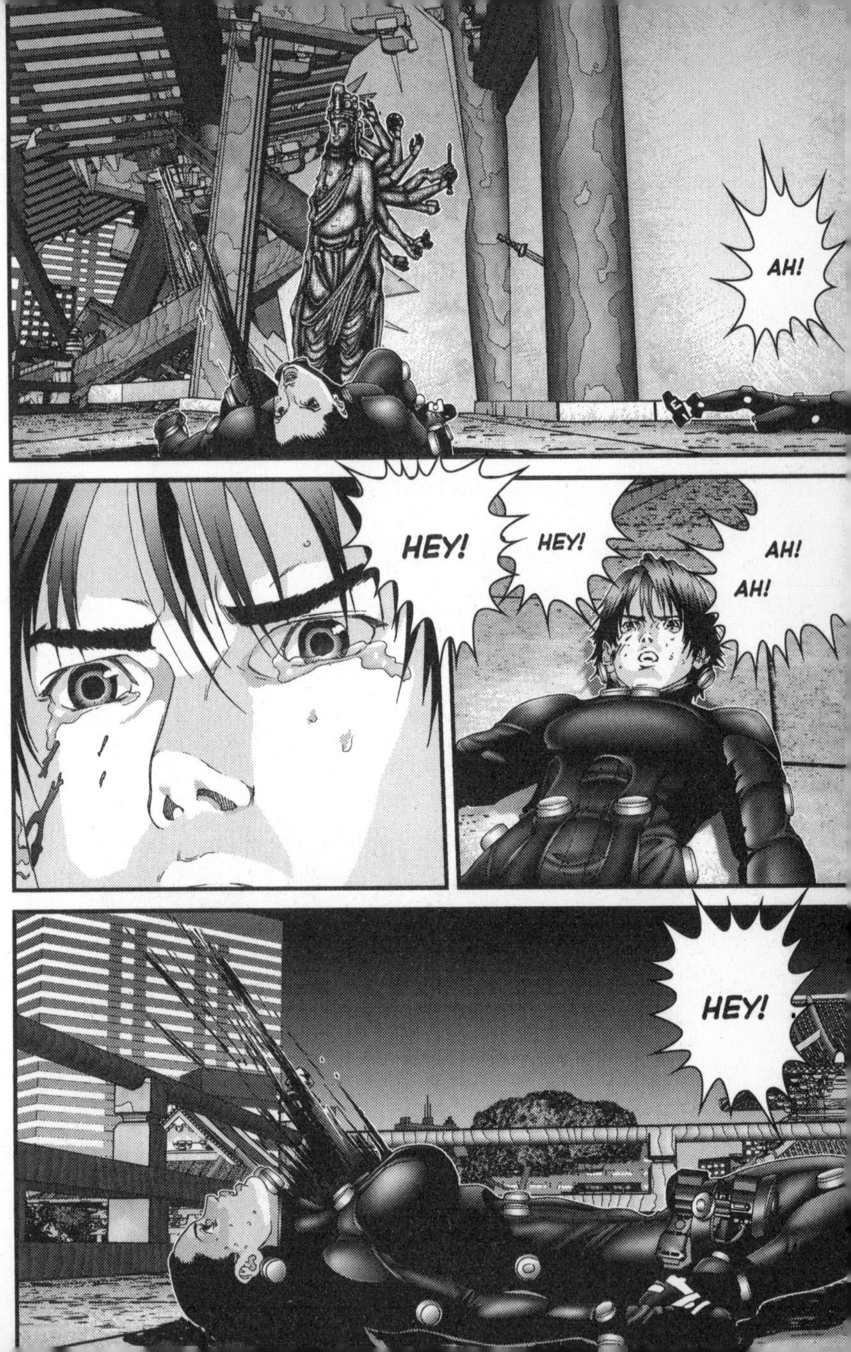
AH!
HEY!
HEY!
AH!
AH!
HEY!

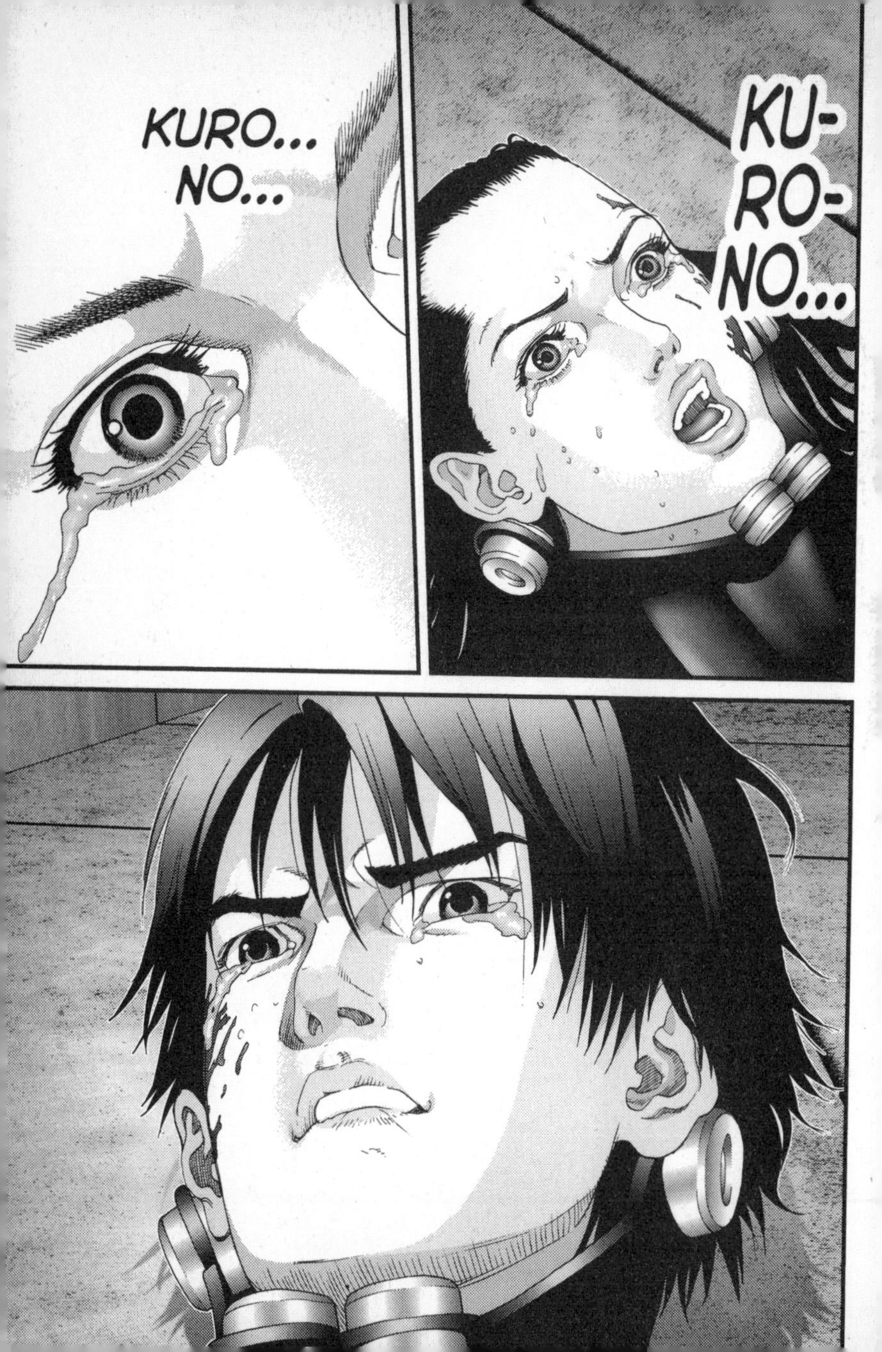
KU-
RO-
NO...
KURO...
NO...

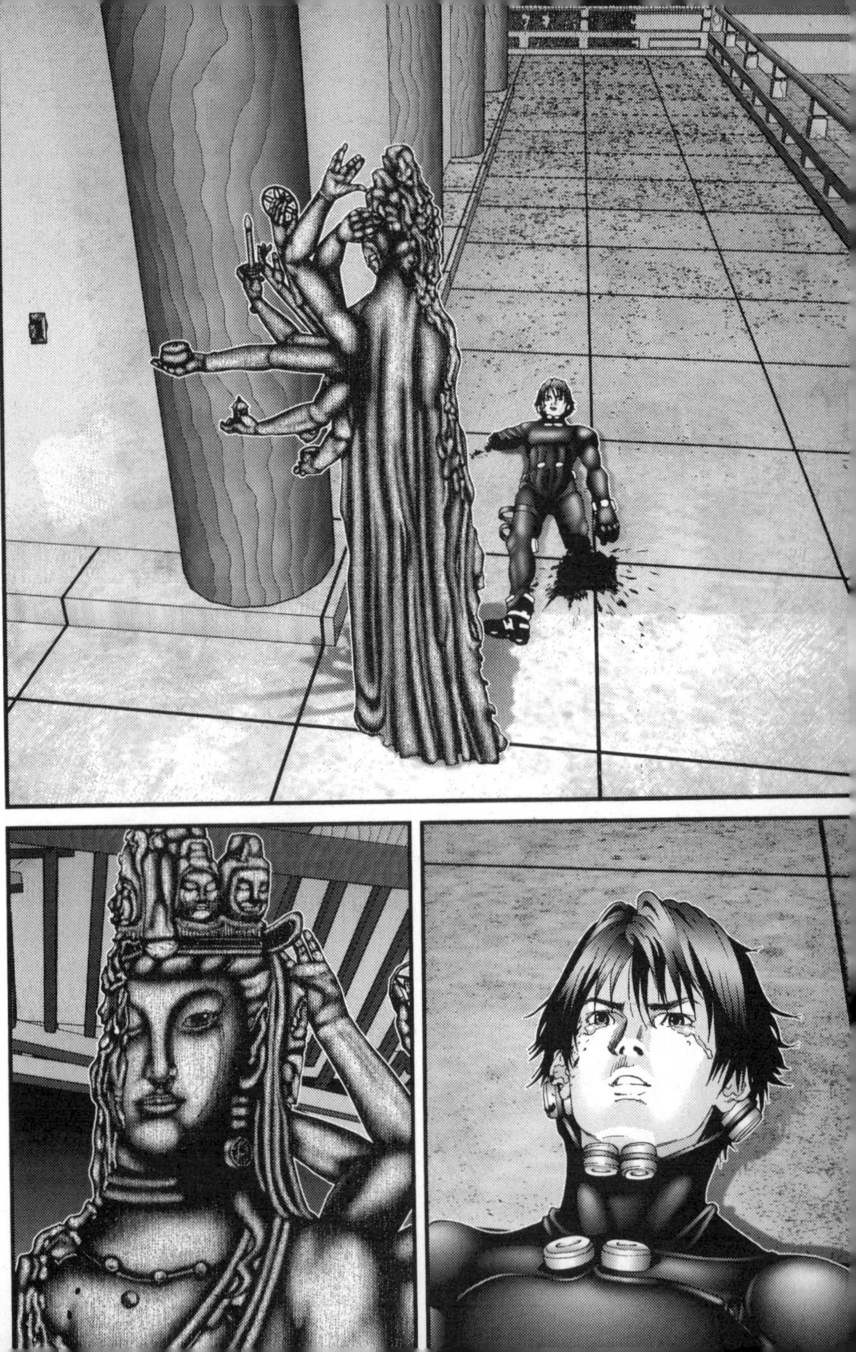

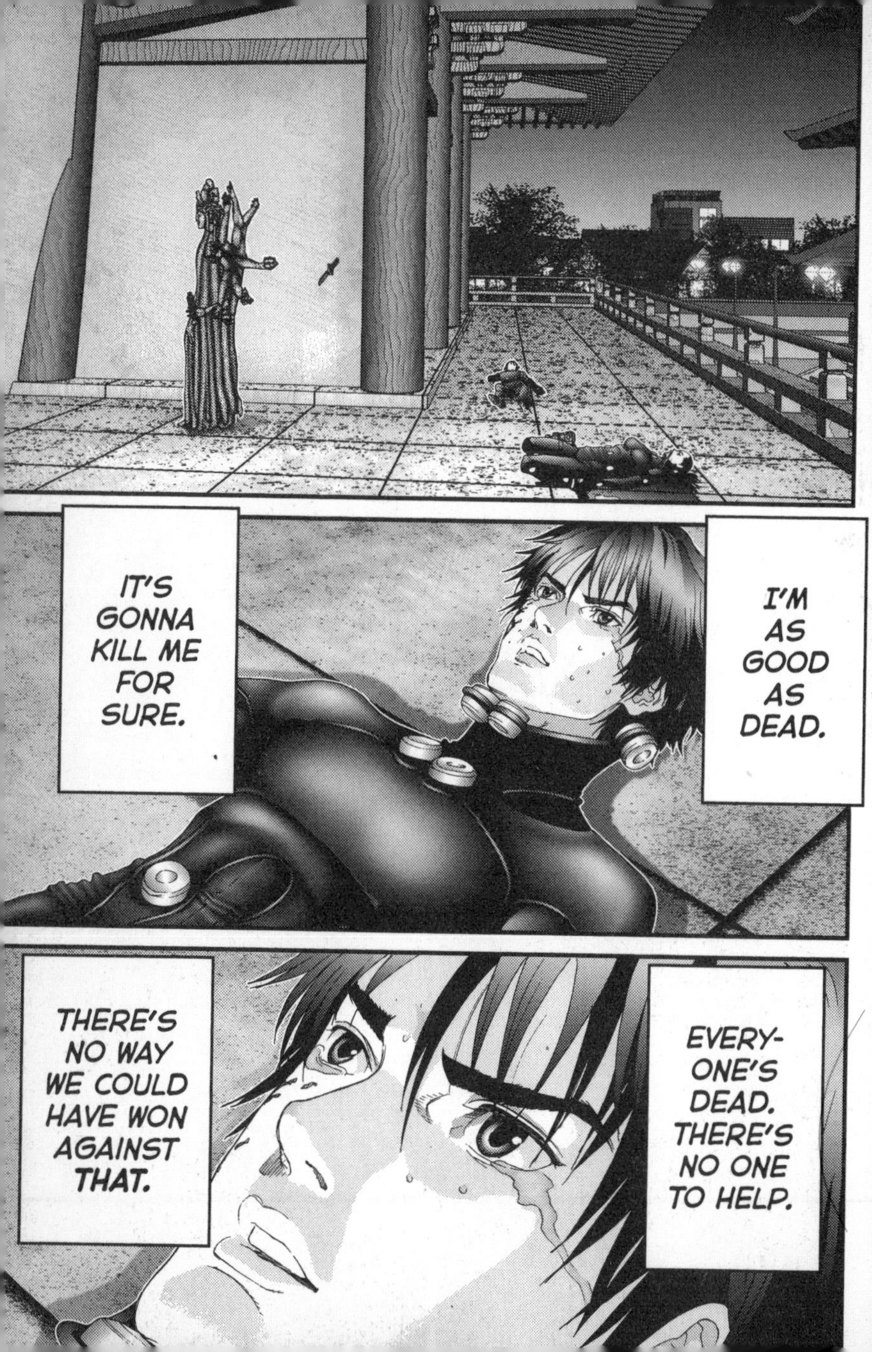
I'M AS GOOD AS DEAD.
IT'S GONNA KILL ME FOR SURE.
EVERY-ONE'S DEAD. THERE'S NO ONE TO HELP.
THERE'S NO WAY WE COULD HAVE WON AGAINST THAT.

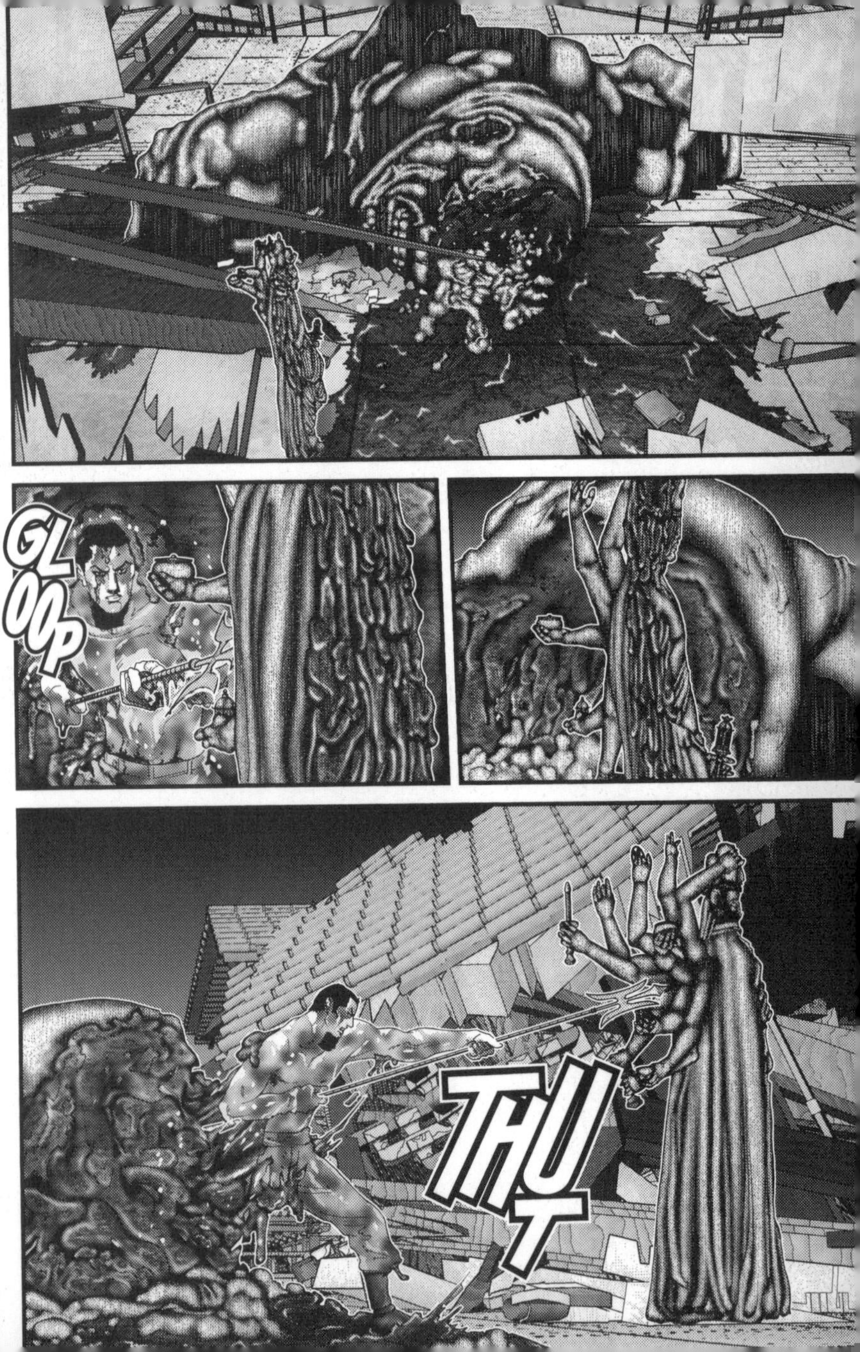
GLOOP
THUT

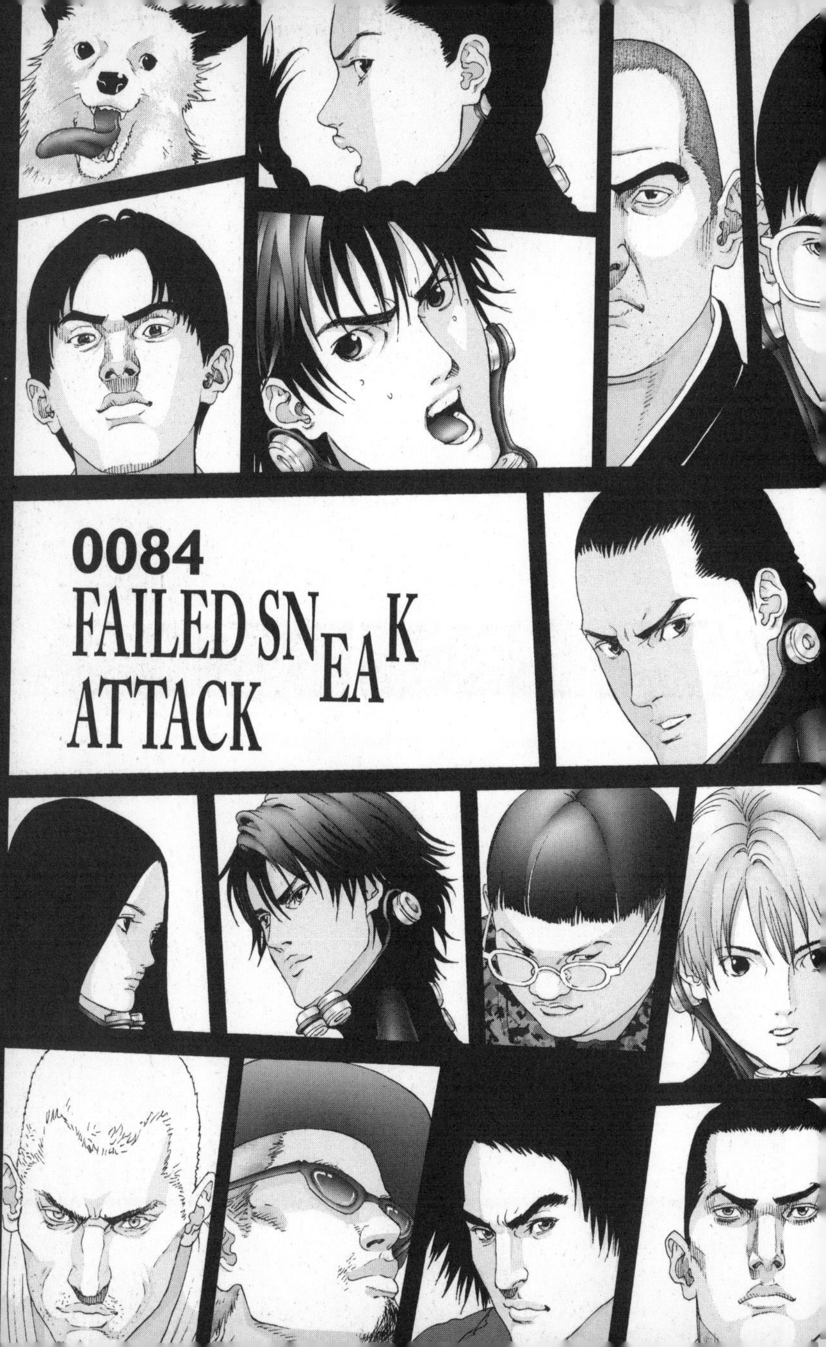
0084
FAILED SNEAK
ATTACK

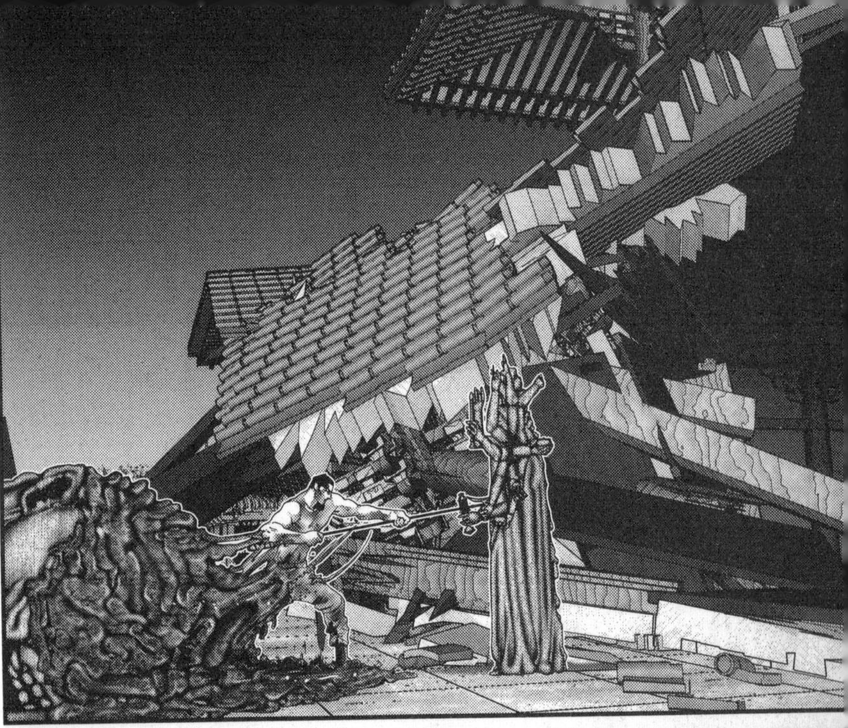
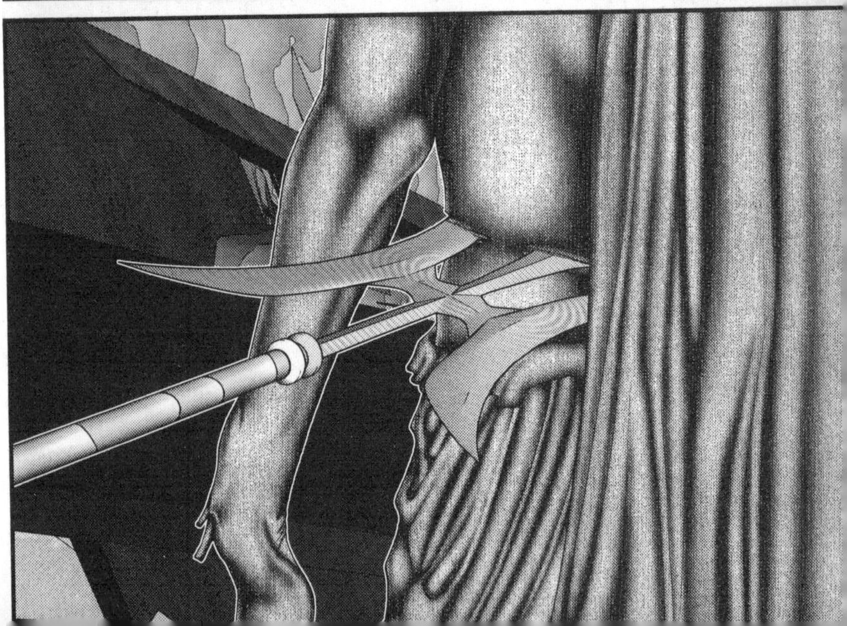

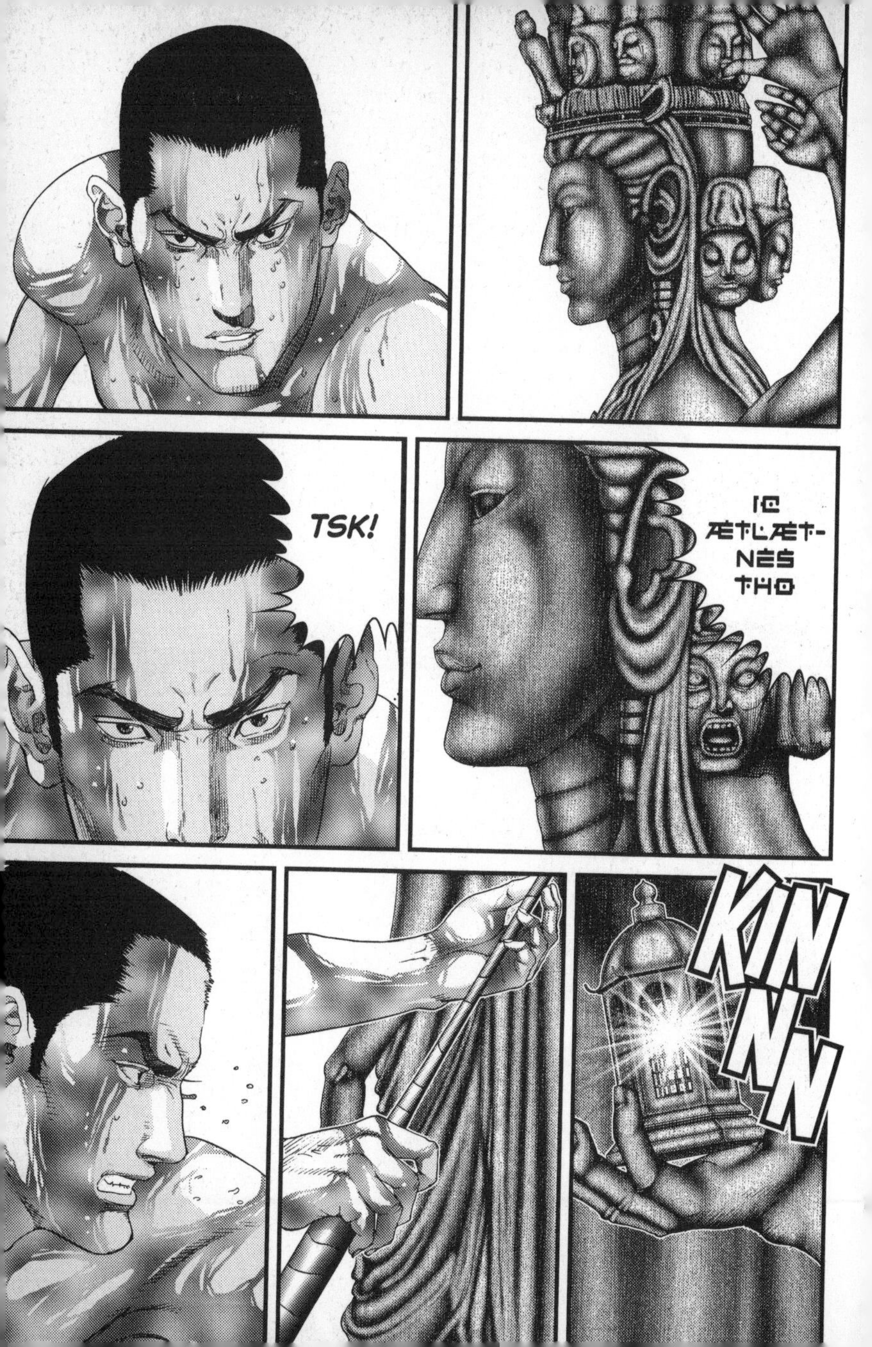
TSK!
IC ÆTLÆT-
NES
THO
KIN
N
N
NN

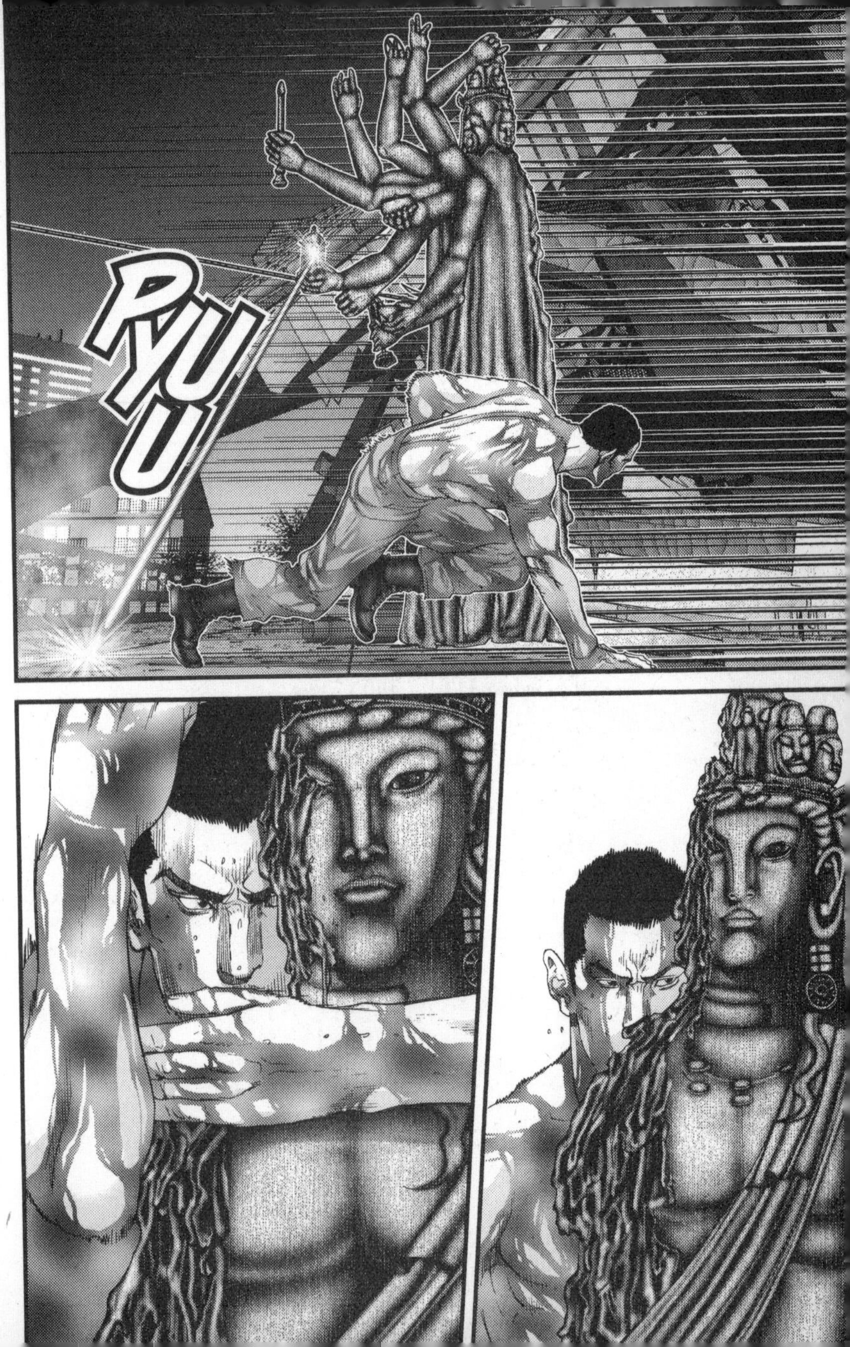
PYUU

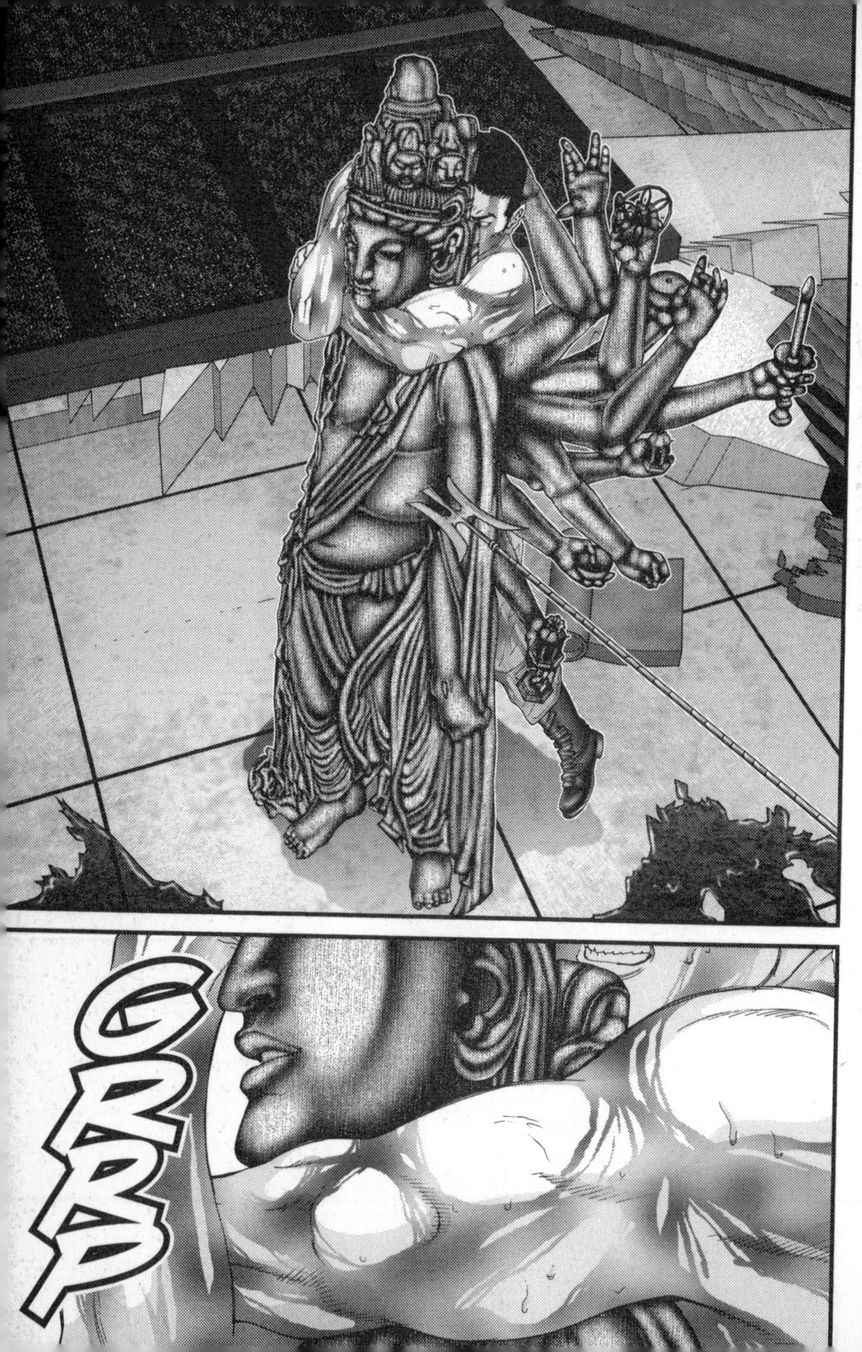
GRRP

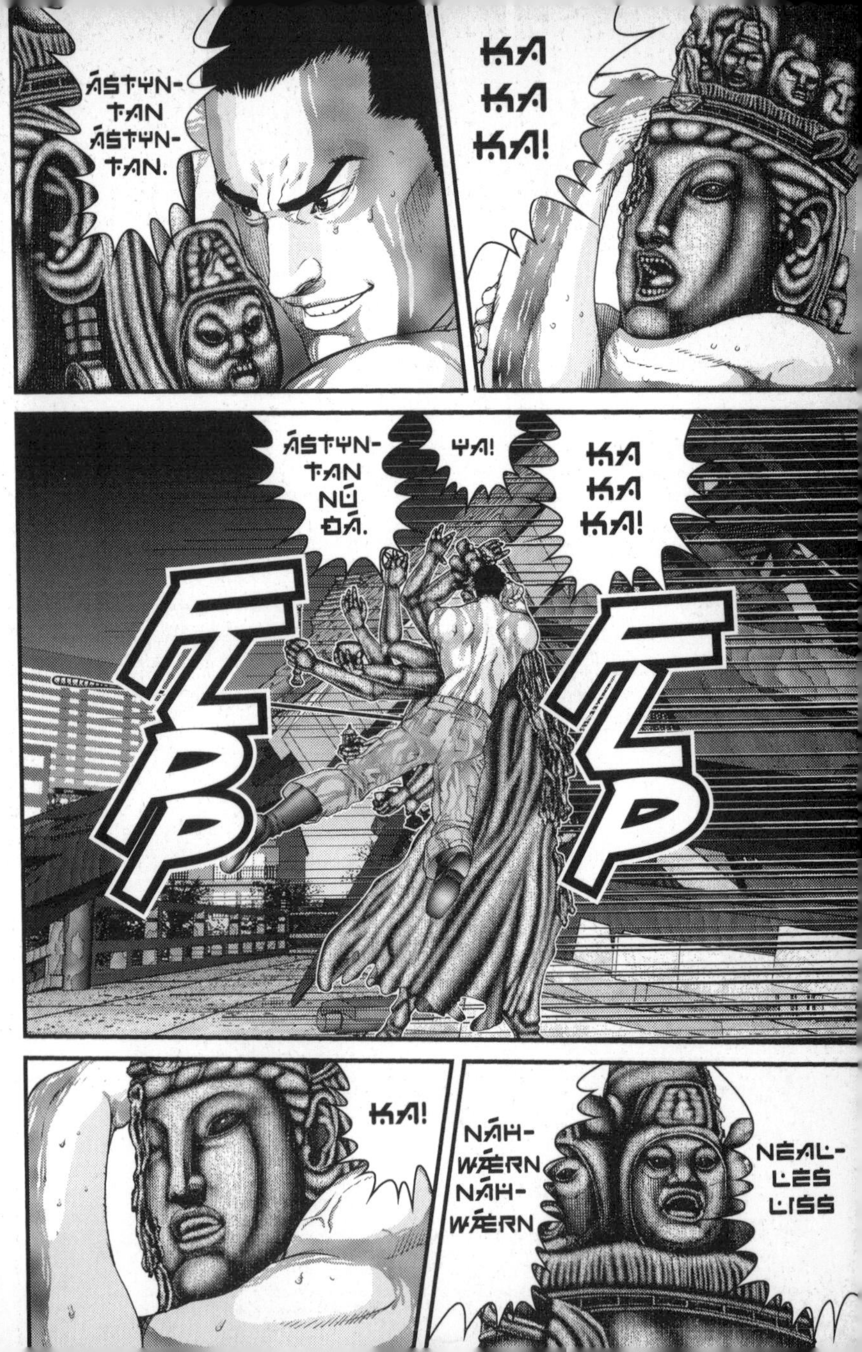
ÁSTYN-TAN ÁSTYN-TAN.
KA KA KA!
ÁSTYN-TAN NÚ ĐÁ.
YA!
KA KA KA!
FLP
FLP
KA!
NÁH-WÆRN NÁH-WÆRN
NEAL-LES LISS

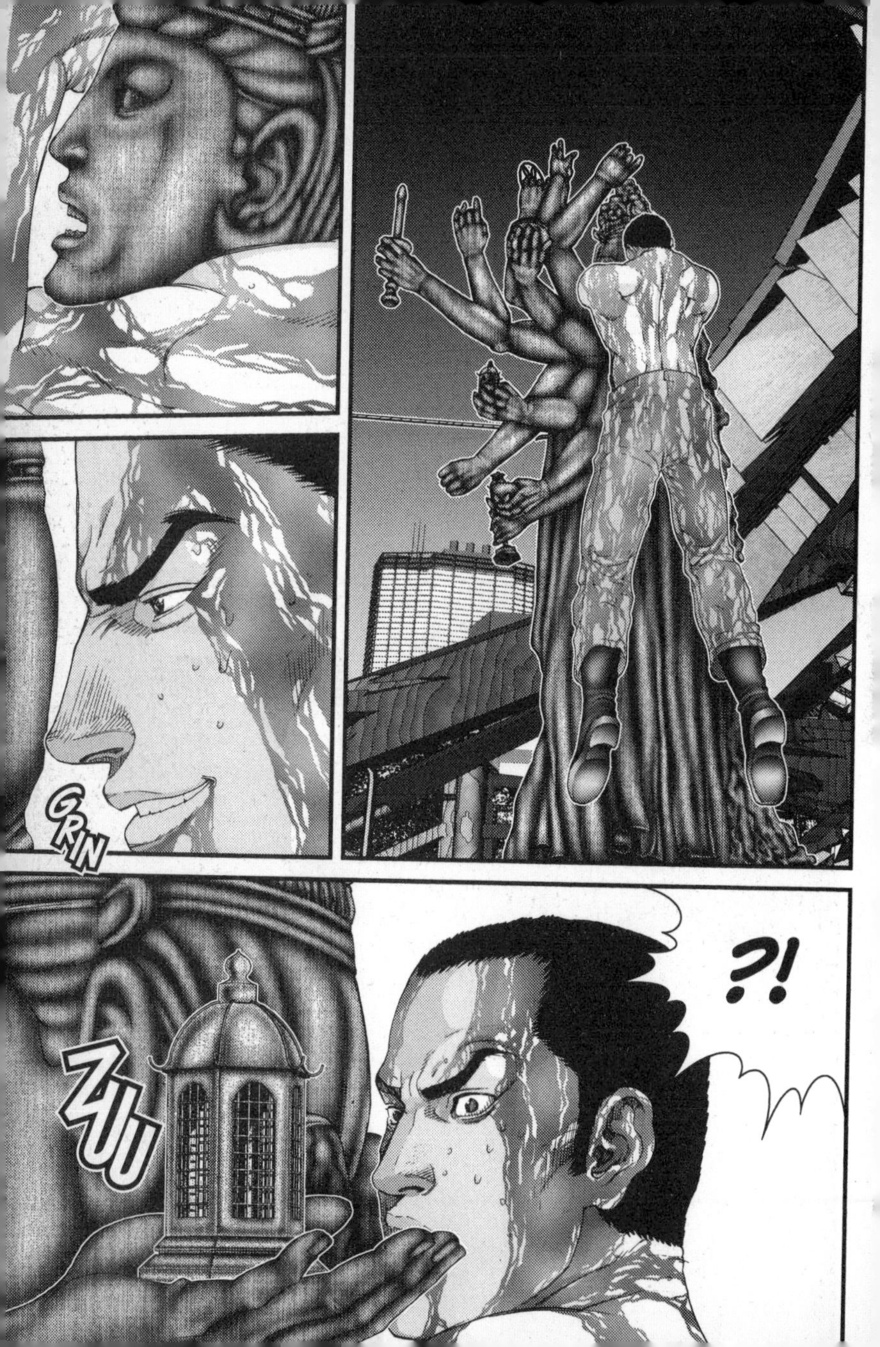
GRIN
?!
ZUU

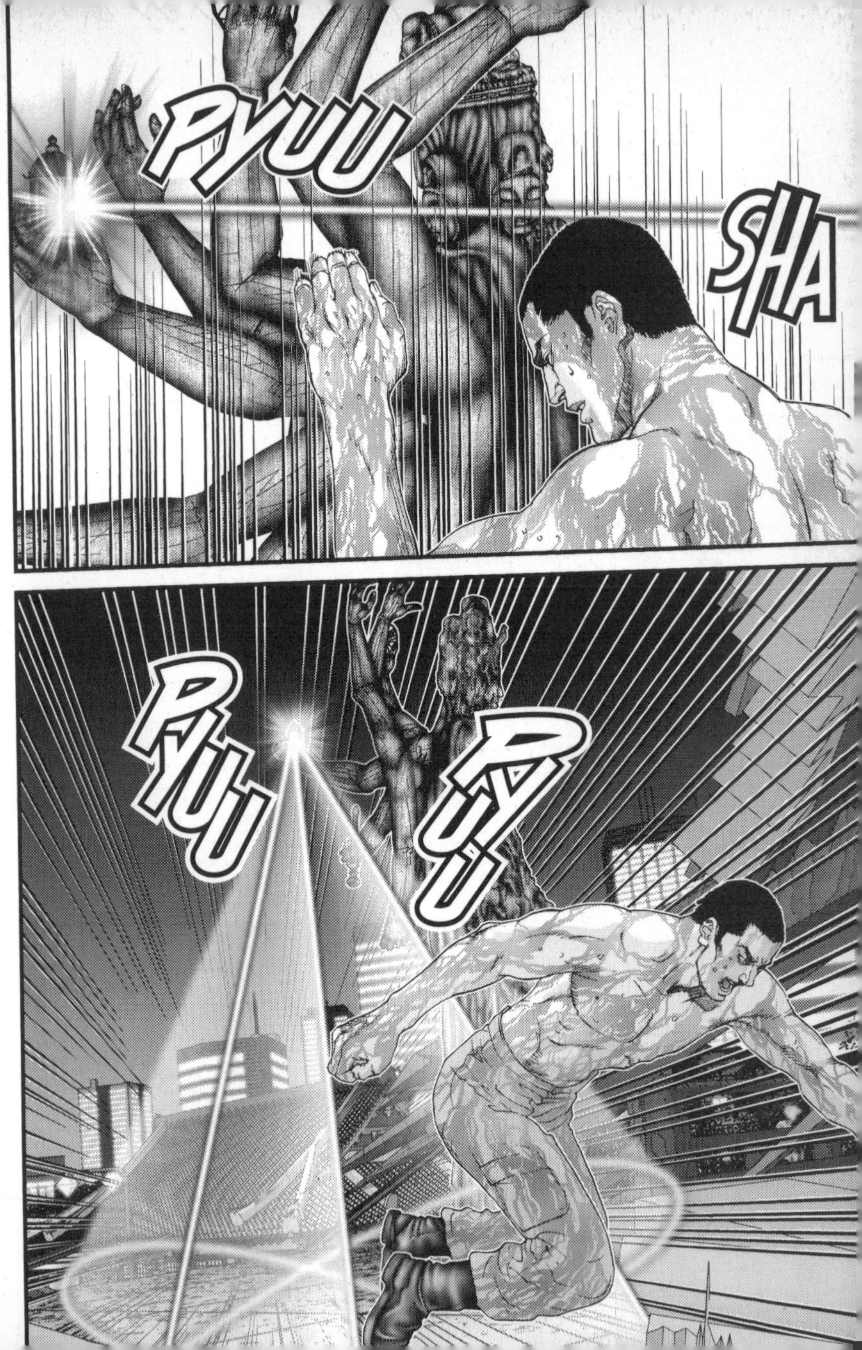
SHA
PYUU
PYUU
PYUU

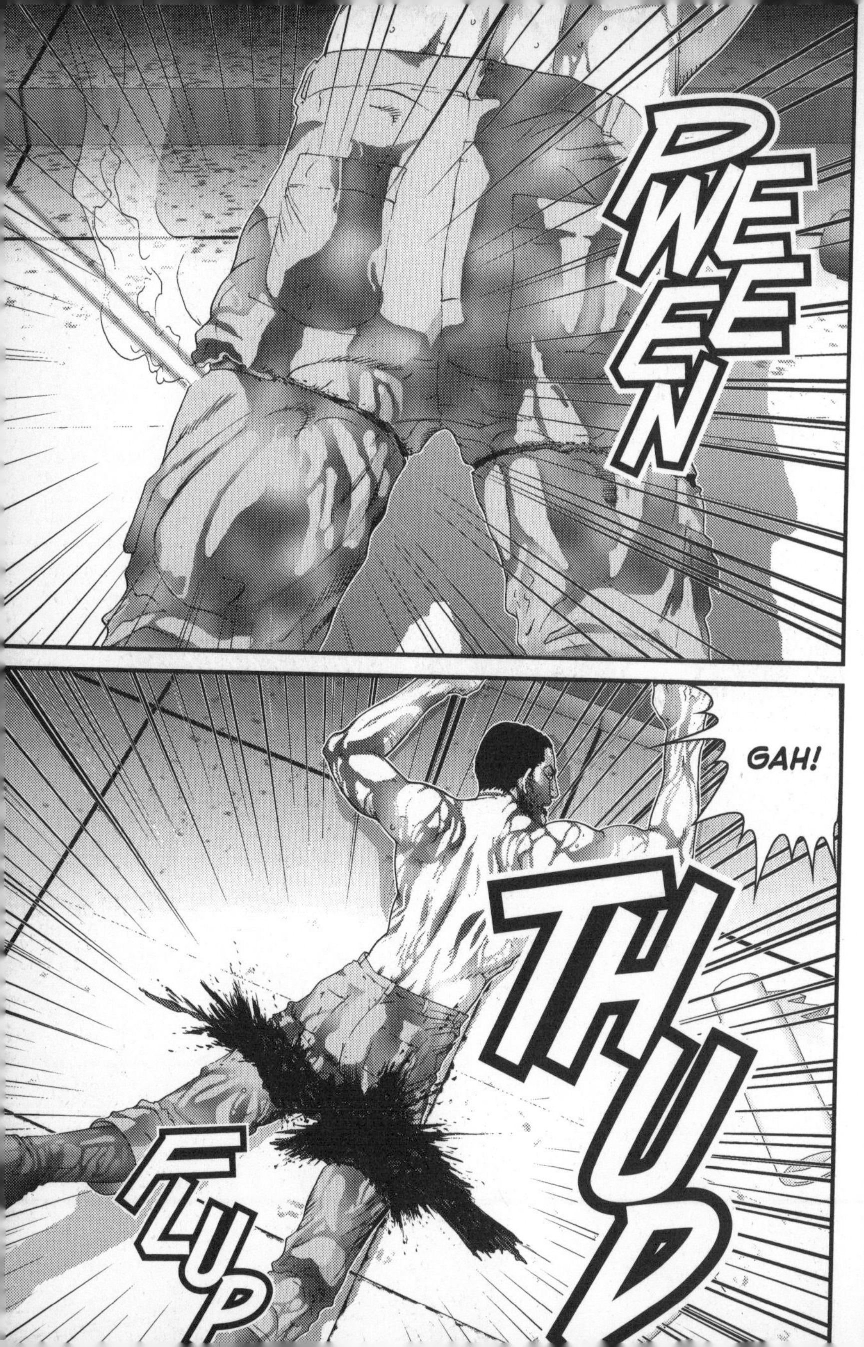
PWEEEN
GAH!
THUD
FLUP

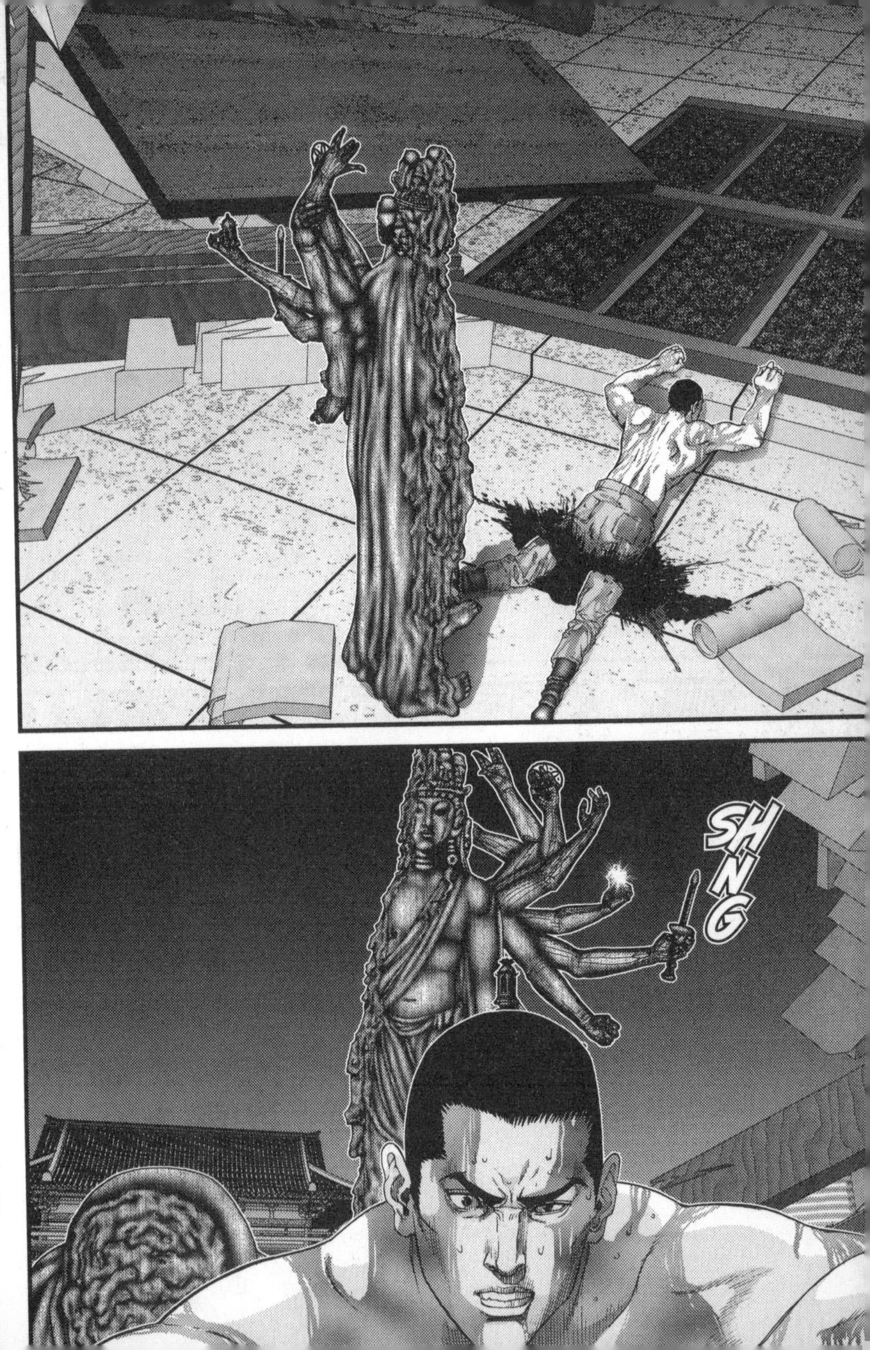
SHNG

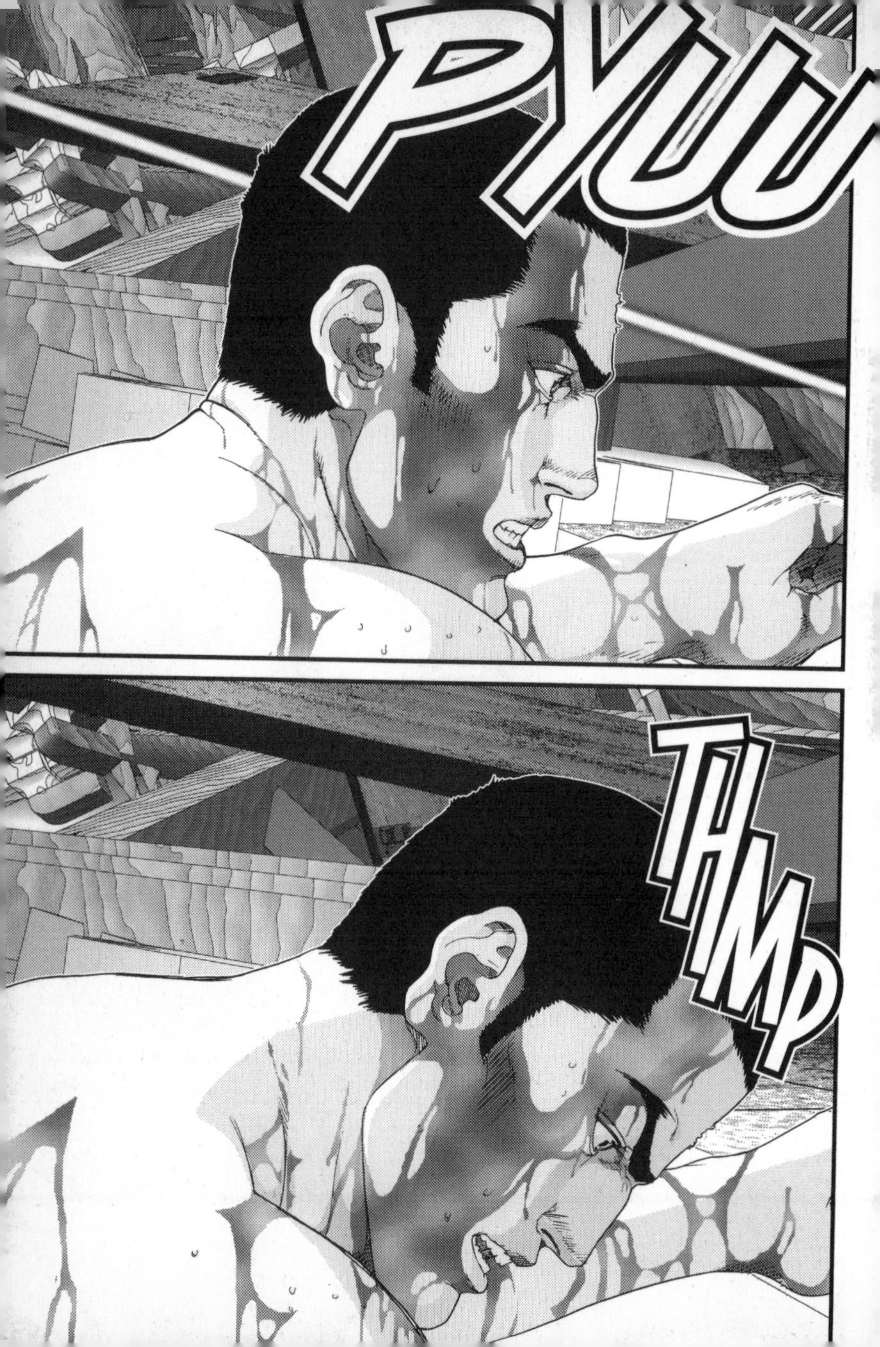
PYUU
THAMP

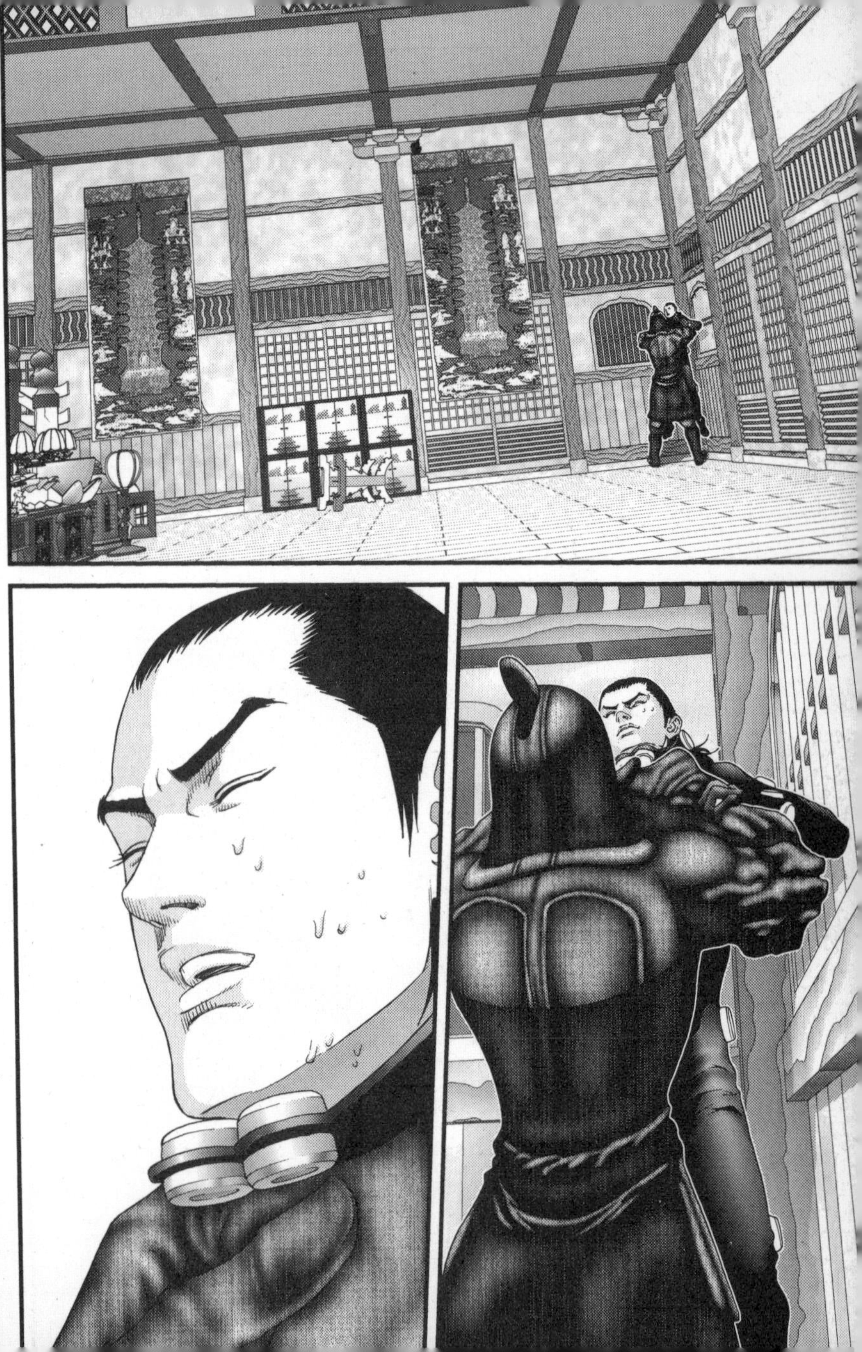

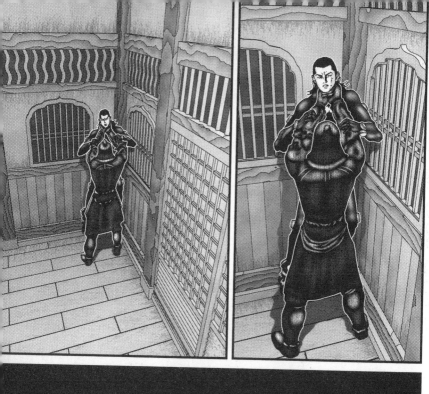

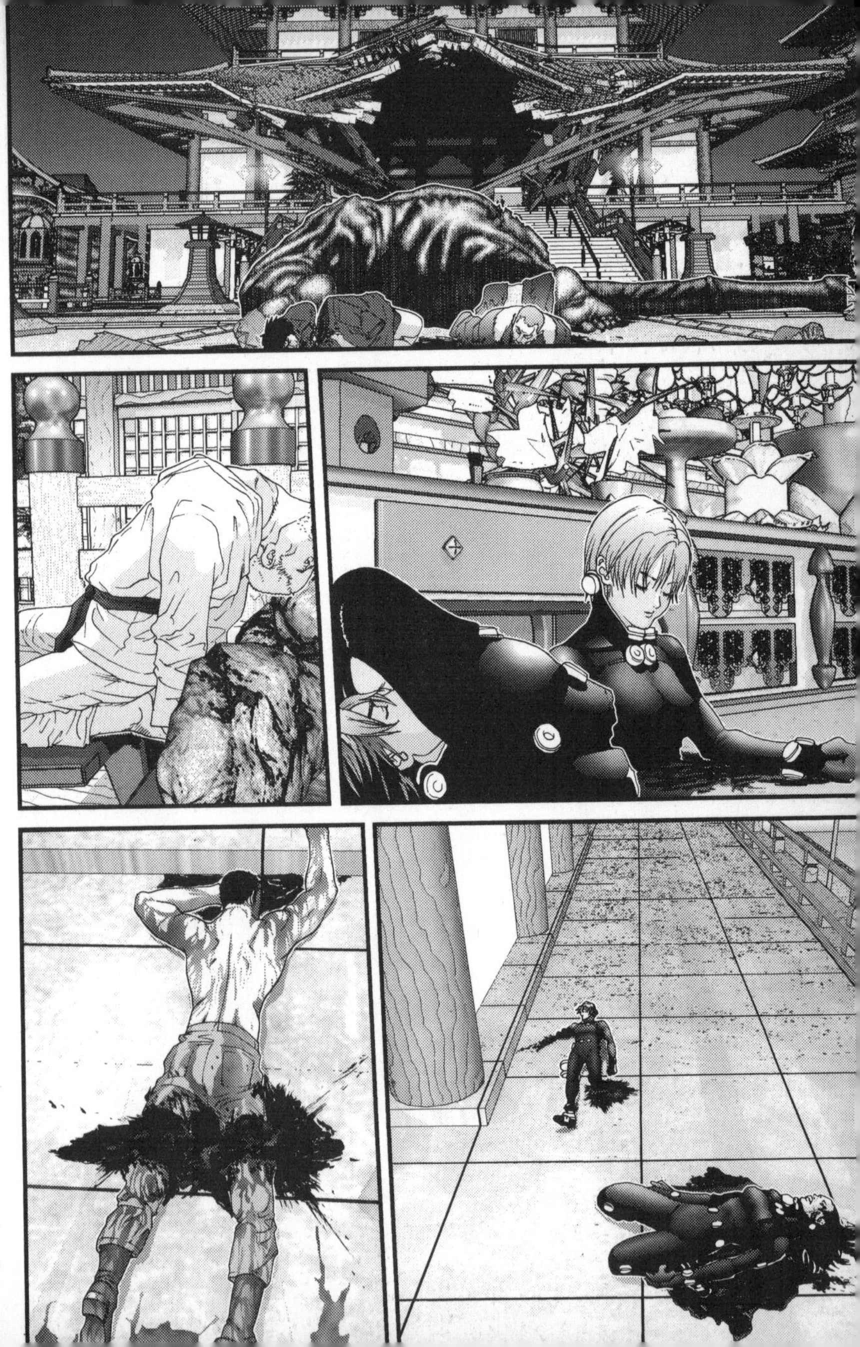

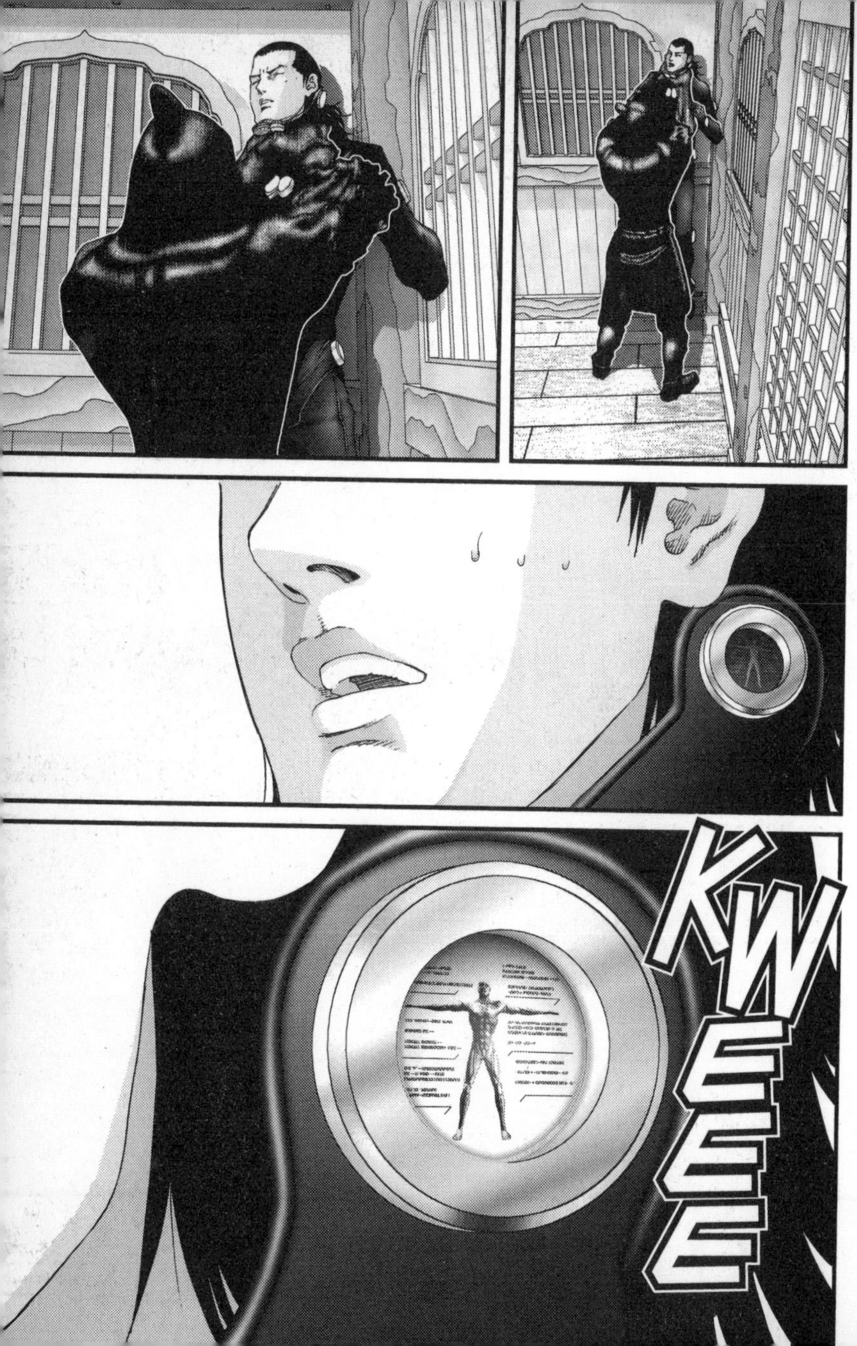
KWEEEE

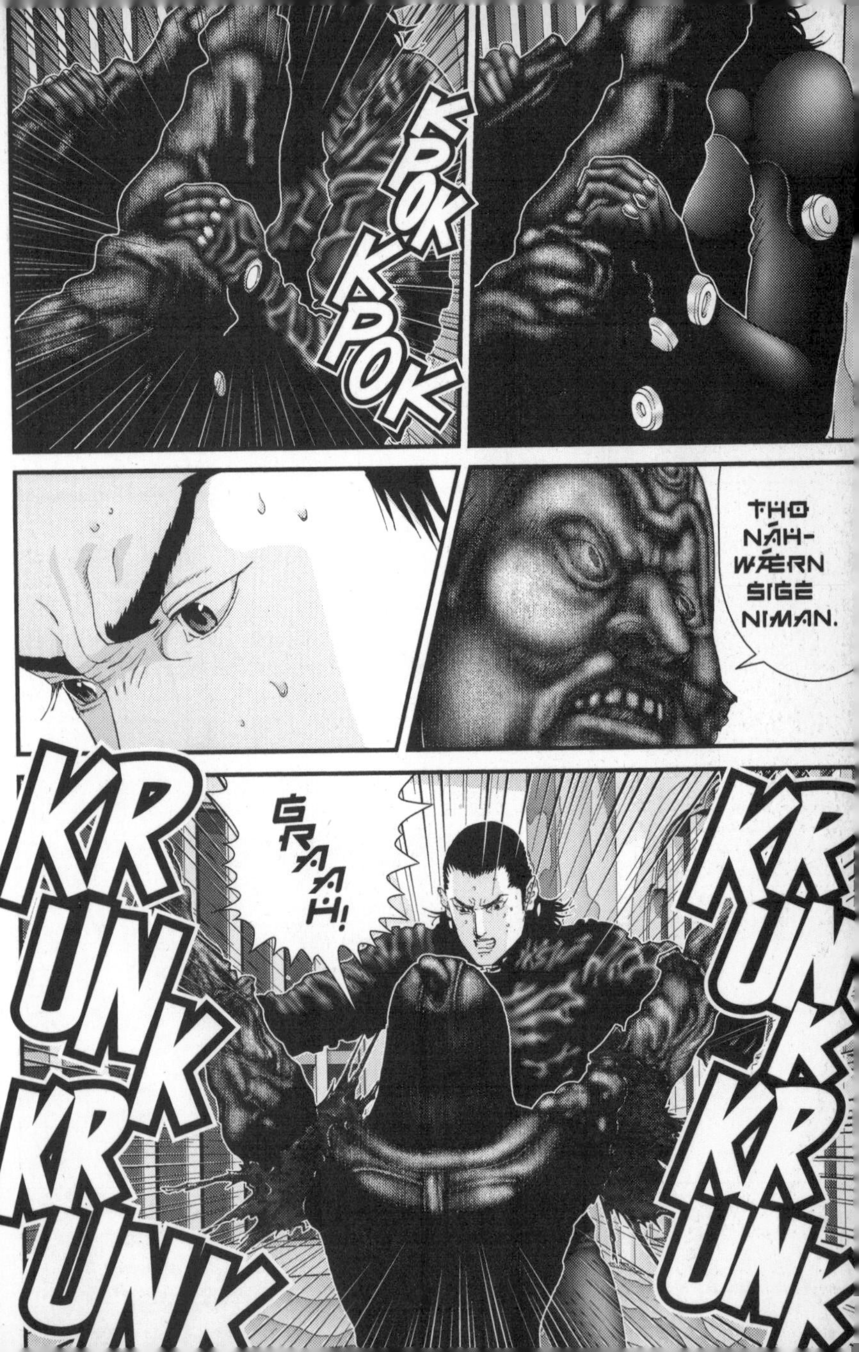
KPOK KPOK
THO NÁH-WÆRN SIGE NIMAN.
KRUNK KRUNK
GRAAH!
KRUNK KRUNK

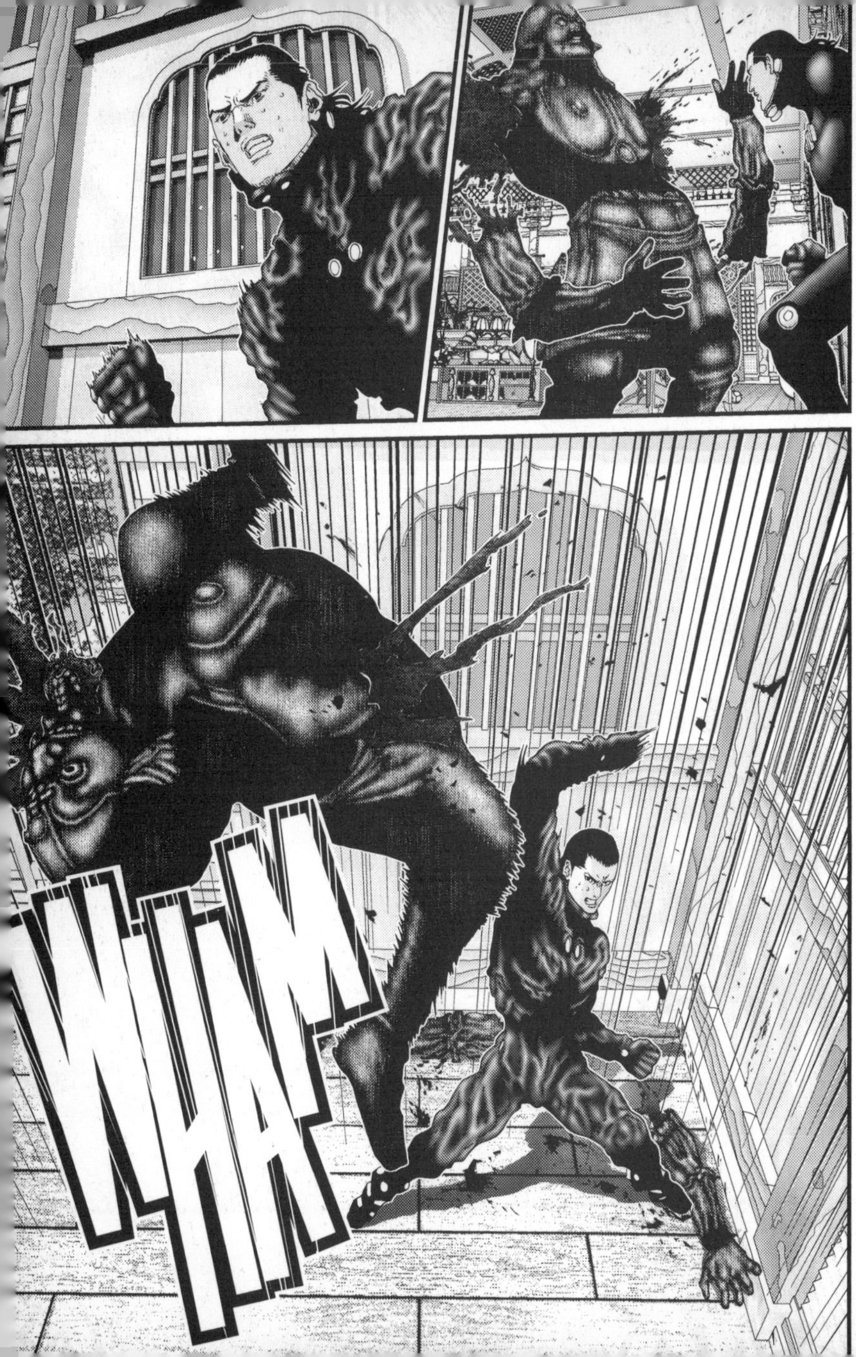
WHAM

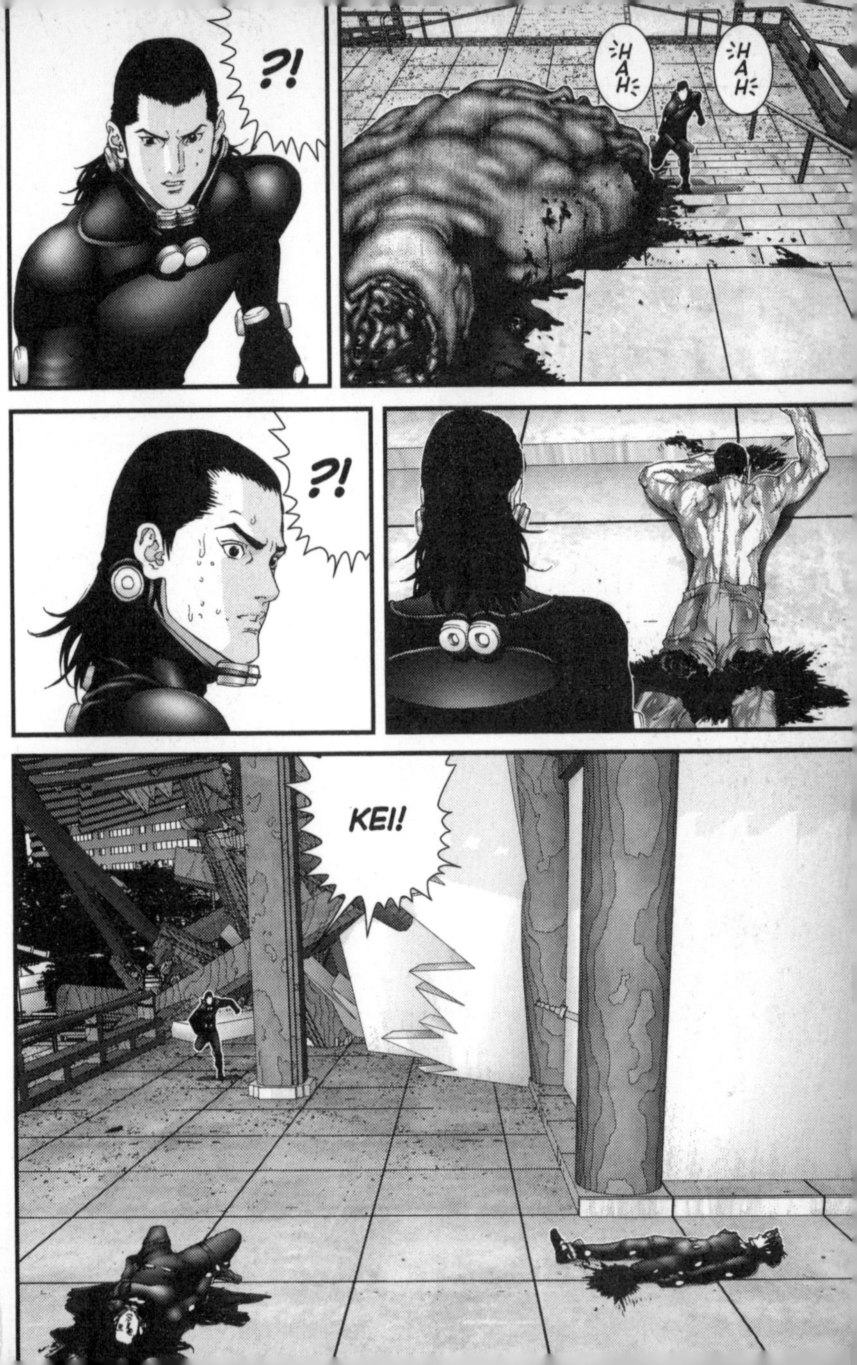

HAH
HAH
?!
?!
KEI!

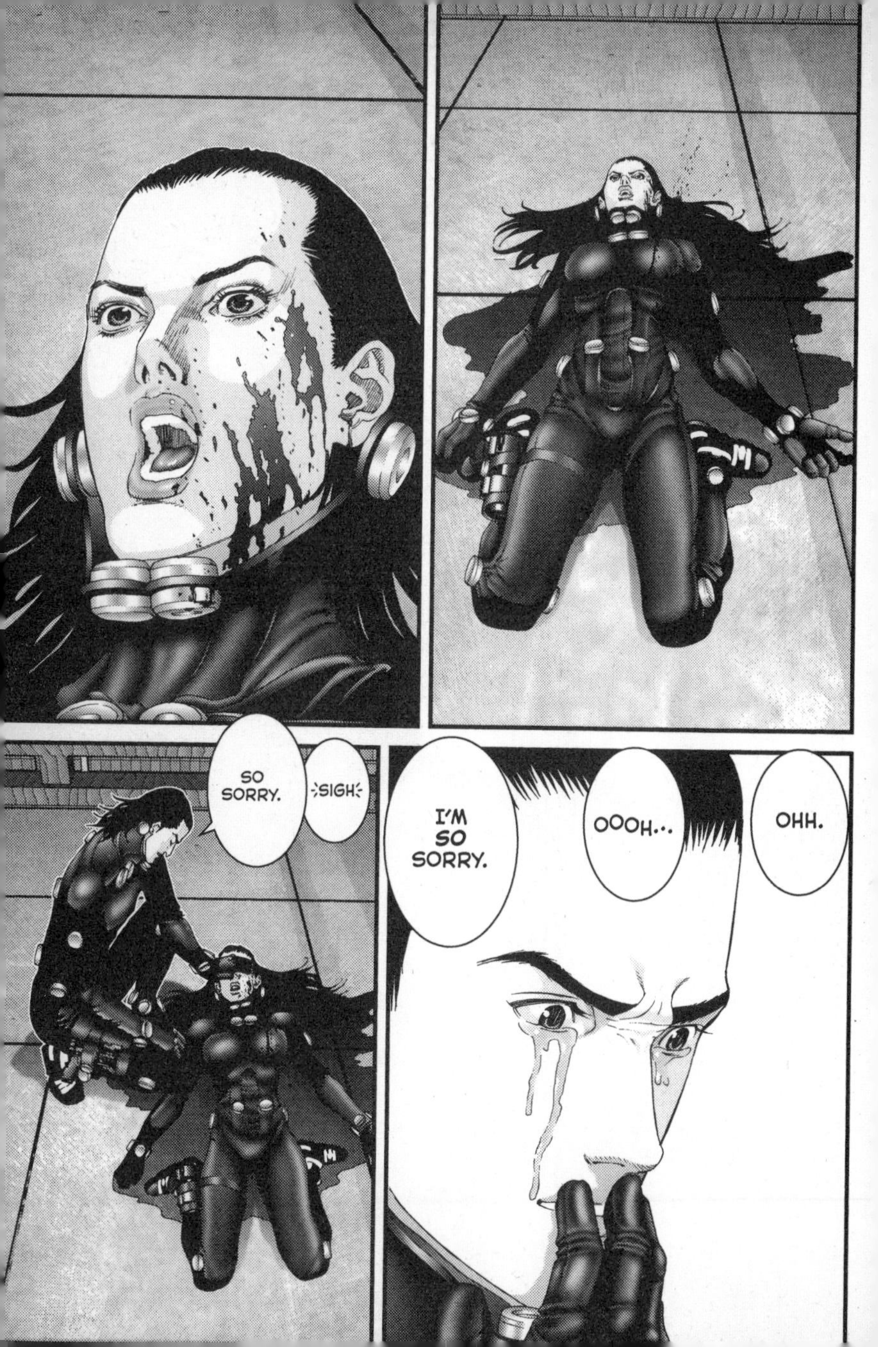
OHH.
OOOH...
I'M SO SORRY.
SIGH
SO SORRY.

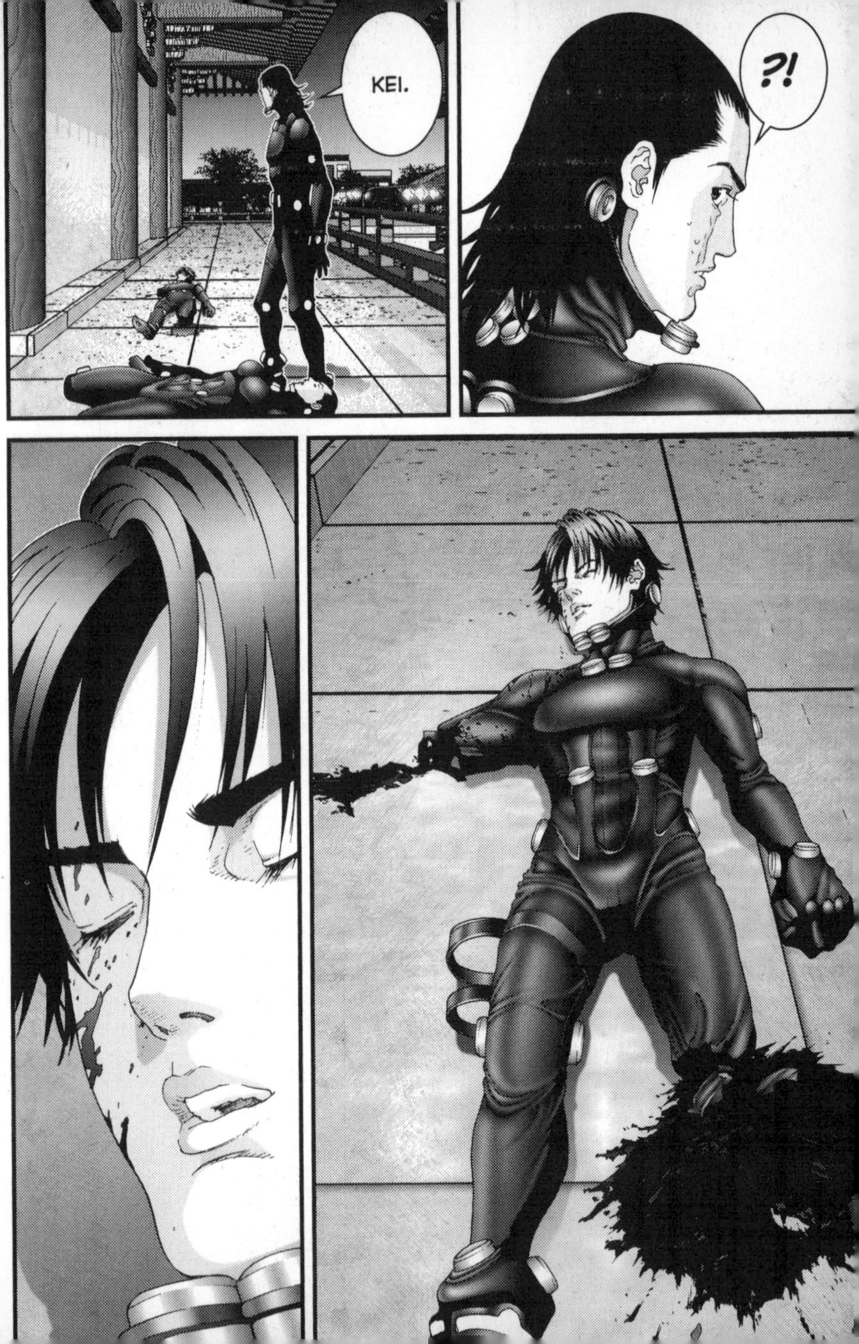
KEI.
?!

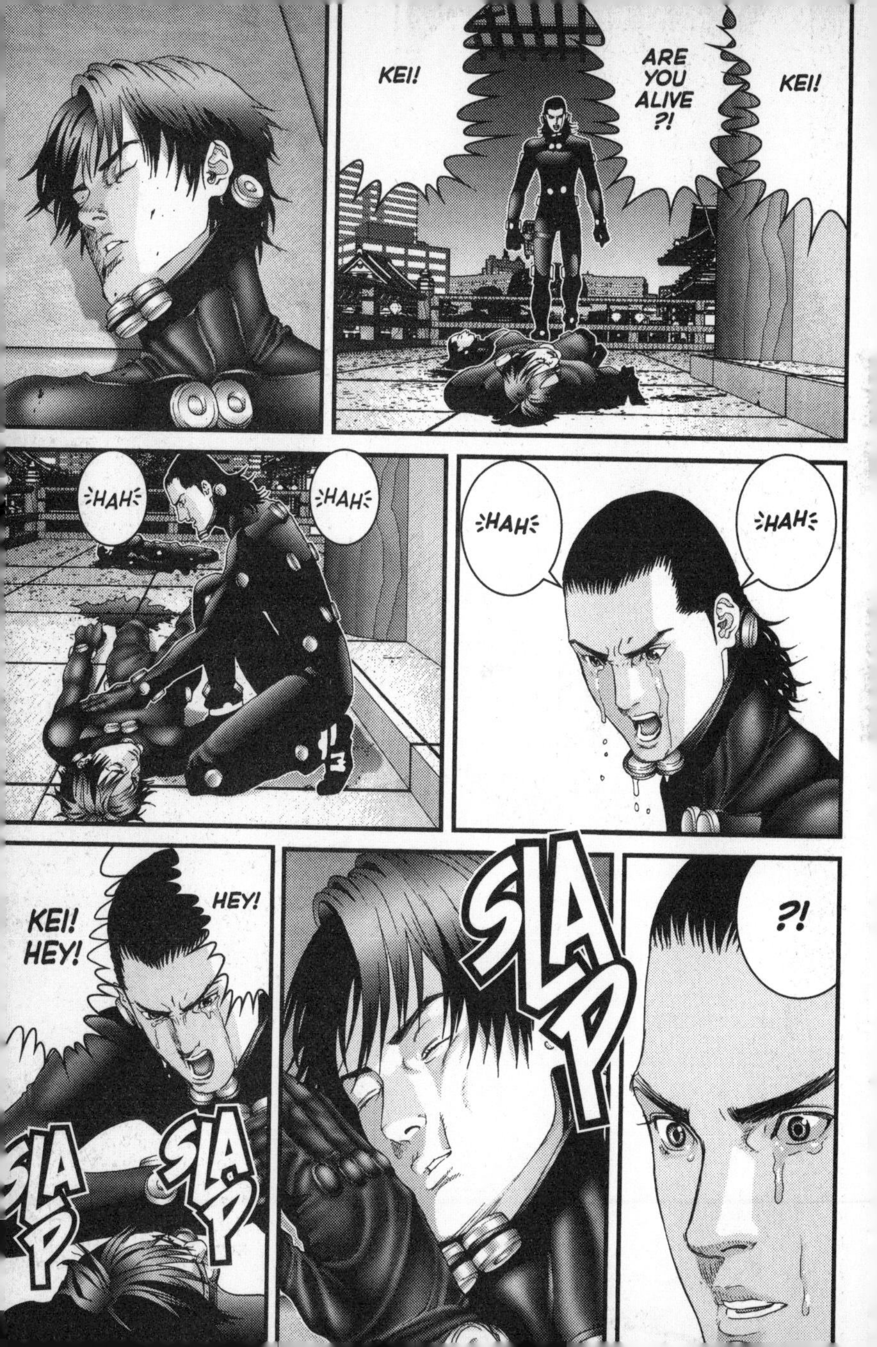
KEI!
ARE YOU ALIVE ?!
KEI!
HAH
HAH
HAH
HAH
KEI! HEY!
HEY!
SLAP
SLAP
SLAP
?!

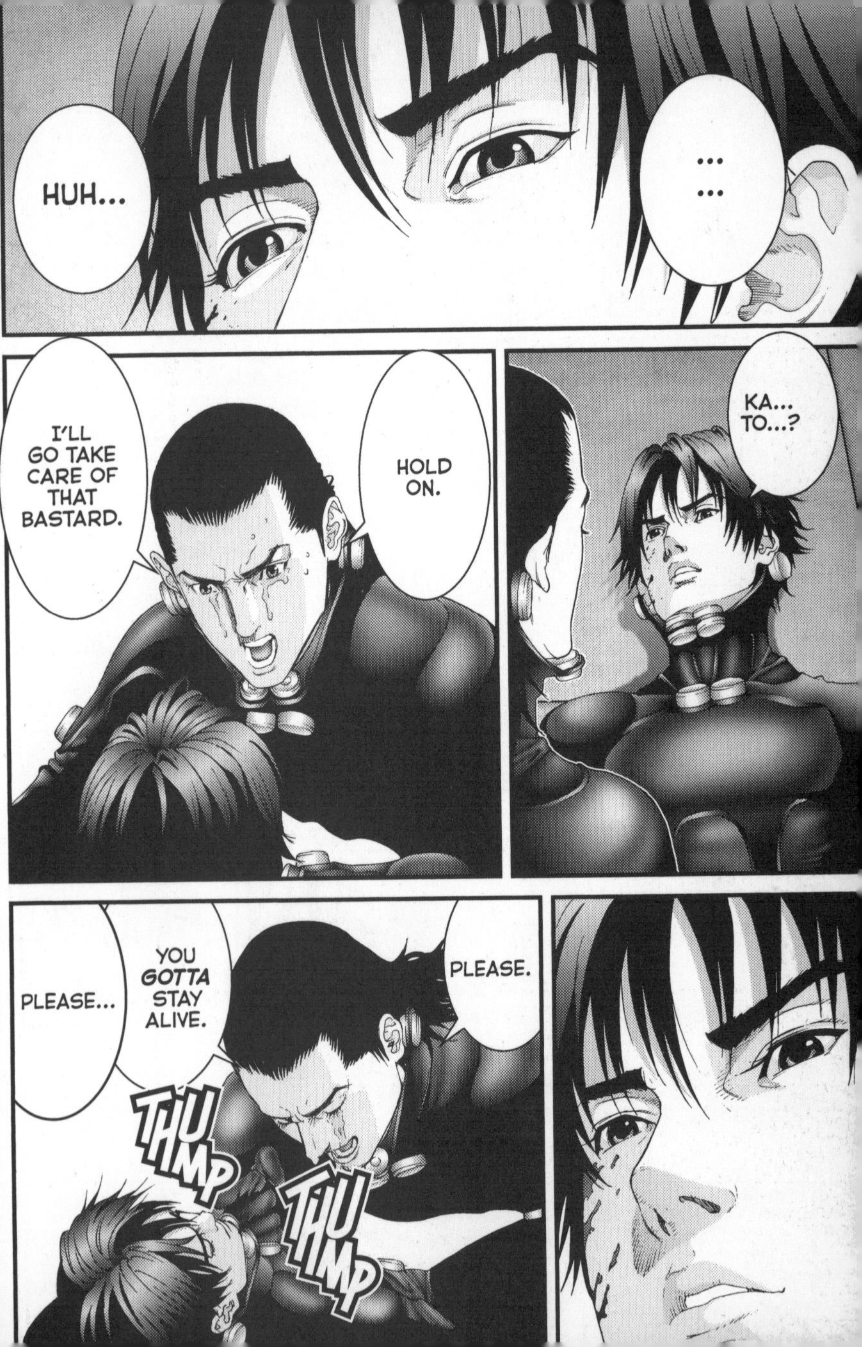
...
...
HUH...
KA... TO...?
HOLD ON.
I'LL GO TAKE CARE OF THAT BASTARD.
PLEASE.
YOU GOTTA STAY ALIVE.
PLEASE...
THUMP
THUMP

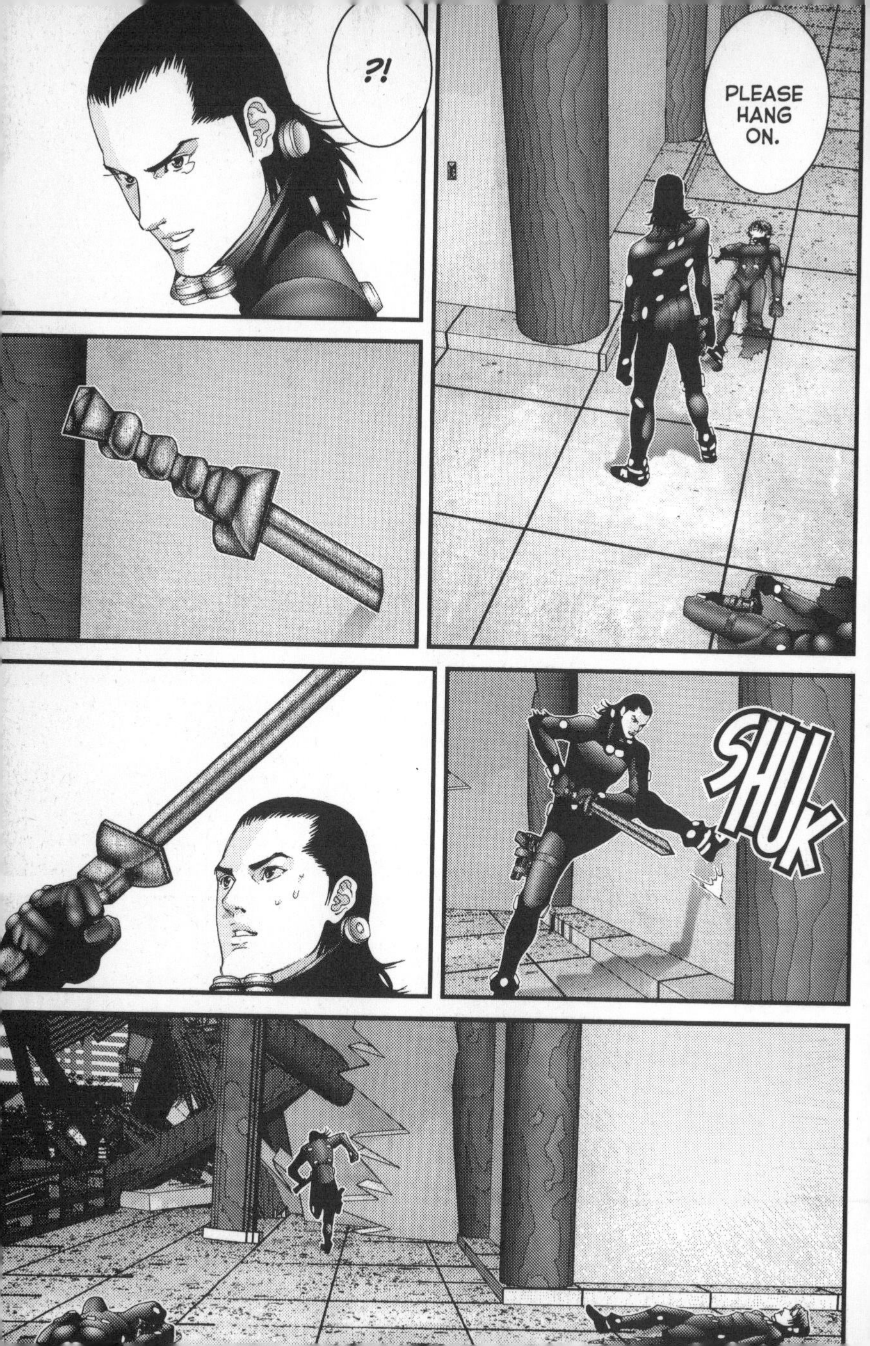
PLEASE HANG ON.
?!
SHUK

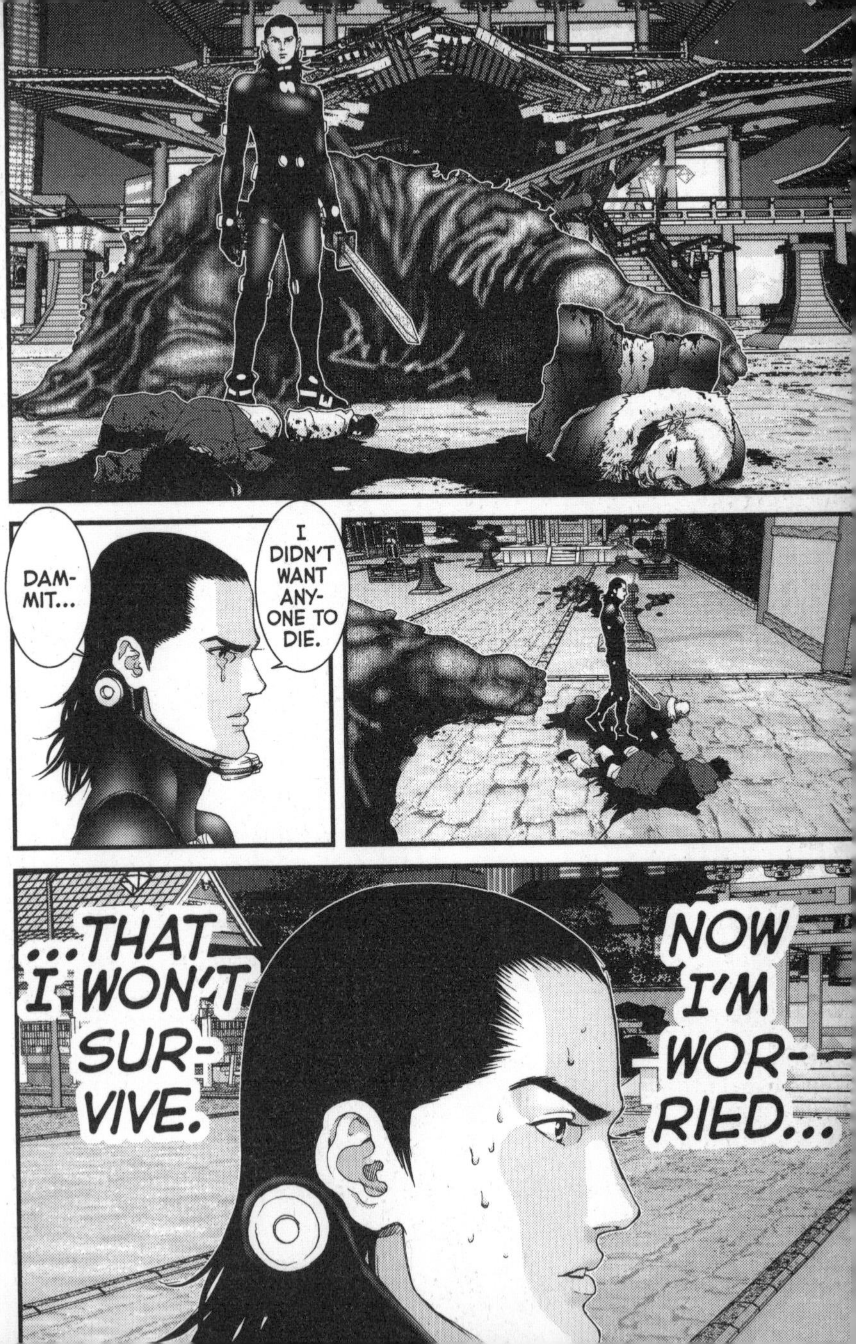
I DIDN'T WANT ANYONE TO DIE.
DAMMIT...
NOW I'M WORRIED...
...THAT I WON'T SURVIVE.

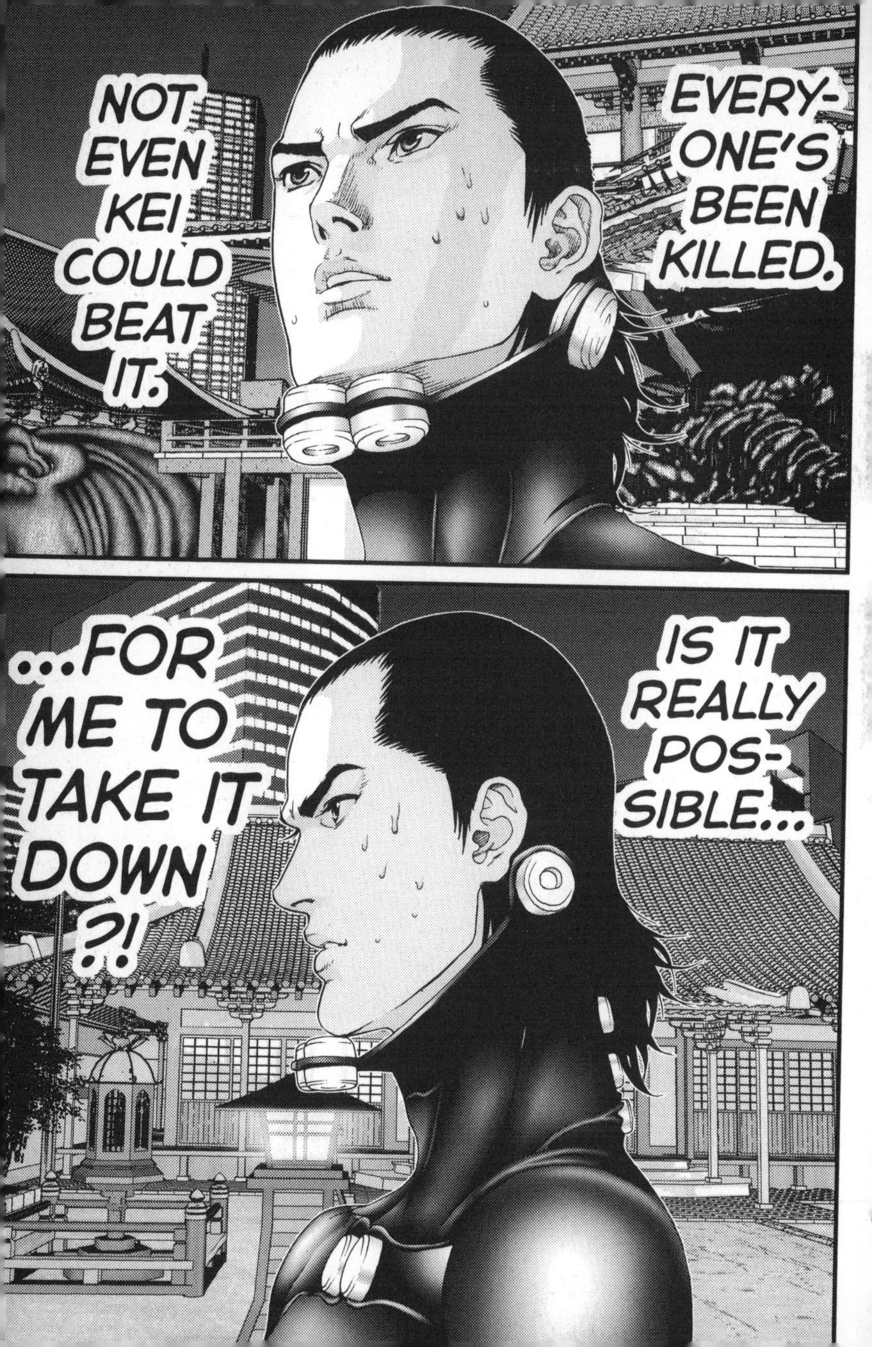
EVERY-ONE'S BEEN KILLED.
NOT EVEN KEI COULD BEAT IT.
IS IT REALLY POS-SIBLE...
...FOR ME TO TAKE IT DOWN?!

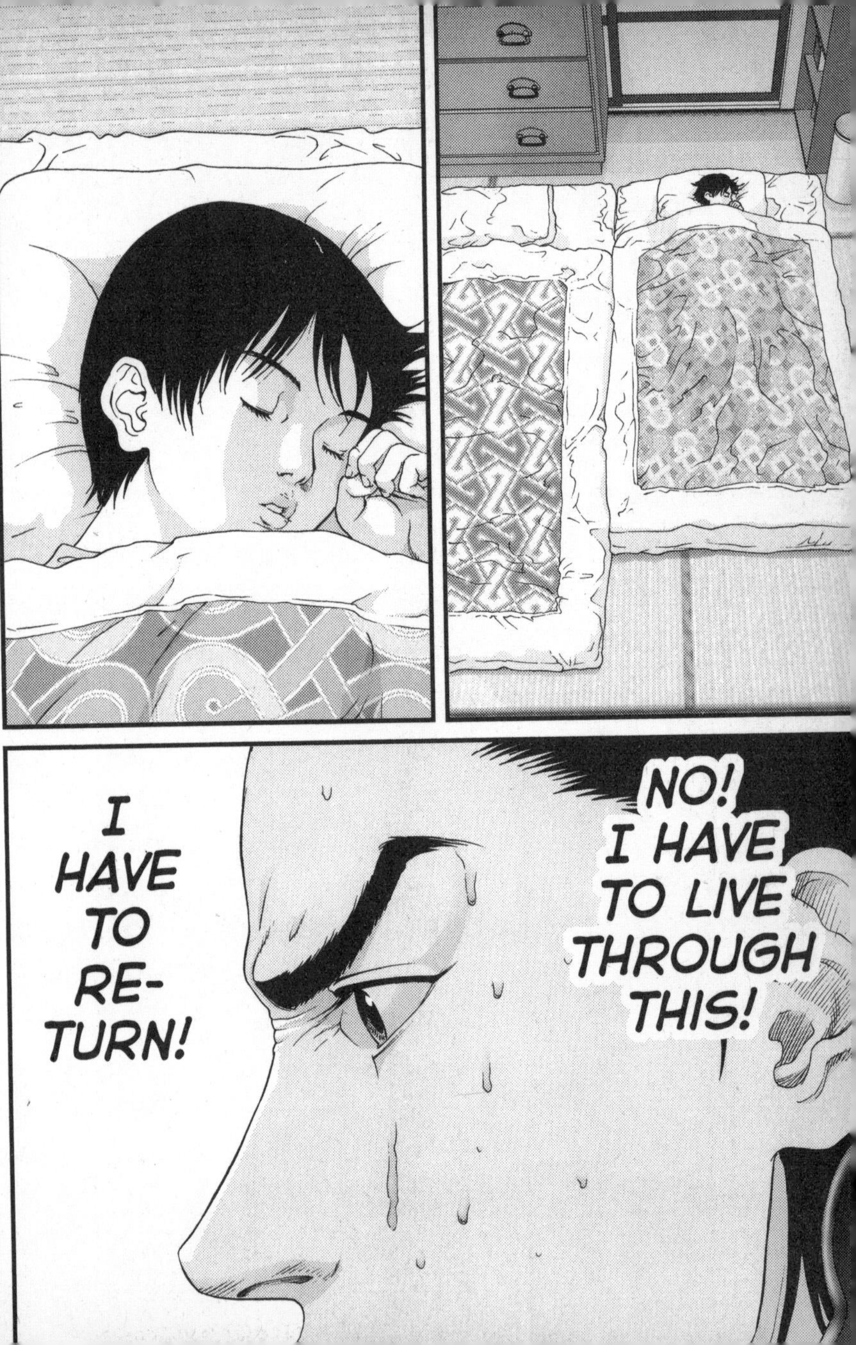
NO! I HAVE TO LIVE THROUGH THIS!
I HAVE TO RE-TURN!

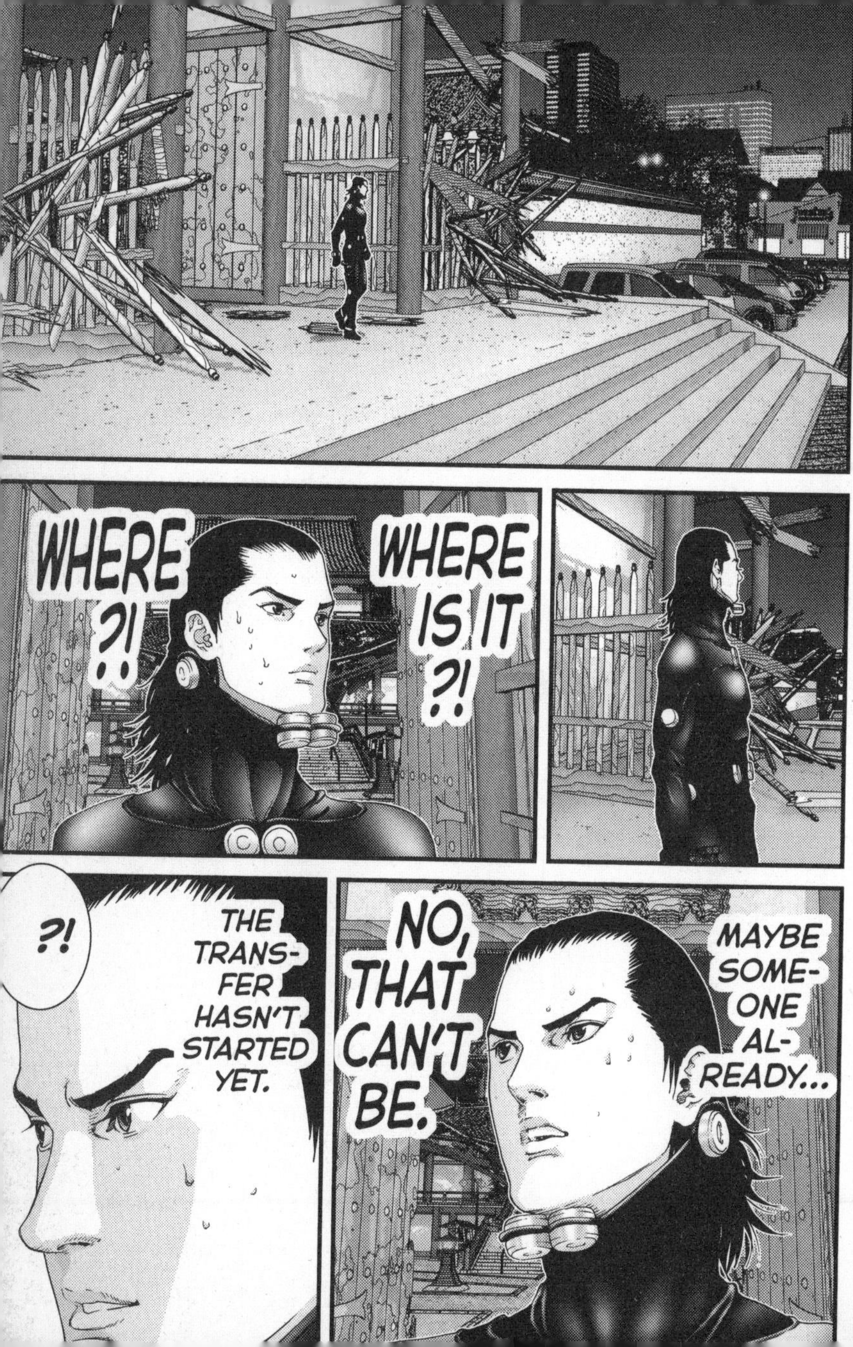
WHERE IS IT ?!
WHERE ?!
MAYBE SOME-ONE AL-READY...
NO, THAT CAN'T BE.
THE TRANS-FER HASN'T STARTED YET.
?!

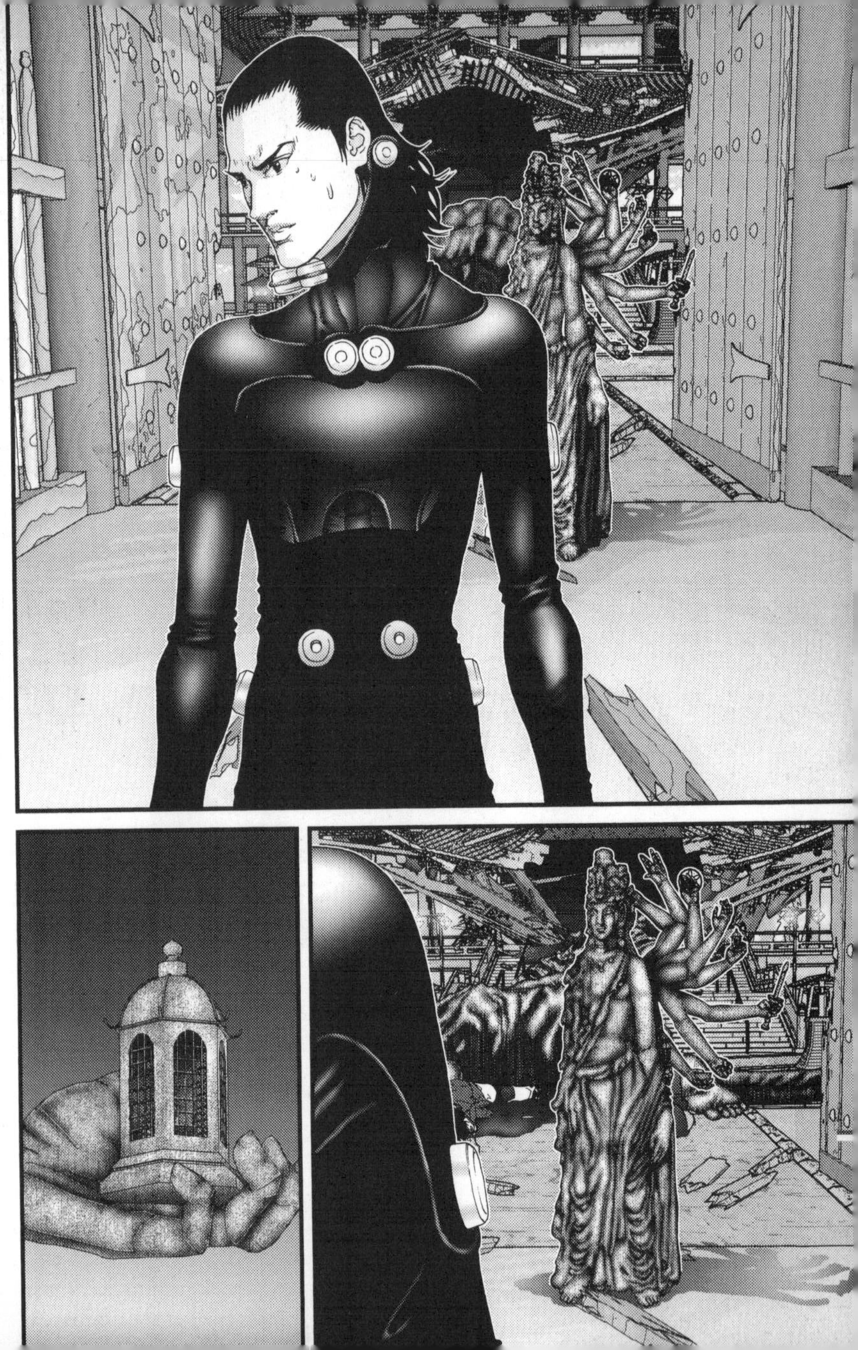

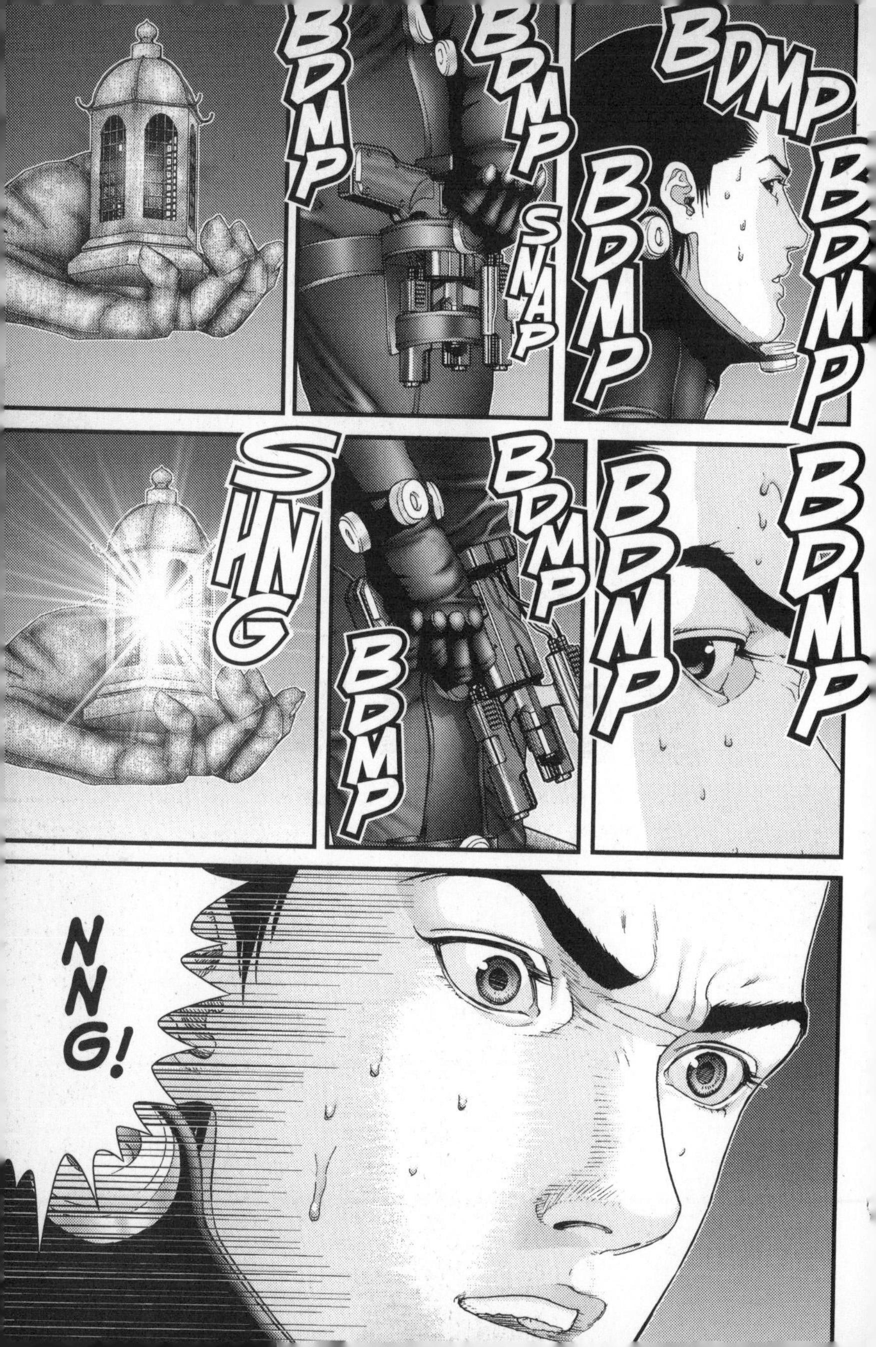
BDMP
BDMP
BDMP
BDMP
SNAP
BDMP
BDMP
BDMP
BDMP
BDMP
SHNG
NNG!

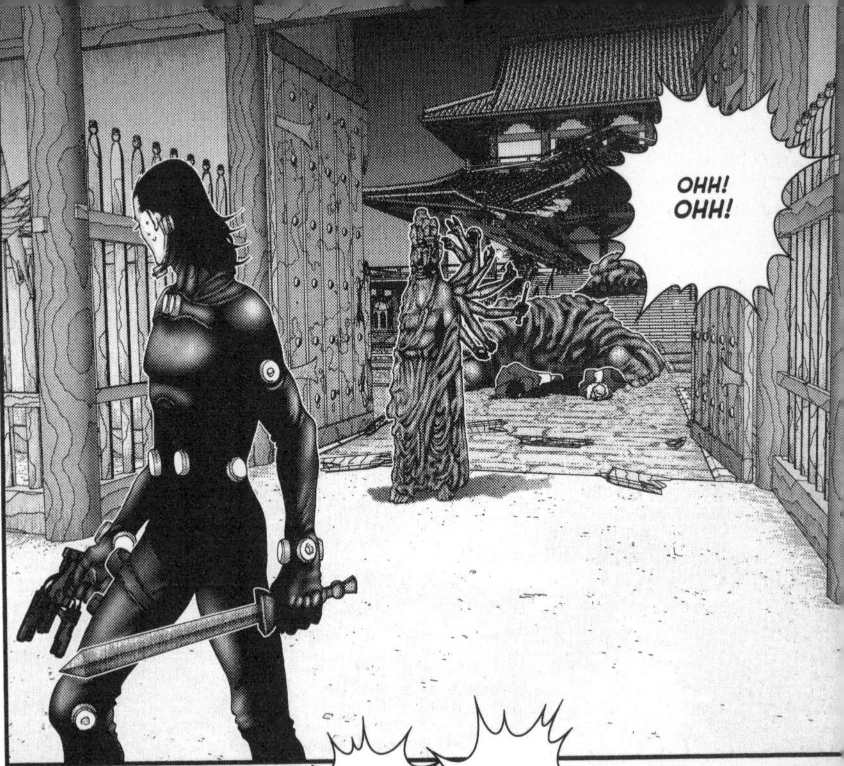
OHH!
OHH!

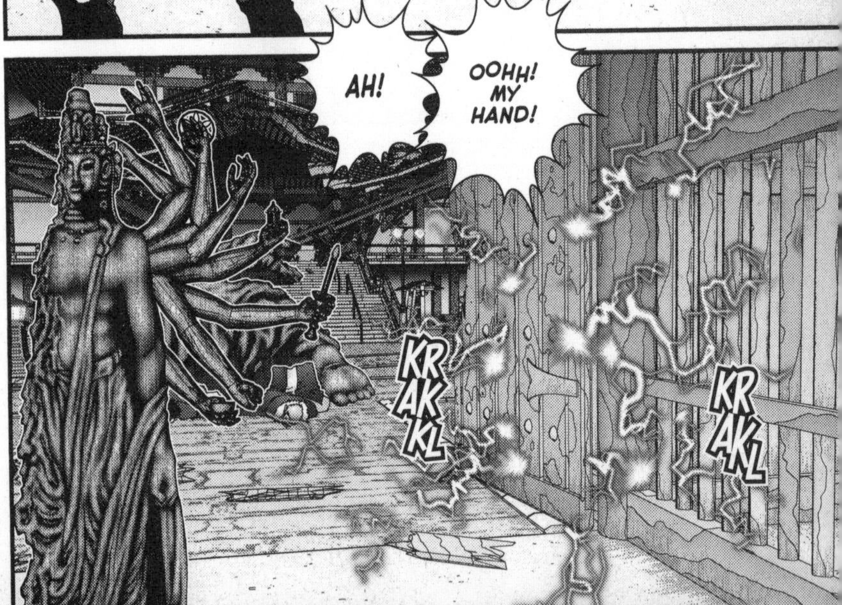
OOHH! MY HAND!
AH!
KRAKL
KRAKL

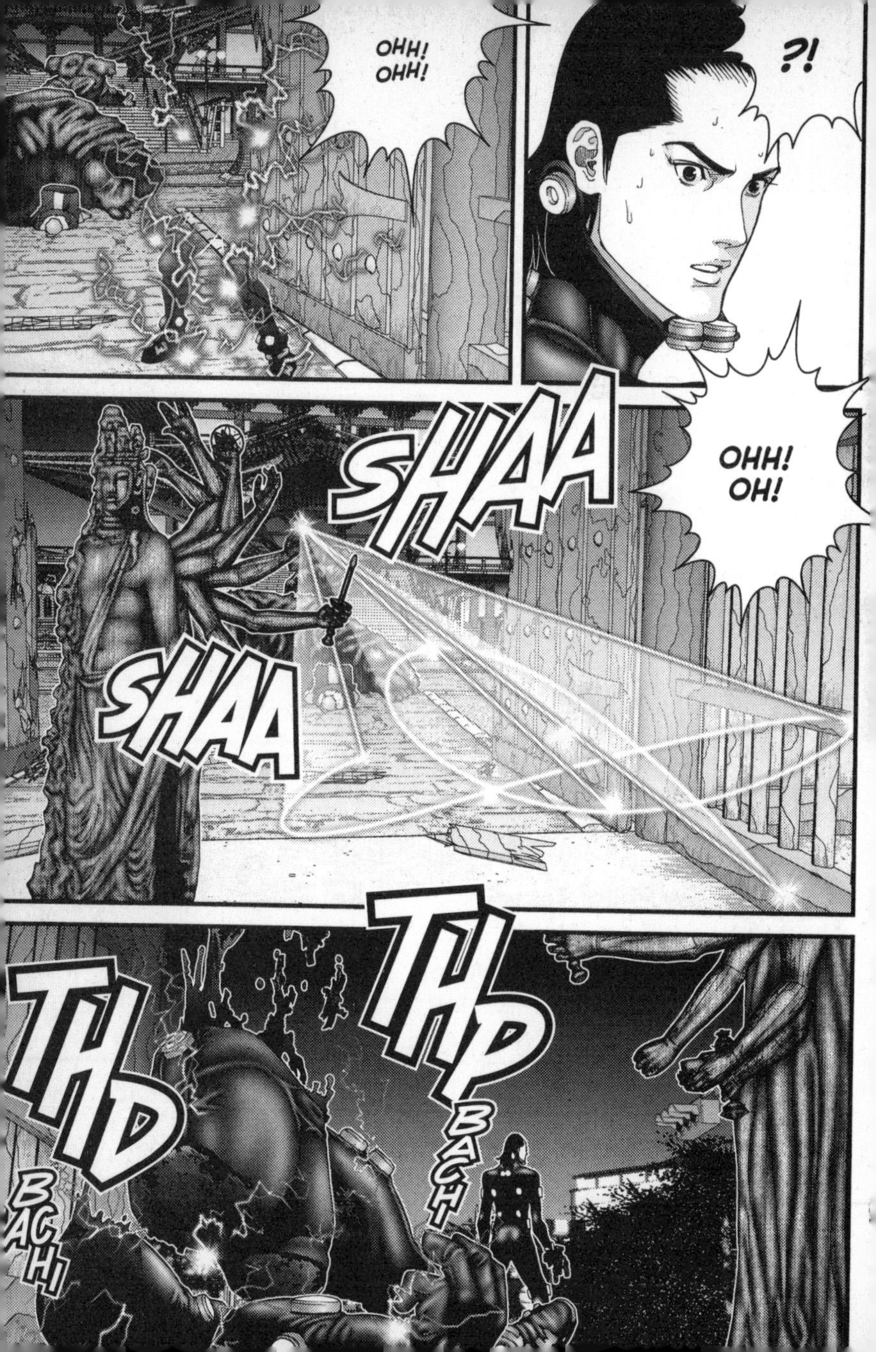

?!
OHH! OHH!
OHH! OH!
SHAA
SHAA
THP
BACHI
THD
BACHI

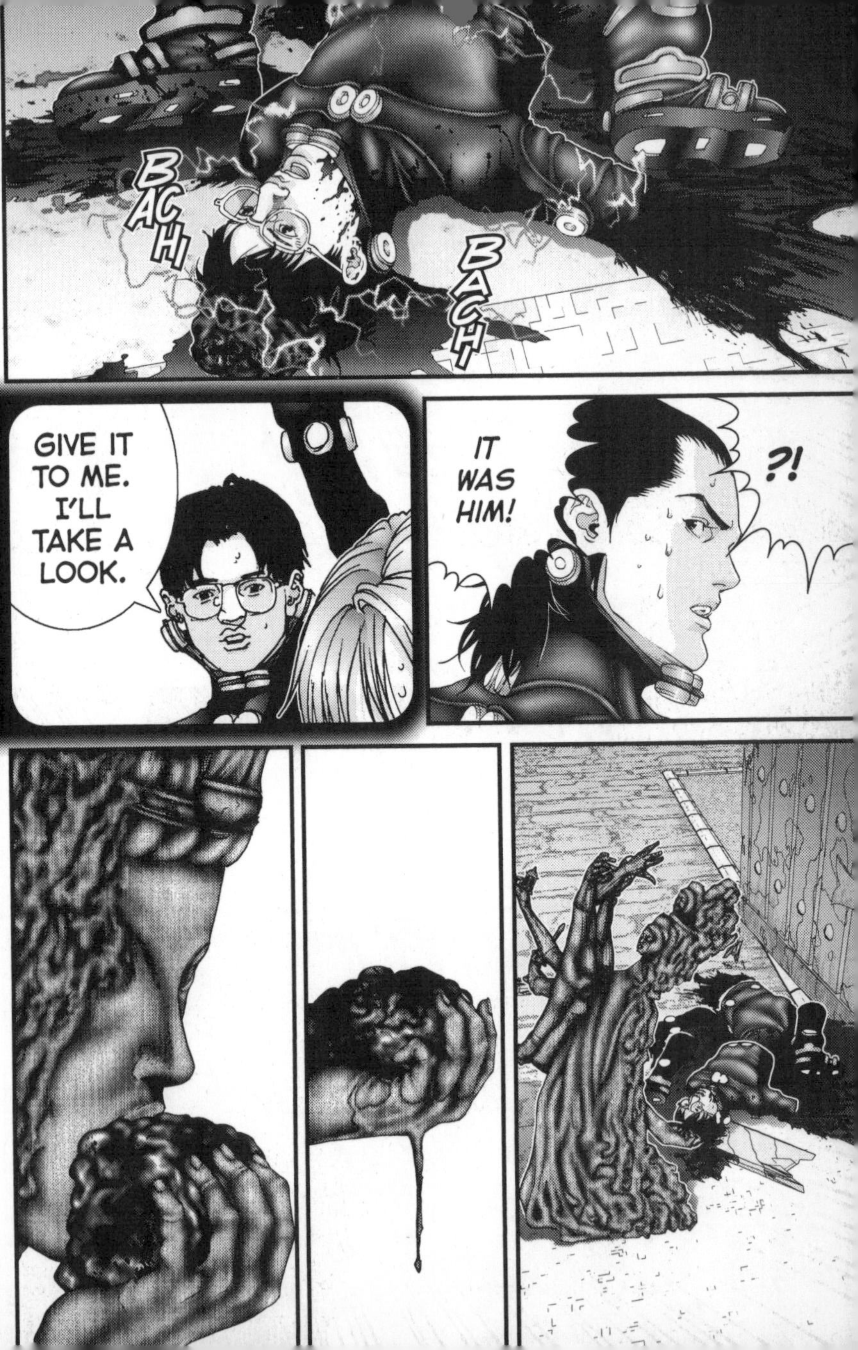
BACHI
BACHI
GIVE IT TO ME. I'LL TAKE A LOOK.
IT WAS HIM!
?!

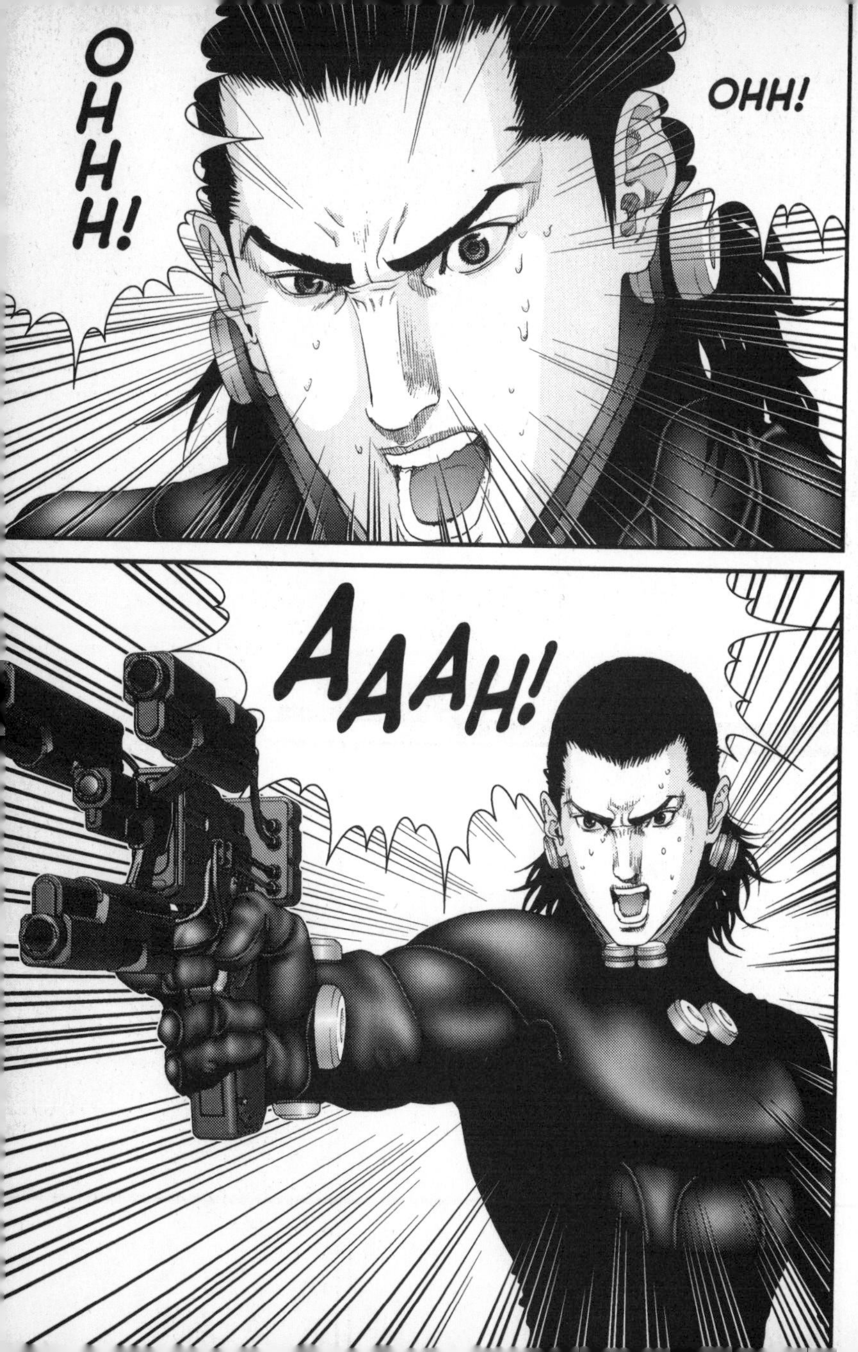
OHH!
OHHH!
AAAH!

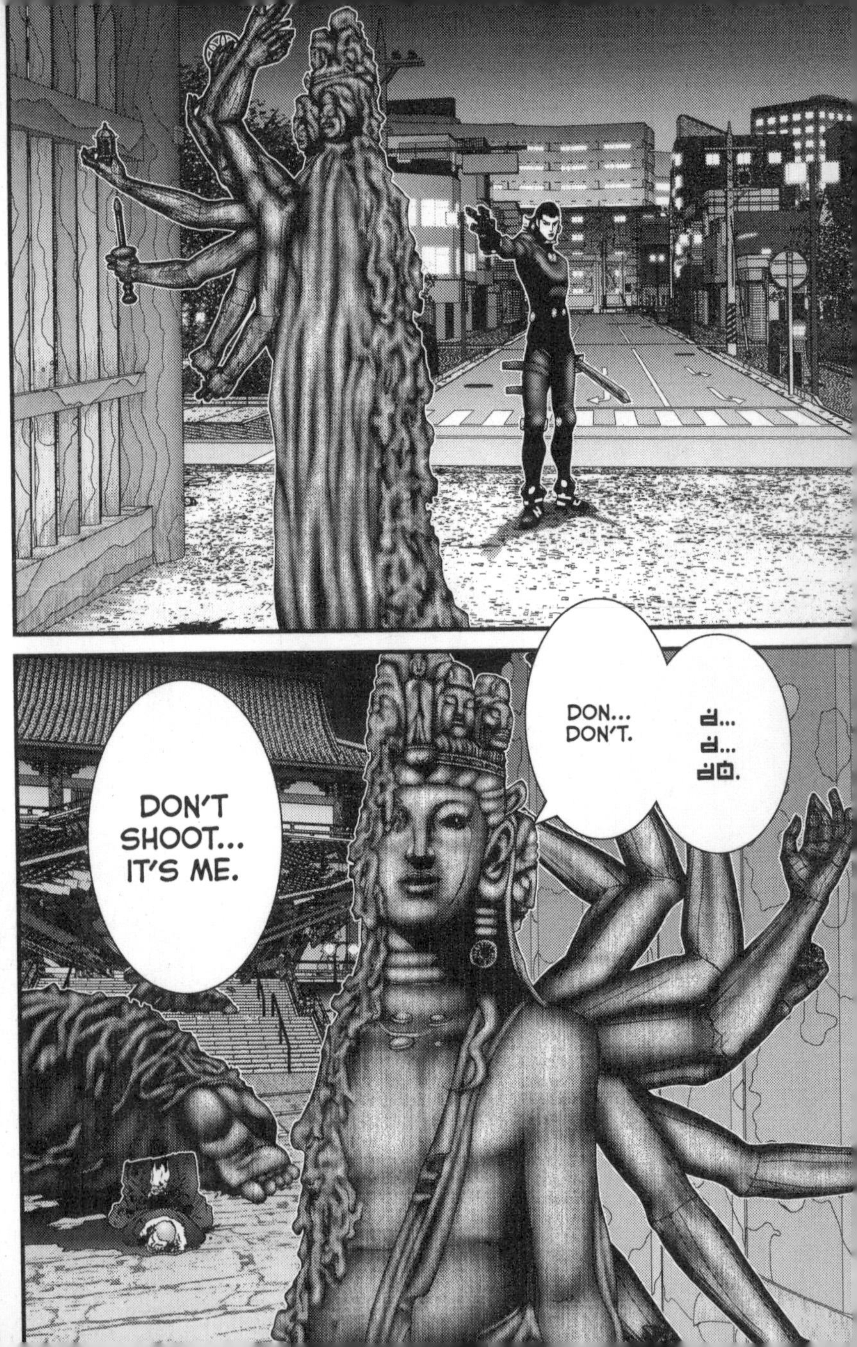
d... d... do.
DON... DON'T.
DON'T SHOOT... IT'S ME.

COMMUNICATION
0086

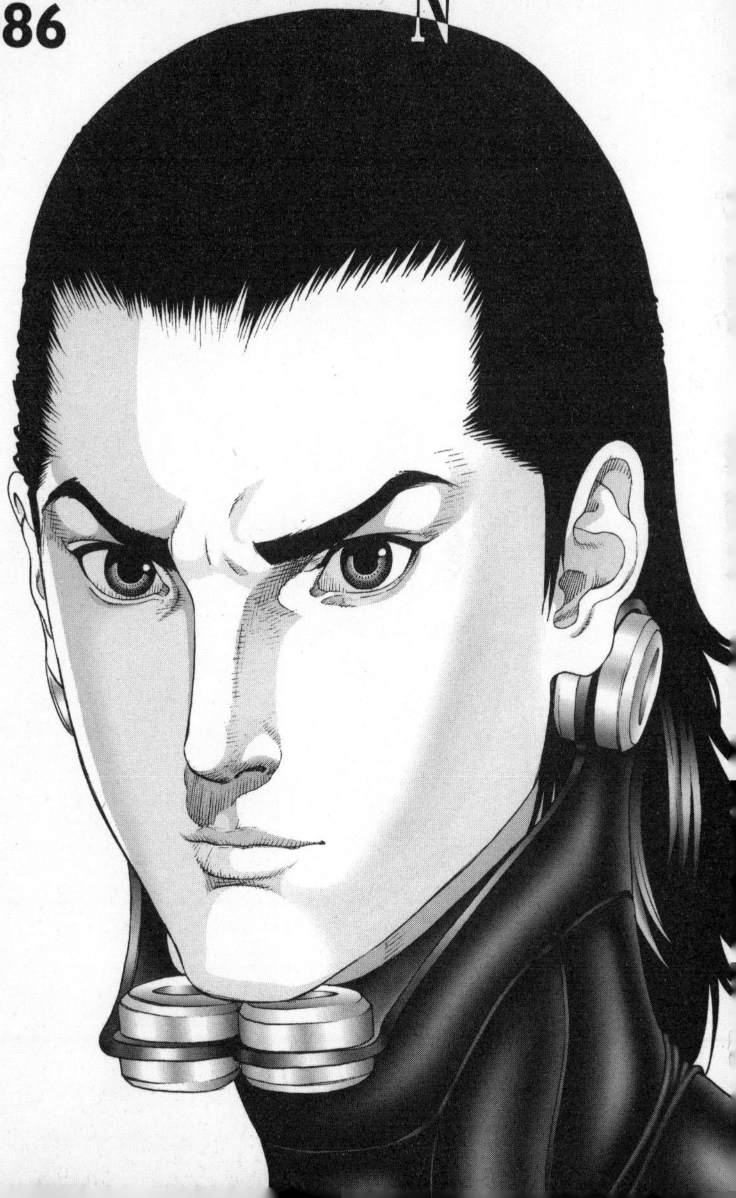

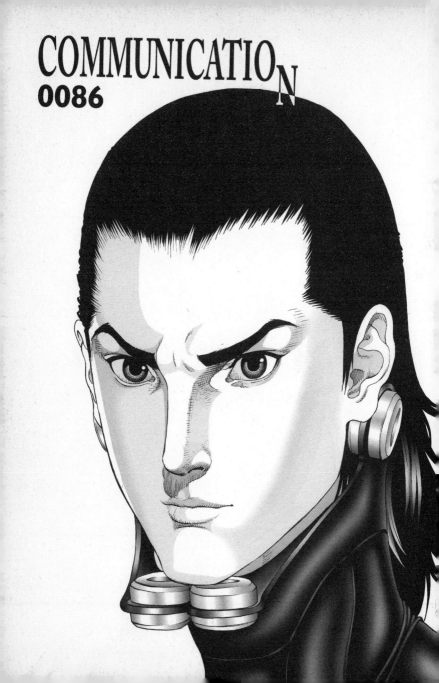

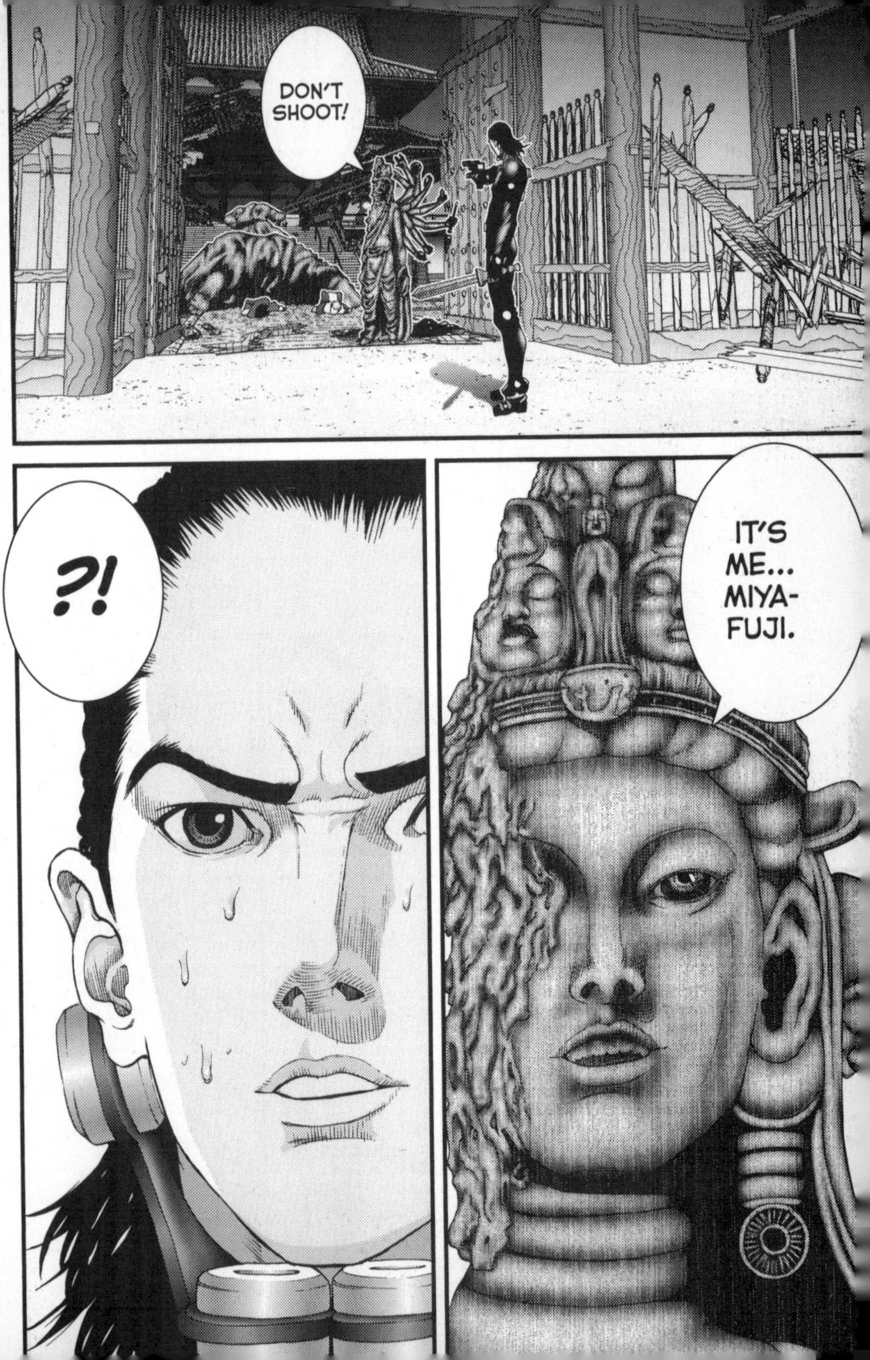
DON'T SHOOT!
IT'S ME... MIYA-FUJI.
?!

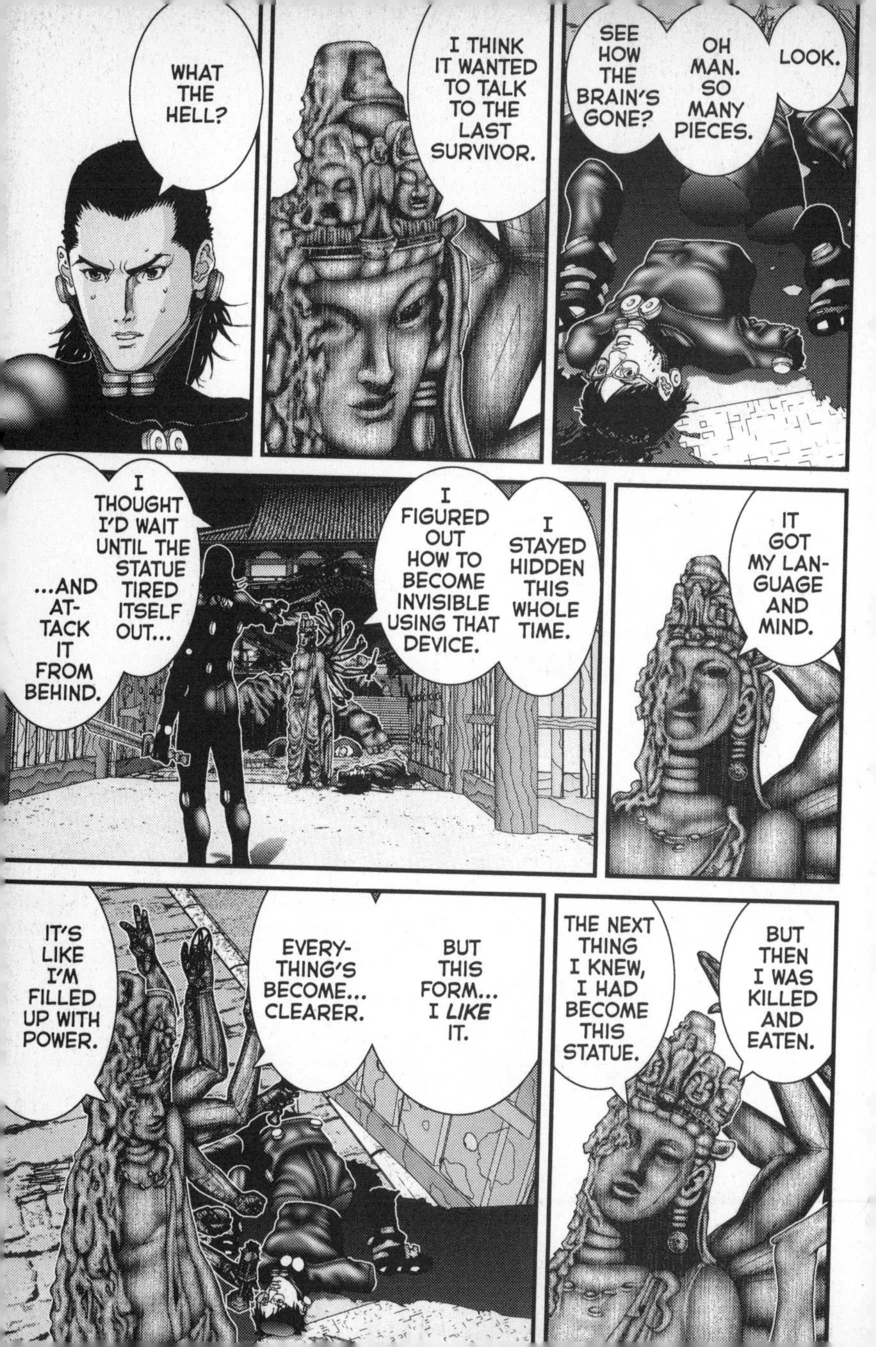

LOOK.
OH MAN. SO MANY PIECES.
SEE HOW THE BRAIN'S GONE?
I THINK IT WANTED TO TALK TO THE LAST SURVIVOR.
WHAT THE HELL?
IT GOT MY LAN-GUAGE AND MIND.
I STAYED HIDDEN THIS WHOLE TIME.
I FIGURED OUT HOW TO BECOME INVISIBLE USING THAT DEVICE.
I THOUGHT I'D WAIT UNTIL THE STATUE TIRED ITSELF OUT...
...AND AT-TACK IT FROM BEHIND.
BUT THEN I WAS KILLED AND EATEN.
THE NEXT THING I KNEW, I HAD BECOME THIS STATUE.
BUT THIS FORM... I *LIKE* IT.
EVERY-THING'S BECOME... CLEARER.
IT'S LIKE I'M FILLED UP WITH POWER.

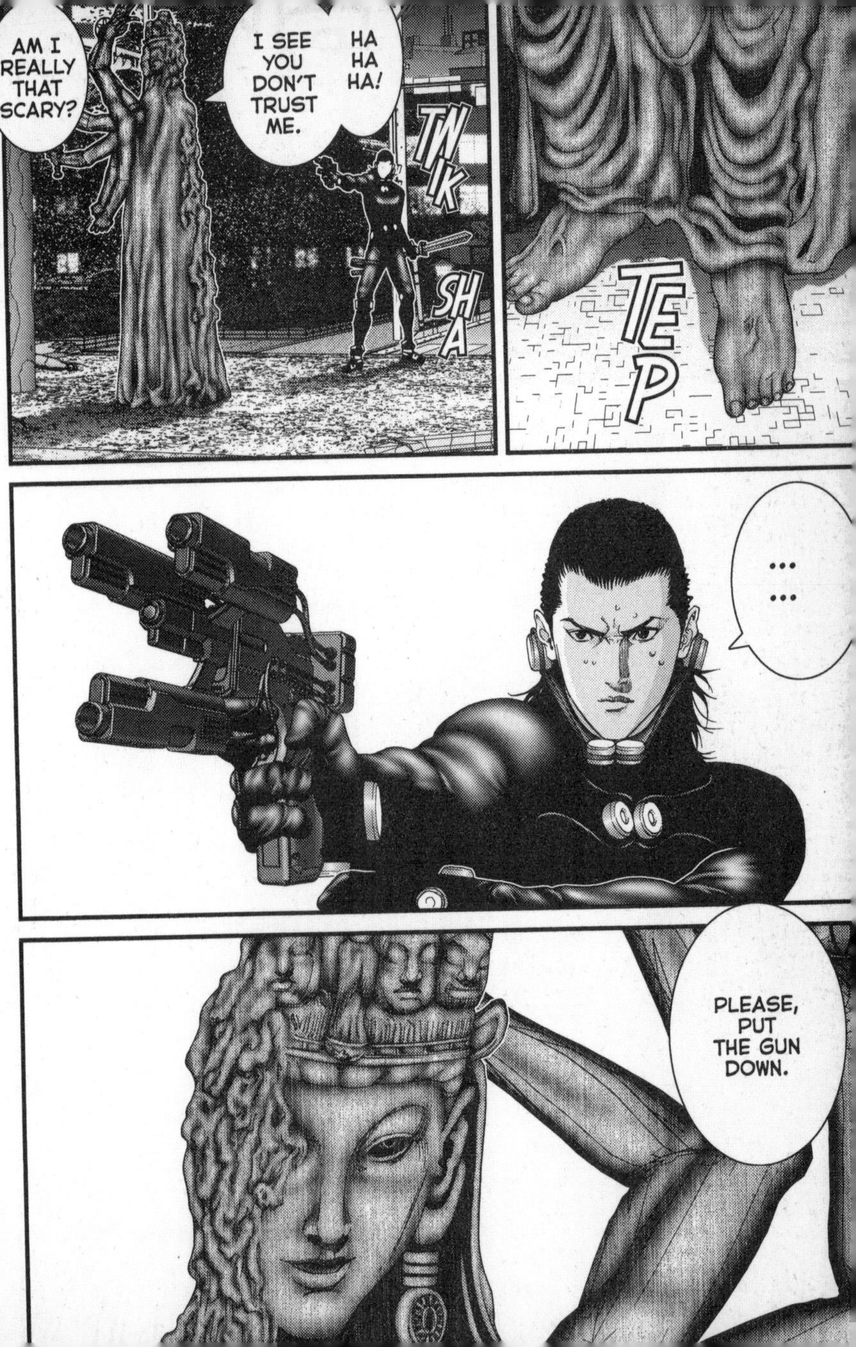
HA HA HA!
I SEE YOU DON'T TRUST ME.
AM I REALLY THAT SCARY?
TWIK
SHA
TEP
... ...
PLEASE, PUT THE GUN DOWN.

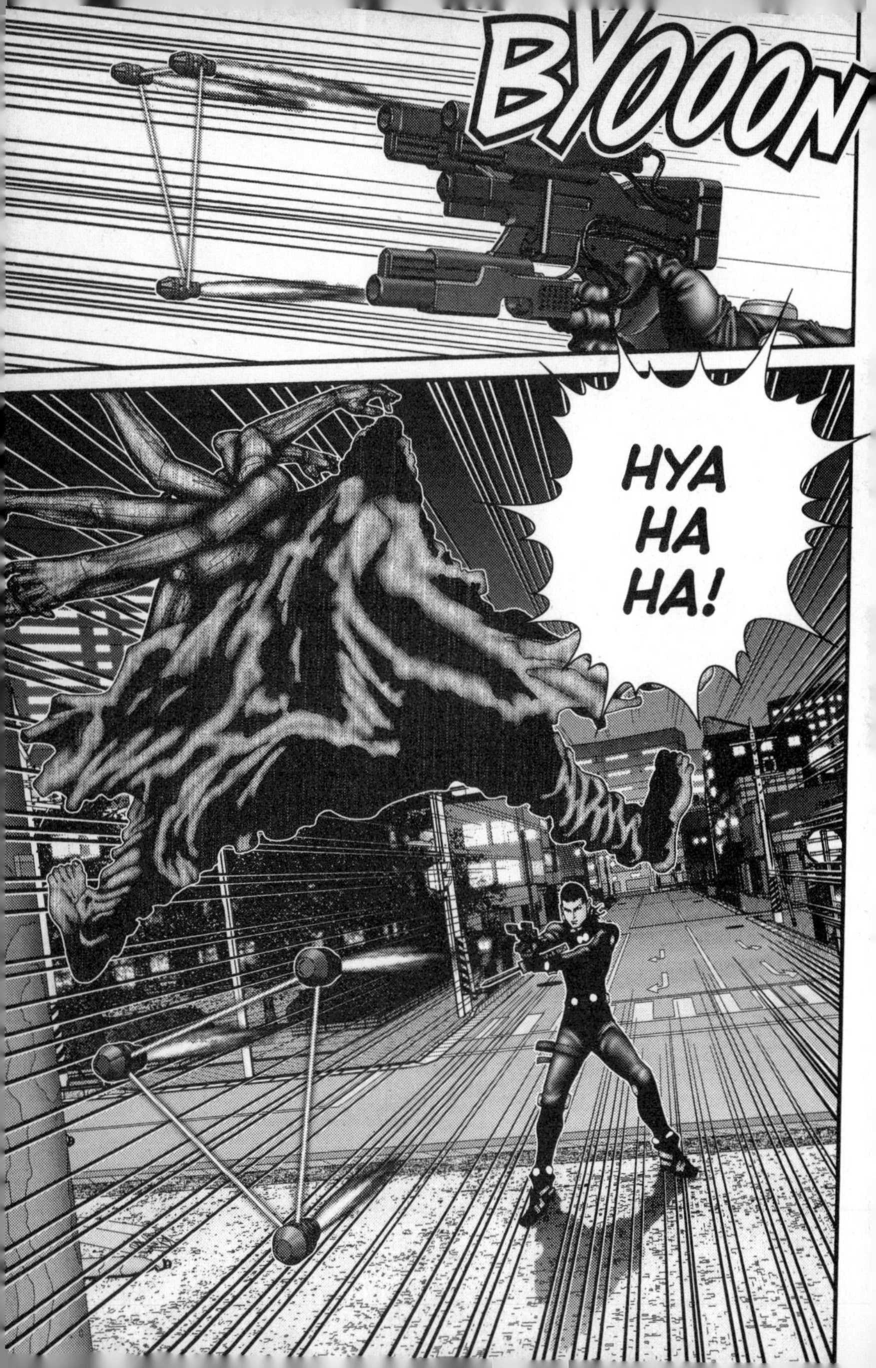
BYOOON
HYA HA HA!

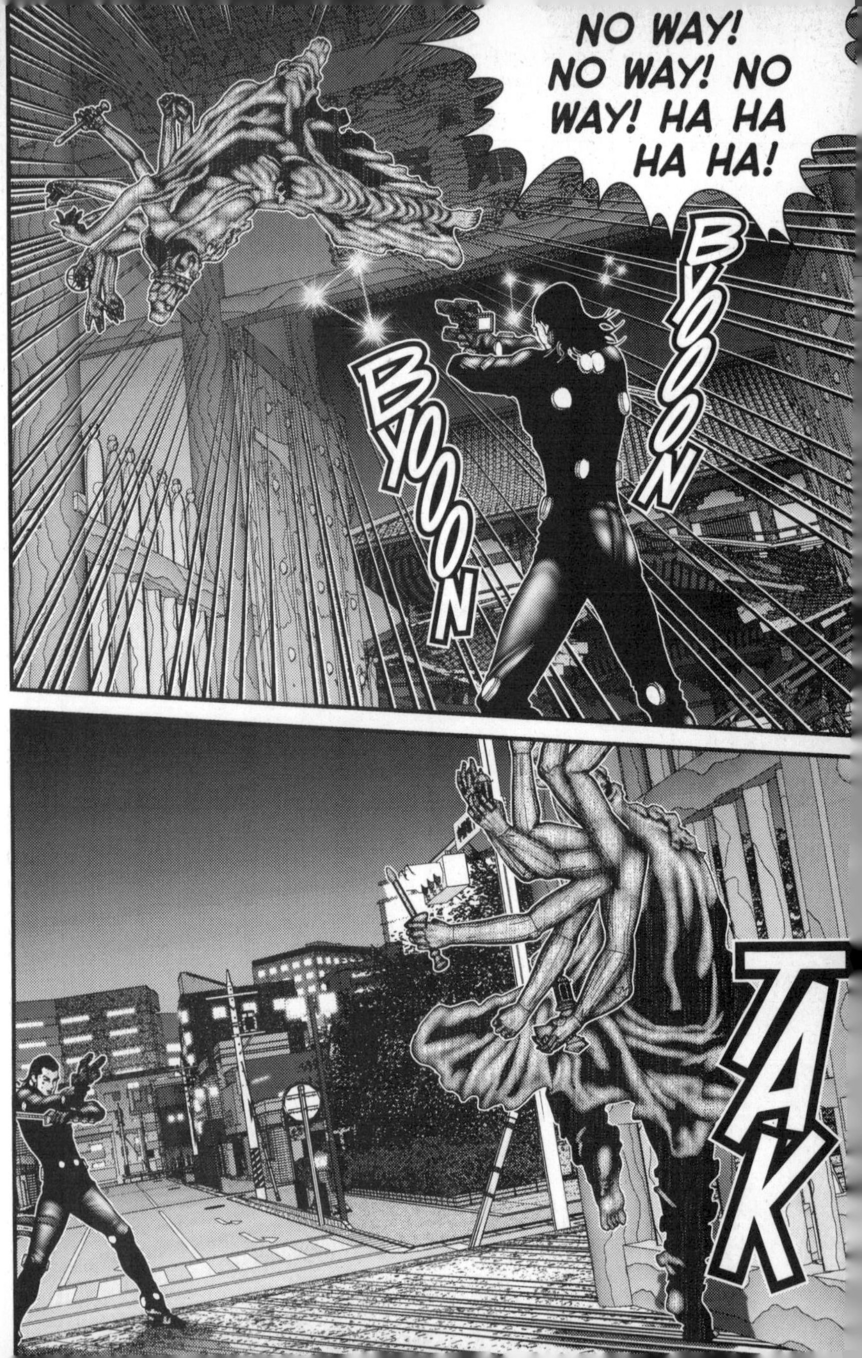
NO WAY! NO WAY! NO WAY! HA HA HA HA!
BYOOOON
BYOOOON
TAK

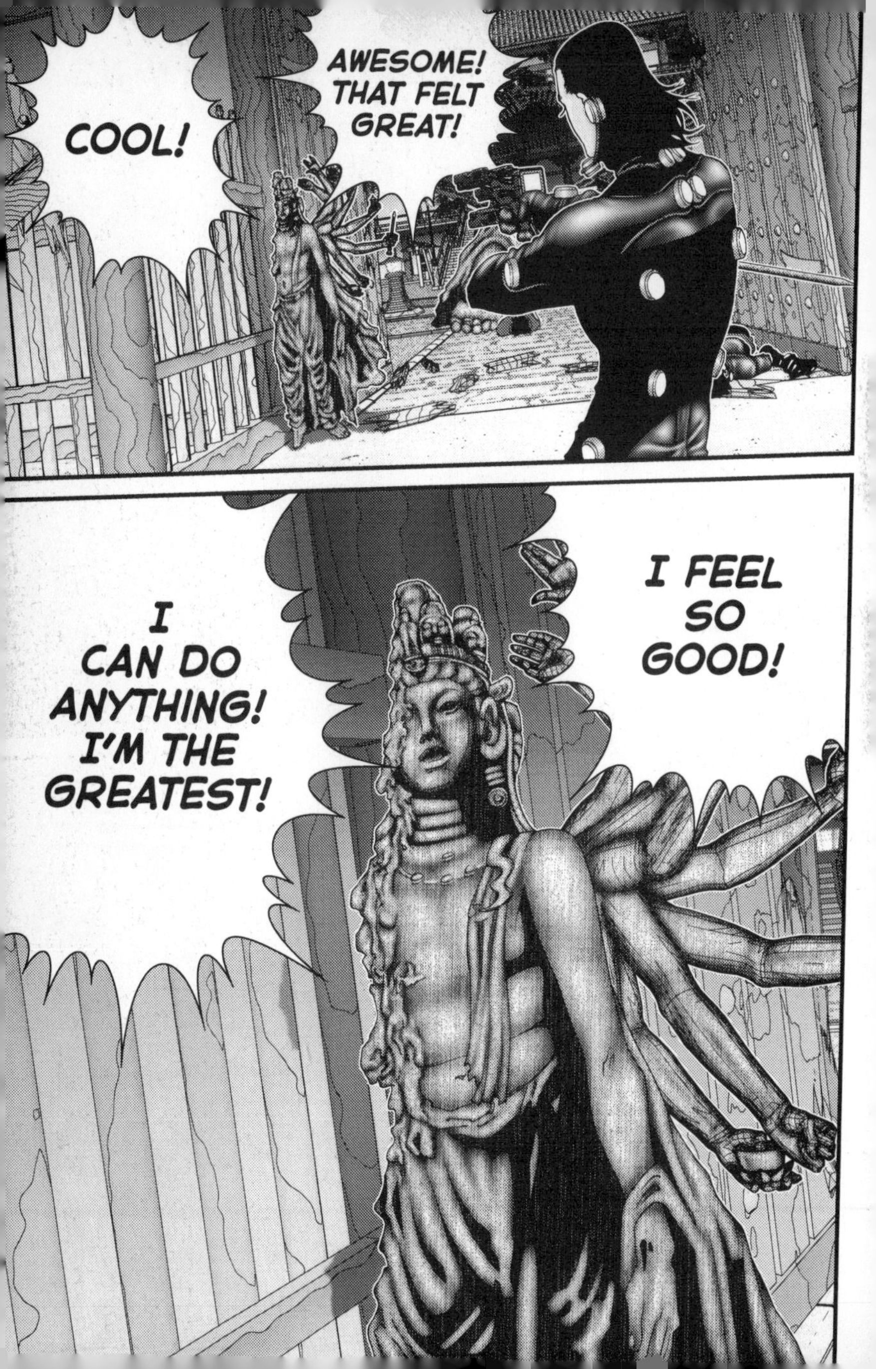
AWESOME! THAT FELT GREAT!
COOL!
I FEEL SO GOOD!
I CAN DO ANYTHING! I'M THE GREATEST!

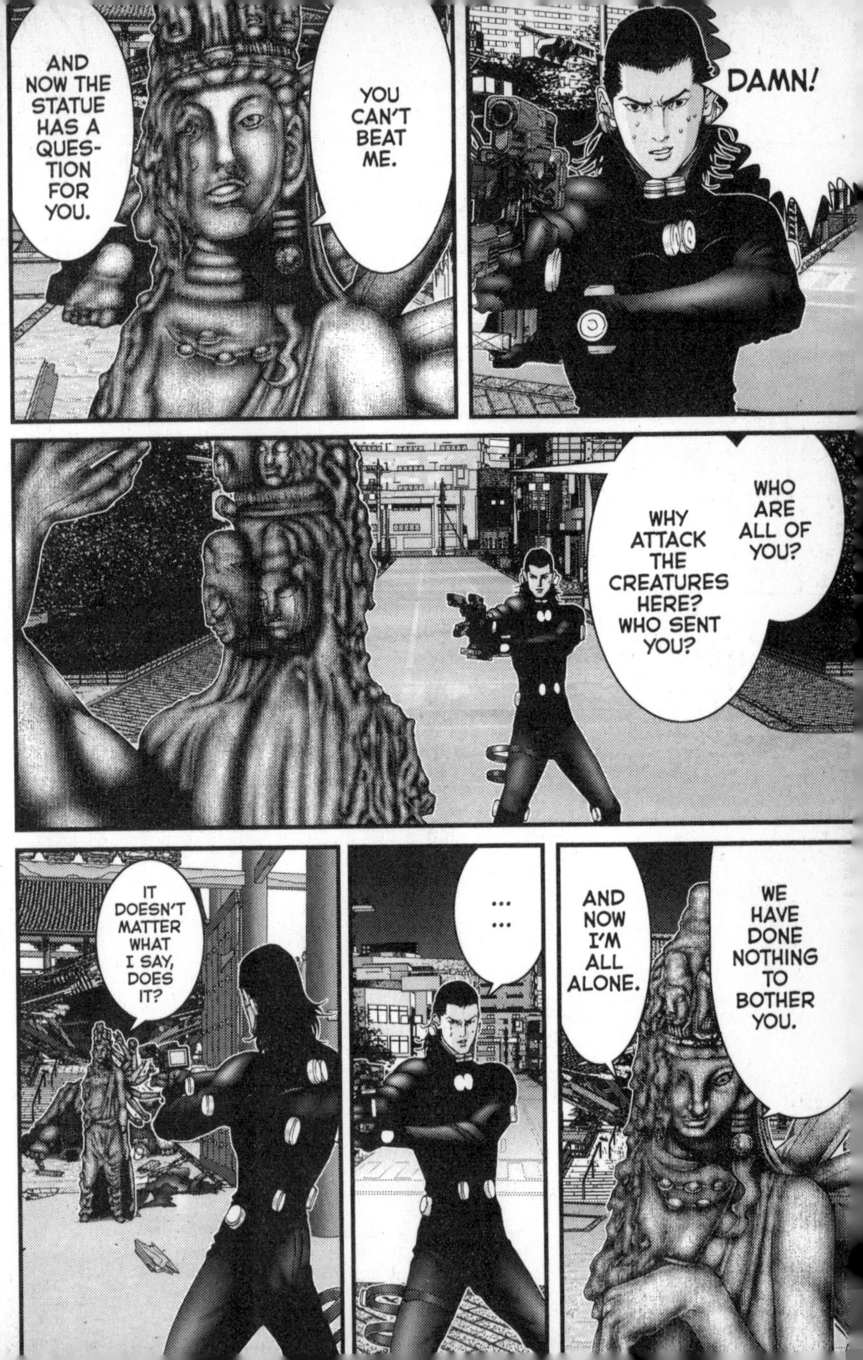
DAMN!
YOU CAN'T BEAT ME.
AND NOW THE STATUE HAS A QUES-TION FOR YOU.
WHO ARE ALL OF YOU?
WHY ATTACK THE CREATURES HERE? WHO SENT YOU?
WE HAVE DONE NOTHING TO BOTHER YOU.
AND NOW I'M ALL ALONE.
... ...
IT DOESN'T MATTER WHAT I SAY, DOES IT?

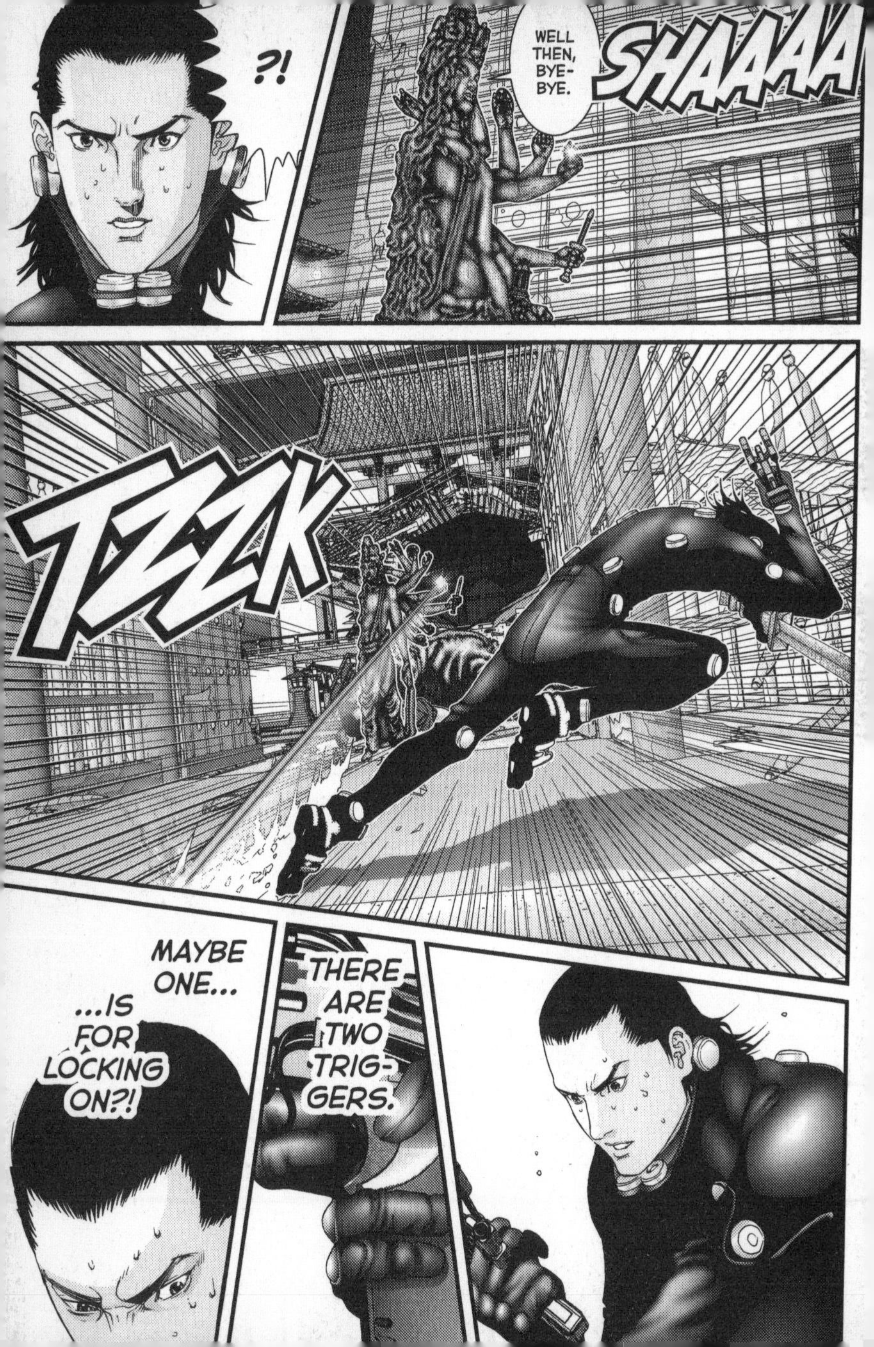
?!
WELL THEN, BYE-BYE.
SHAAAAA
TZZK
MAYBE ONE...
...IS FOR LOCKING ON?!
THERE ARE TWO TRIG-GERS.

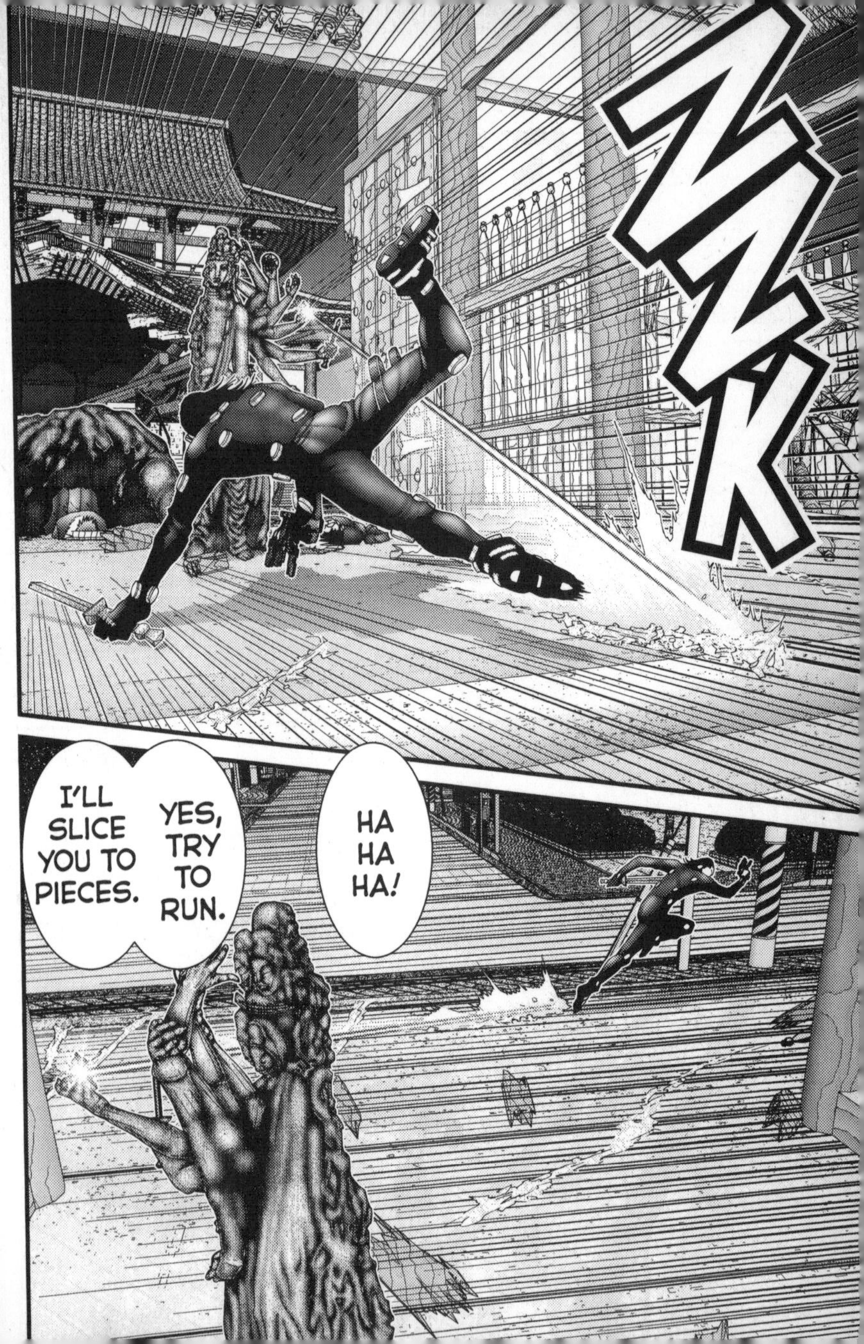
NNK
HA HA HA!
YES, TRY TO RUN.
I'LL SLICE YOU TO PIECES.

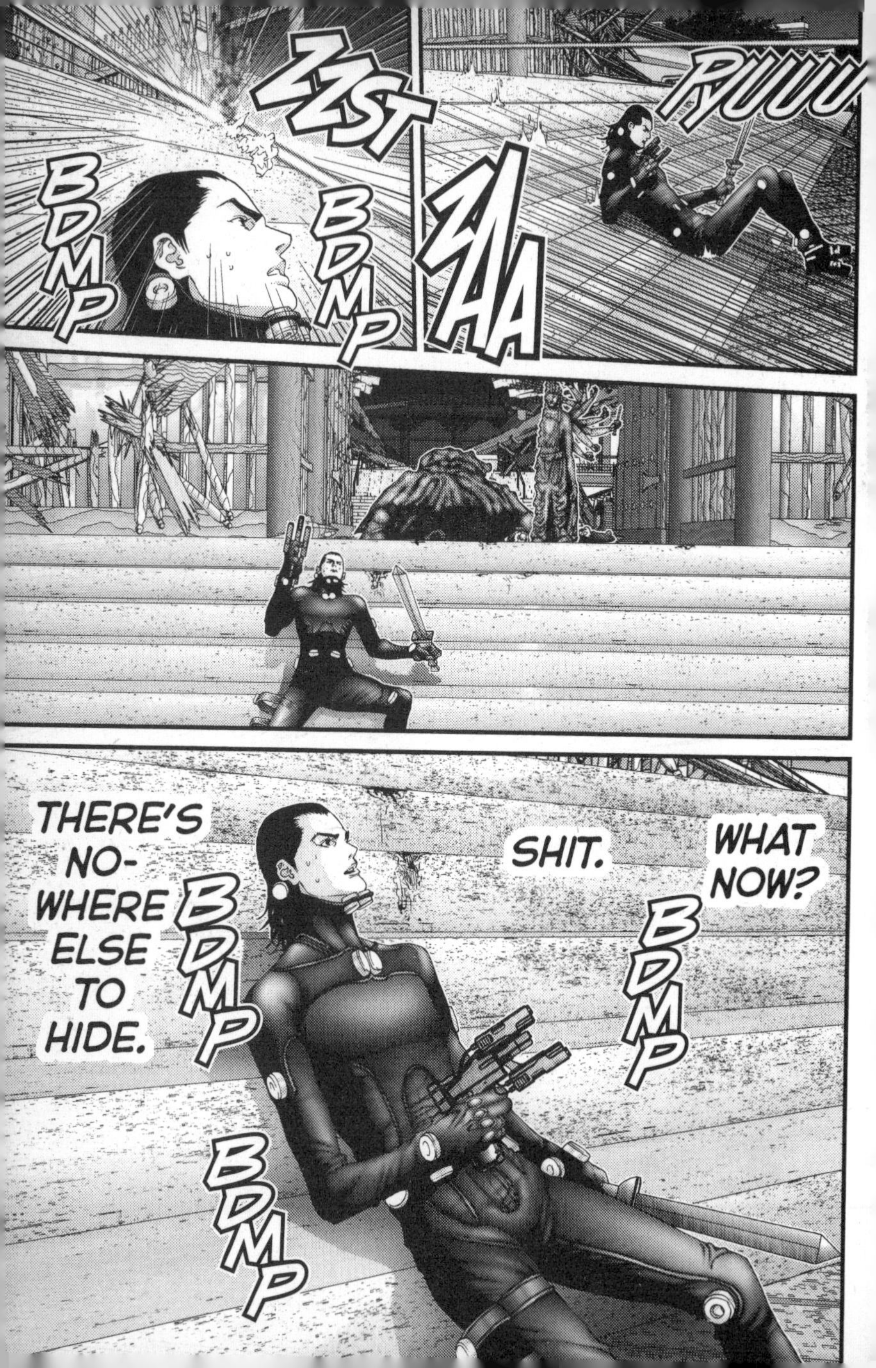
ZZST
BDMP
BDMP
RYUUU
ZAAA
THERE'S NO-WHERE ELSE TO HIDE.
BDMP
SHIT.
WHAT NOW?
BDMP
BDMP

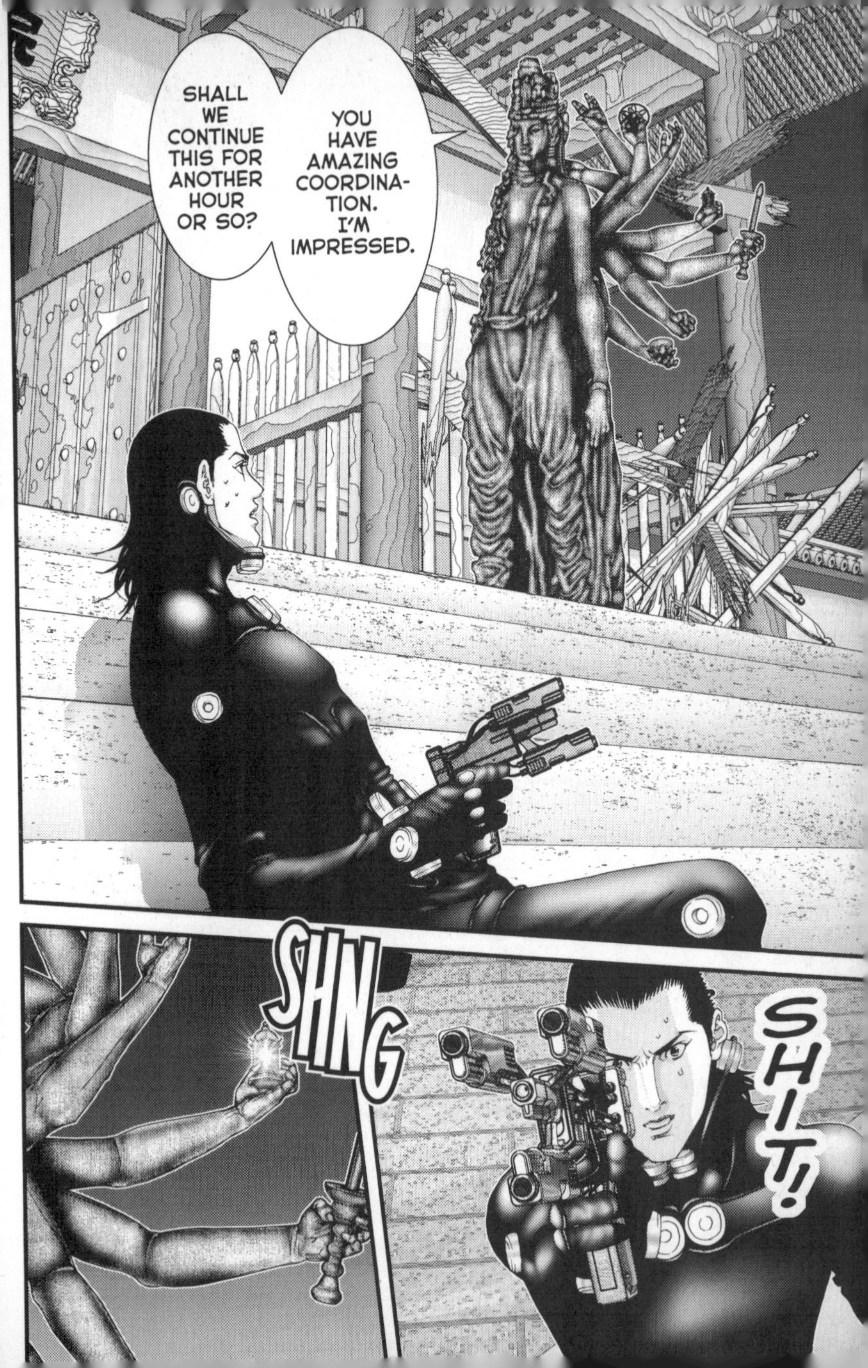
SHALL WE CONTINUE THIS FOR ANOTHER HOUR OR SO?
YOU HAVE AMAZING COORDINA-TION. I'M IMPRESSED.
SHING
SHIT!

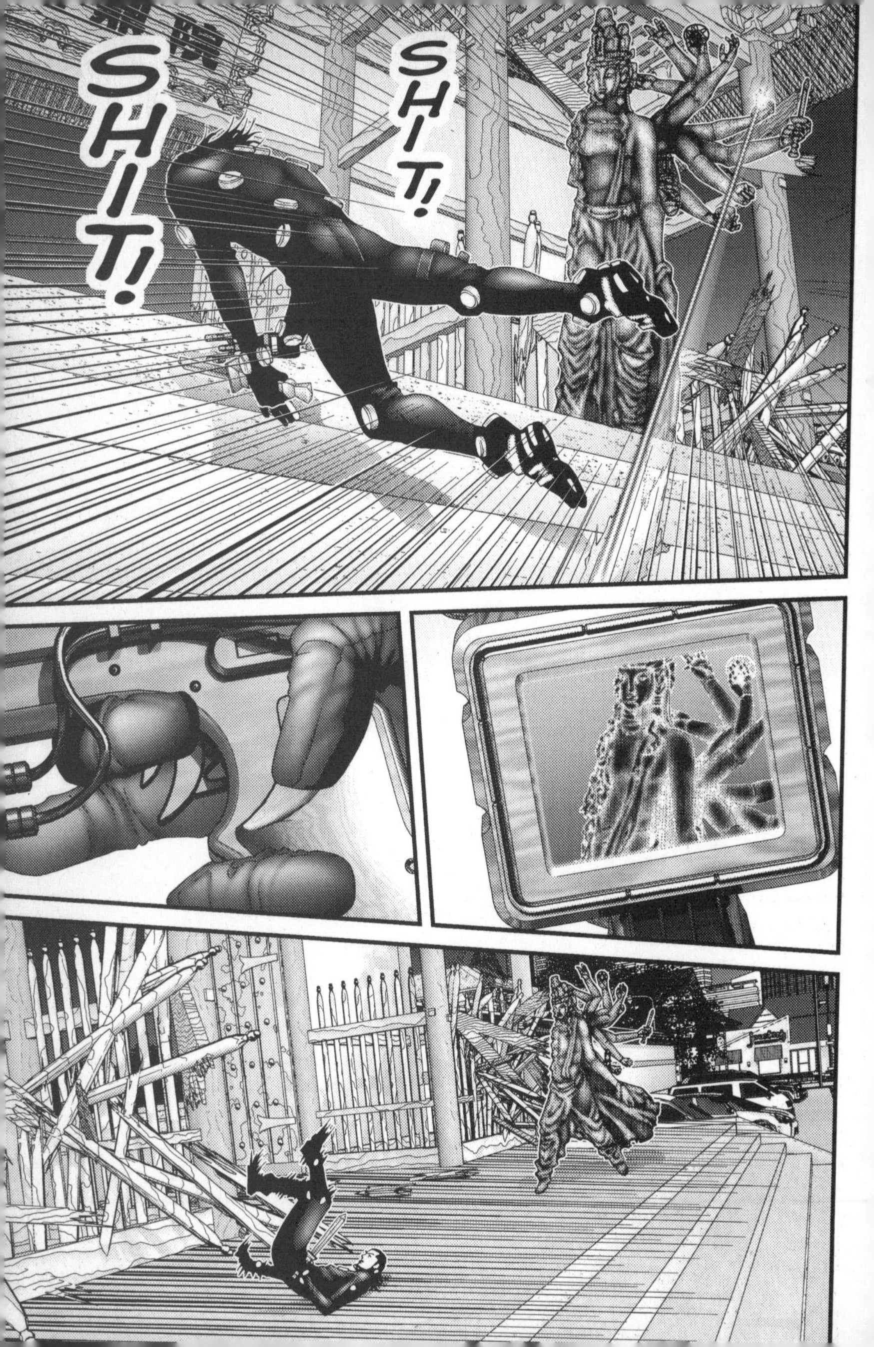
SHIT!
SHIT!

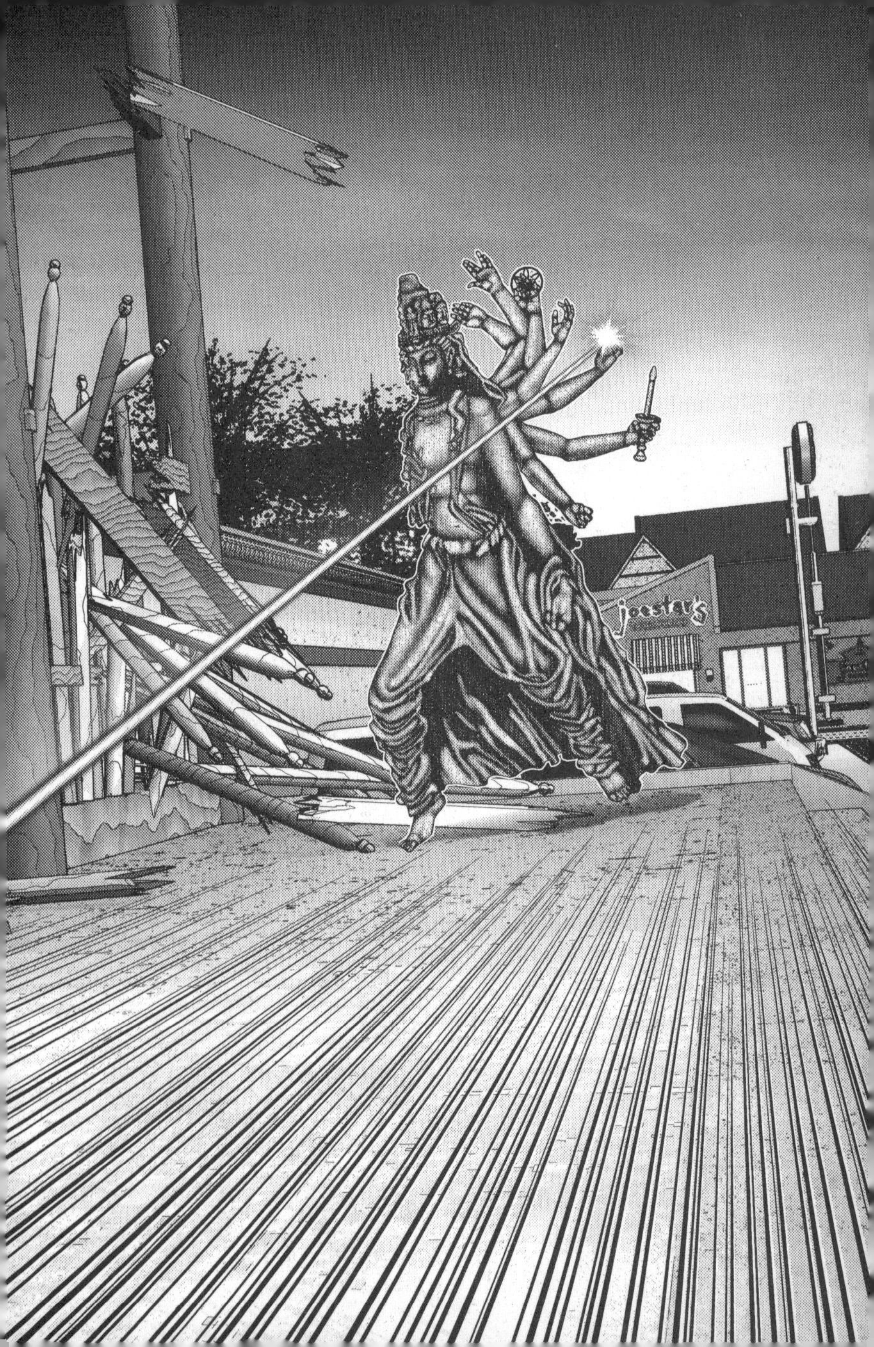
joestar's

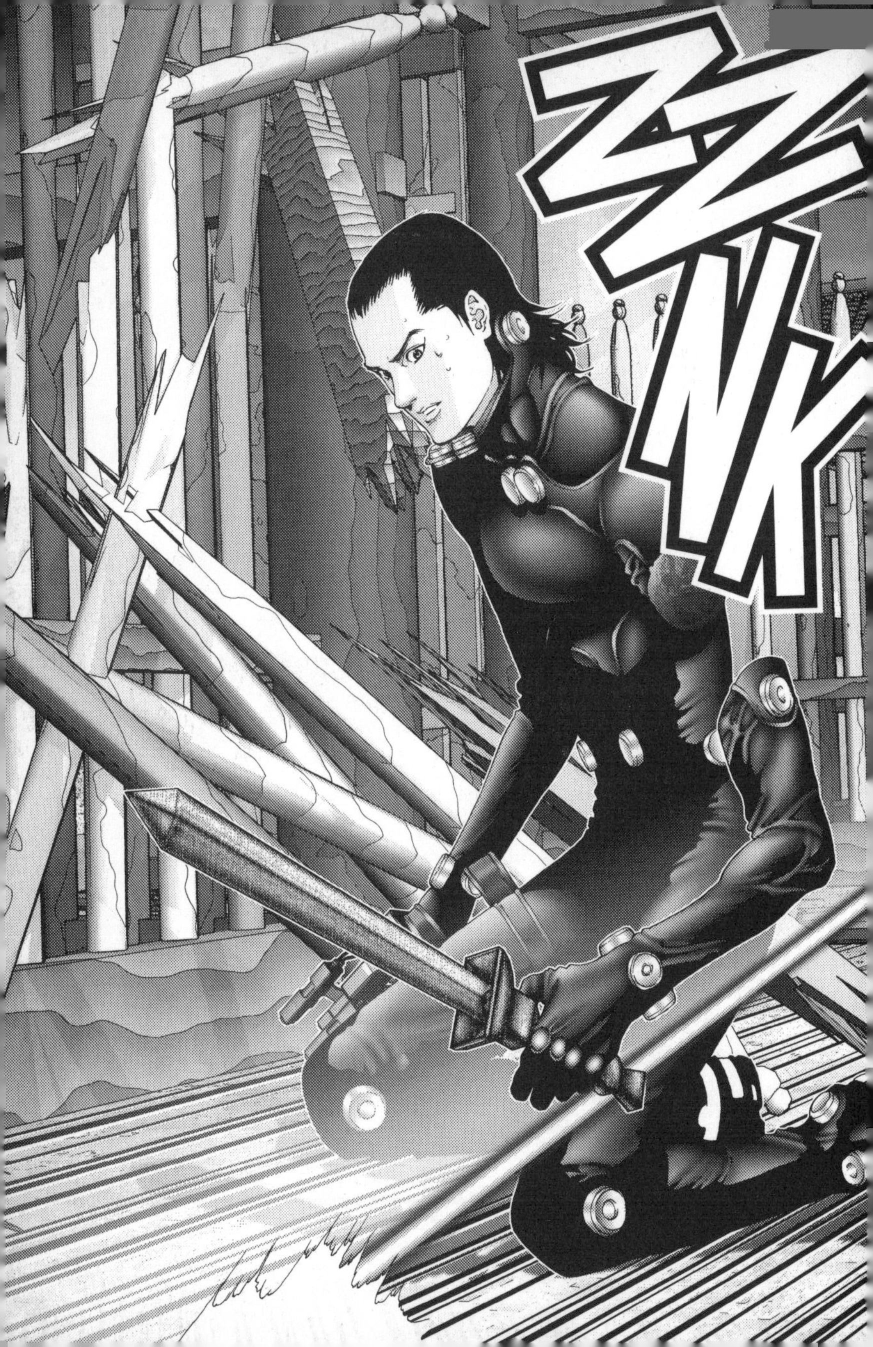
ZZNK

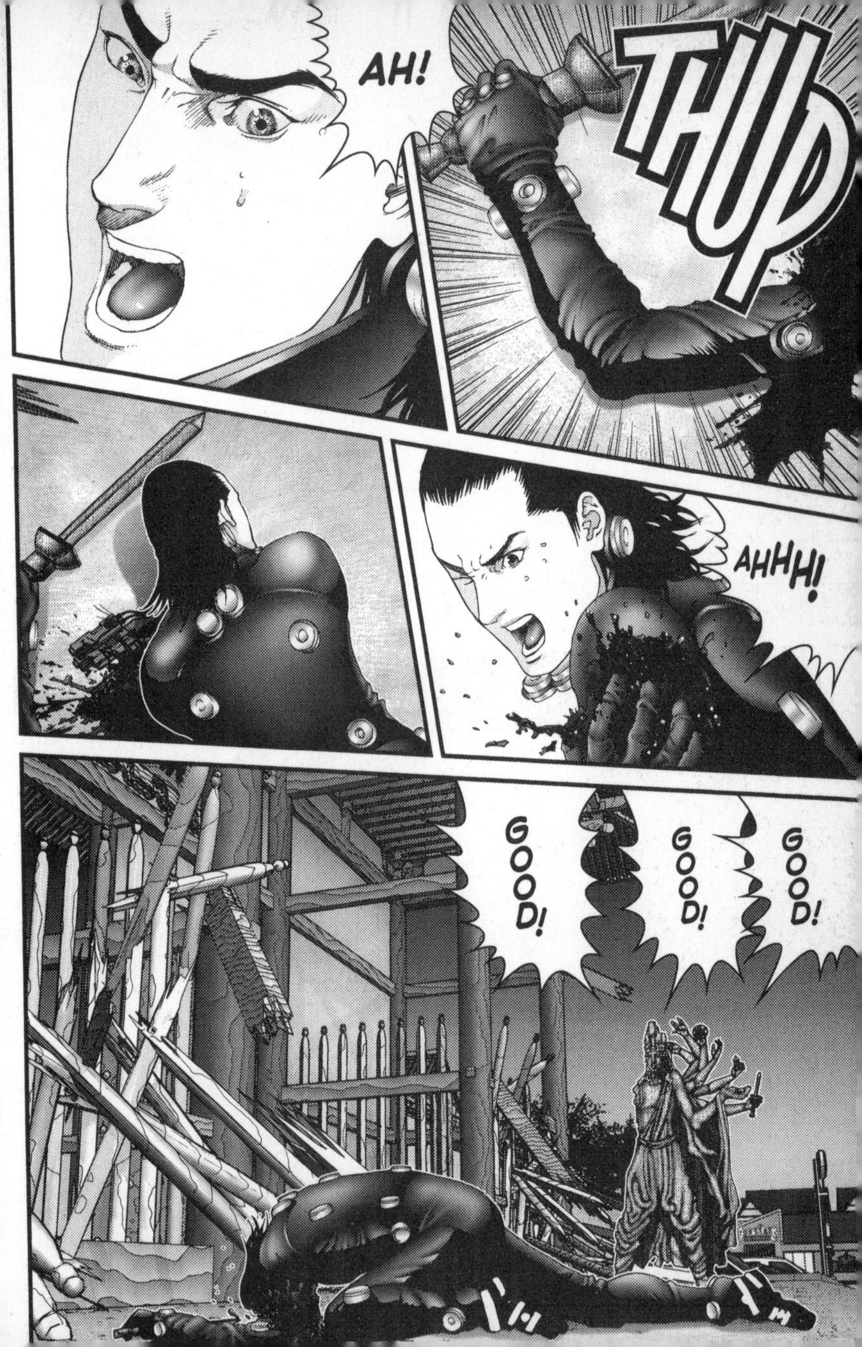
THUP
AH!
AHHH!
GOOD!
GOOD!
GOOD!

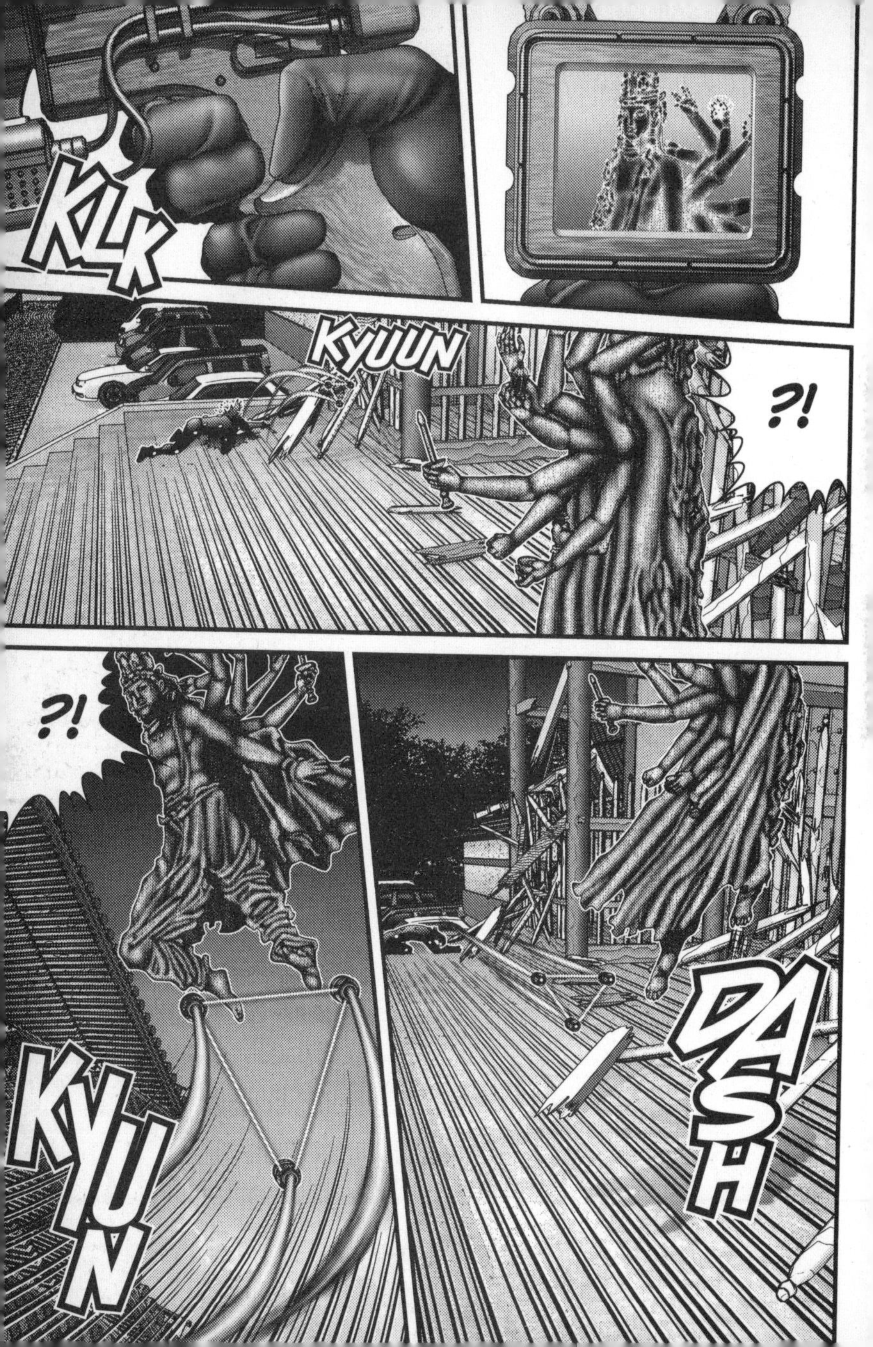

KLIK
KYUUN
?!
?!
KYUN
DASH

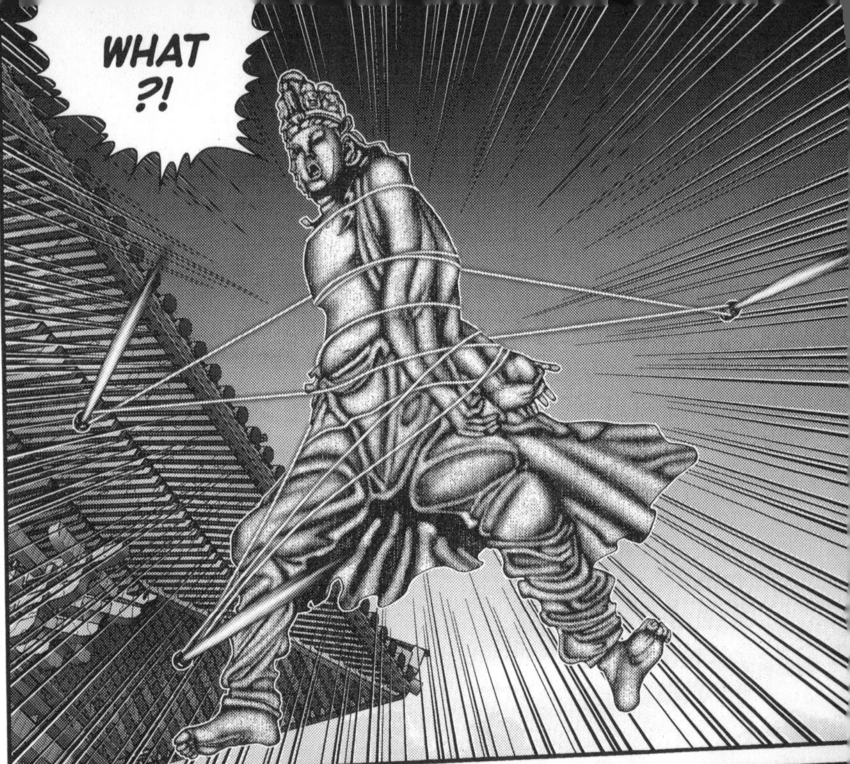
WHAT ?!

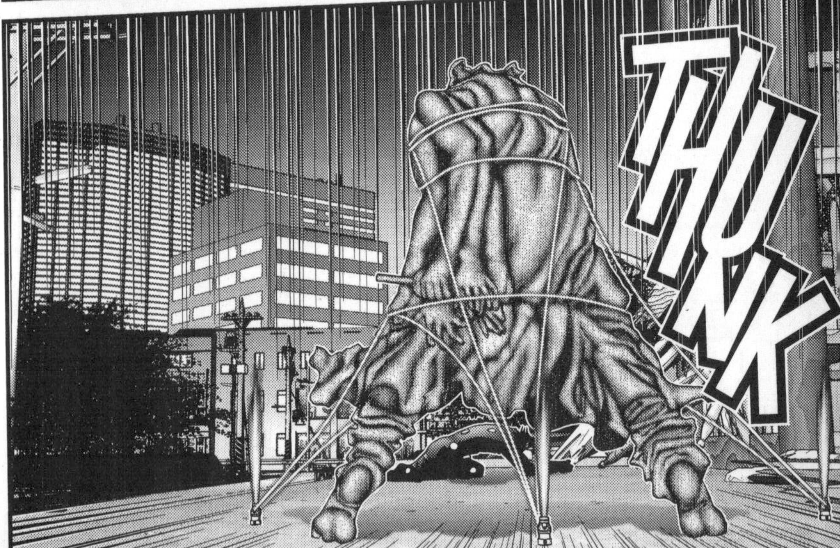
THUNK

0087
TRUE FORM

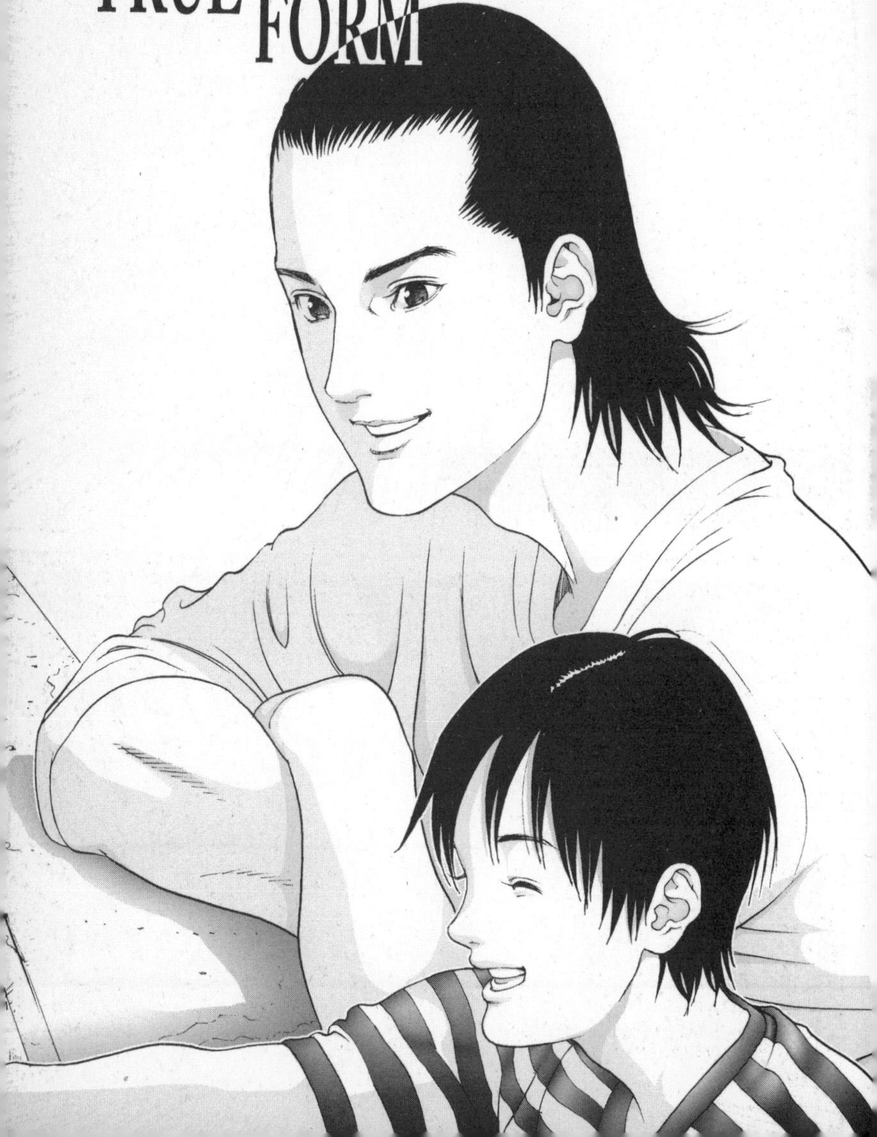

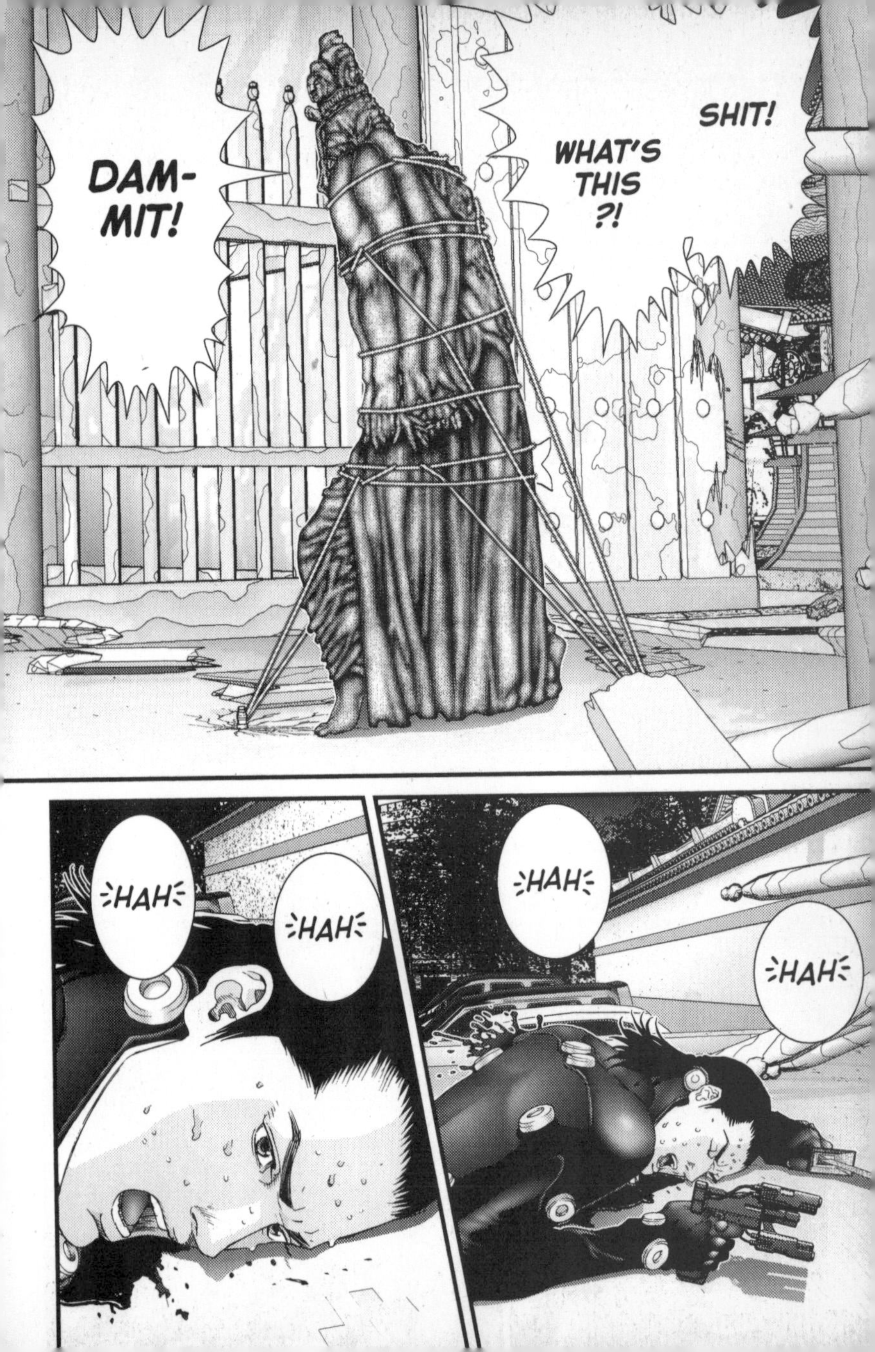

SHIT!
WHAT'S THIS ?!
DAM-MIT!
HAH
HAH
HAH
HAH

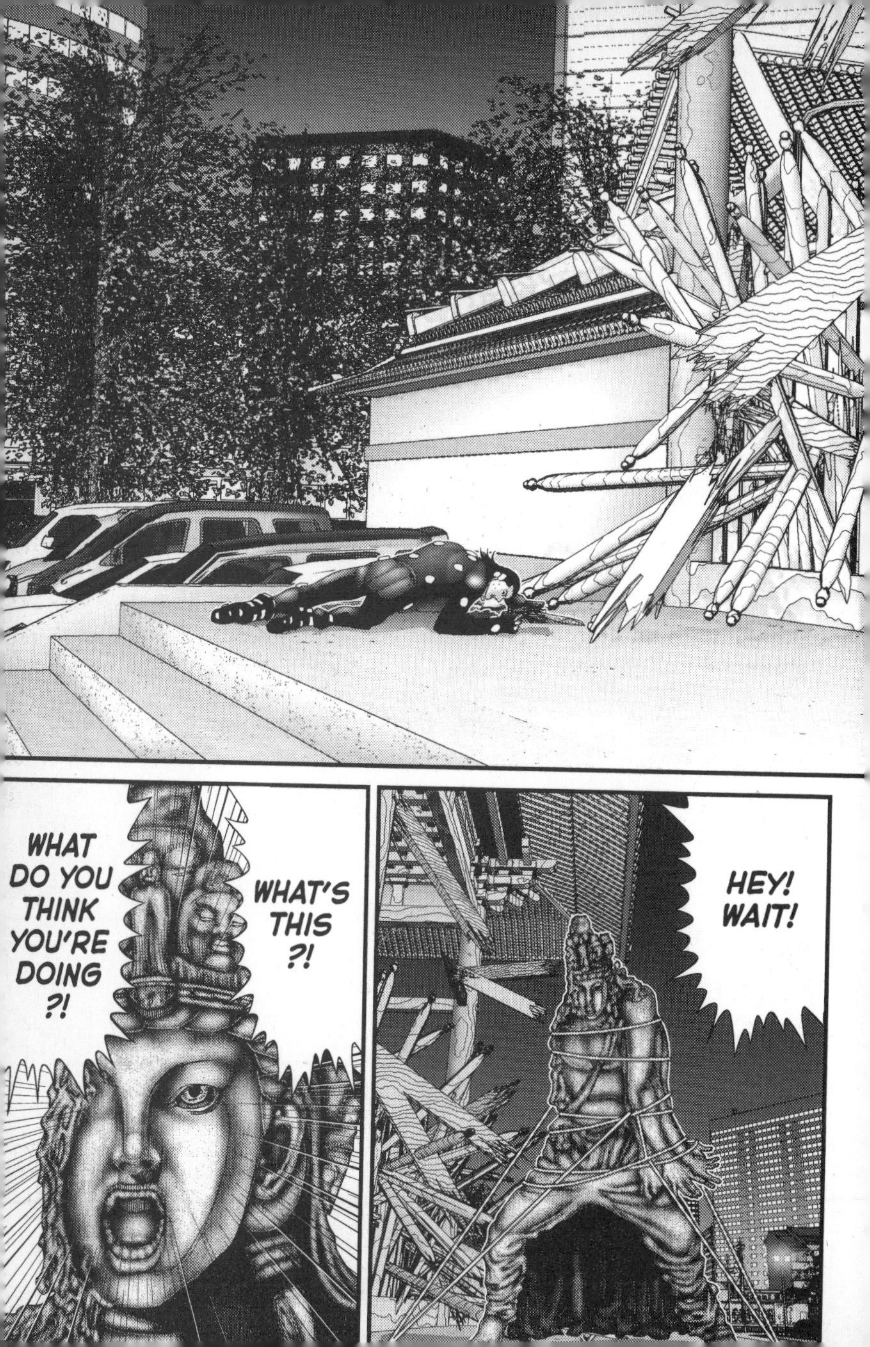
HEY! WAIT!
WHAT'S THIS ?!
WHAT DO YOU THINK YOU'RE DOING ?!

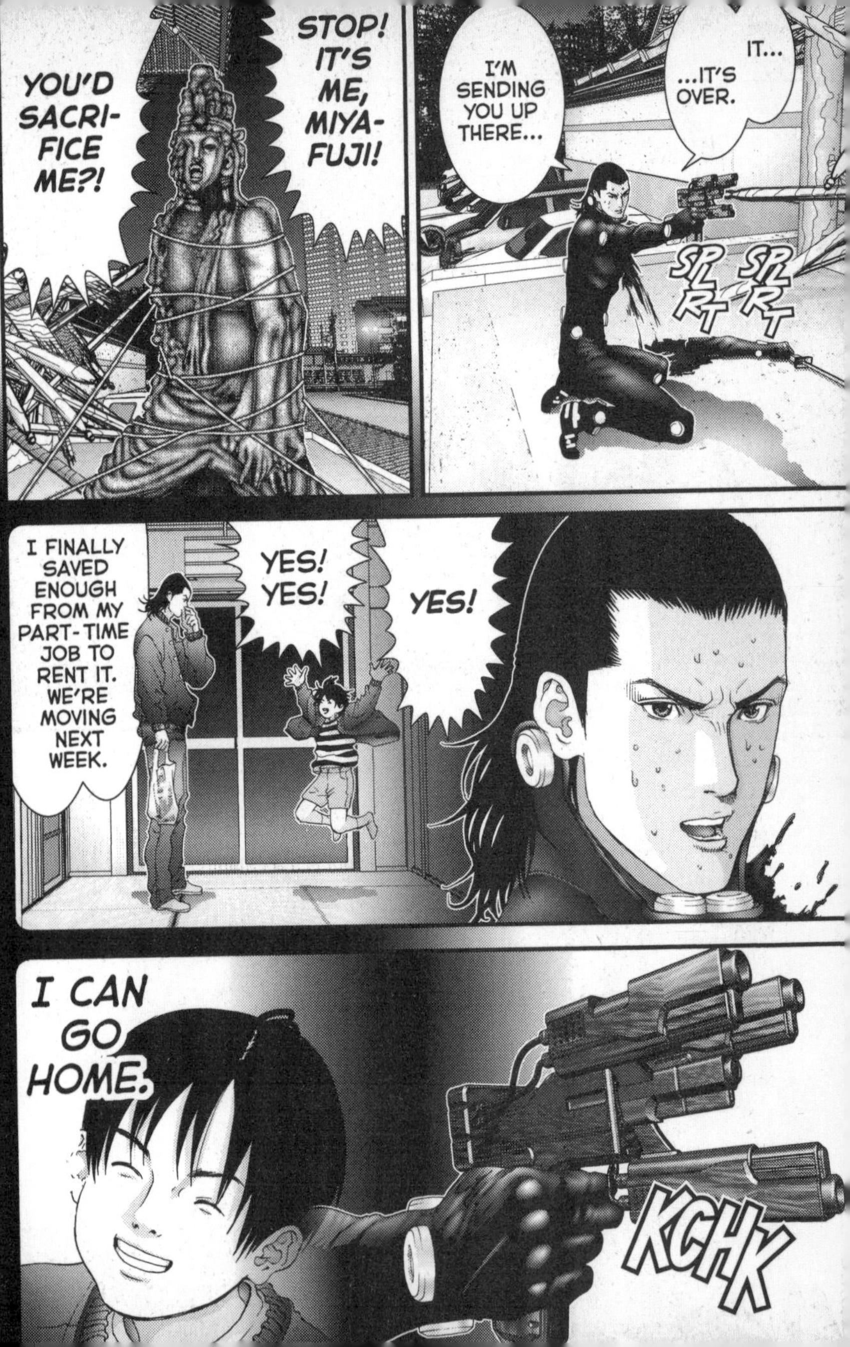
IT...
...IT'S OVER.
I'M SENDING YOU UP THERE...
SPLRT SPLRT
STOP! IT'S ME, MIYA-FUJI!
YOU'D SACRI-FICE ME?!
YES!
YES! YES!
I FINALLY SAVED ENOUGH FROM MY PART-TIME JOB TO RENT IT. WE'RE MOVING NEXT WEEK.
I CAN GO HOME.
KCHK

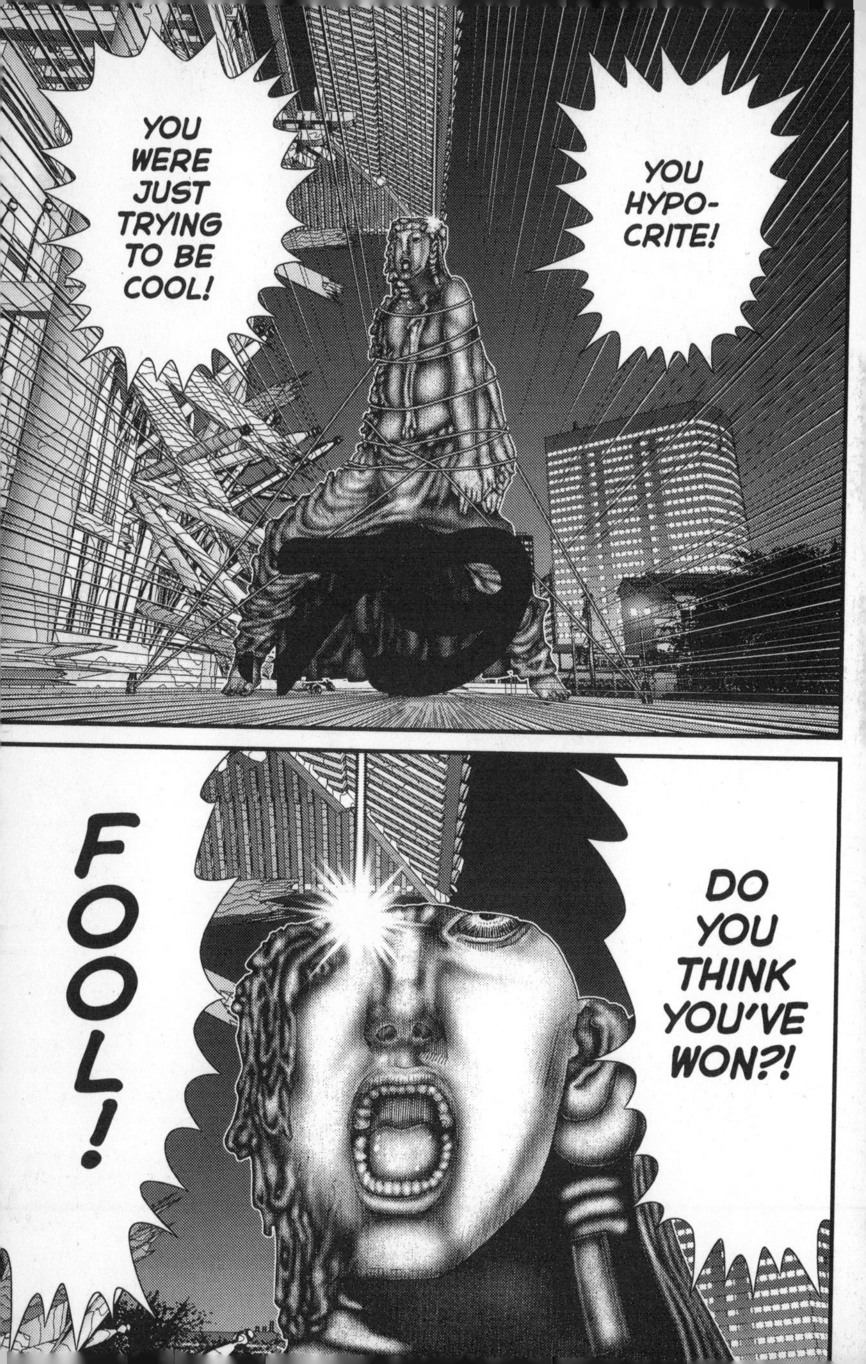
YOU HYPO-CRITE!
YOU WERE JUST TRYING TO BE COOL!
DO YOU THINK YOU'VE WON?!
FOOL!

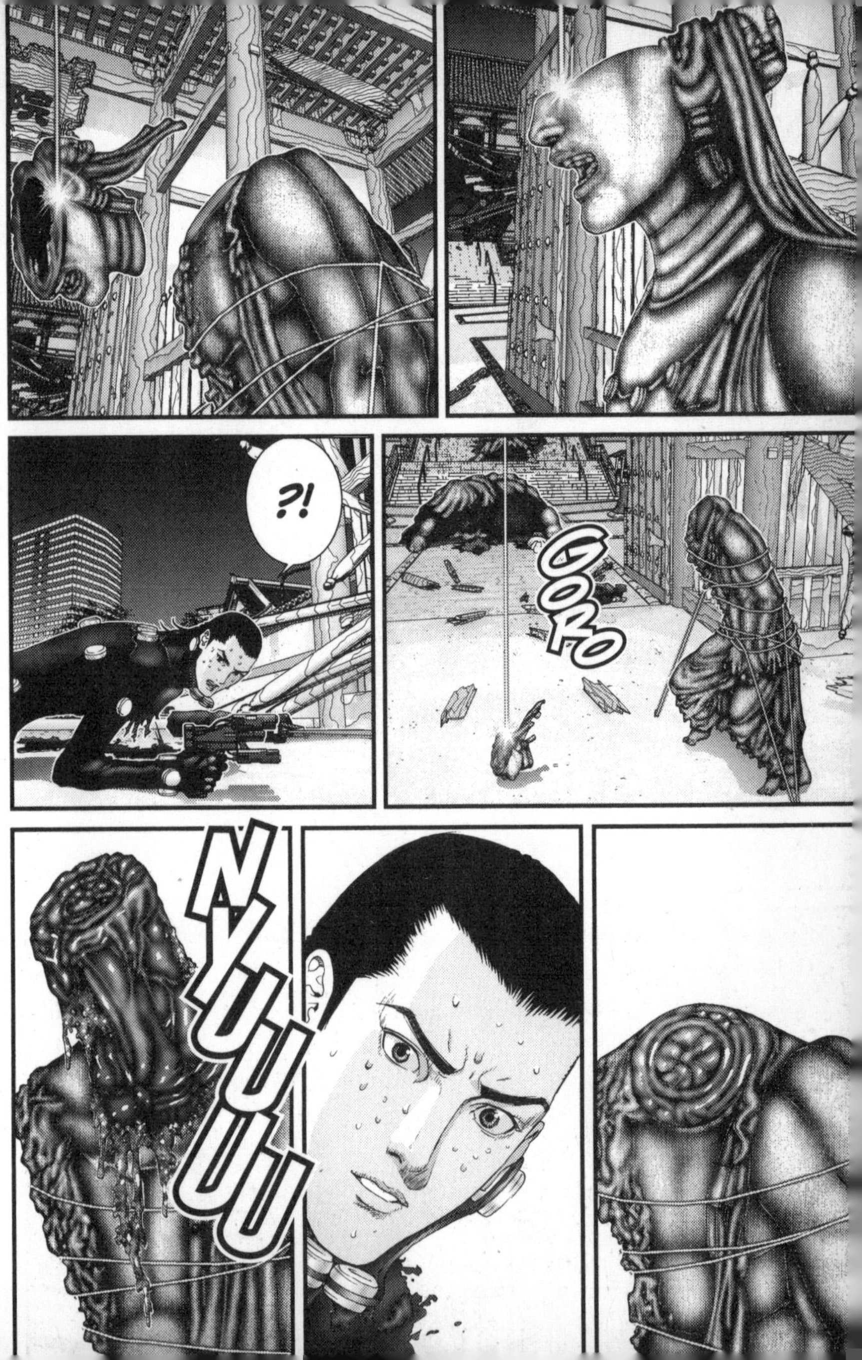

?!
GORO
NYUUUU

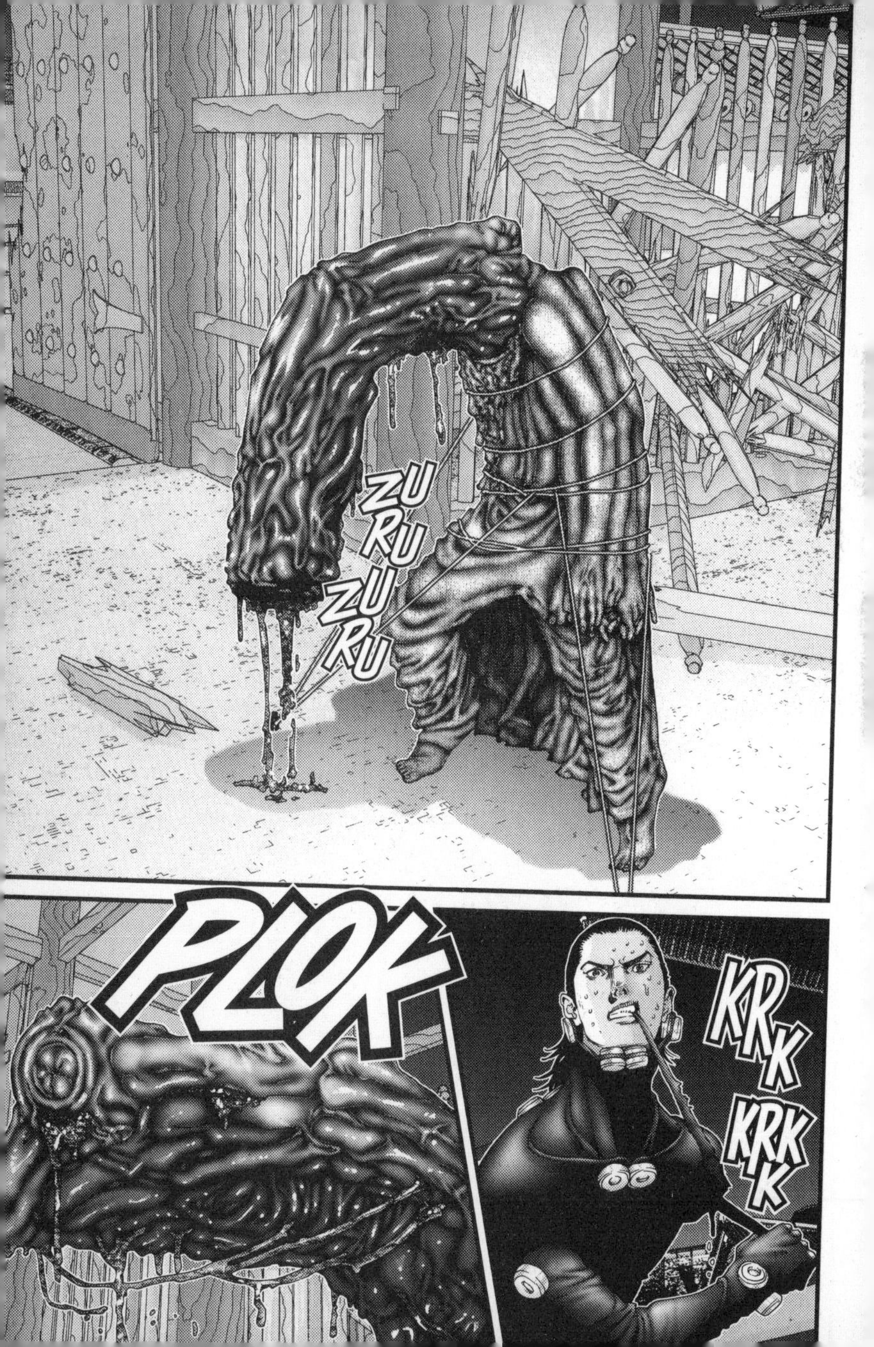

ZURUZURUZURUZURU
PLOK
KRK
KRK
KRK
K

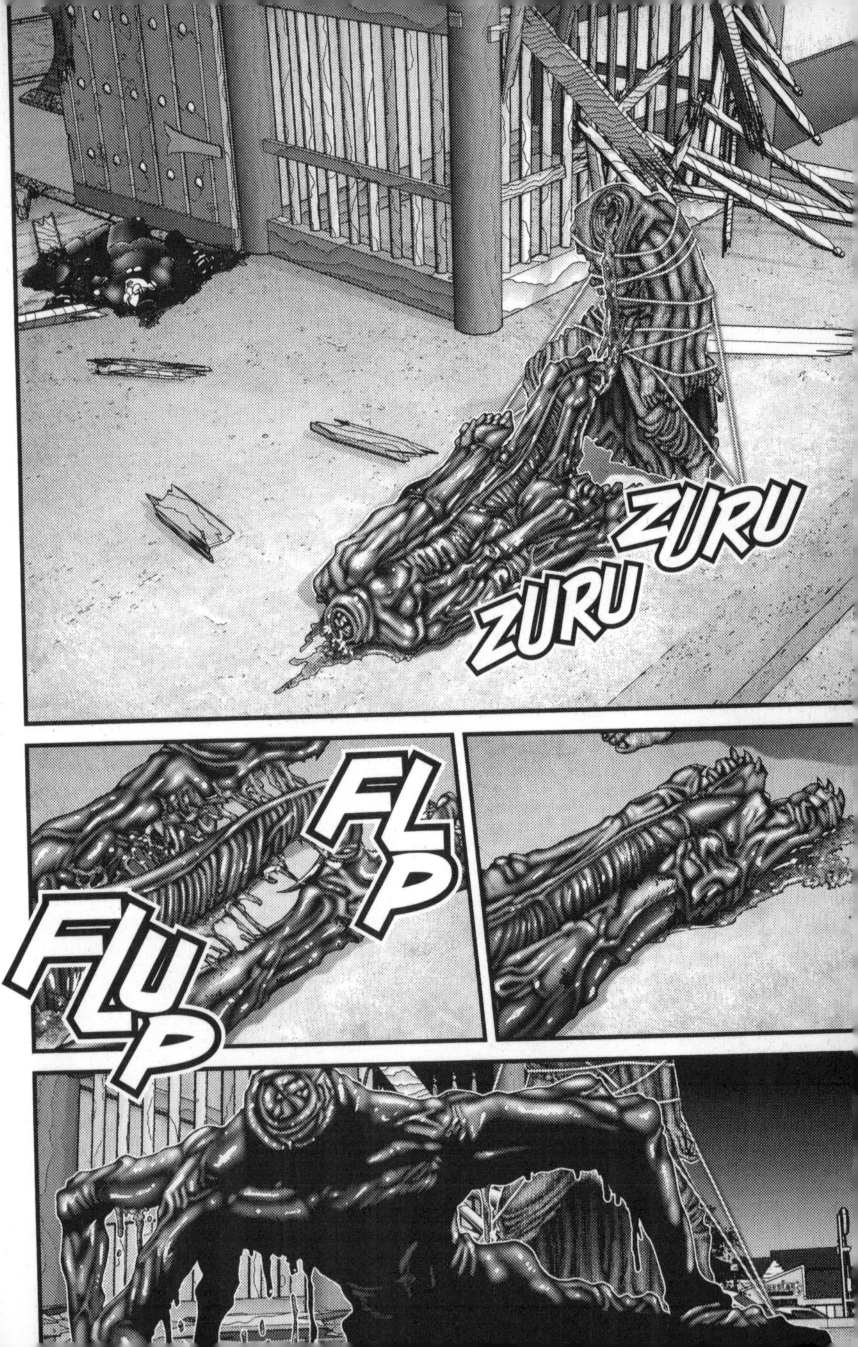
ZURU ZURU
FLIP
FLUP

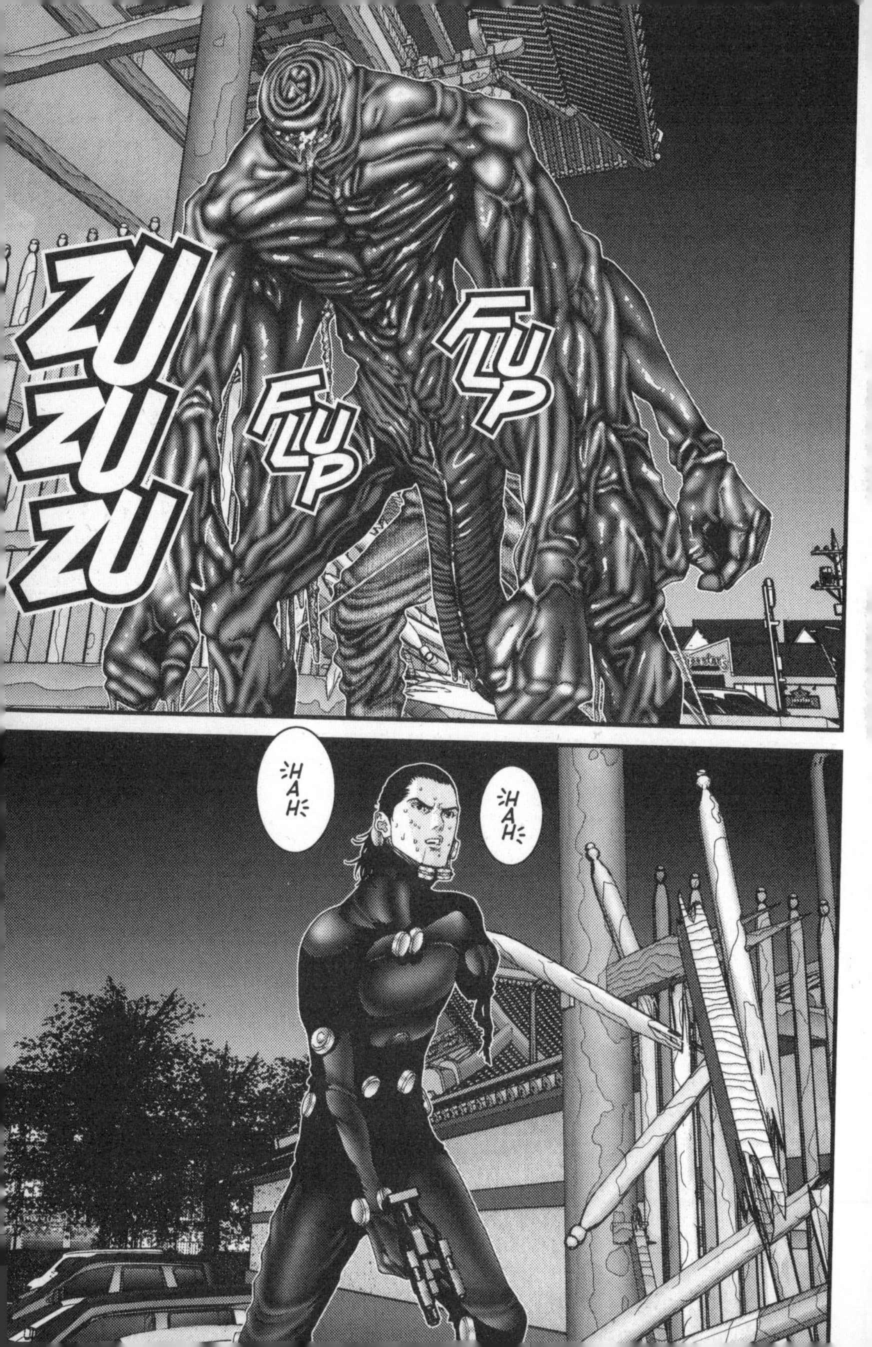
ZU ZU ZU ZU
FLUP
FLUP
HAH
HAH

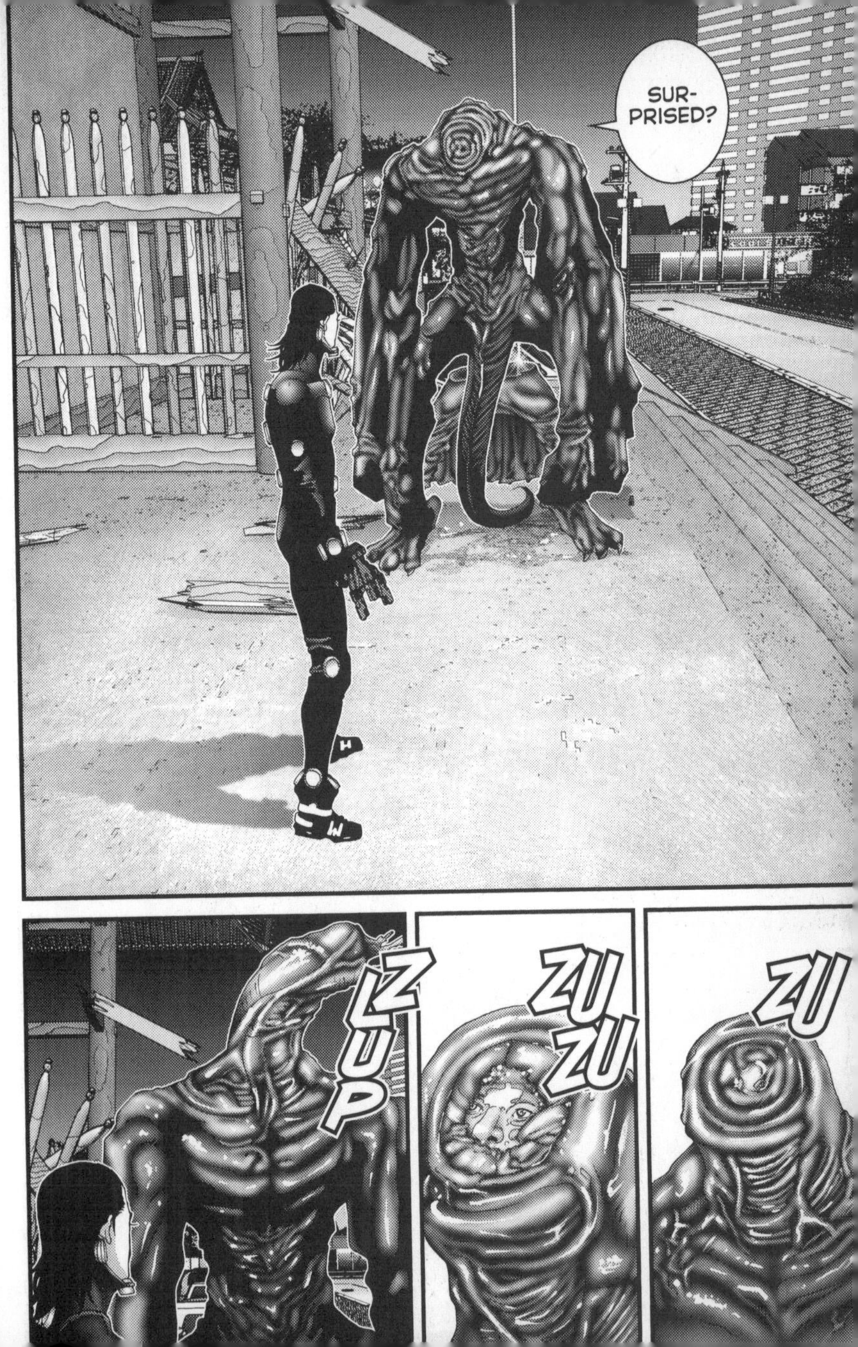
SUR-
PRISED?
ZLUP
ZU ZU
ZU

I'M NOT GONNA HOLD BACK.

FLRRP

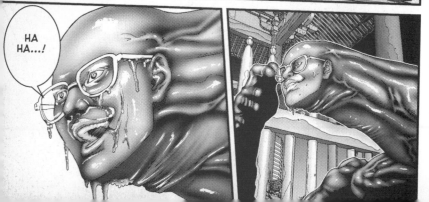

HA HA...!

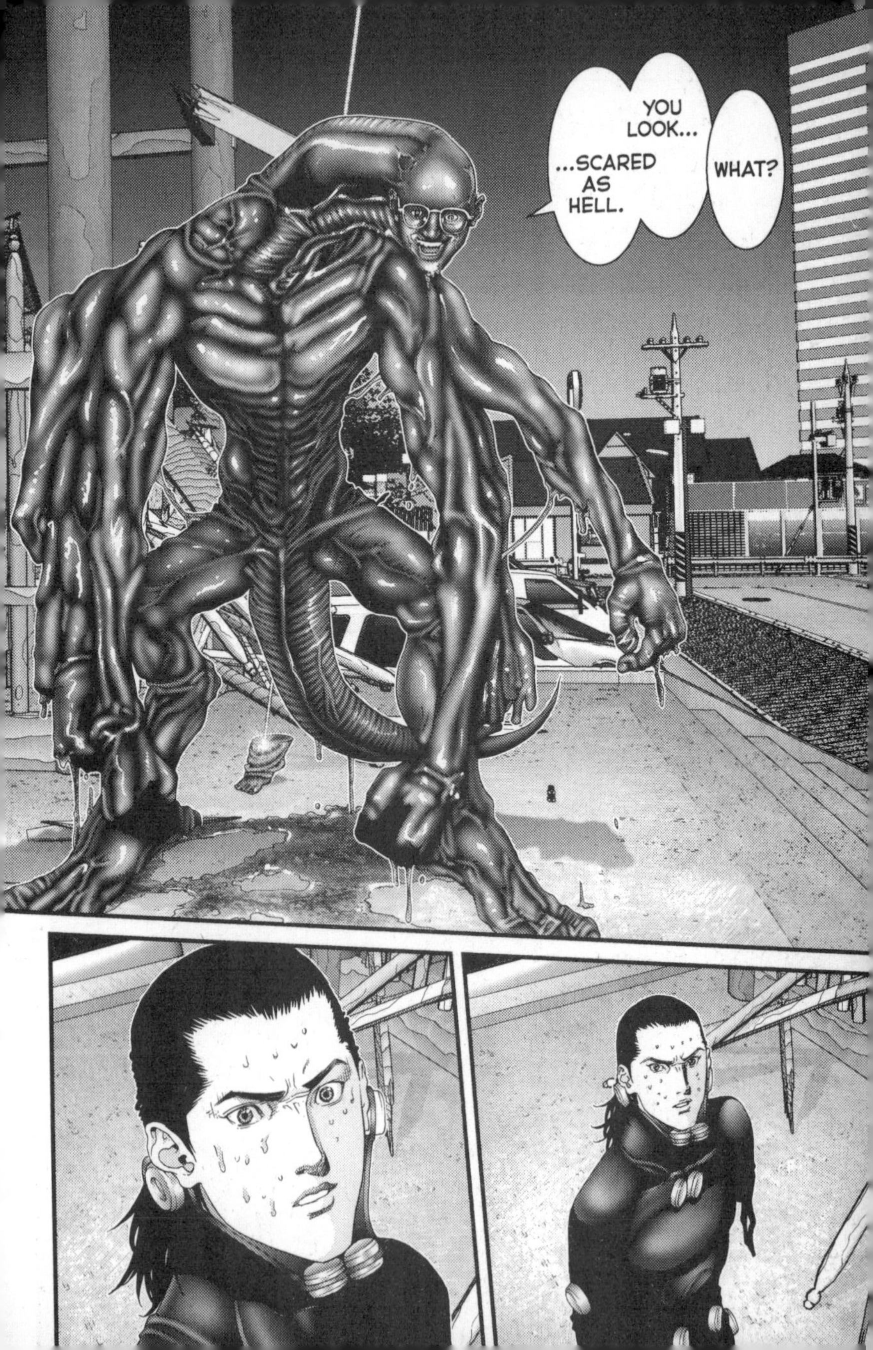
WHAT?
YOU LOOK...
...SCARED AS HELL.

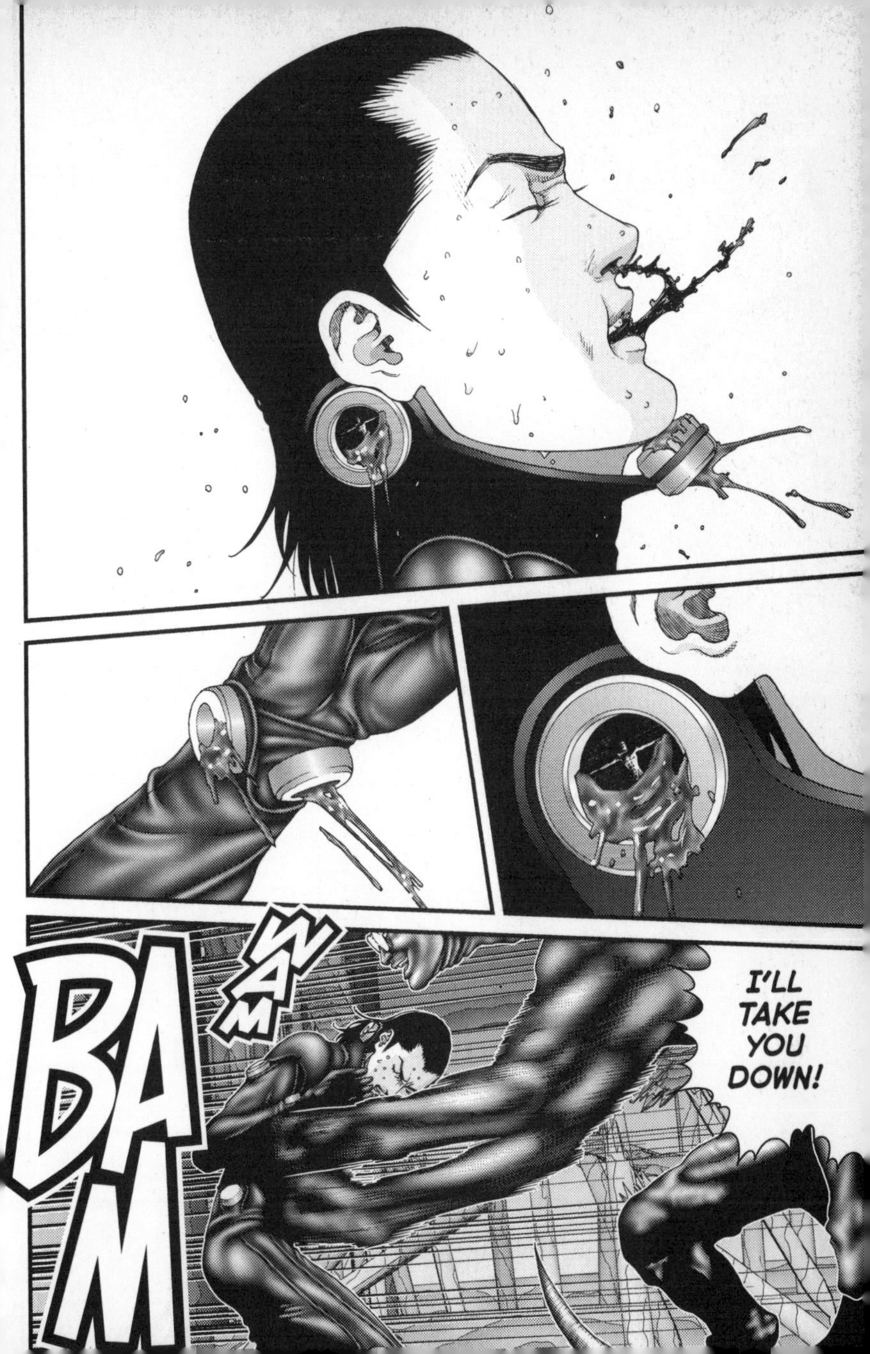
BAM
WAM
I'LL TAKE YOU DOWN!

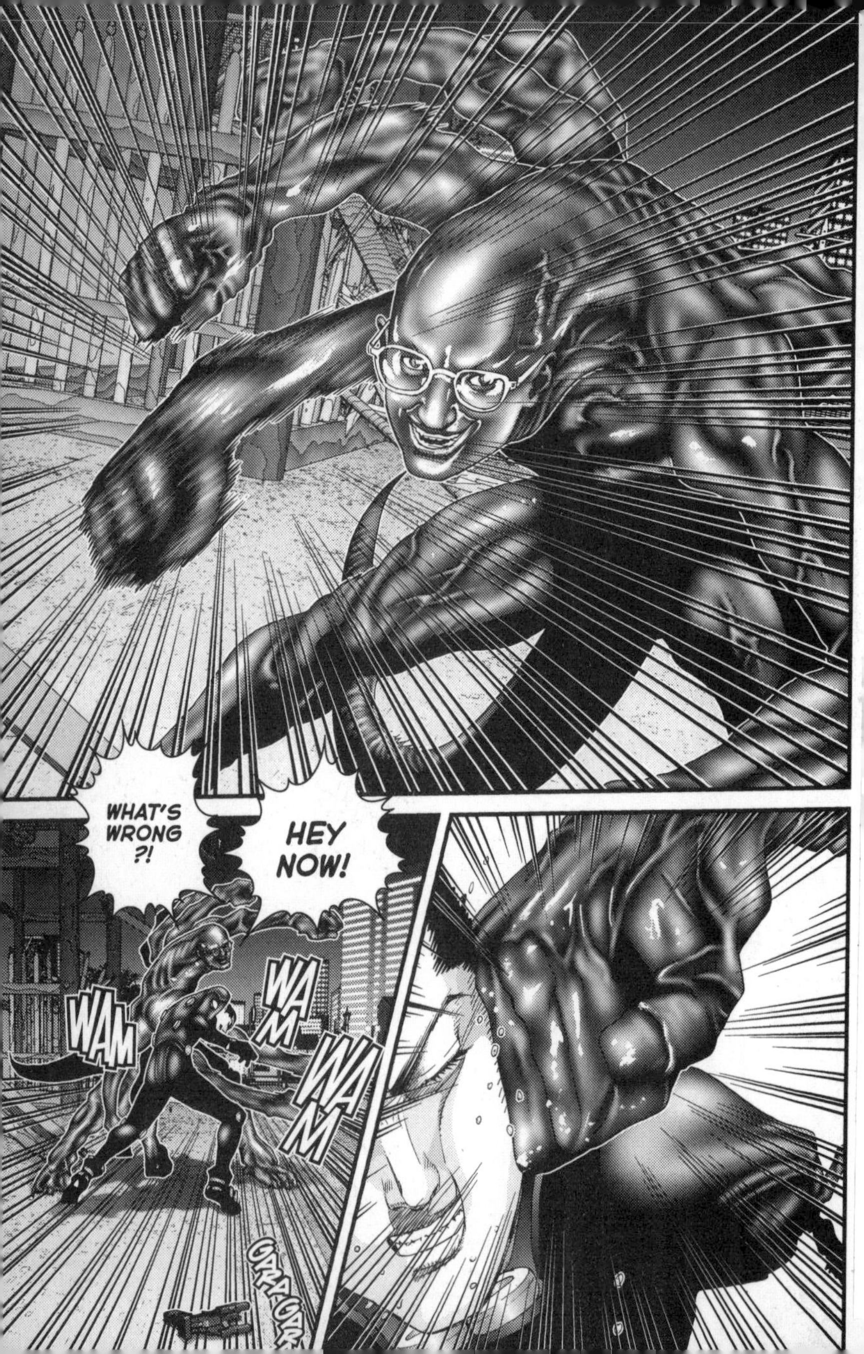
HEY NOW!
WHAT'S WRONG ?!
WAM
WAM
WAM
WAM

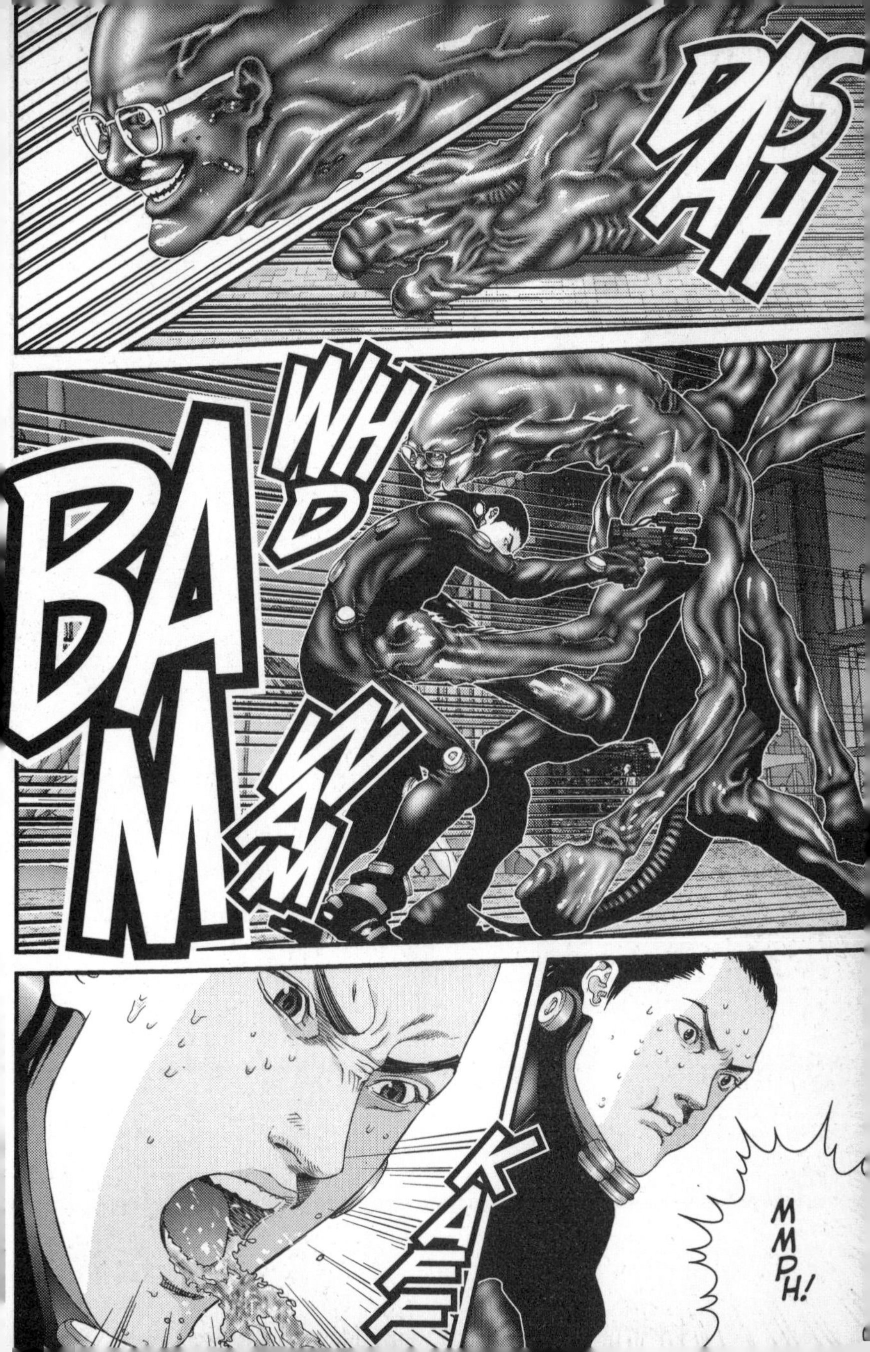
DASAH
BADAM
WHDWAM
KAFF
MMPH!

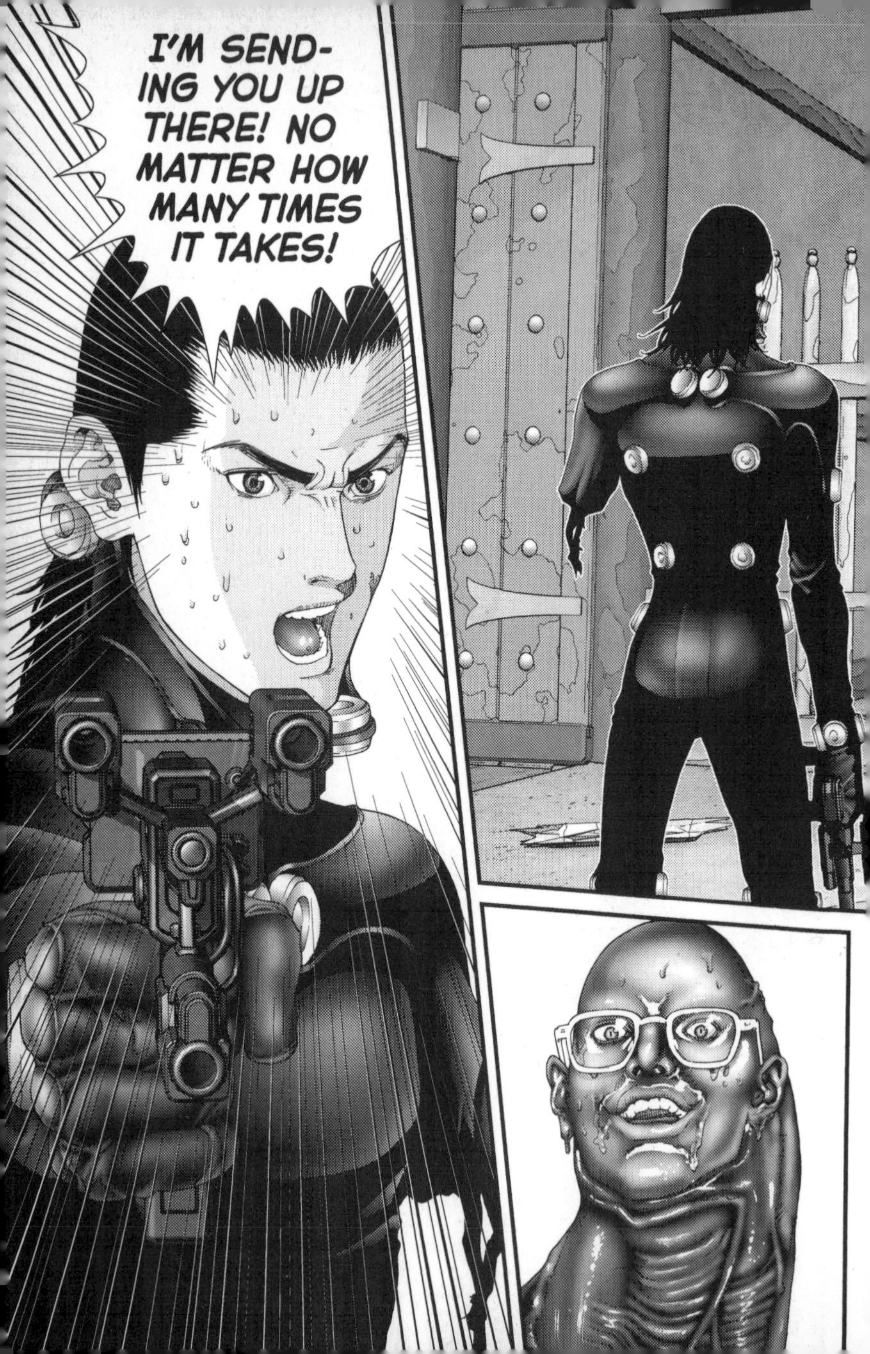
I'M SENDING YOU UP THERE! NO MATTER HOW MANY TIMES IT TAKES!

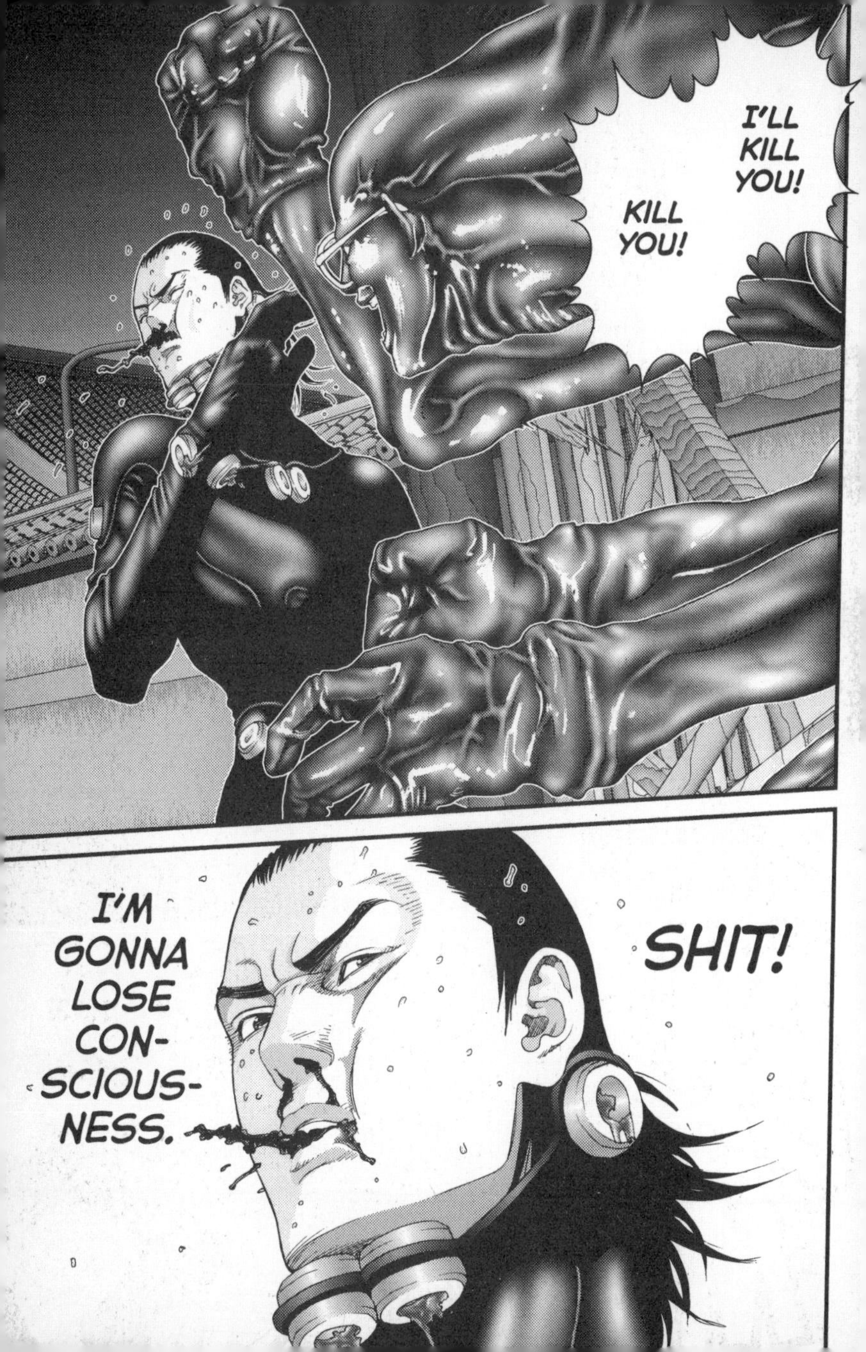
I'LL KILL YOU!
KILL YOU!
SHIT!
I'M GONNA LOSE CON-SCIOUS-NESS.

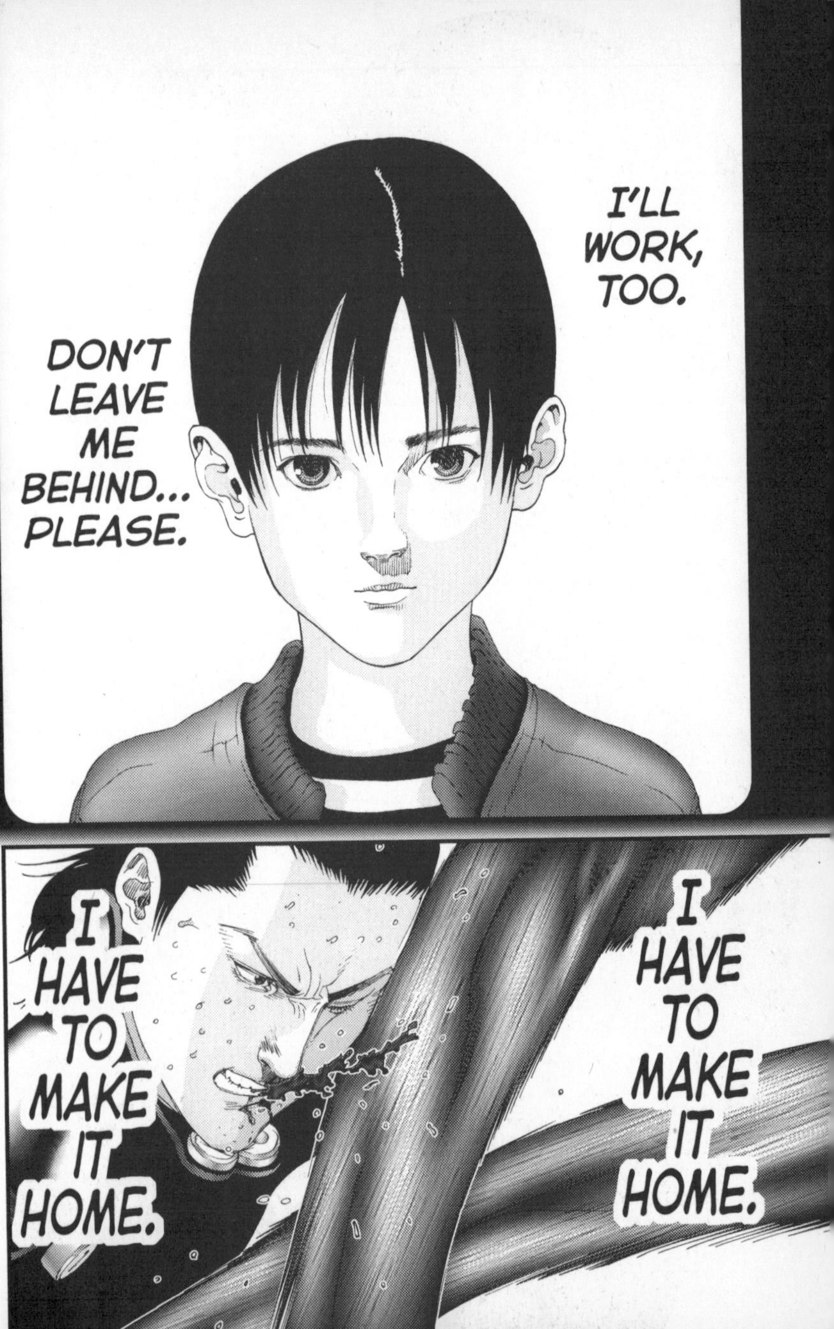
I'LL WORK, TOO.
DON'T LEAVE ME BEHIND... PLEASE.
I HAVE TO MAKE IT HOME.
I HAVE TO MAKE IT HOME.

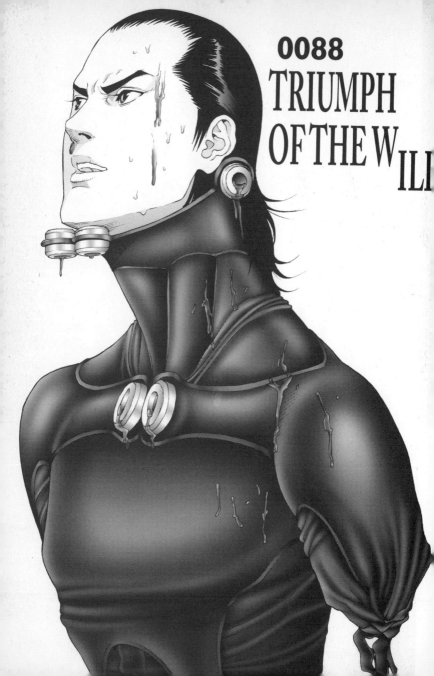

0088
TRIUMPH
OF THE W ILL

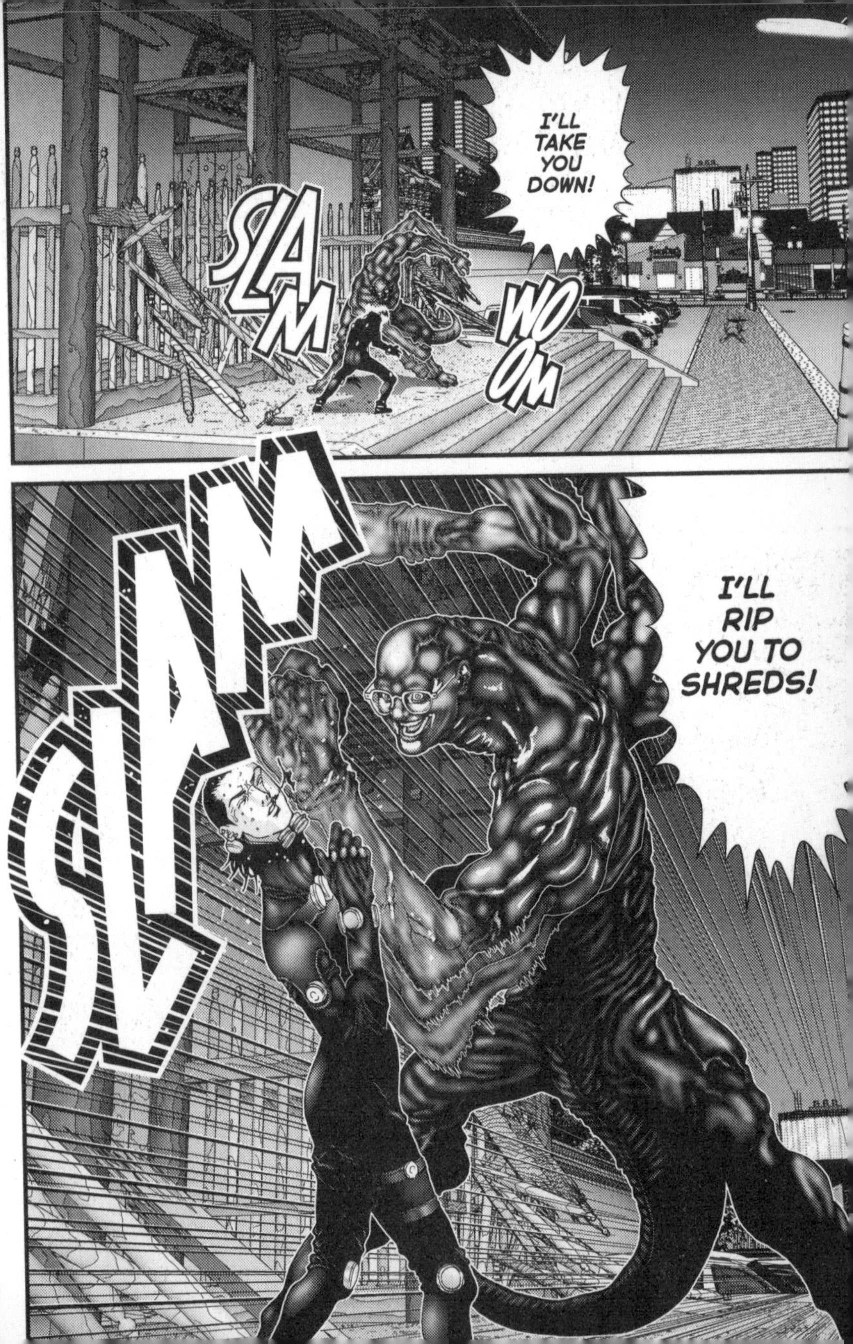
I'LL TAKE YOU DOWN!
SLAM
WOOM
SLAM
I'LL RIP YOU TO SHREDS!

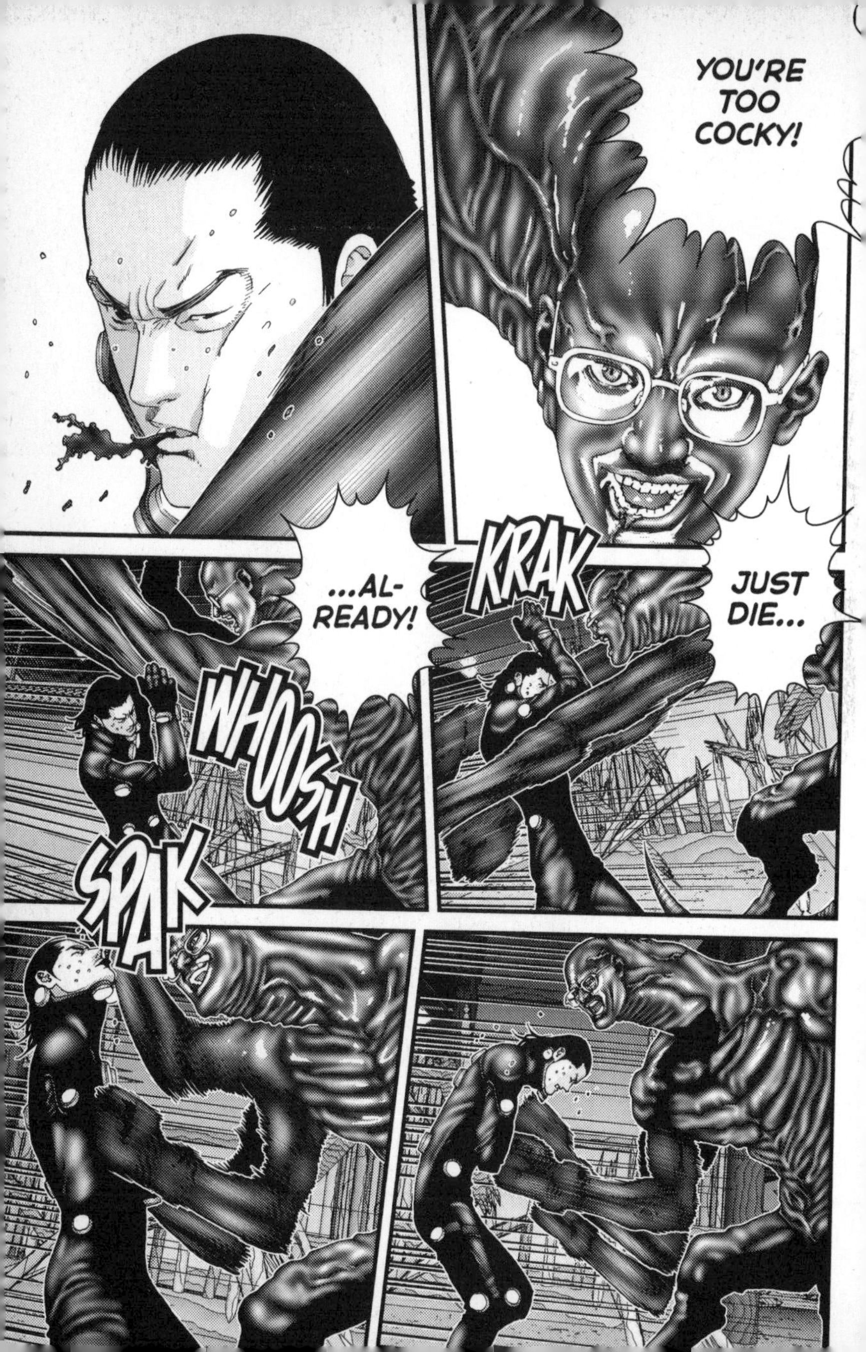

YOU'RE TOO COCKY!
JUST DIE...
...AL-READY!
KRAK
WHOOSH
SPAK

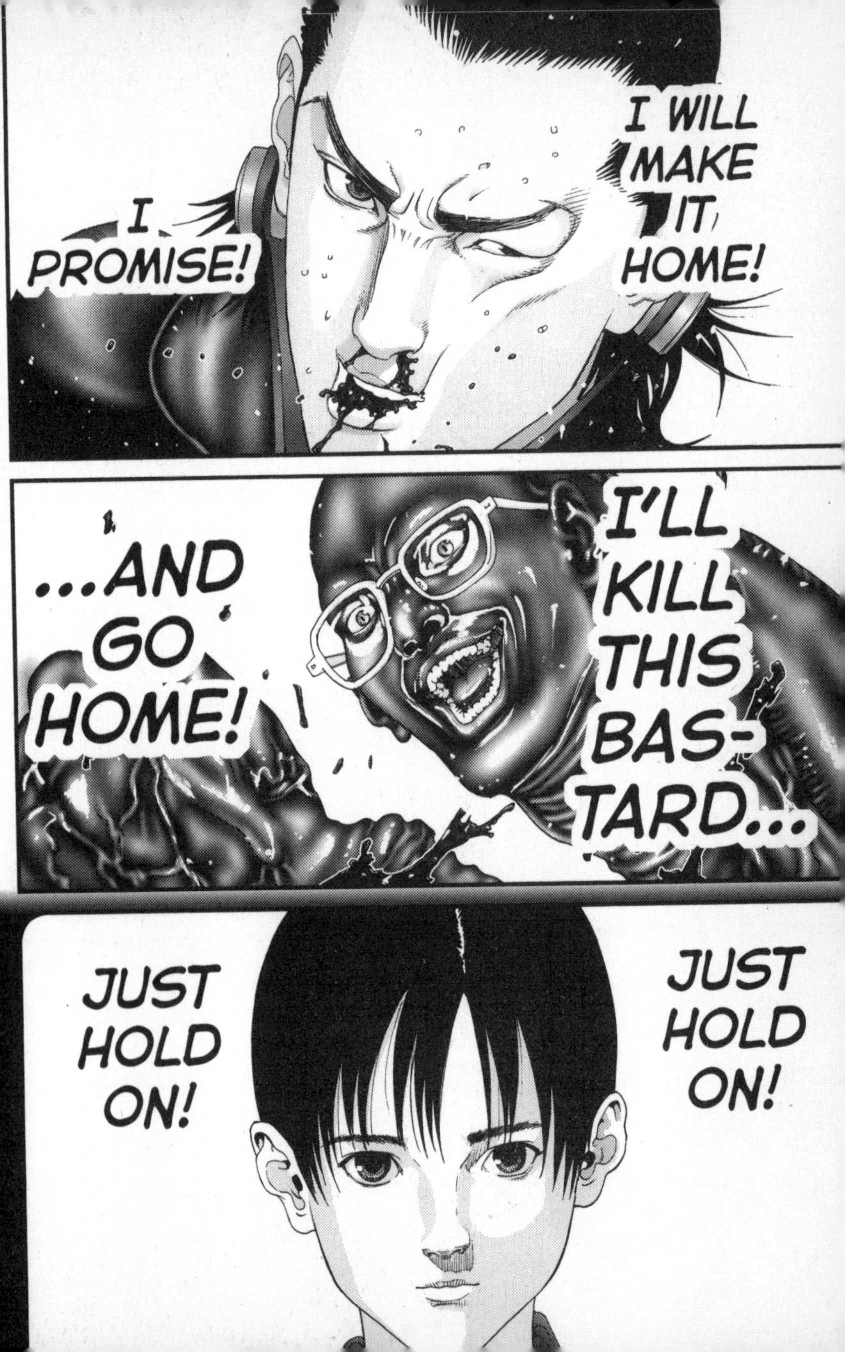
I WILL MAKE IT HOME!
I PROMISE!
I'LL KILL THIS BASTARD...
...AND GO HOME!
JUST HOLD ON!
JUST HOLD ON!

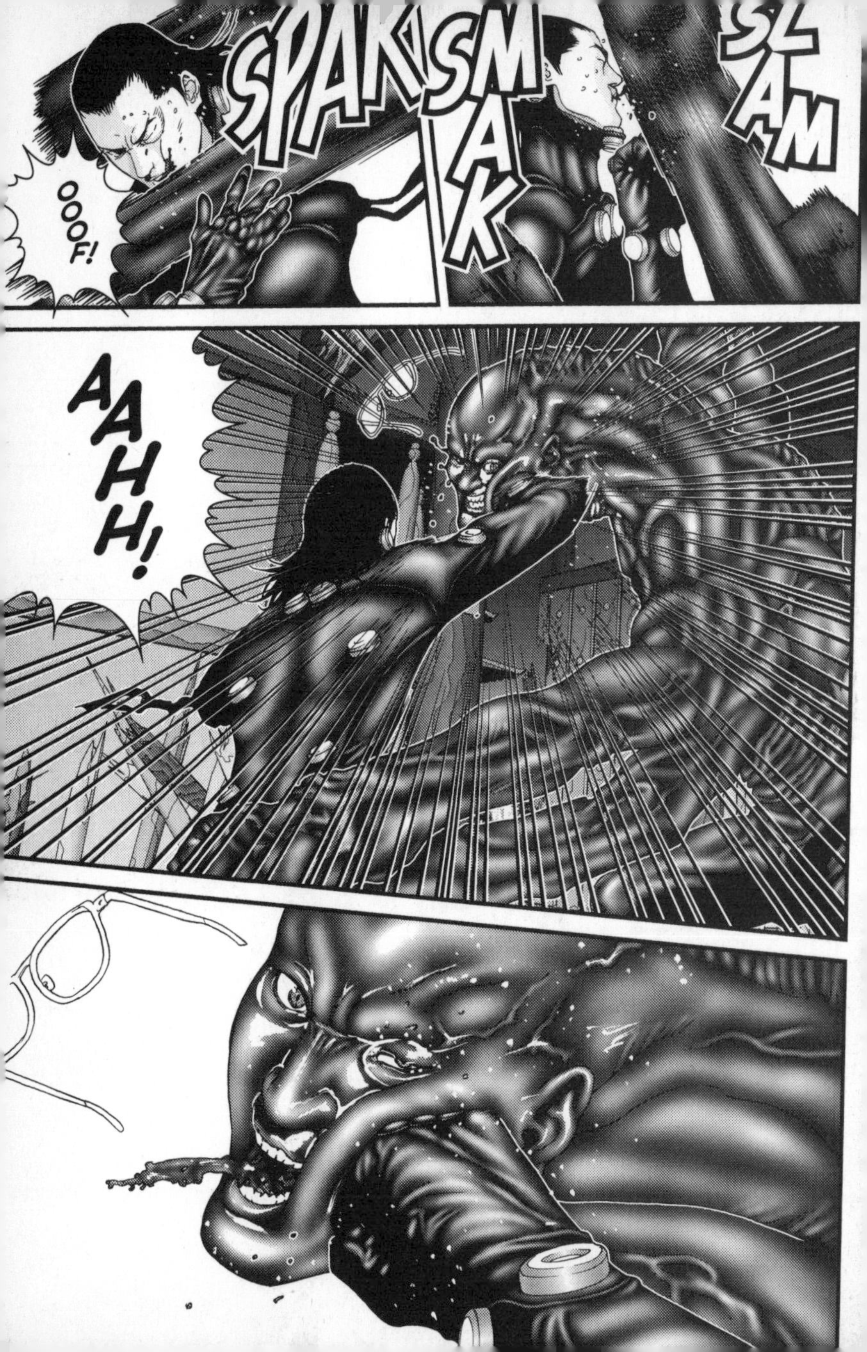

OOOF!
SPAK
SMAK
SLAM
AAHH!

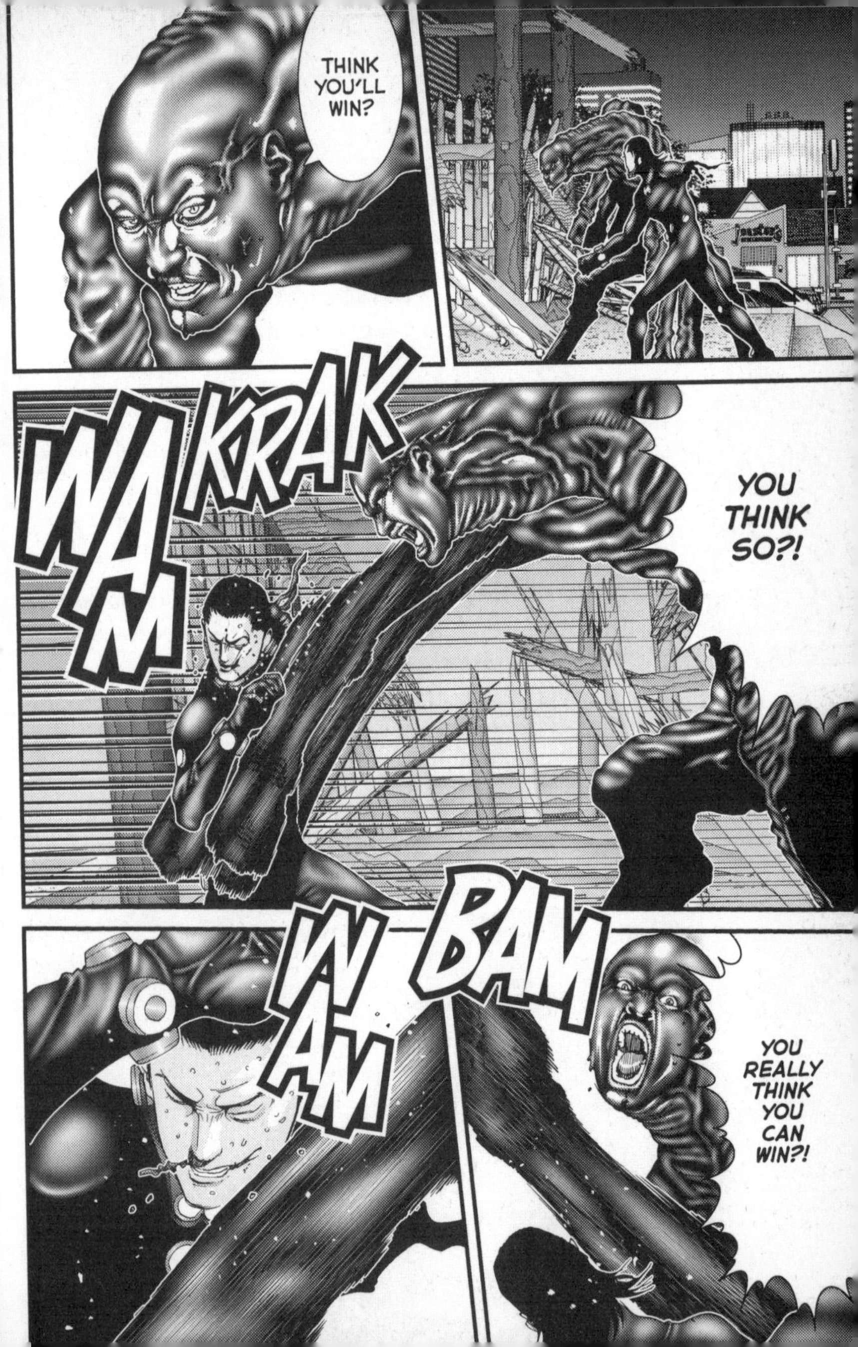
THINK YOU'LL WIN?
WAM
KRAK
YOU THINK SO?!
WAM
BAM
YOU REALLY THINK YOU CAN WIN?!

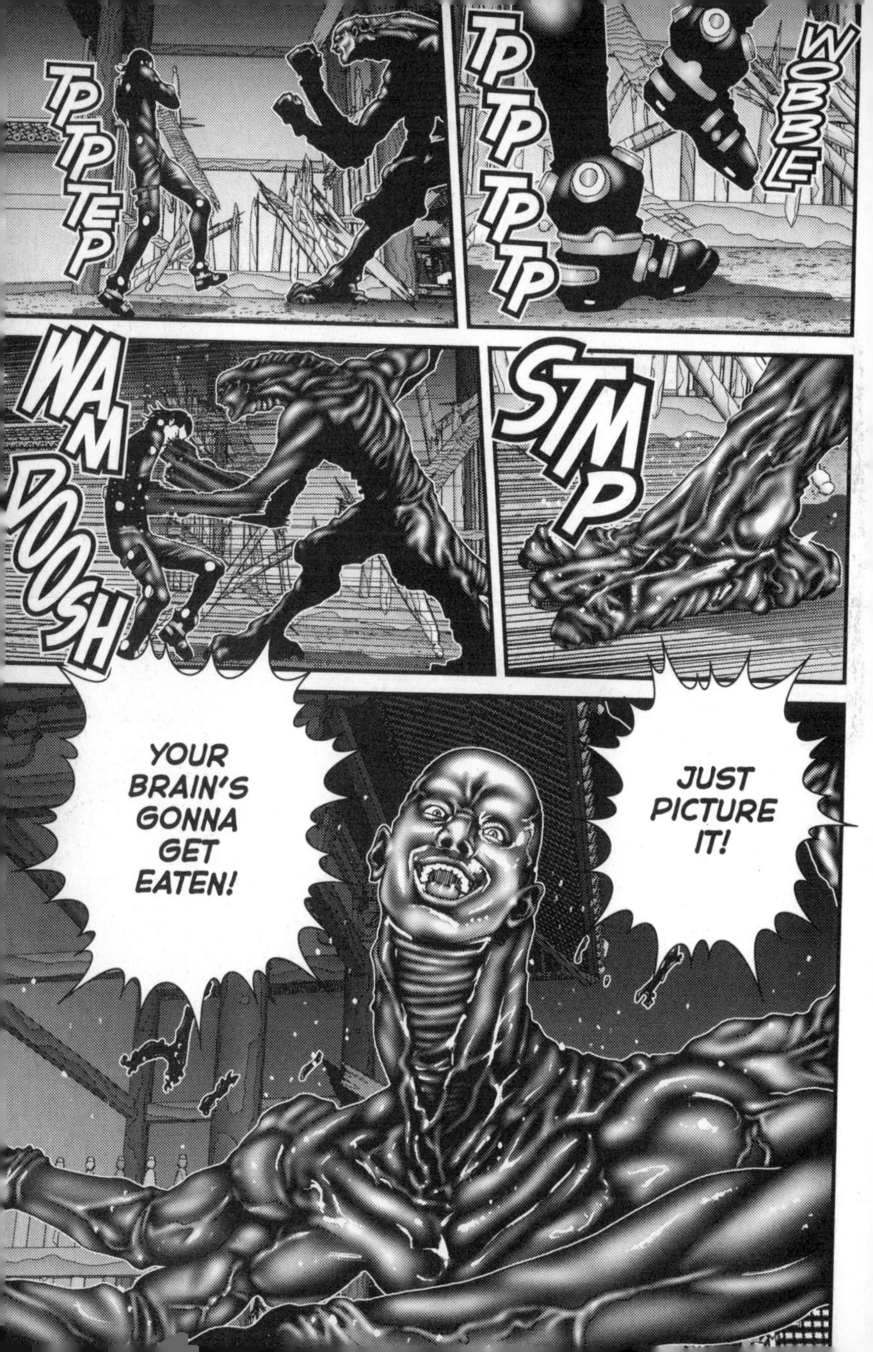

WOBBLE
TPTPTP TPTP
TPTPTEP
STMP
WAM
DOOOSH
JUST PICTURE IT!
YOUR BRAIN'S GONNA GET EATEN!

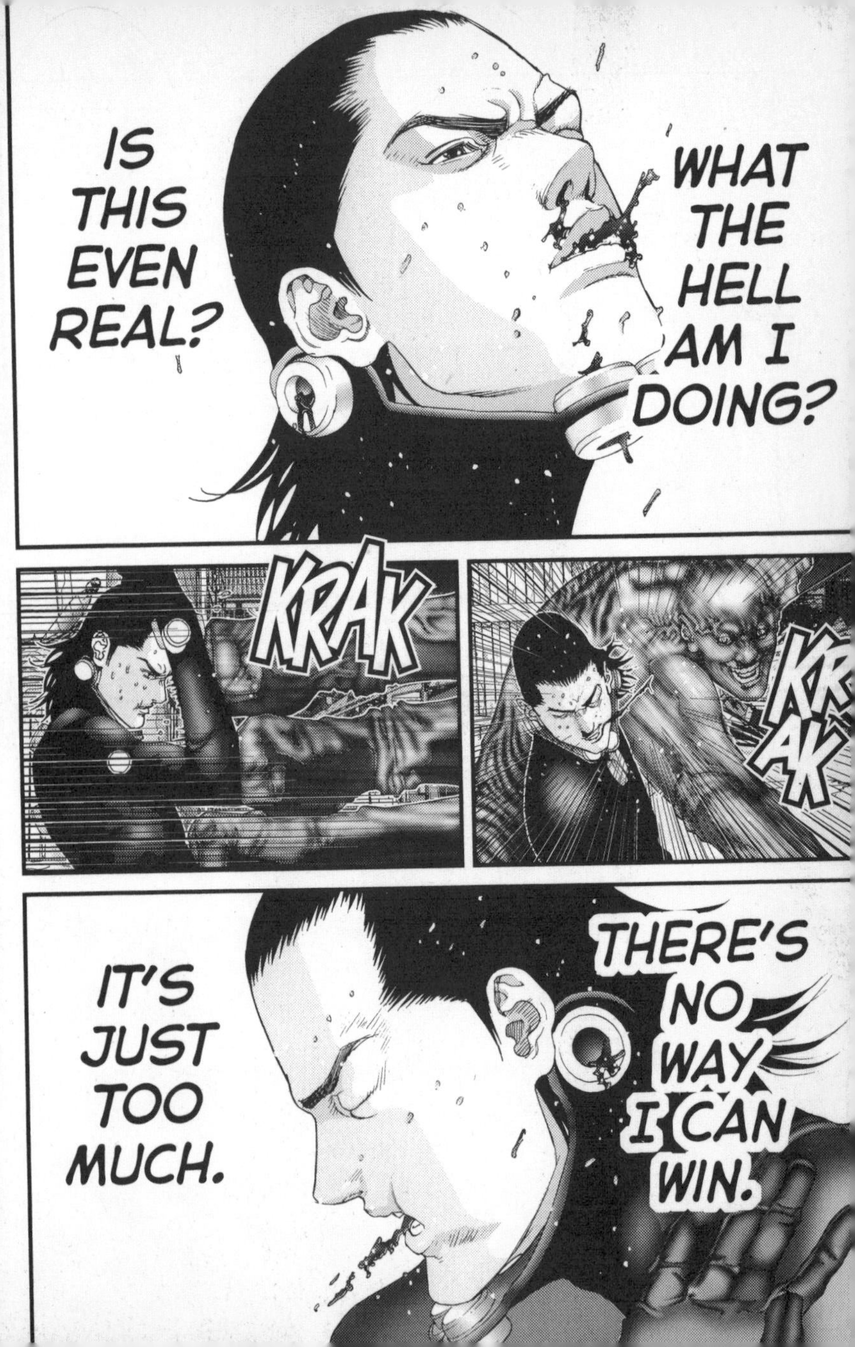
WHAT THE HELL AM I DOING?
IS THIS EVEN REAL?
KRAK
THERE'S NO WAY I CAN WIN.
IT'S JUST TOO MUCH.

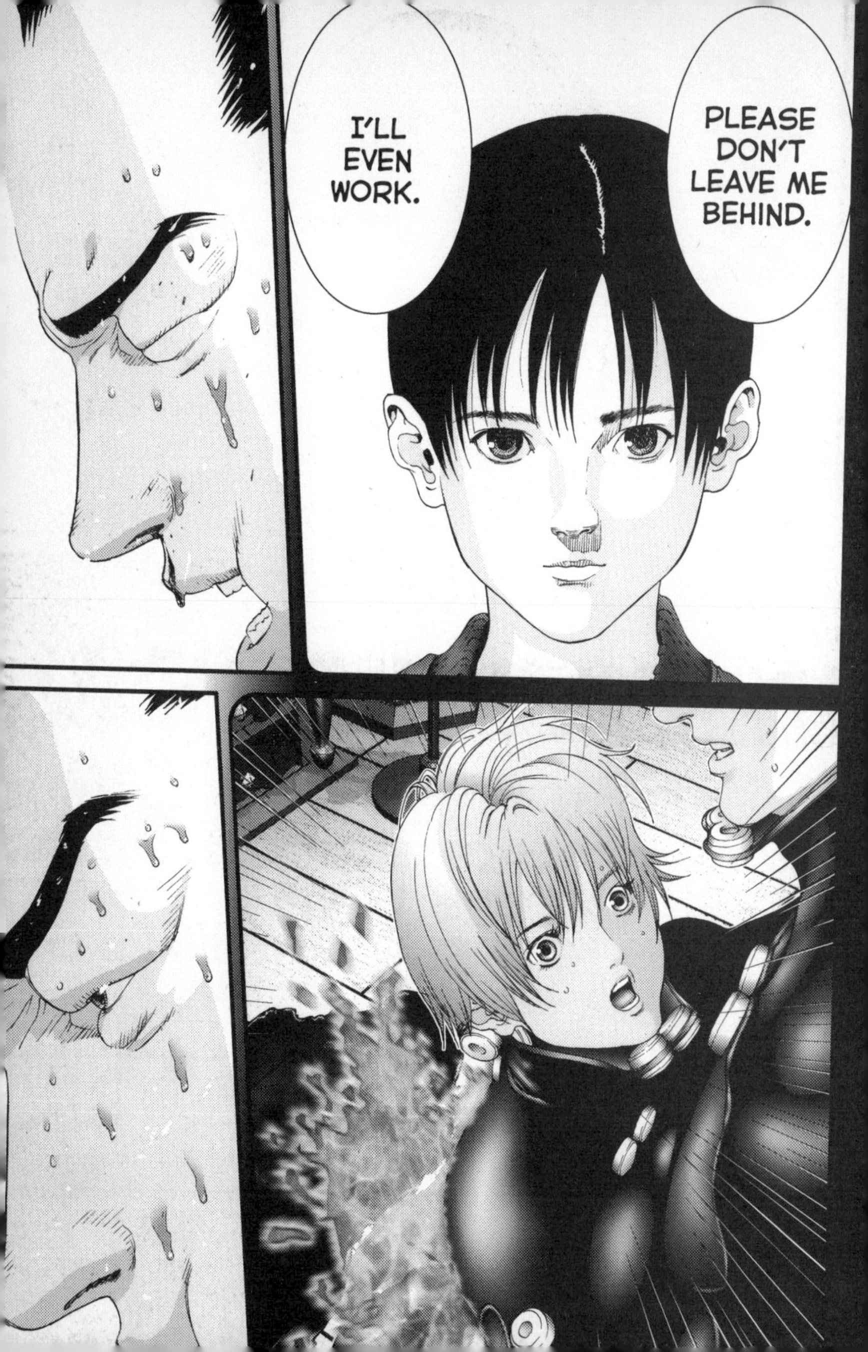
PLEASE DON'T LEAVE ME BEHIND.
I'LL EVEN WORK.

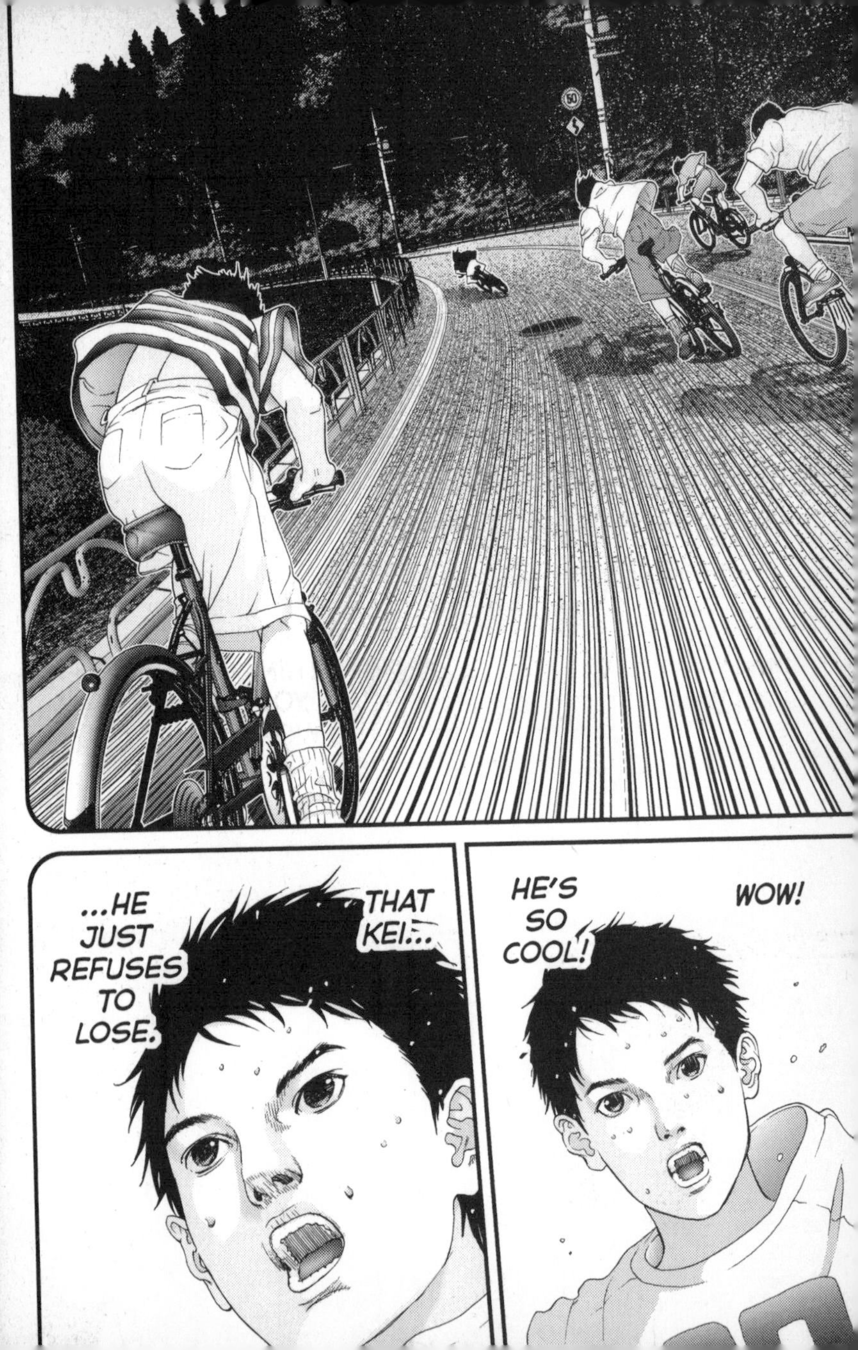
WOW!
HE'S SO COOL!
THAT KEI...
...HE JUST REFUSES TO LOSE.

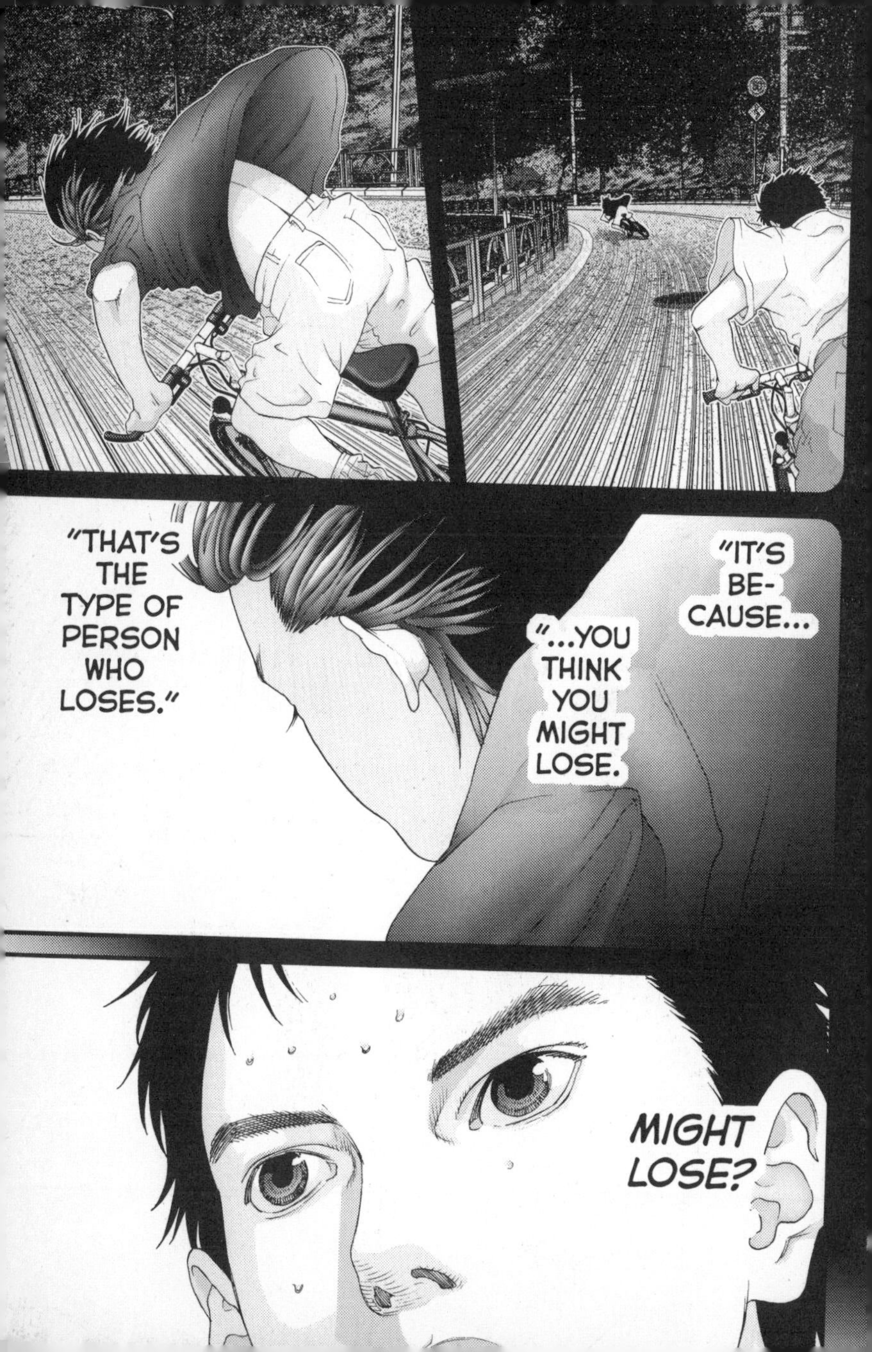
"IT'S BE-CAUSE...
"...YOU THINK YOU MIGHT LOSE.
"THAT'S THE TYPE OF PERSON WHO LOSES."
MIGHT LOSE?

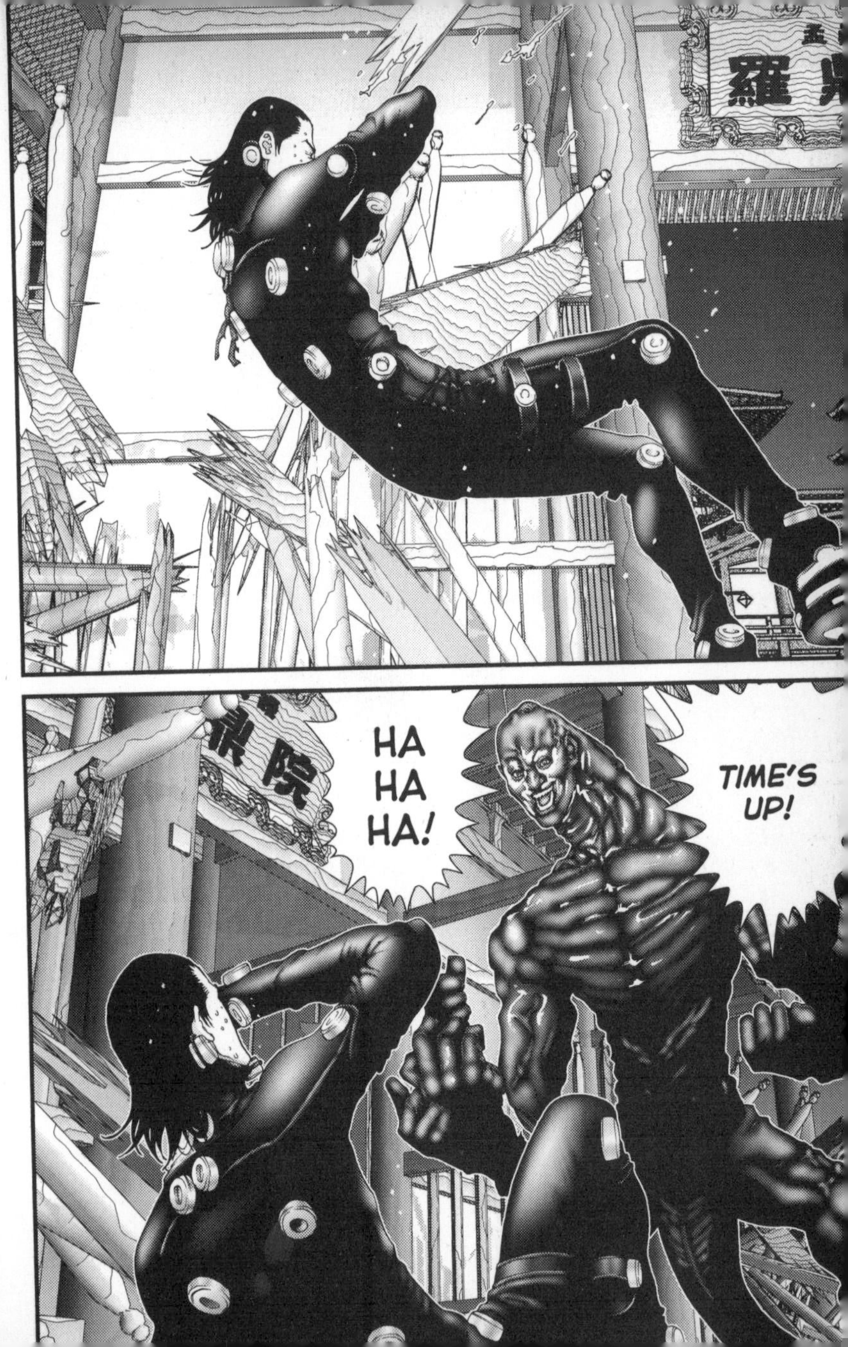
羅
院
HA HA HA!
TIME'S UP!

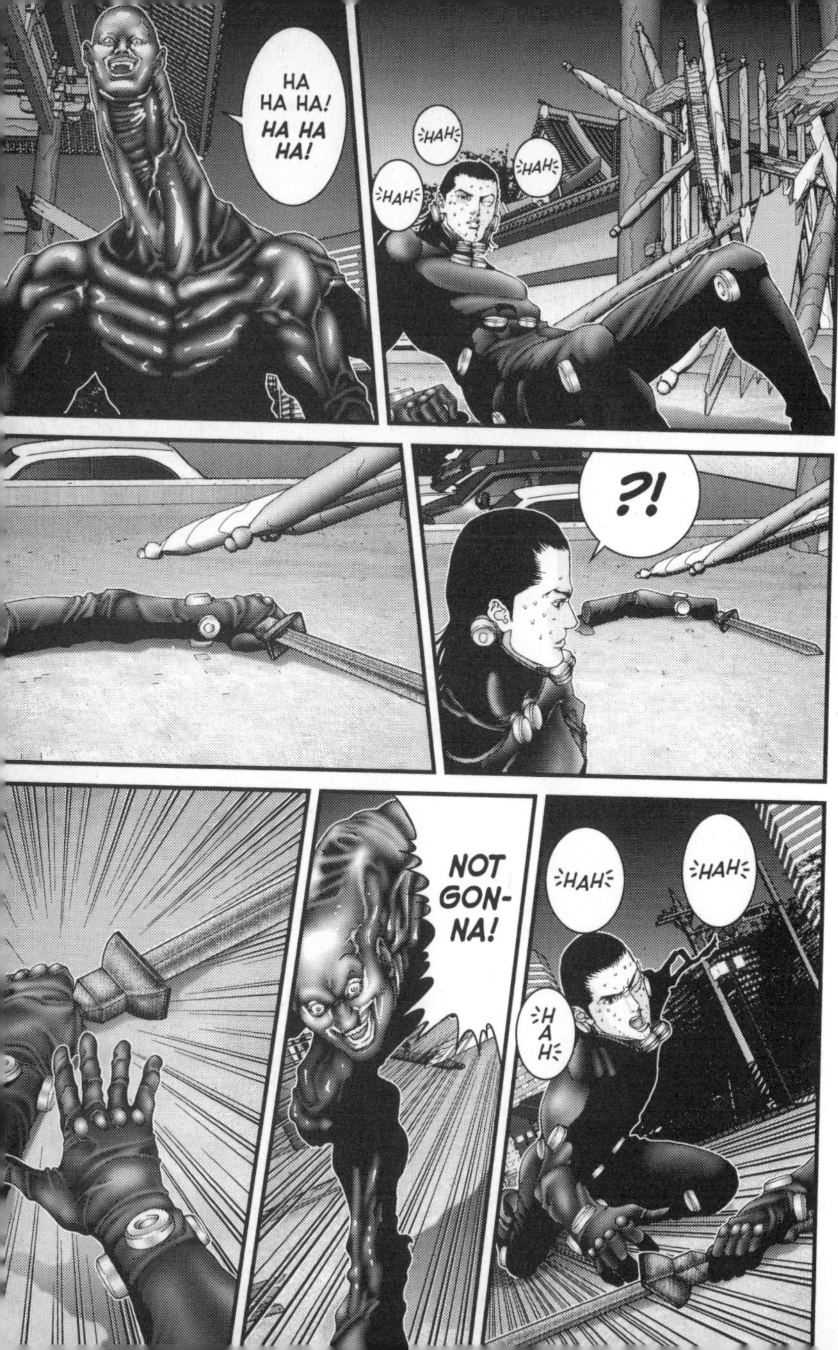
HAH
HAH
HAH
HA HA HA! HA HA HA!
?!
HAH
HAH
HAH
NOT GONNA!

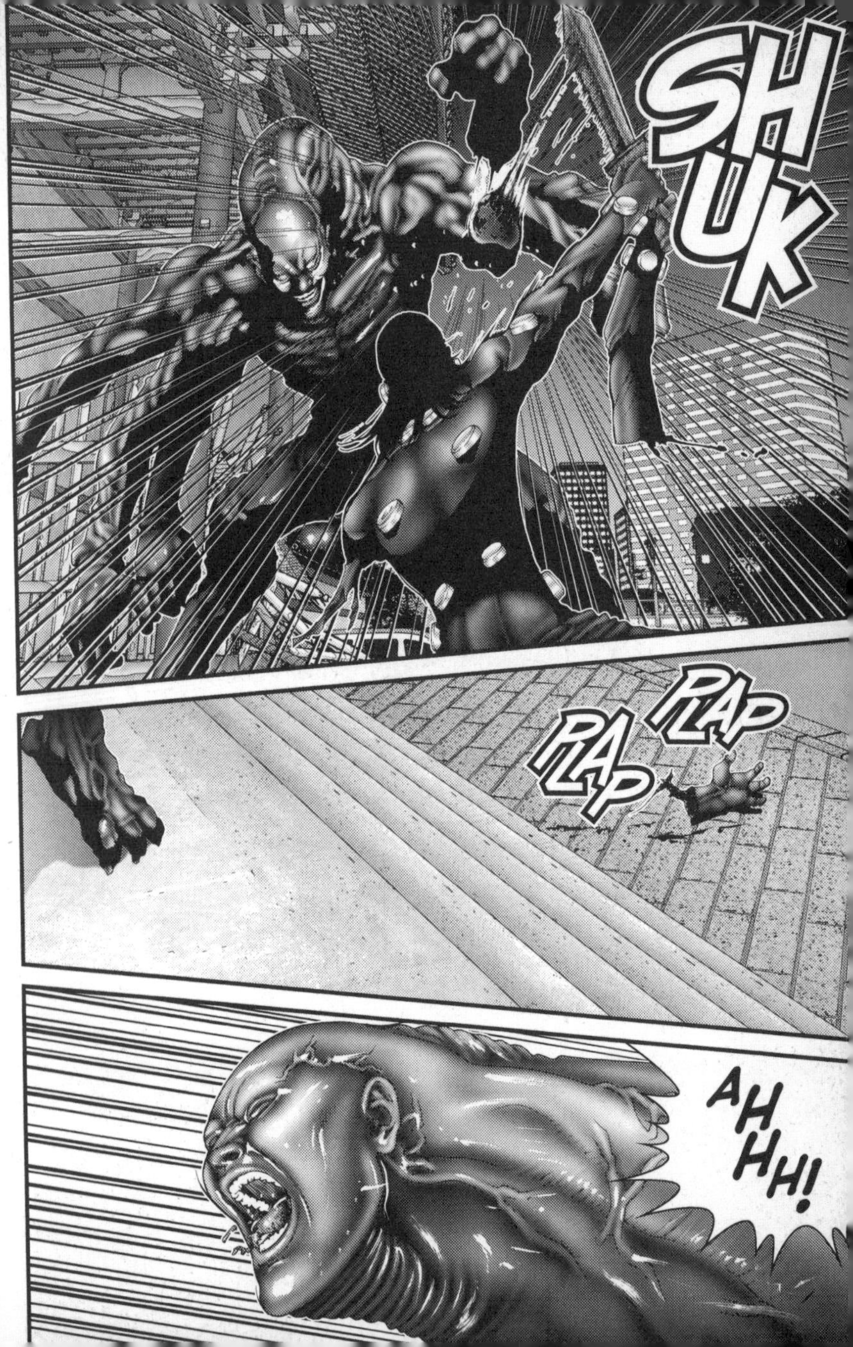
SHUK
PLAP
PLAP
AHHH!

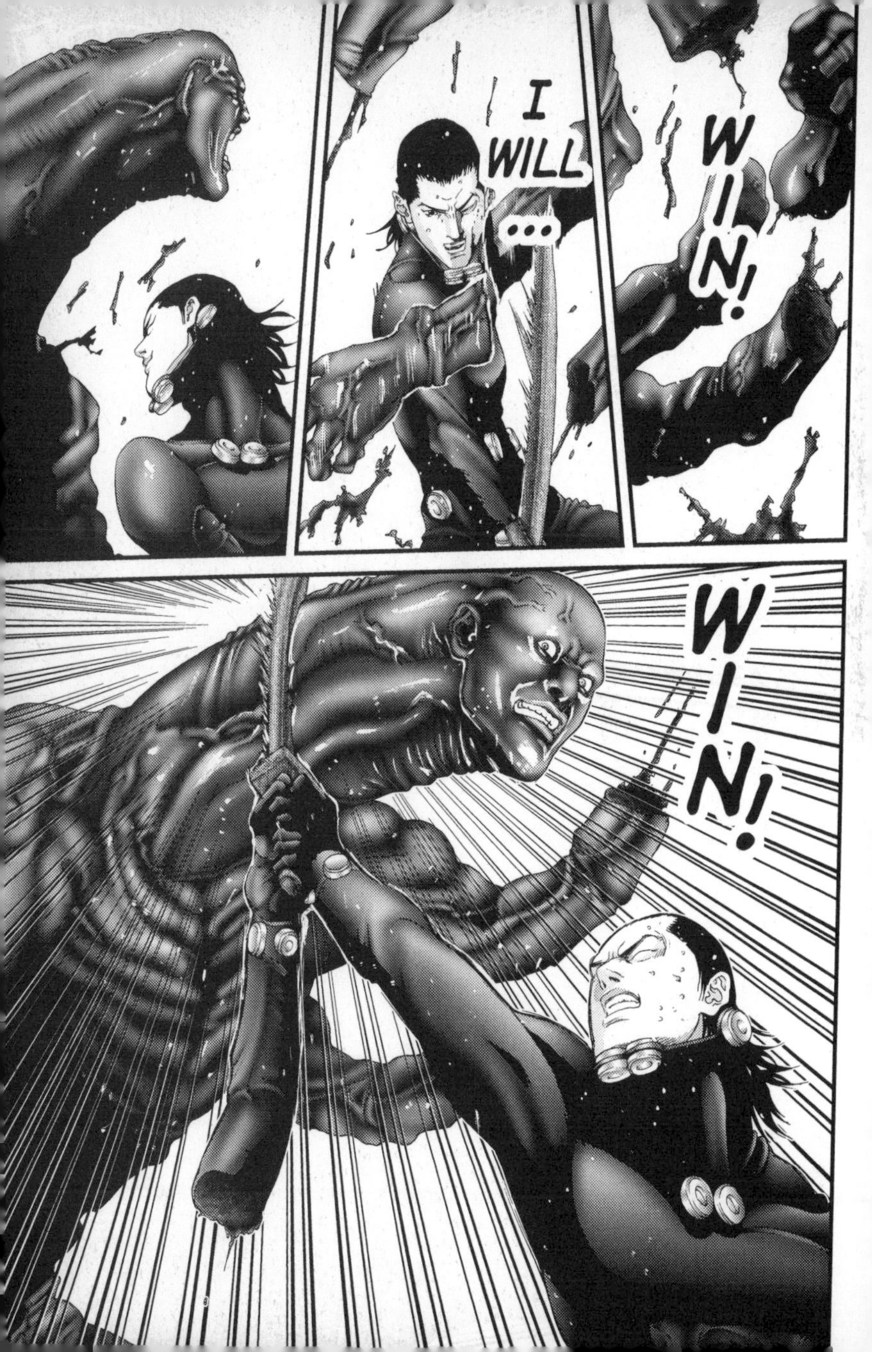
I WILL ...
WIN!
WIN!

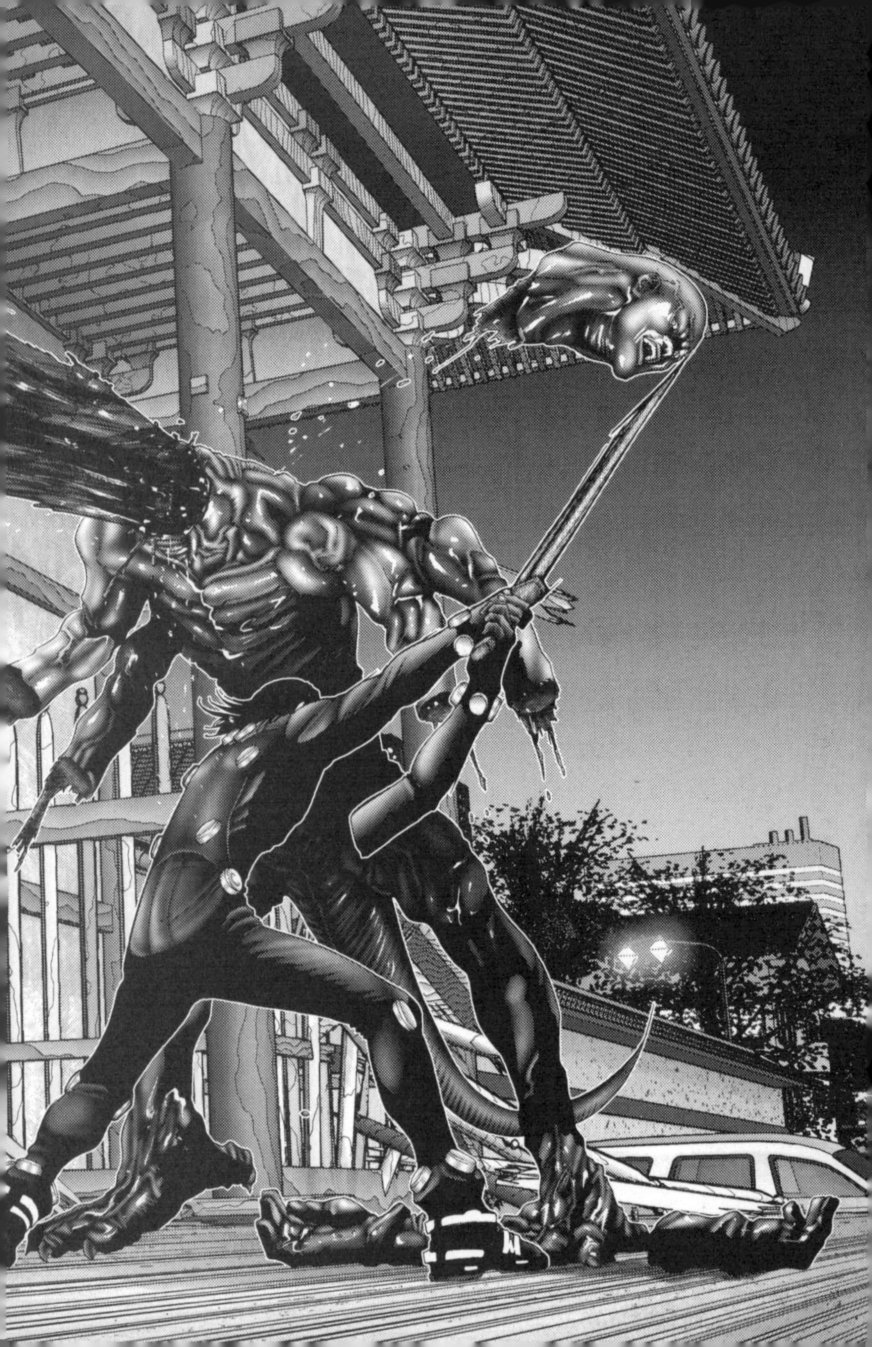

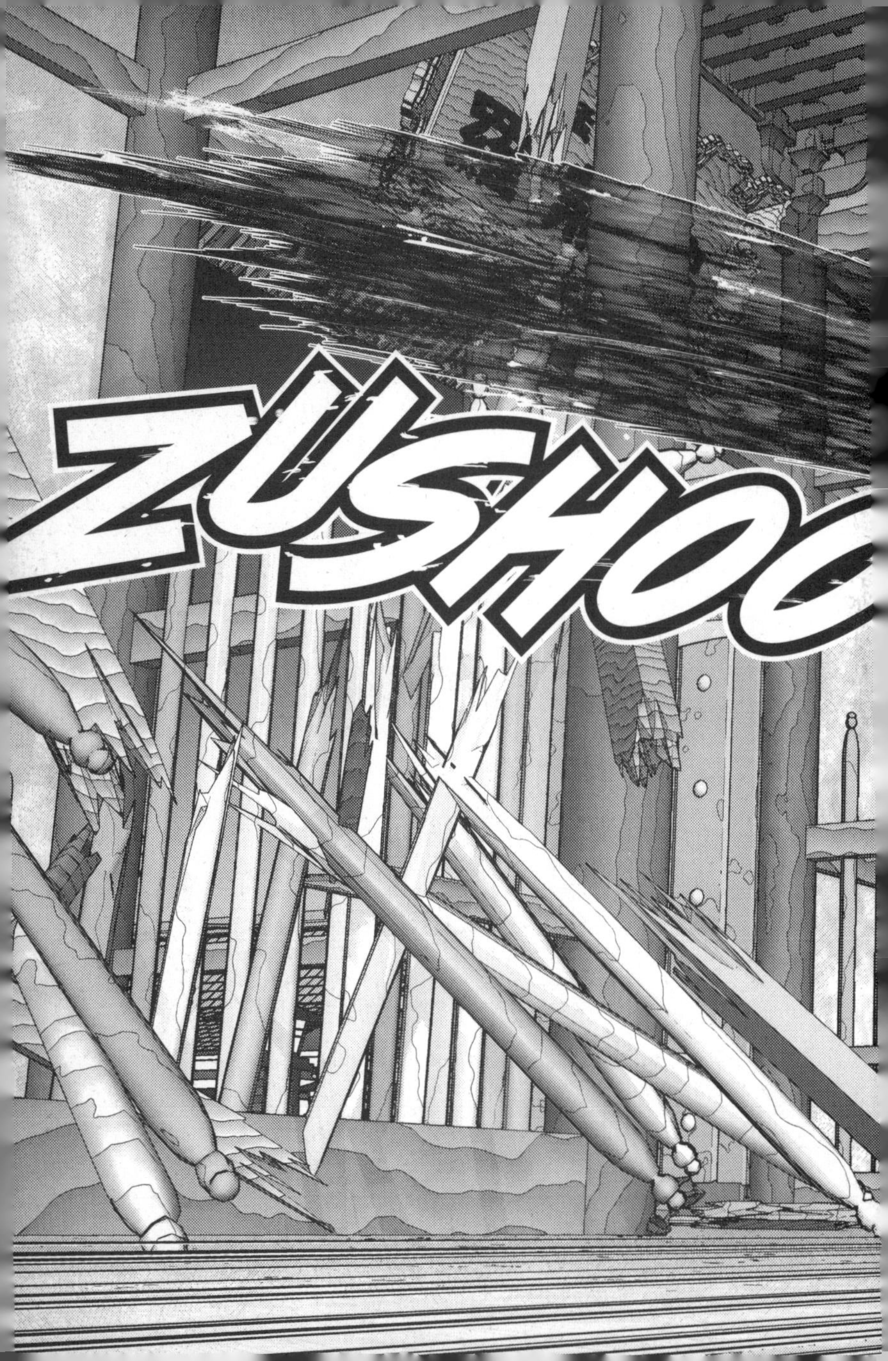
ZUSHOO

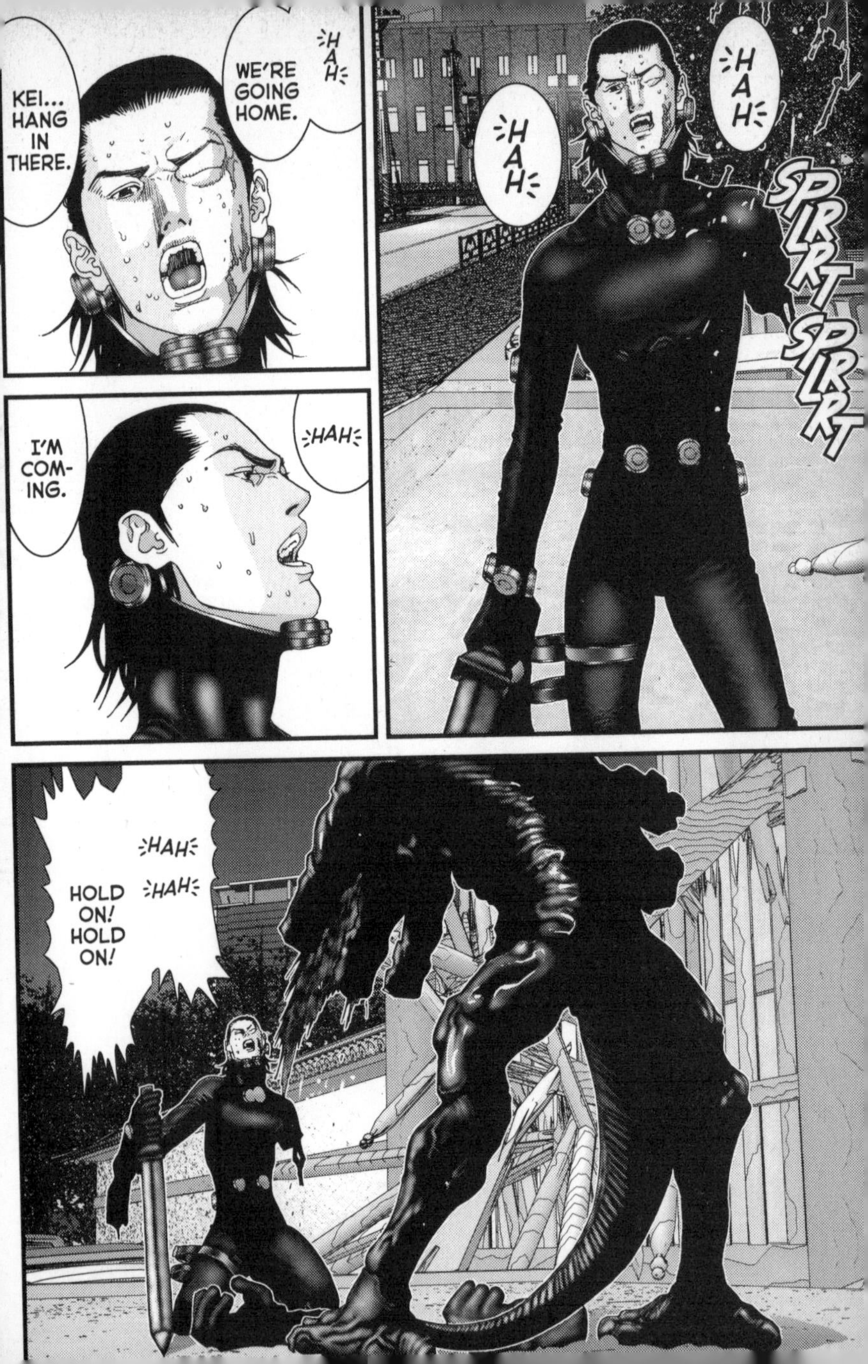
HAH HAH
HAH HAH
SPLRT SPLRT
HAH
WE'RE GOING HOME.
KEI... HANG IN THERE.
HAH
I'M COM-ING.
HAH
HAH
HOLD ON! HOLD ON!

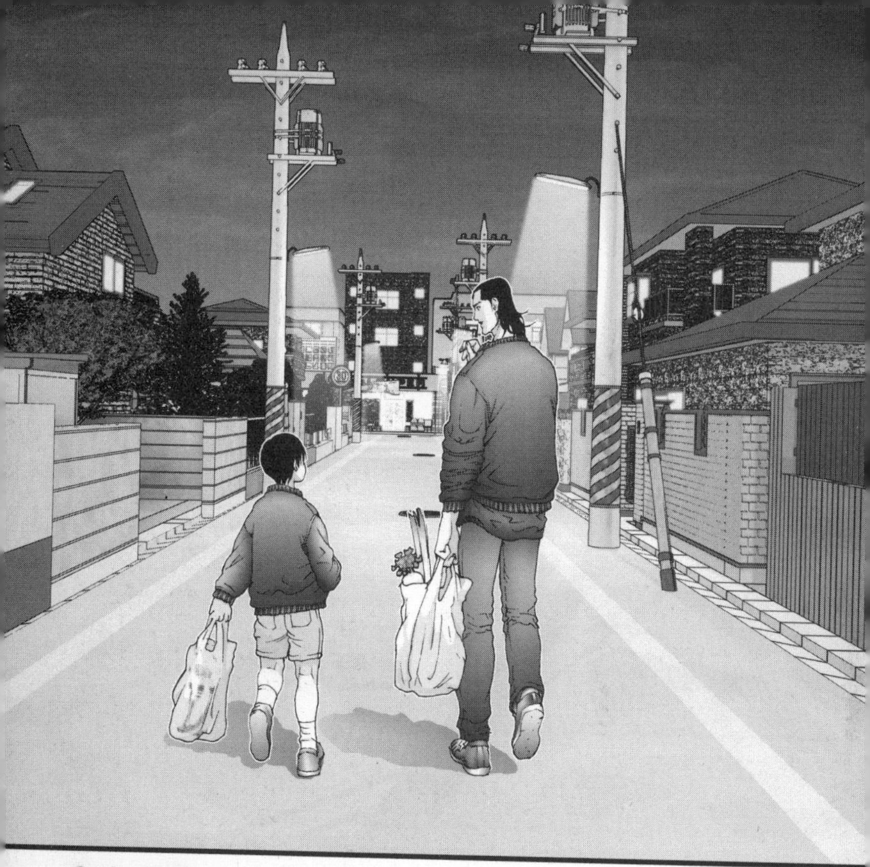

0089

BROTHER

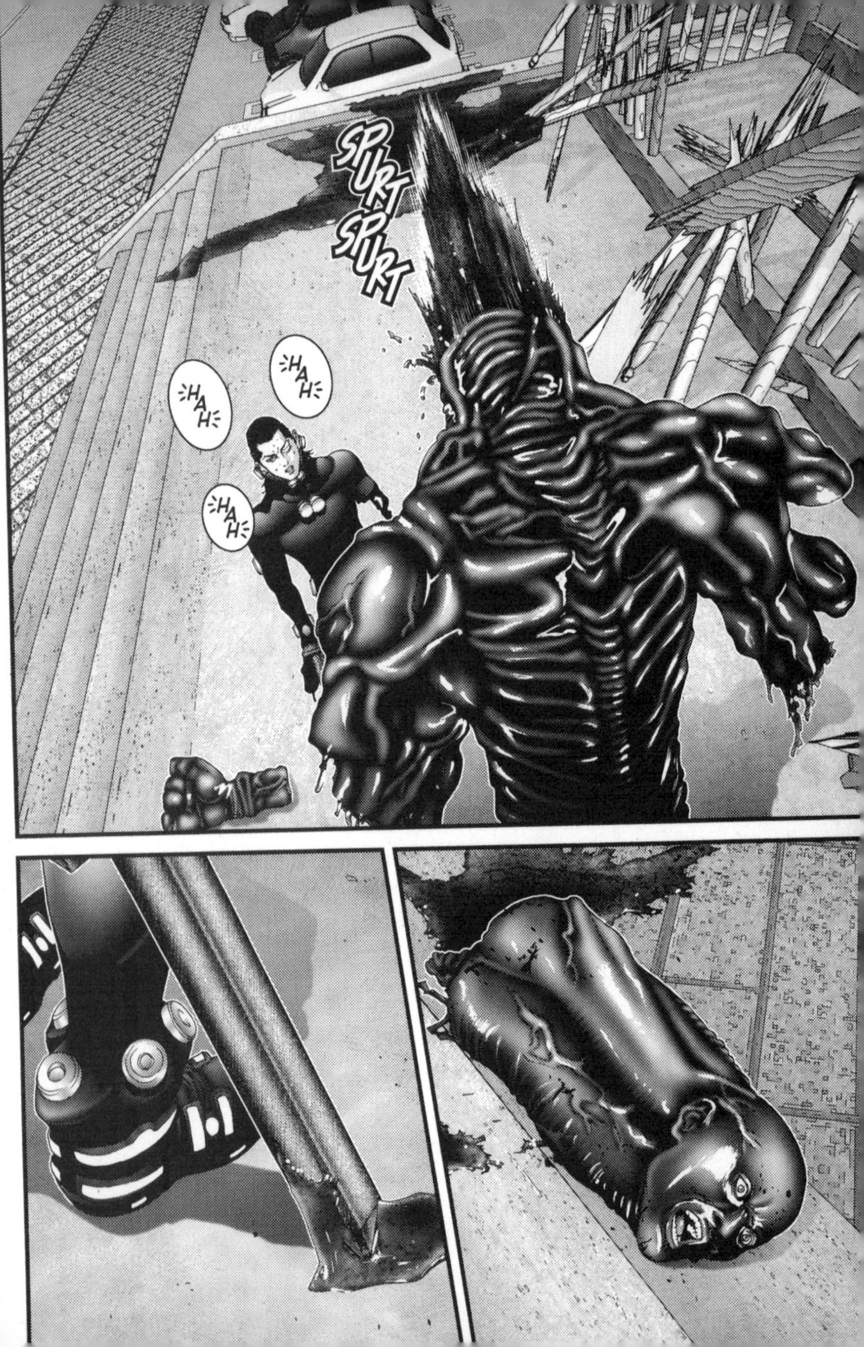
SPURT SPURT
HAH
HAH
HAH

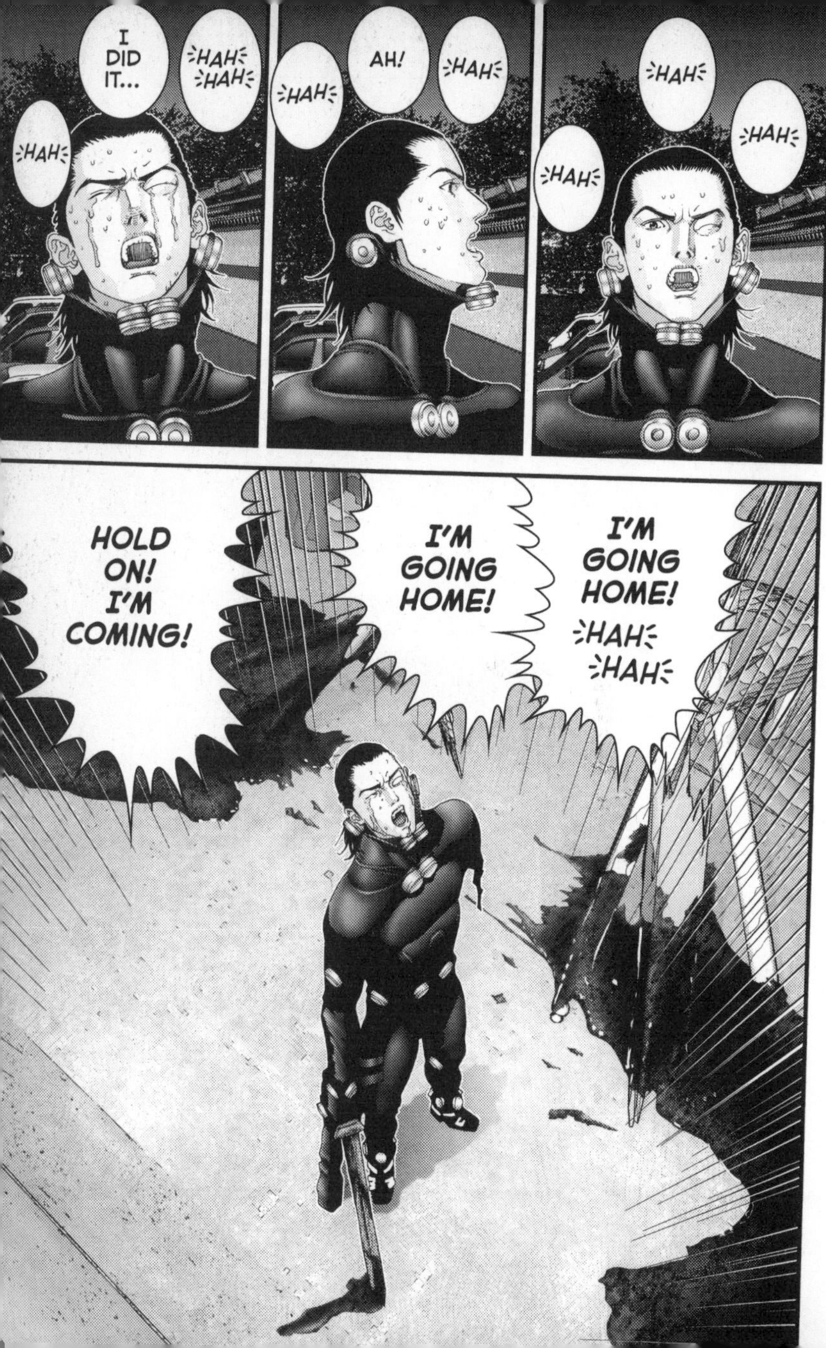
HAH
I DID IT...
HAH HAH
HAH
AH!
HAH
HAH
HAH
HAH
HOLD ON! I'M COMING!
I'M GOING HOME!
I'M GOING HOME!
HAH HAH

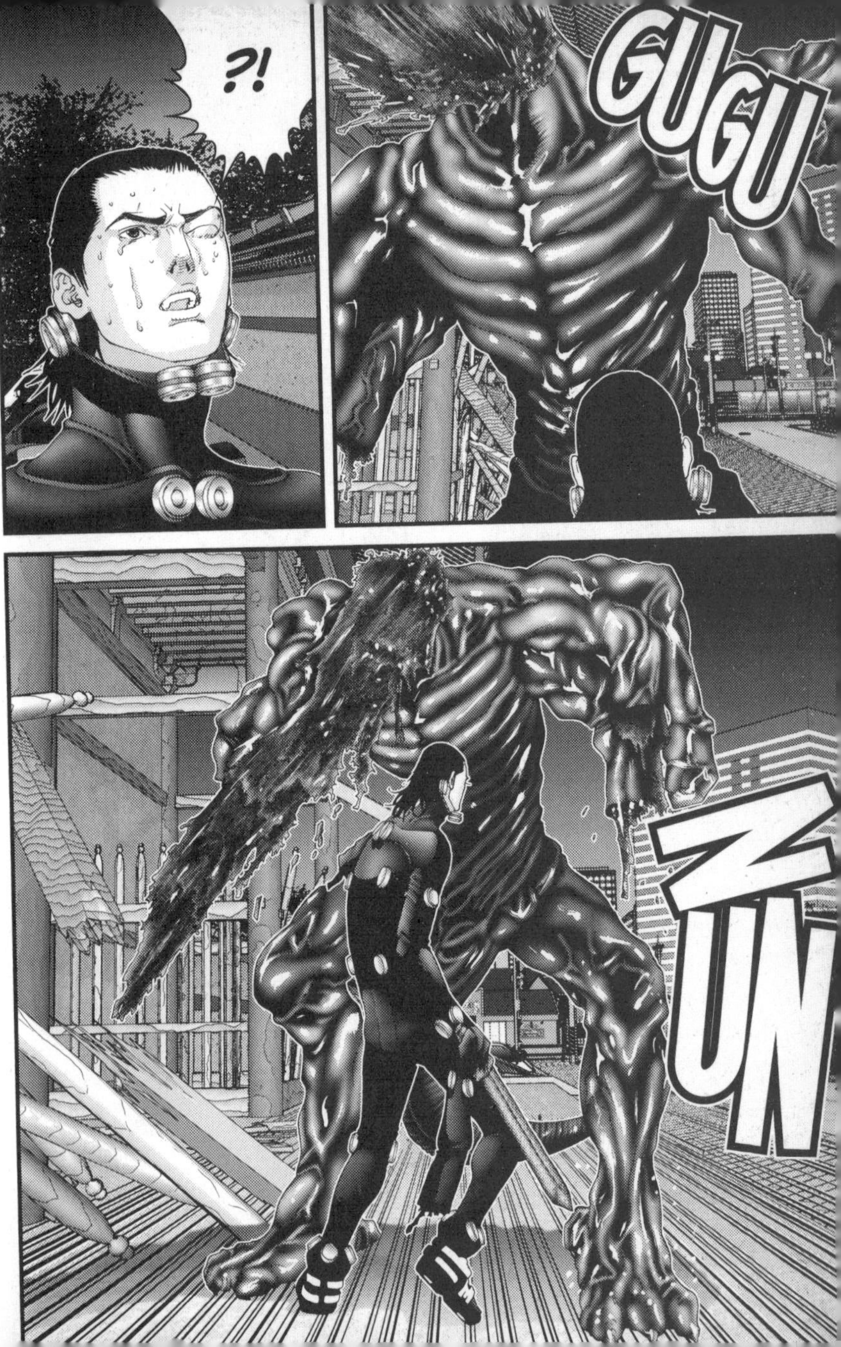

?!
GUGU
ZUN

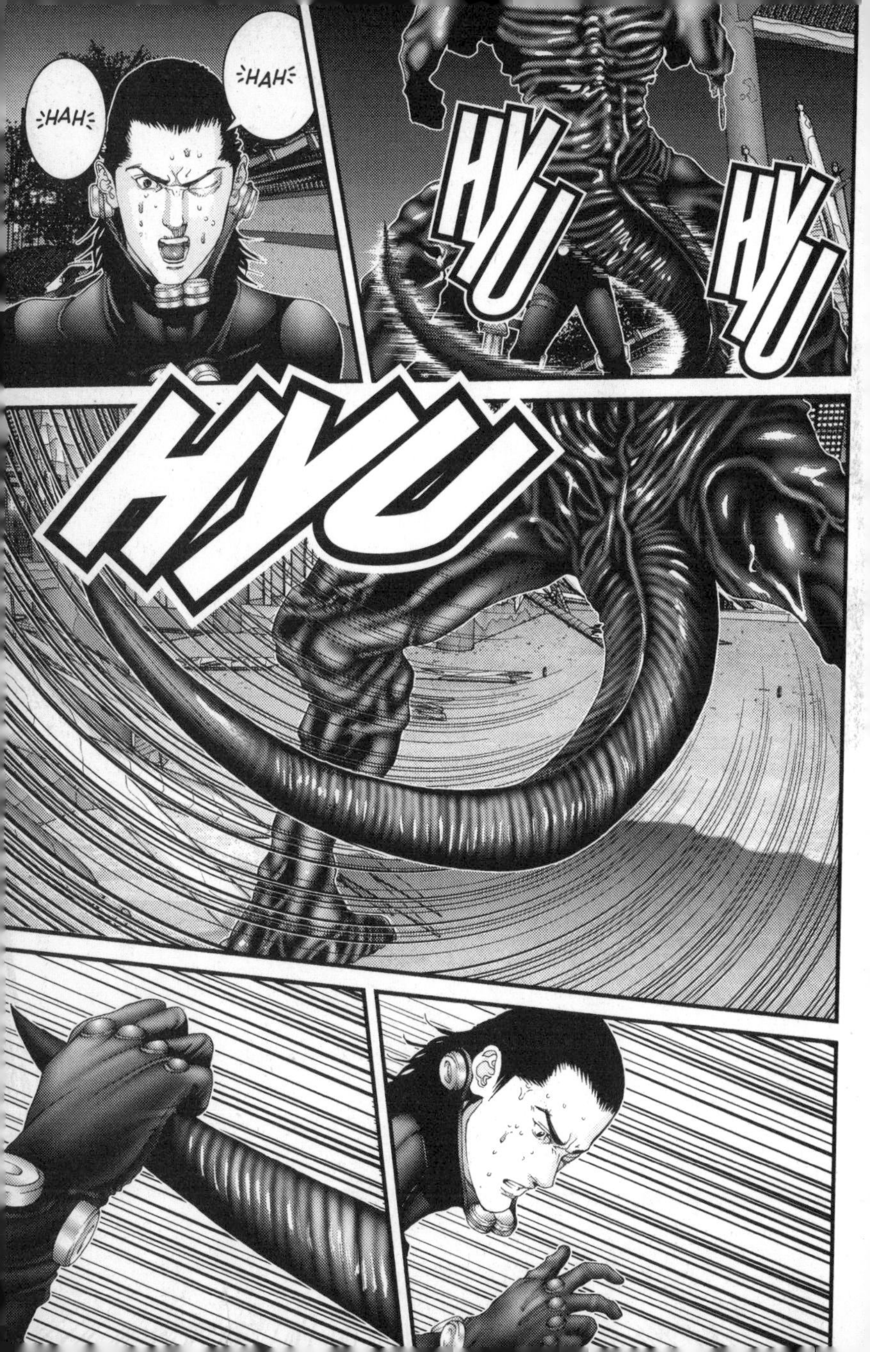

HAH
HAH
HYU
HYU
HYU

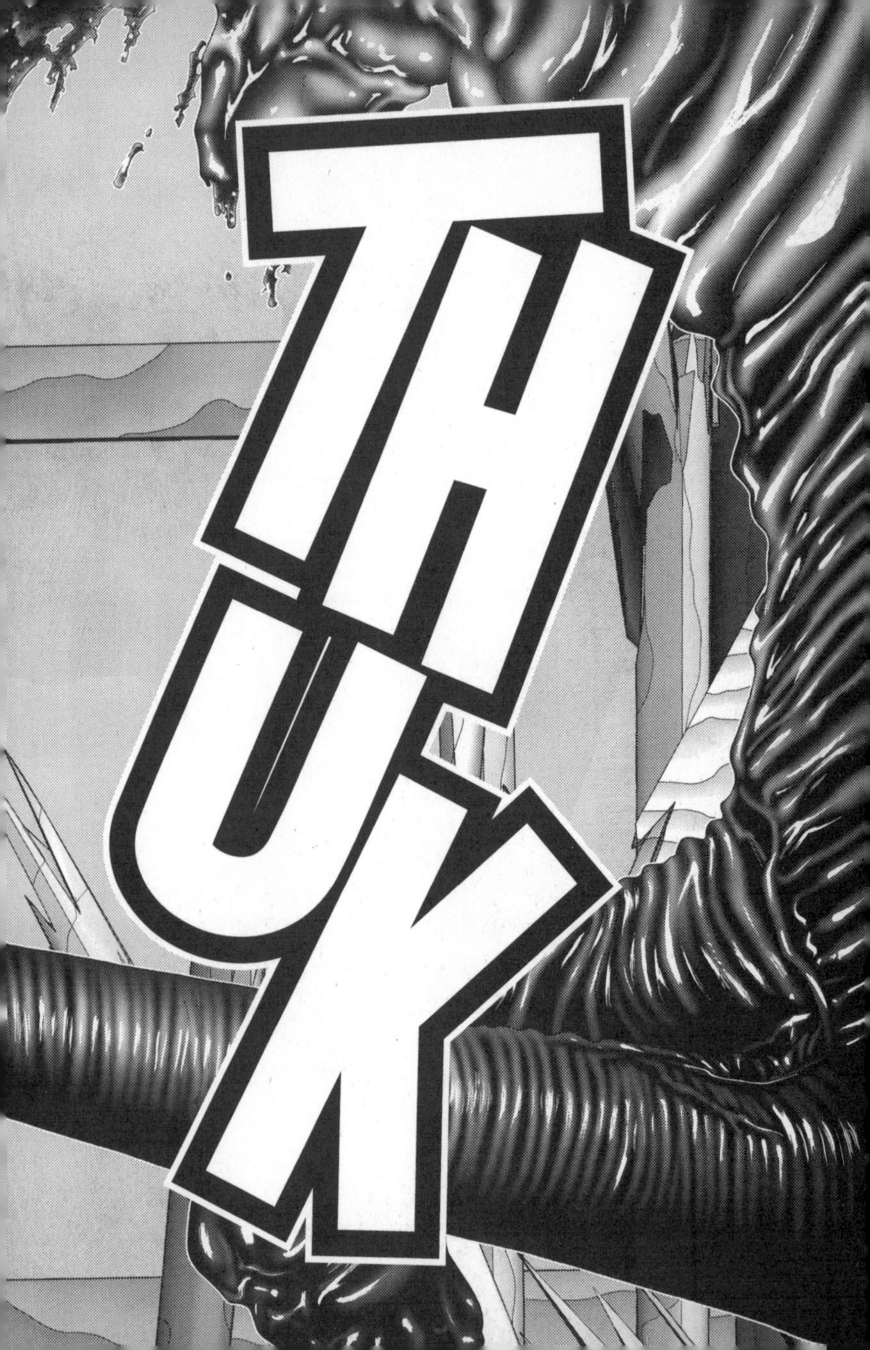
THUK

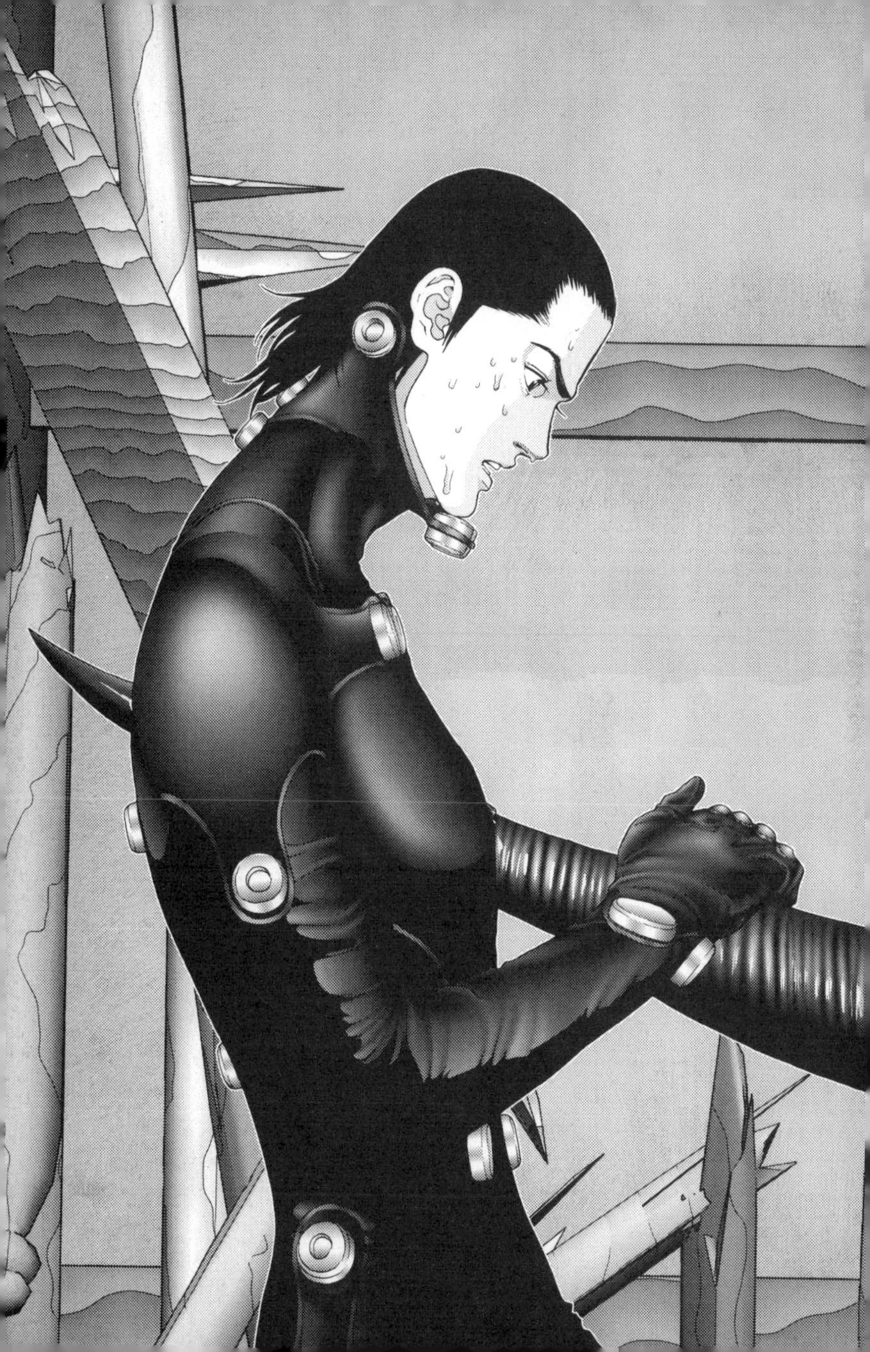

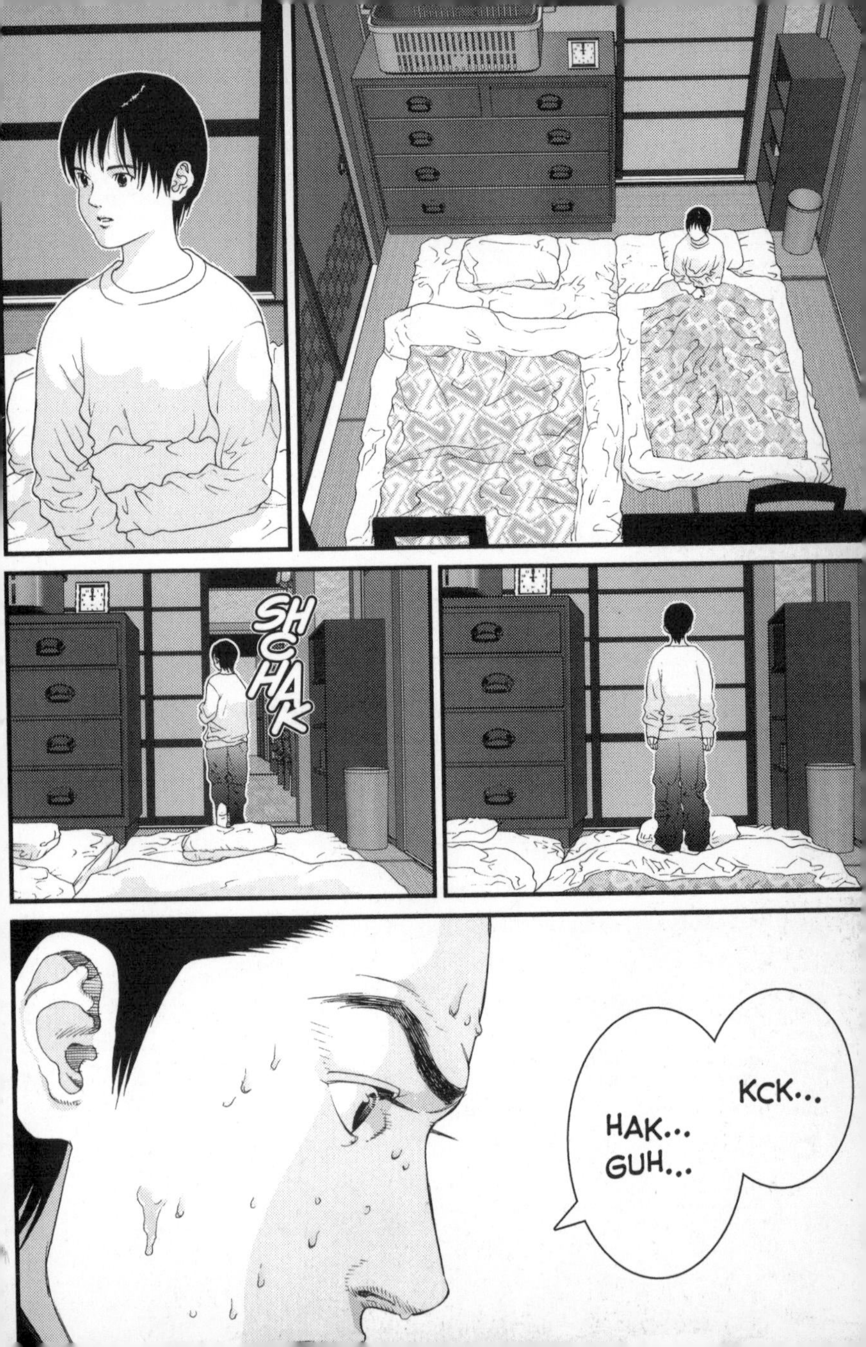
SHCHAK
KCK...
HAK...
GUH...

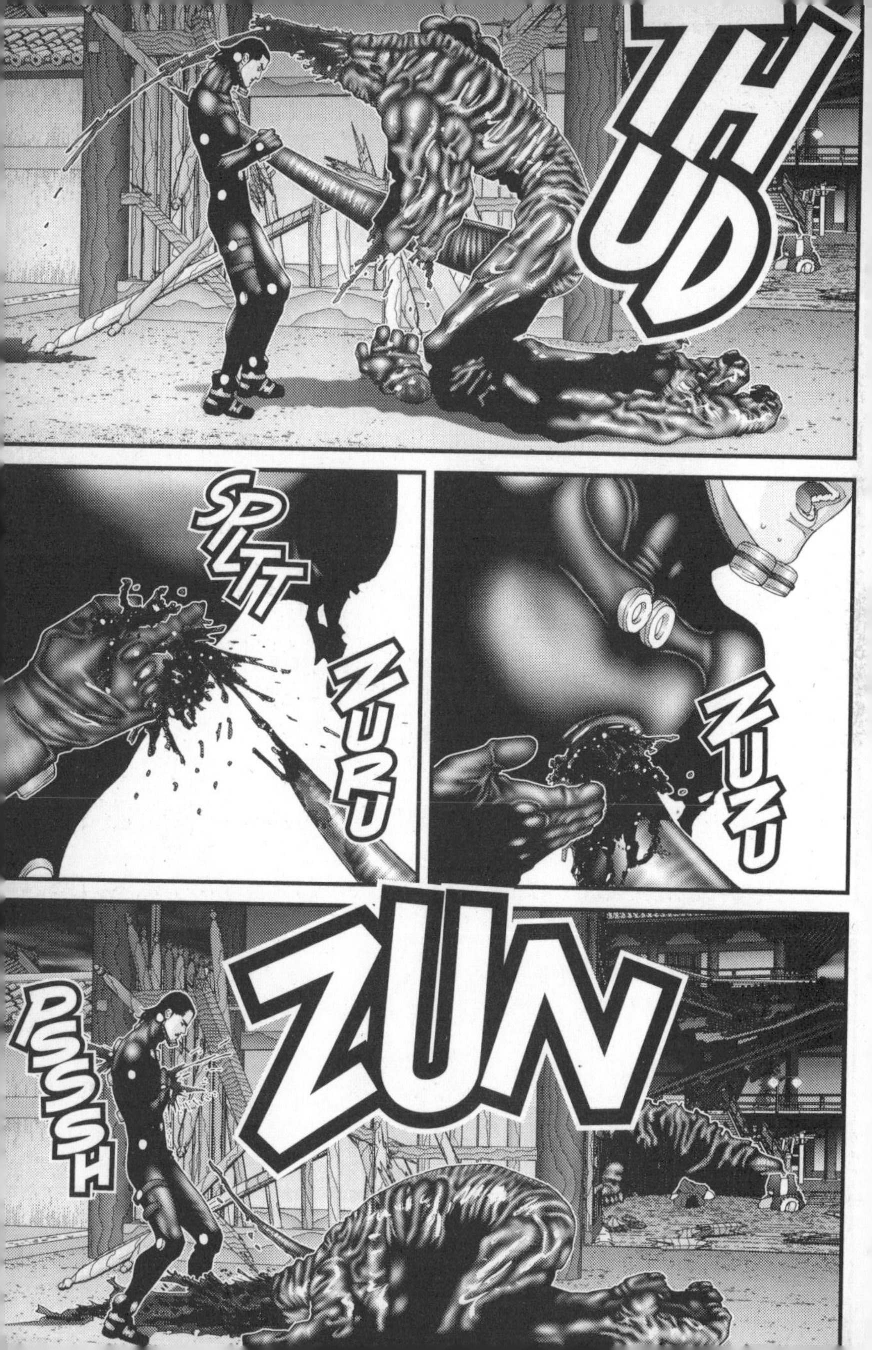
THUD
SPLTT
NURU
NURU
ZUN
PSSSH

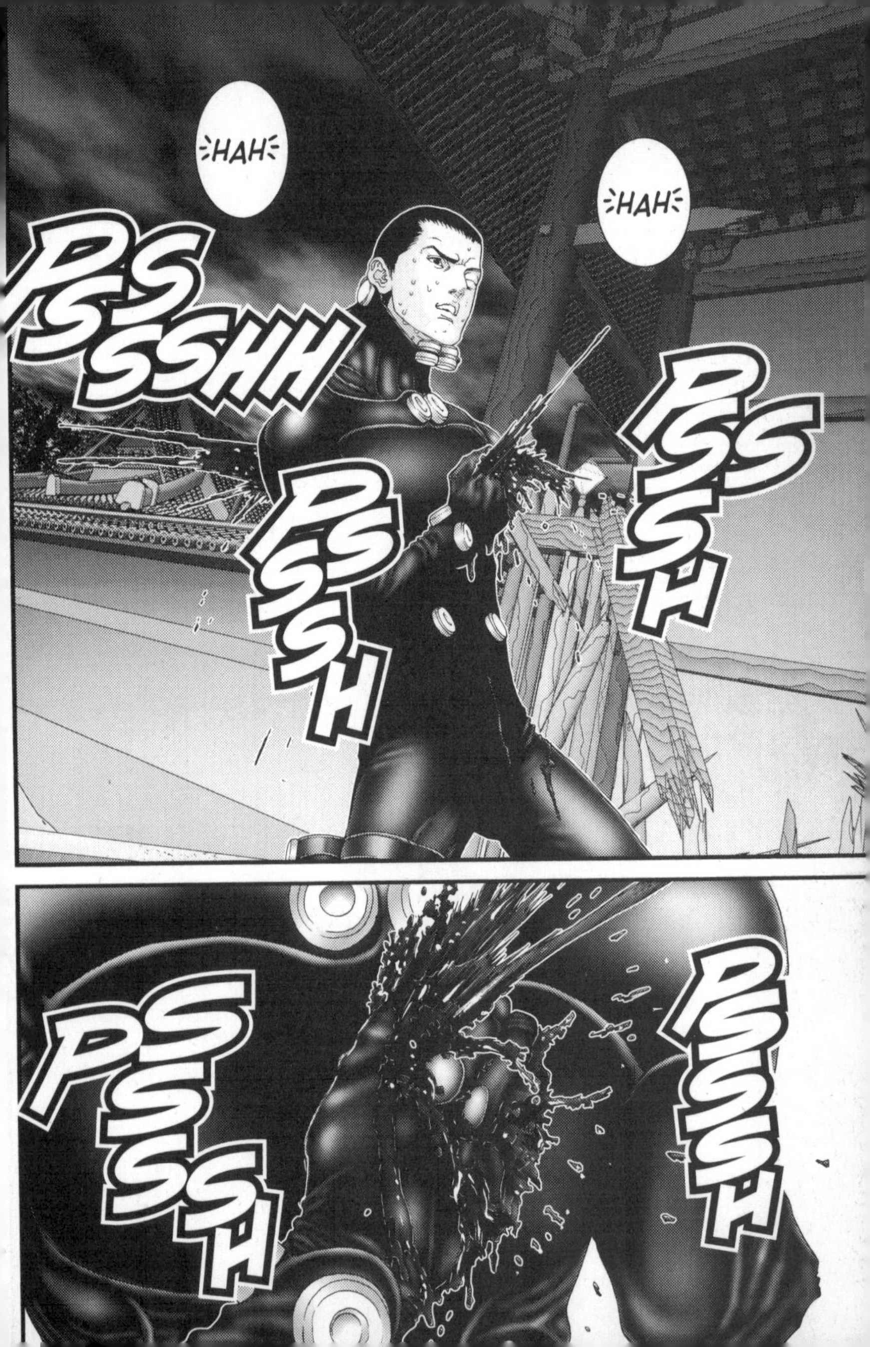
HAH
HAH
PSSSSHH
PSSSH
PSSSH
PSSSH
PSSSSH

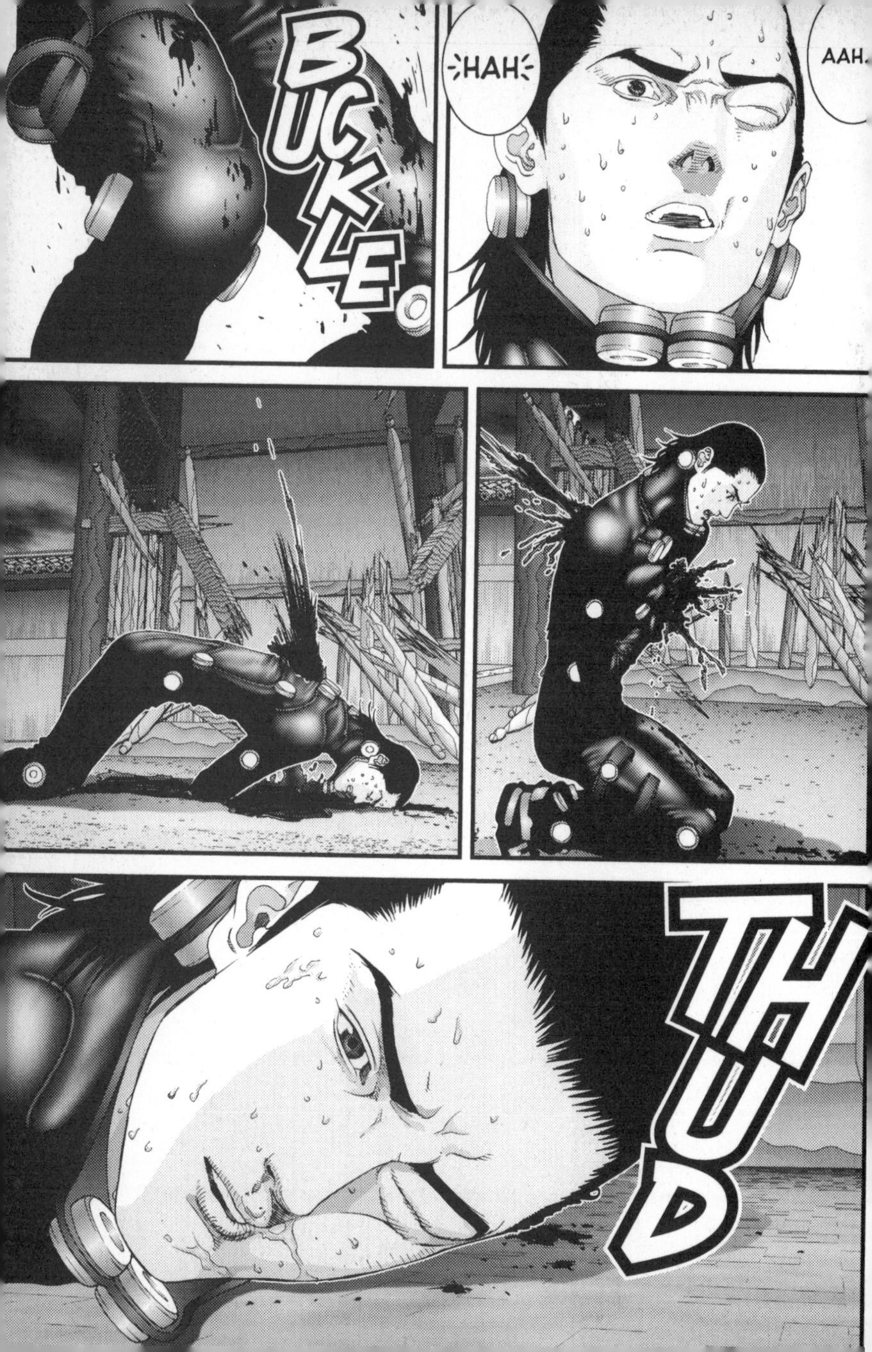
AAH.
HAH
BUCKLE
THUD

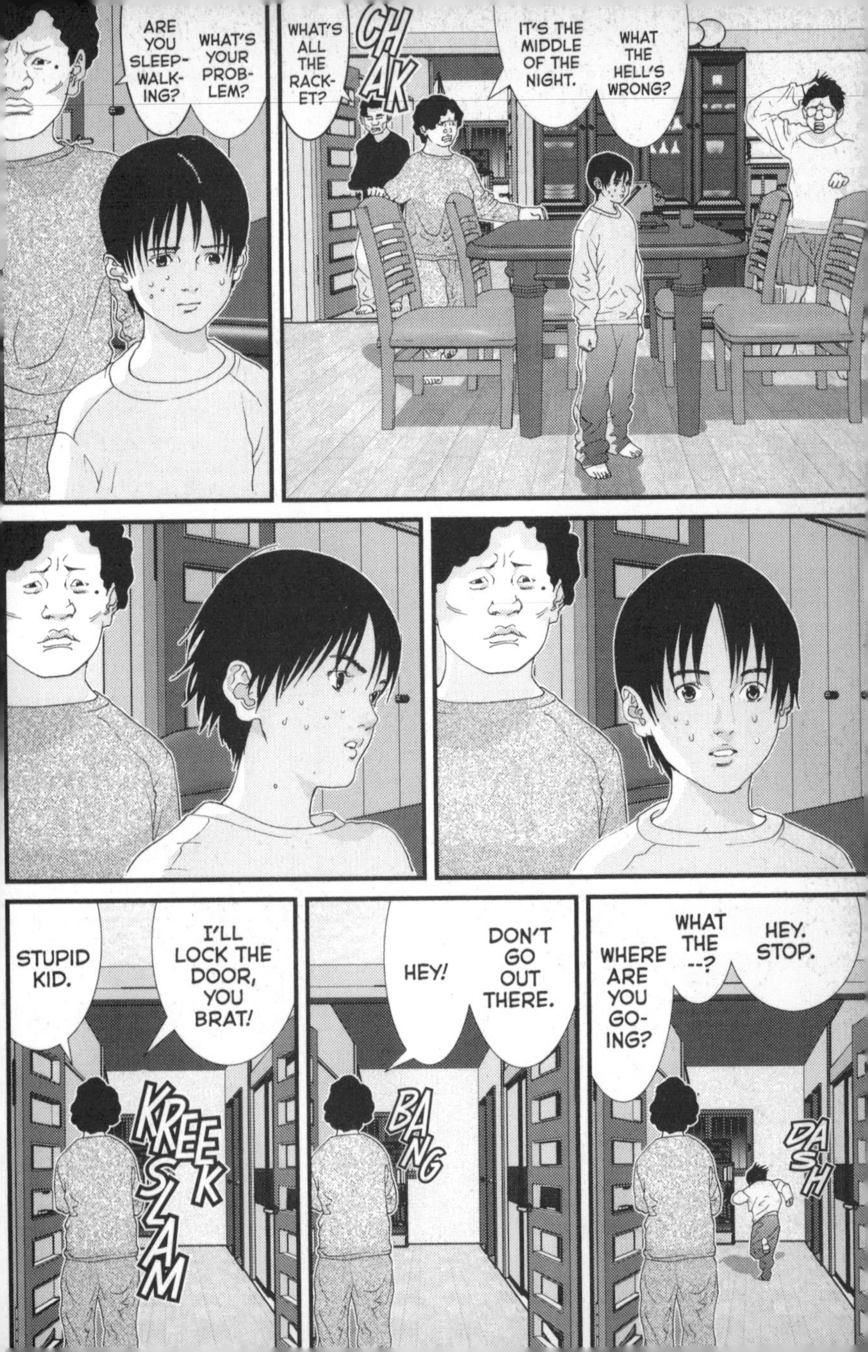
WHAT THE HELL'S WRONG?
IT'S THE MIDDLE OF THE NIGHT.
CHAK
WHAT'S ALL THE RACK-ET?
WHAT'S YOUR PROB-LEM?
ARE YOU SLEEP-WALK-ING?
HEY. STOP.
WHAT THE --?
WHERE ARE YOU GO-ING?
DASH
DON'T GO OUT THERE.
HEY!
BANG
I'LL LOCK THE DOOR, YOU BRAT!
STUPID KID.
KREEEK
SLAM

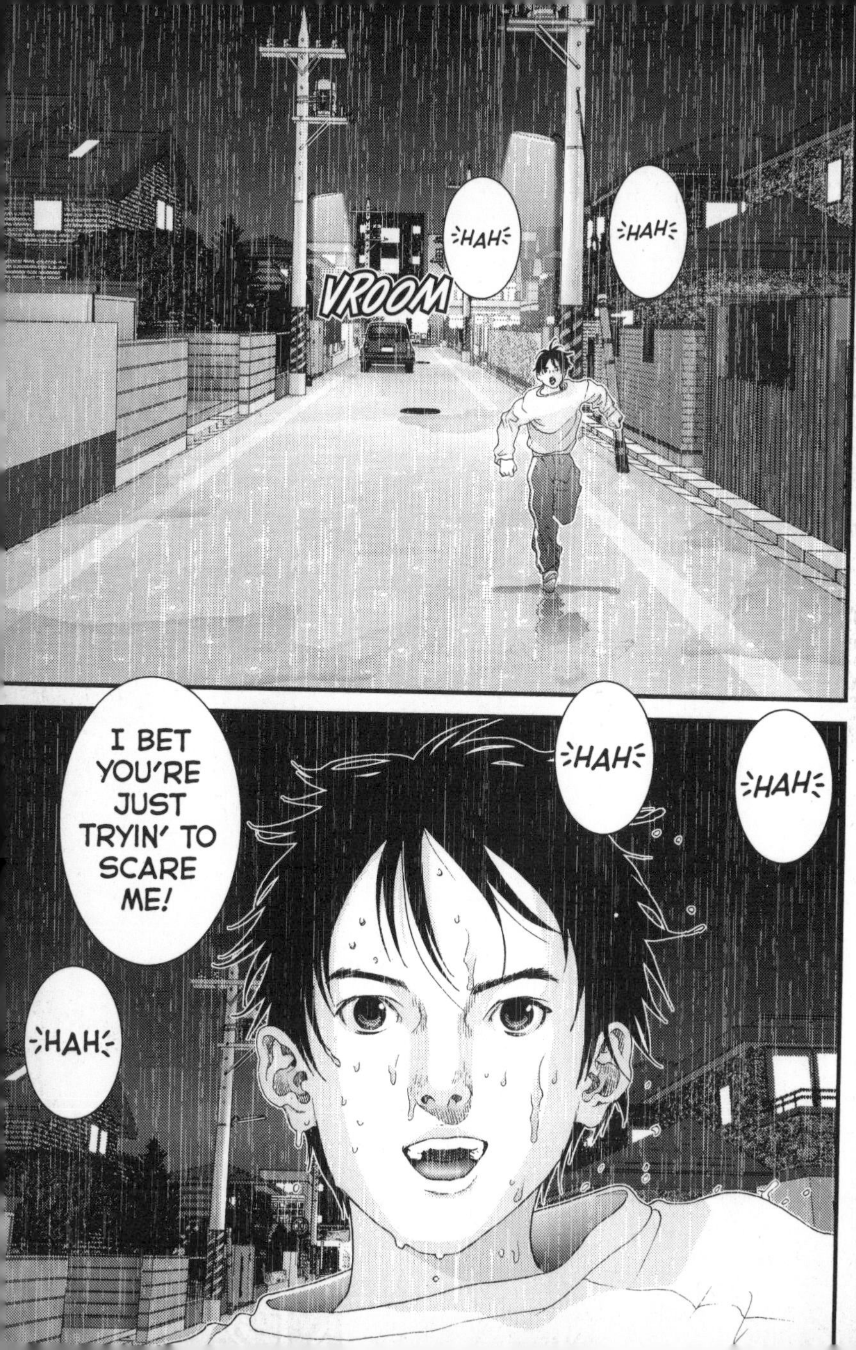
HAH
HAH
VROOM
HAH
HAH
I BET YOU'RE JUST TRYIN' TO SCARE ME!
HAH

=HAH= =HAH= =HAH=

...

GA CHA GA CHA

GA CHA

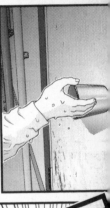

BIG BROTH-ER!

OPEN UP!

THUMP THUMP THUMP

BIG BROTHER! BIG BROTHER!

THUMP

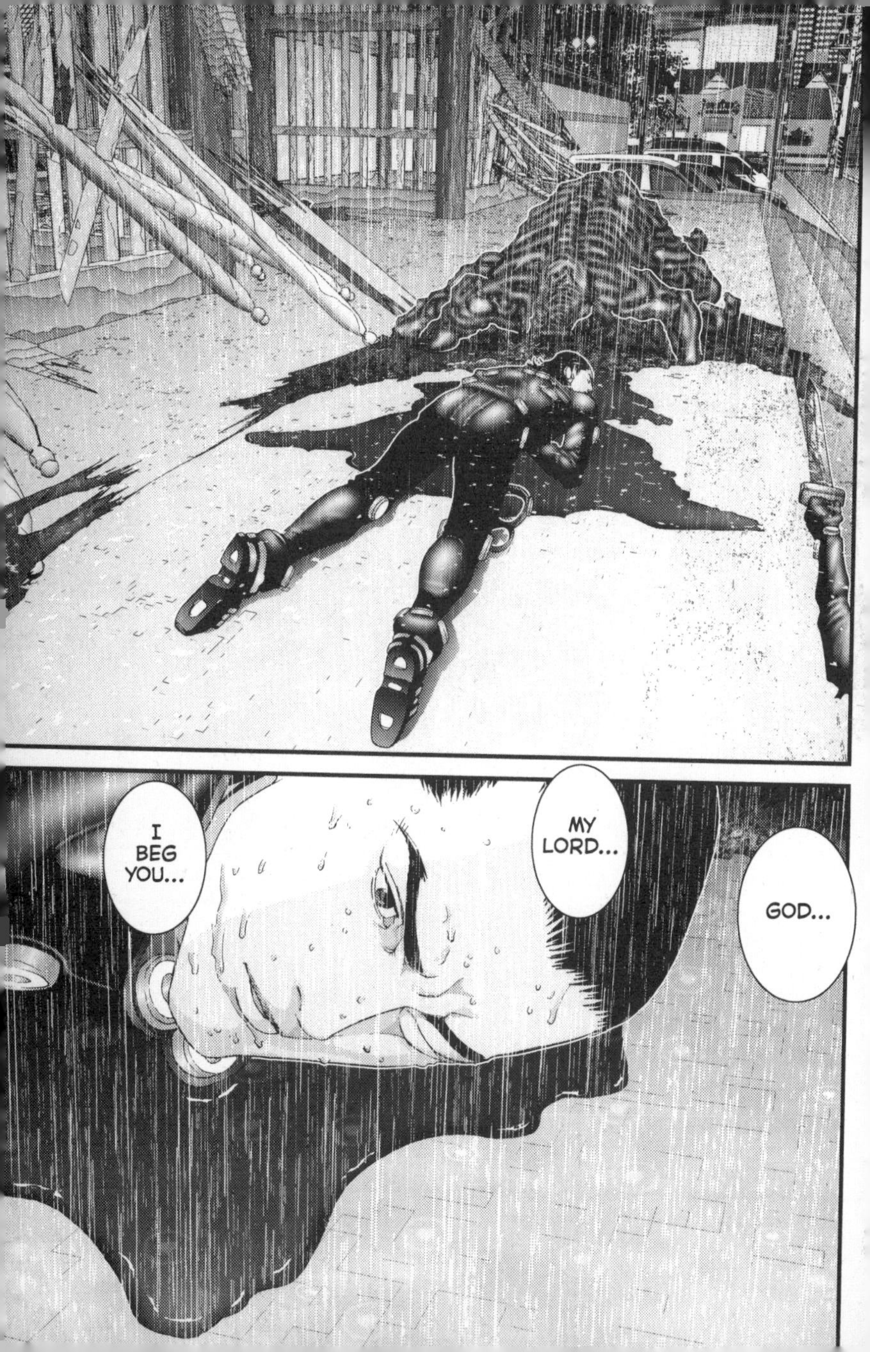
GOD...
MY LORD...
I BEG YOU...

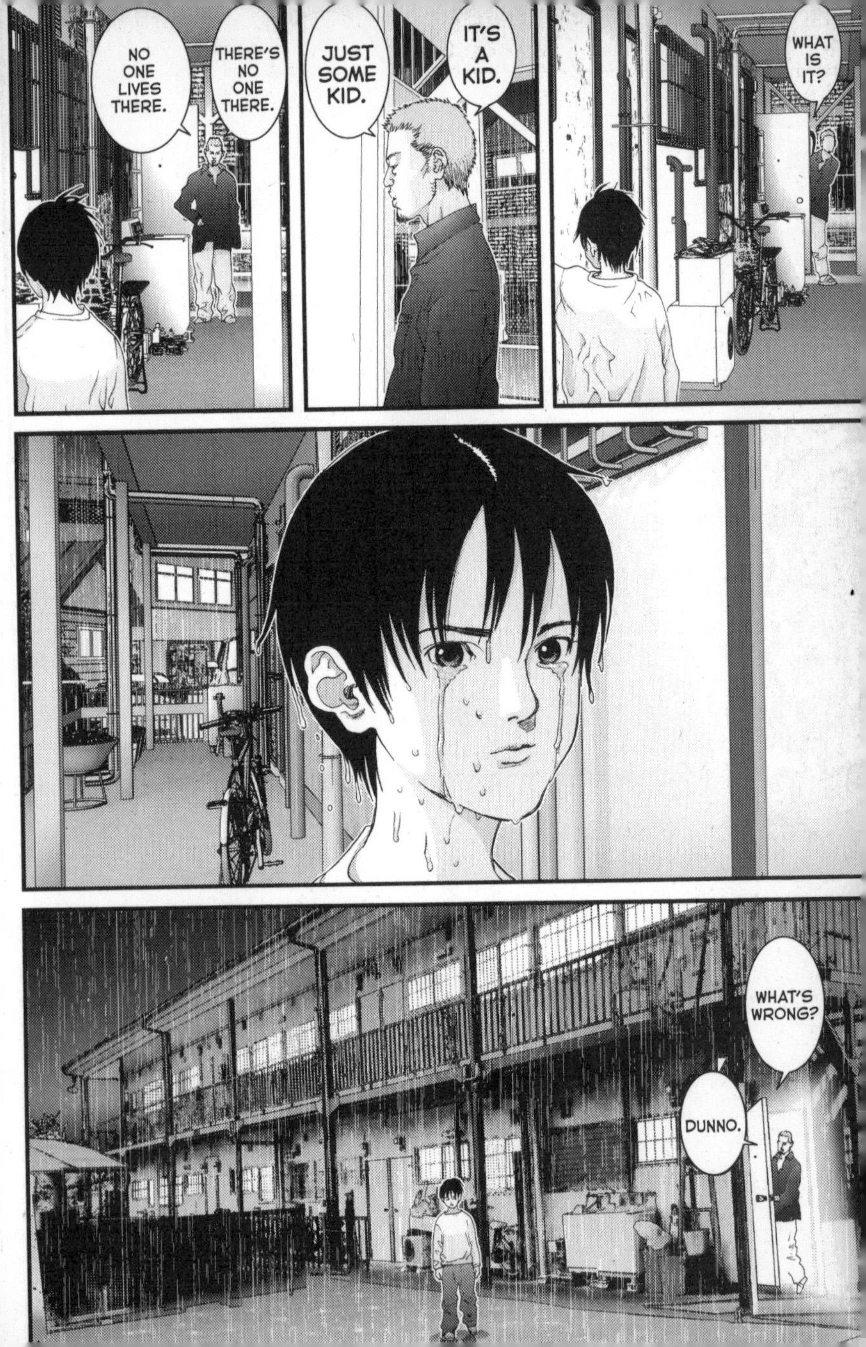
WHAT IS IT?
IT'S A KID.
JUST SOME KID.
THERE'S NO ONE THERE.
NO ONE LIVES THERE.
WHAT'S WRONG?
DUNNO.

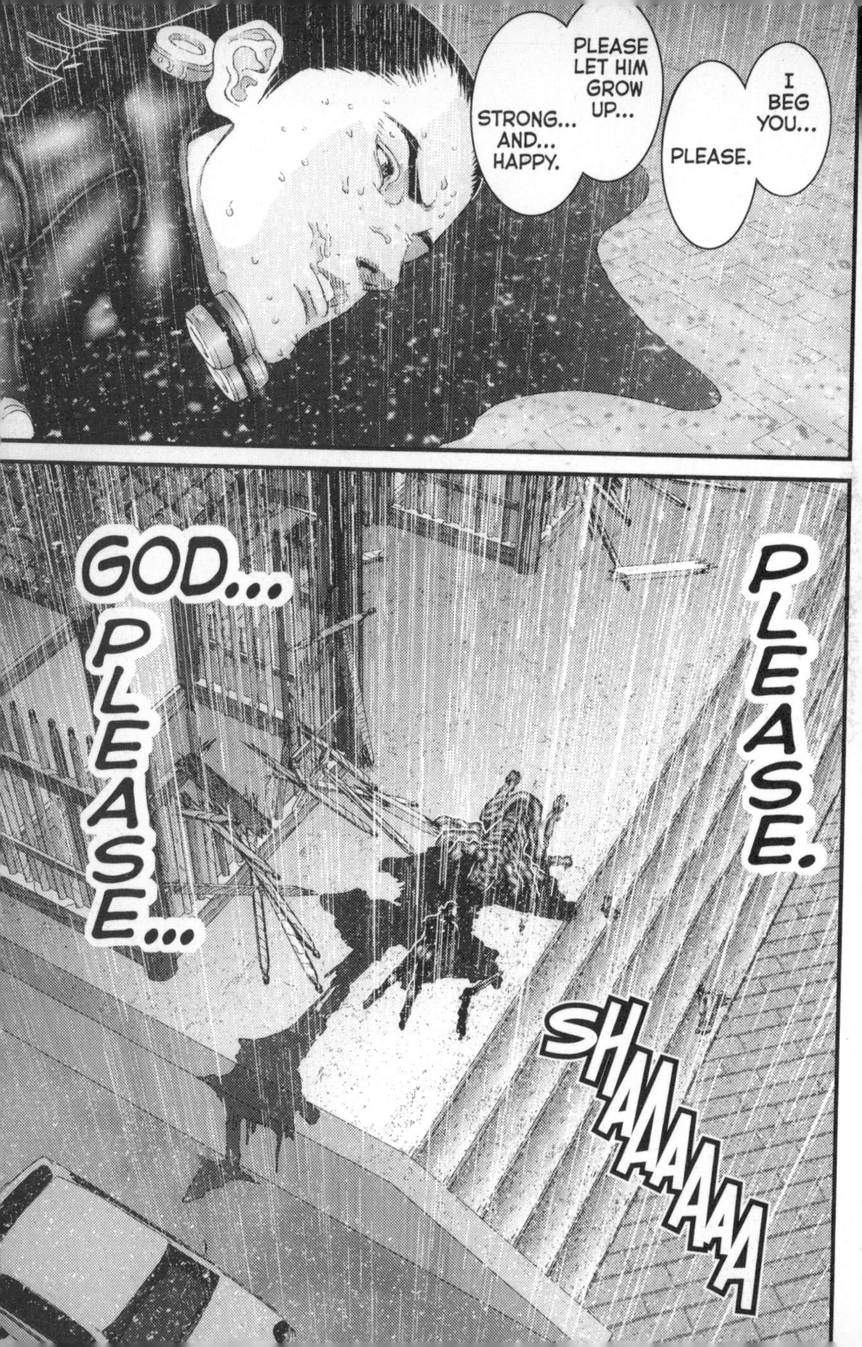
I BEG YOU...
PLEASE.
PLEASE LET HIM GROW UP...
STRONG... AND... HAPPY.
PLEASE.
GOD... PLEASE...
SHAAAAAAA

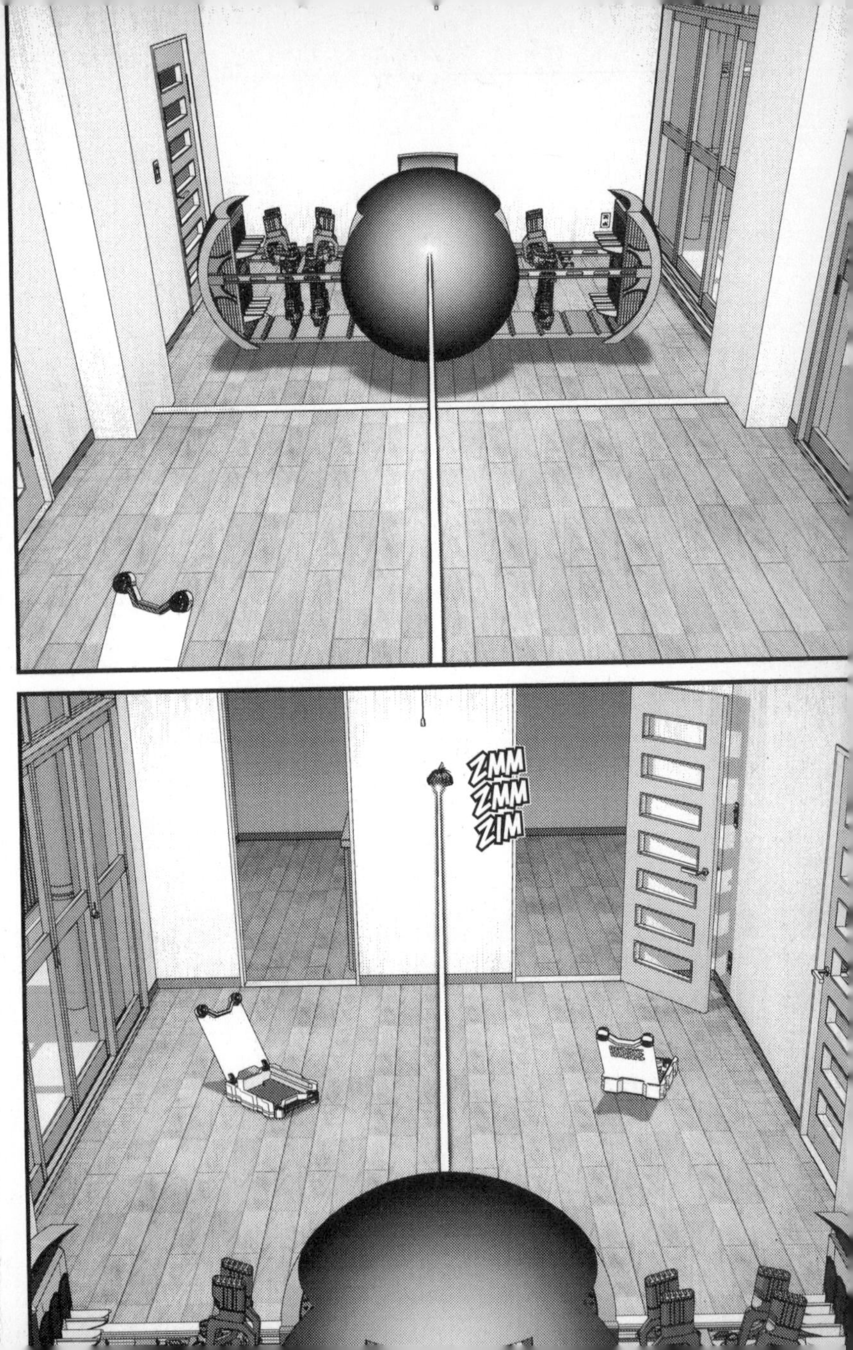
ZMM
ZMM
ZIM

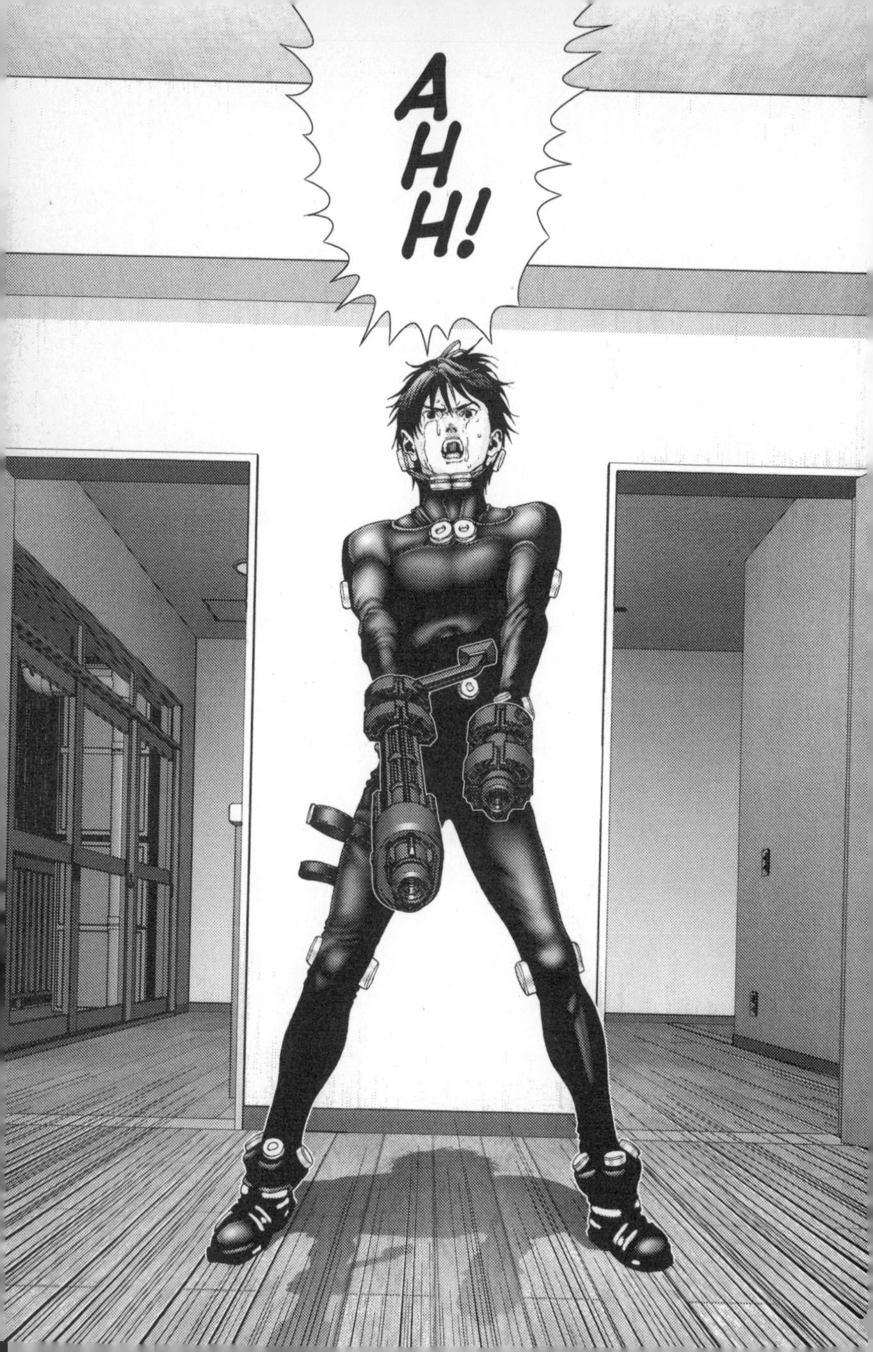
AHH!

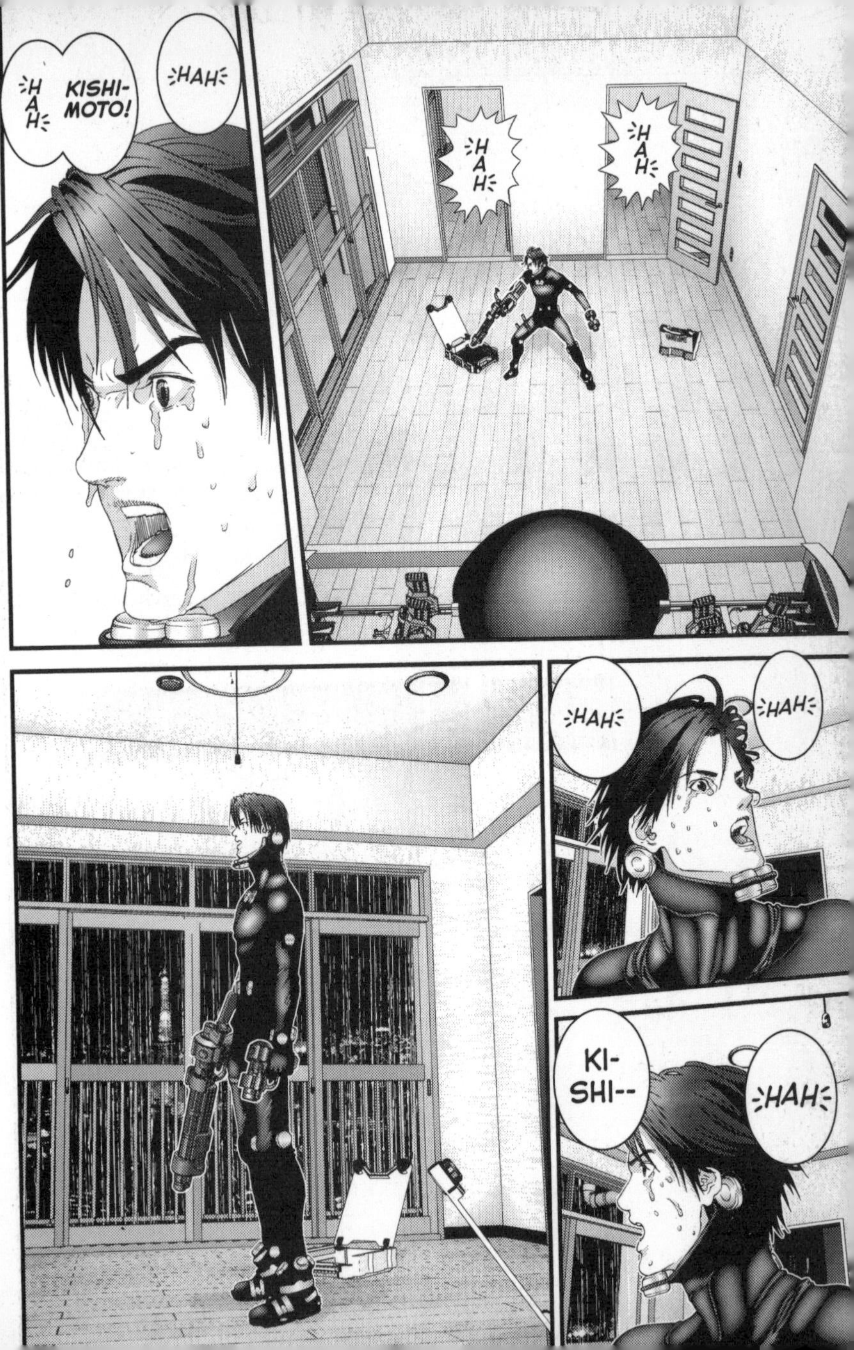
HAH HAH
HAH HAH
HAH
KISHI-MOTO!
HAH HAH
HAH
HAH
HAH
KI-SHI--

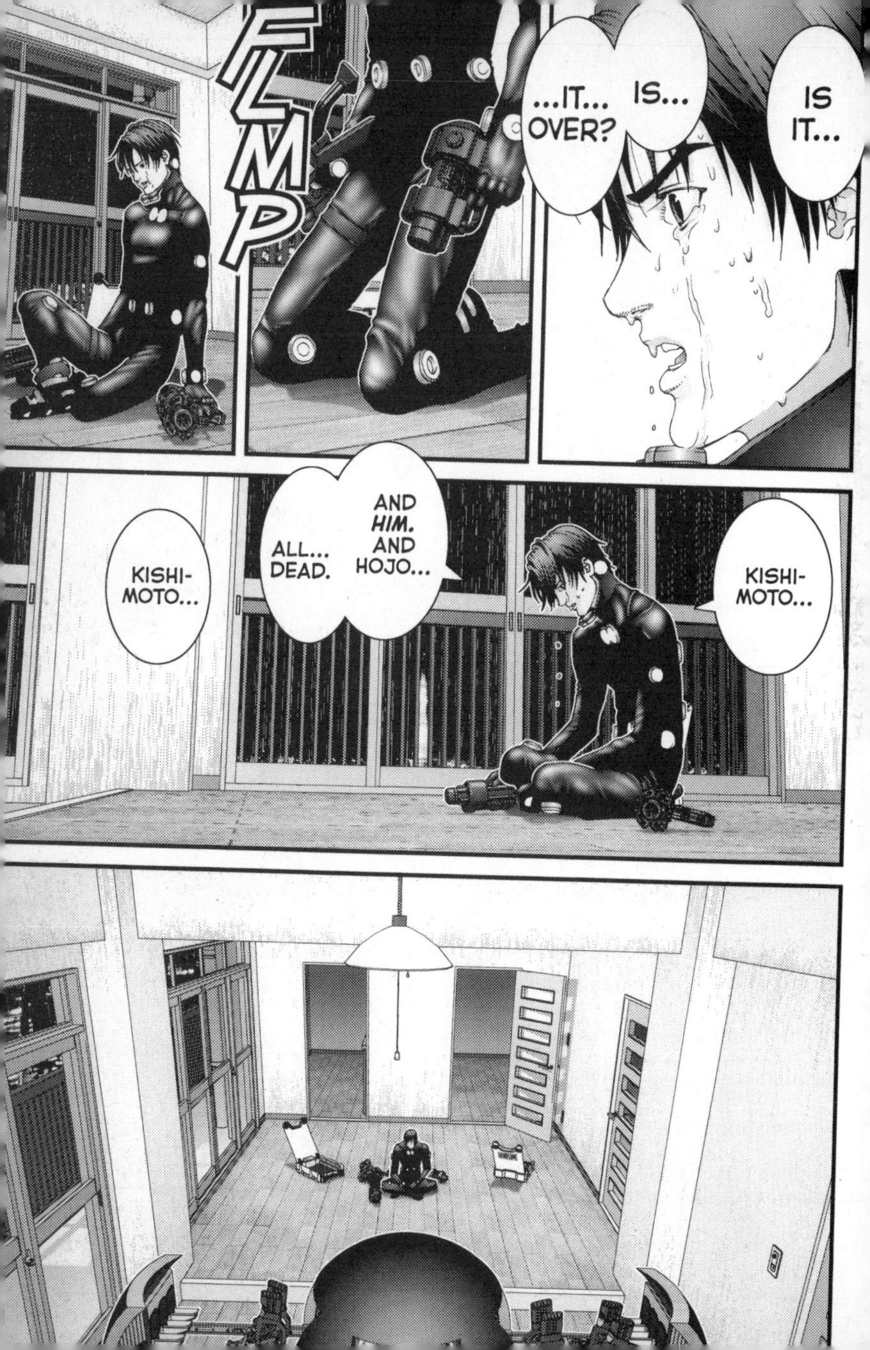
IS IT...
IS...
...IT... OVER?
FLMP
KISHI-MOTO...
AND HIM. AND HOJO...
ALL... DEAD.
KISHI-MOTO...

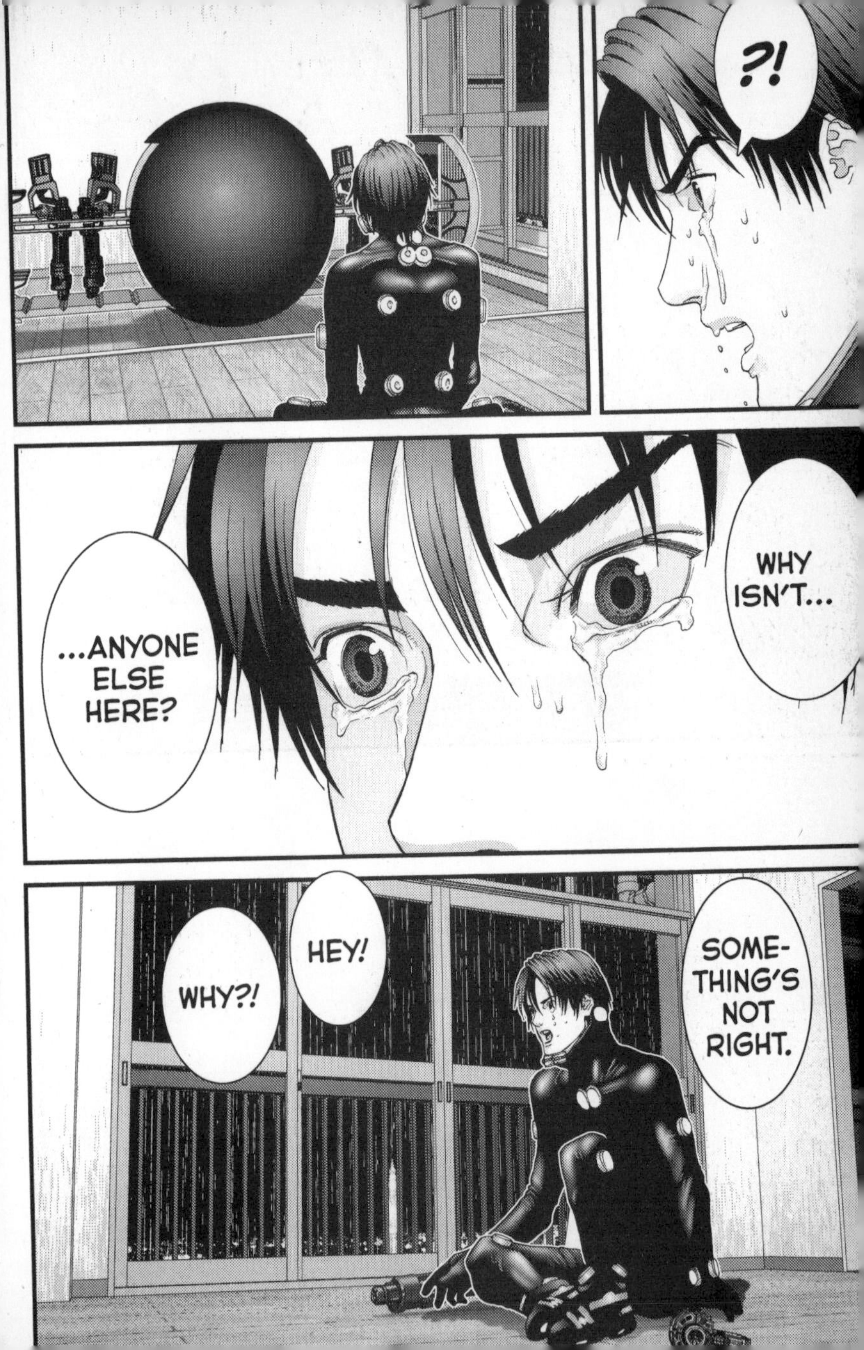
?!
WHY ISN'T...
...ANYONE ELSE HERE?
SOME-THING'S NOT RIGHT.
HEY!
WHY?!

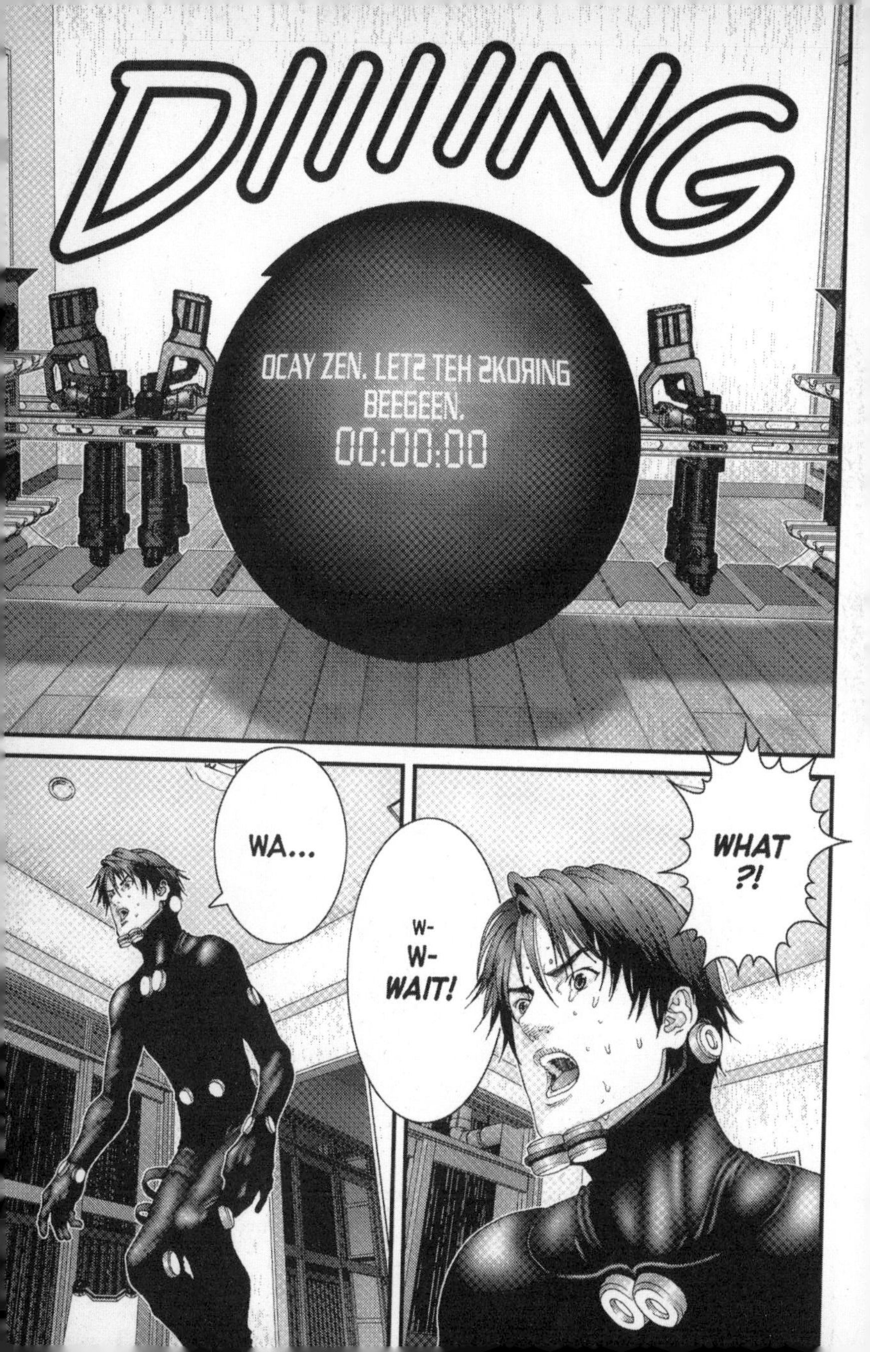
DIIING
OCAY ZEN. LETZ TEH ZKORING BEEGEEN.
00:00:00
WHAT ?!
W- W- WAIT!
WA...

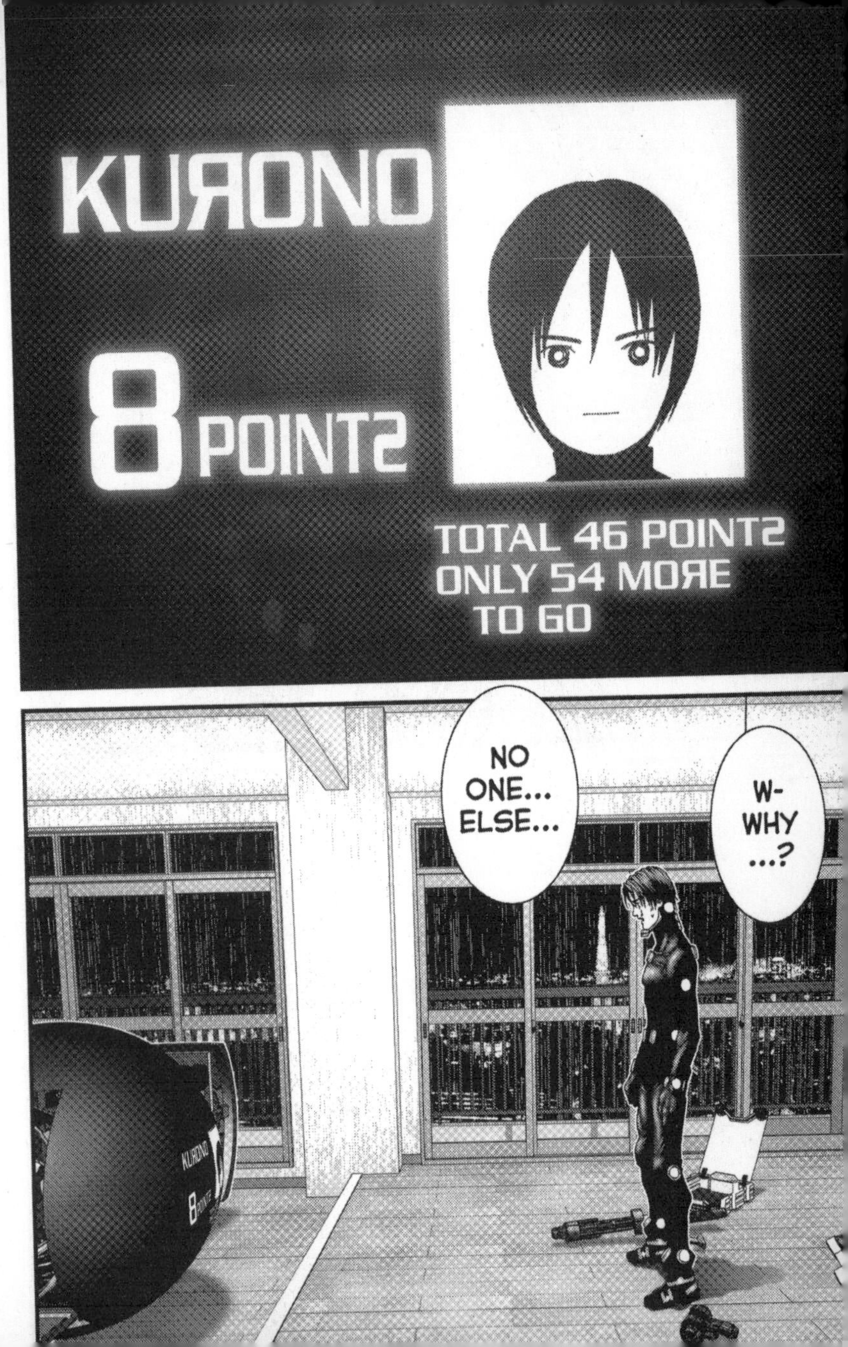
KURONO
8 POINTS
TOTAL 46 POINTS
ONLY 54 MORE
TO GO
W-
WHY
...?
NO
ONE...
ELSE...
KURONO
8 POINTS

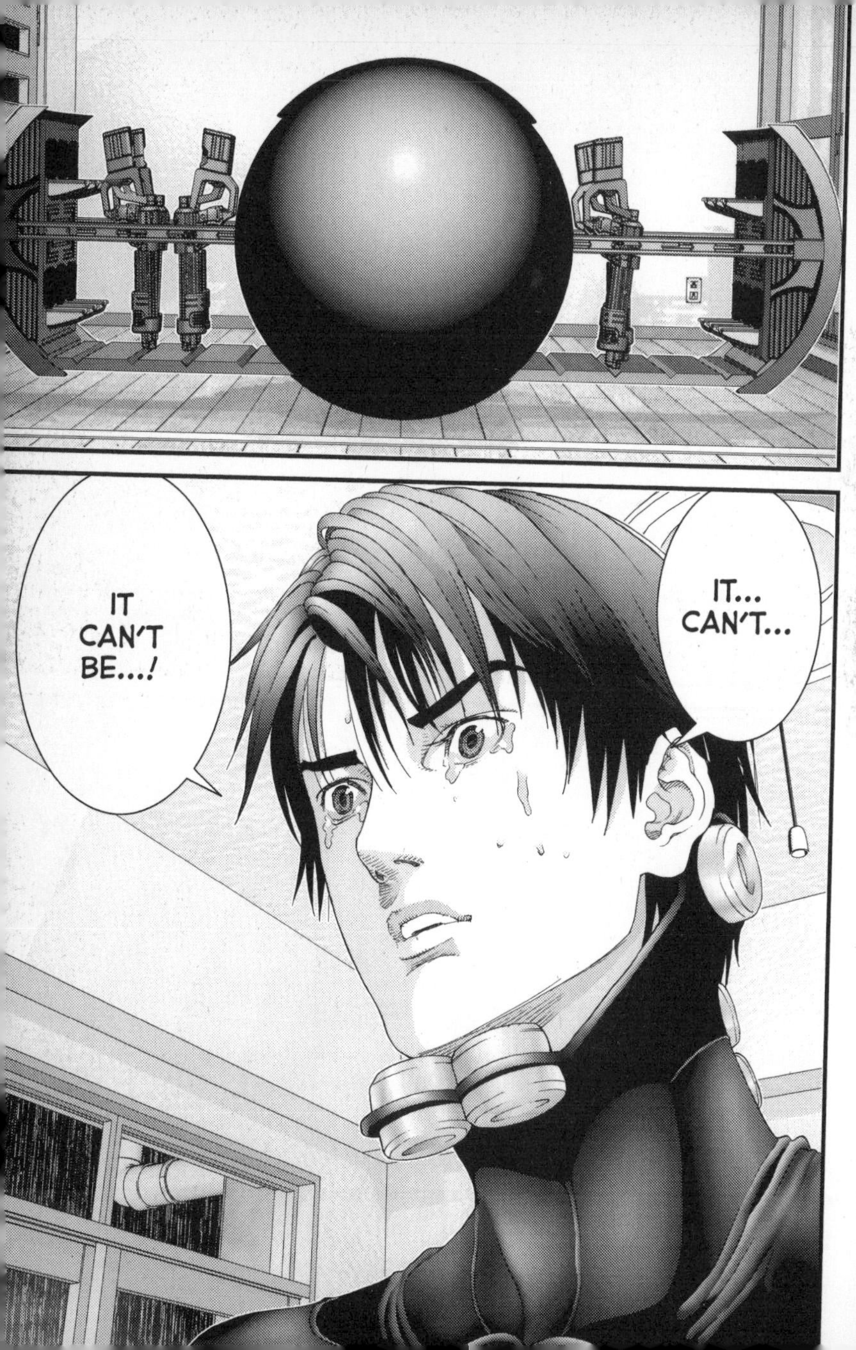
IT... CAN'T...
IT CAN'T BE...!

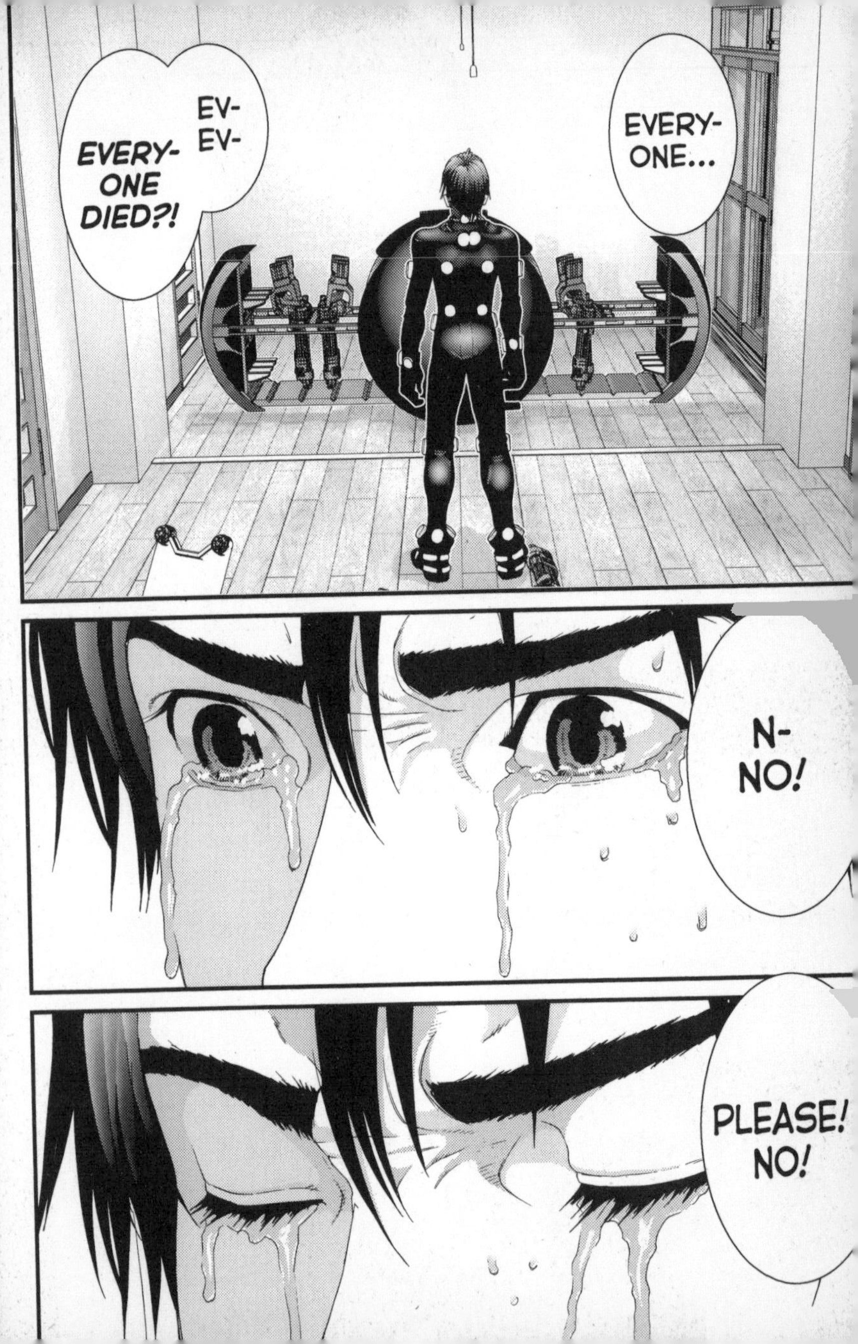
EVERY-ONE...
EV- EV- EVERY-ONE DIED?!
N- NO!
PLEASE! NO!

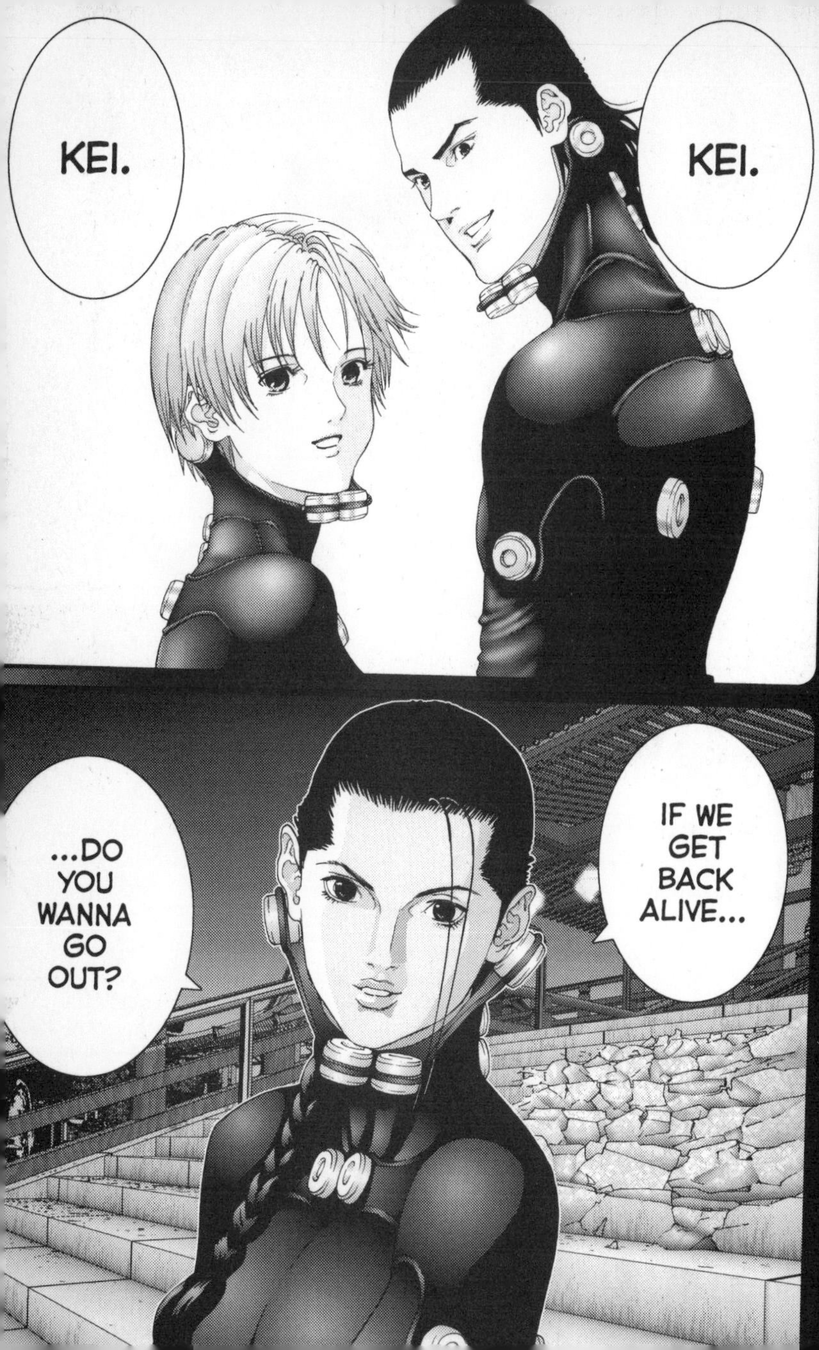
KEI.
KEI.
IF WE GET BACK ALIVE...
...DO YOU WANNA GO OUT?

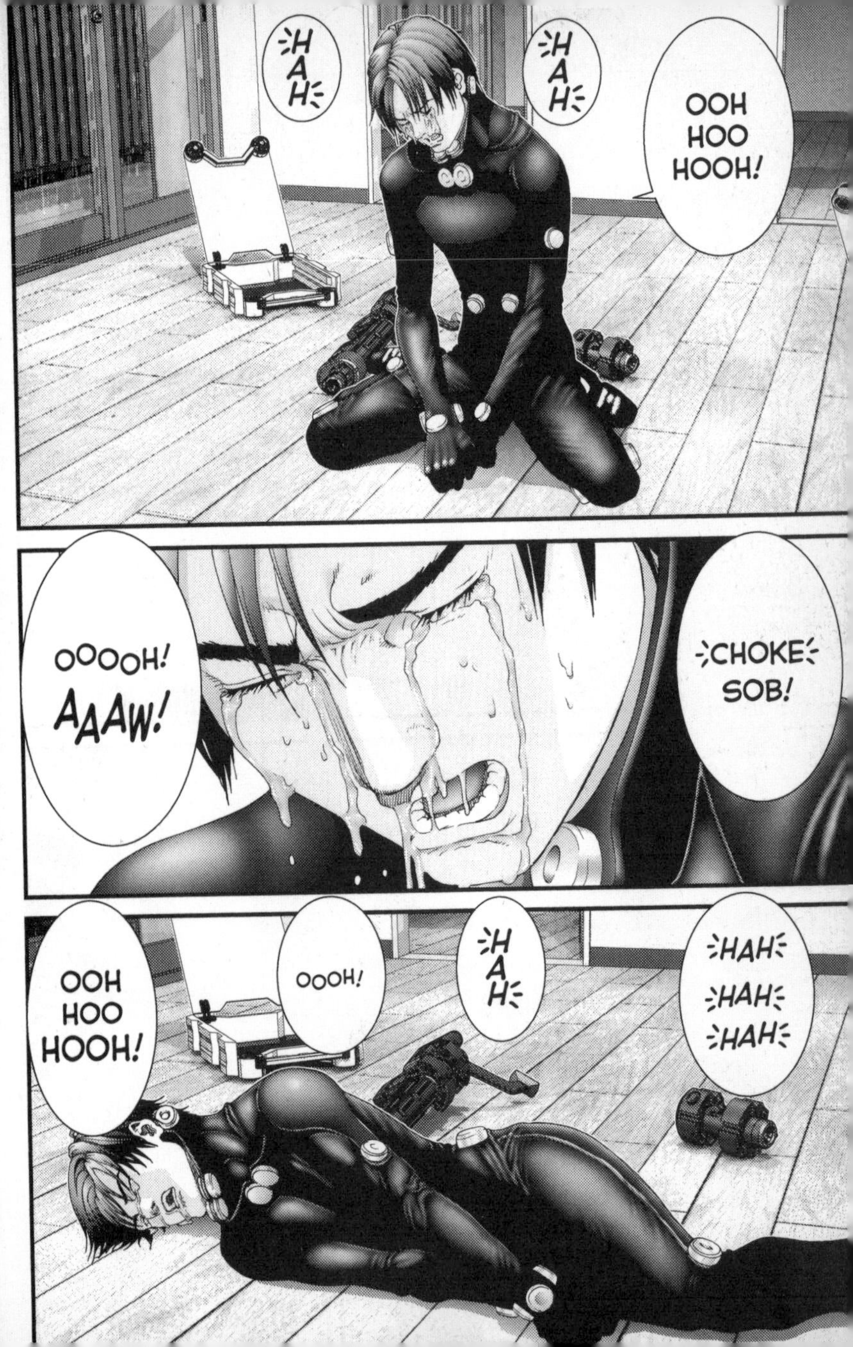

OOH HOO HOOH!
HAH
HAH
CHOKE SOB!
OOOOH! AAAW!
HAH HAH HAH
HAH
OOOH!
OOH HOO HOOH!

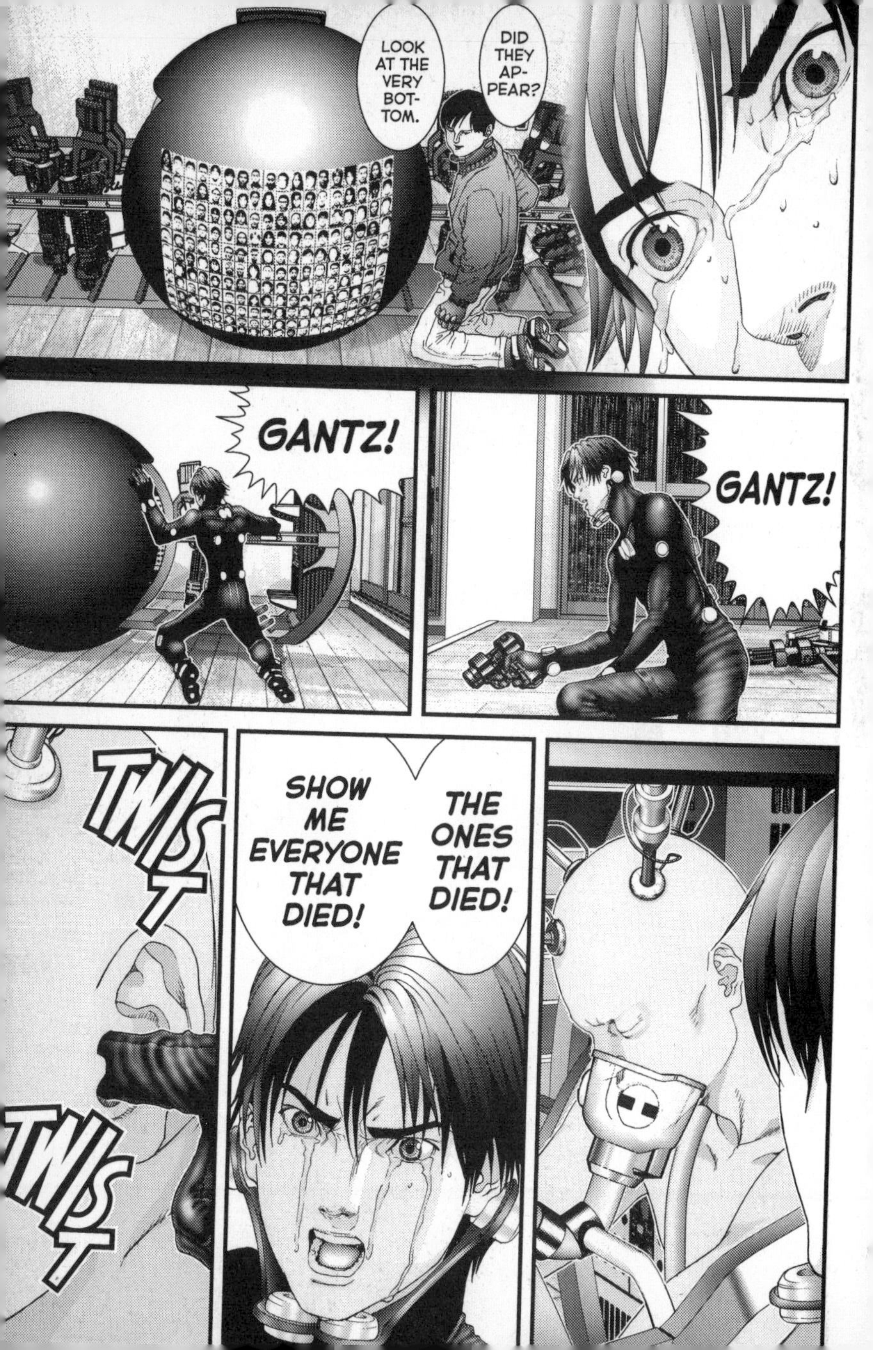
DID THEY AP-PEAR?
LOOK AT THE VERY BOT-TOM.
GANTZ!
GANTZ!
THE ONES THAT DIED!
SHOW ME EVERYONE THAT DIED!
TWIST
TWIST

	YAKUZA A	YAKUZA B	BLONDIE	GANG A	GLA
UG	PRIEST	MISTA KATO (HEEHEE)	TITS	HOMO	SAD

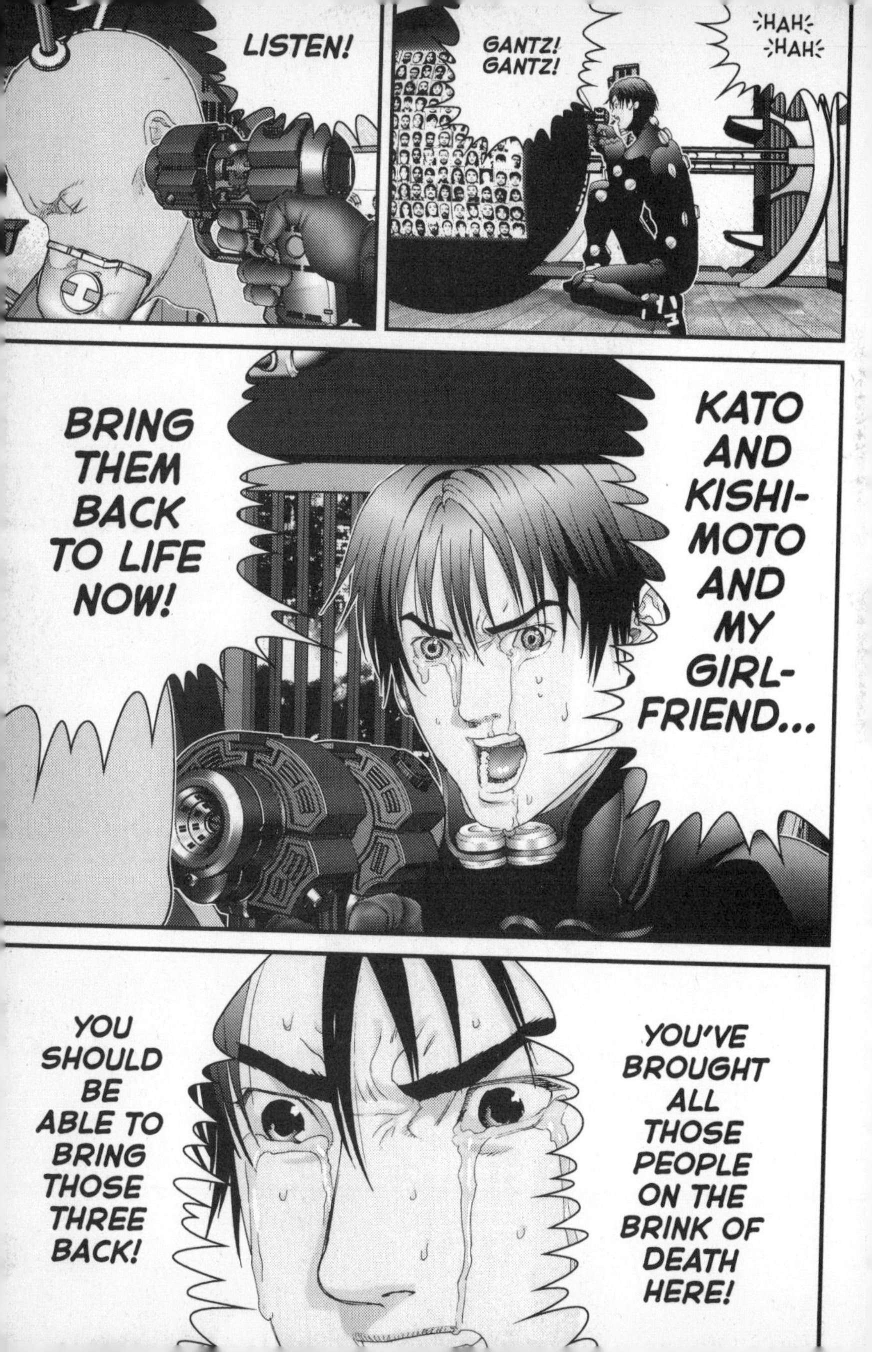

HAH HAH
GANTZ! GANTZ!
LISTEN!
KATO AND KISHI-MOTO AND MY GIRL-FRIEND...
BRING THEM BACK TO LIFE NOW!
YOU'VE BROUGHT ALL THOSE PEOPLE ON THE BRINK OF DEATH HERE!
YOU SHOULD BE ABLE TO BRING THOSE THREE BACK!

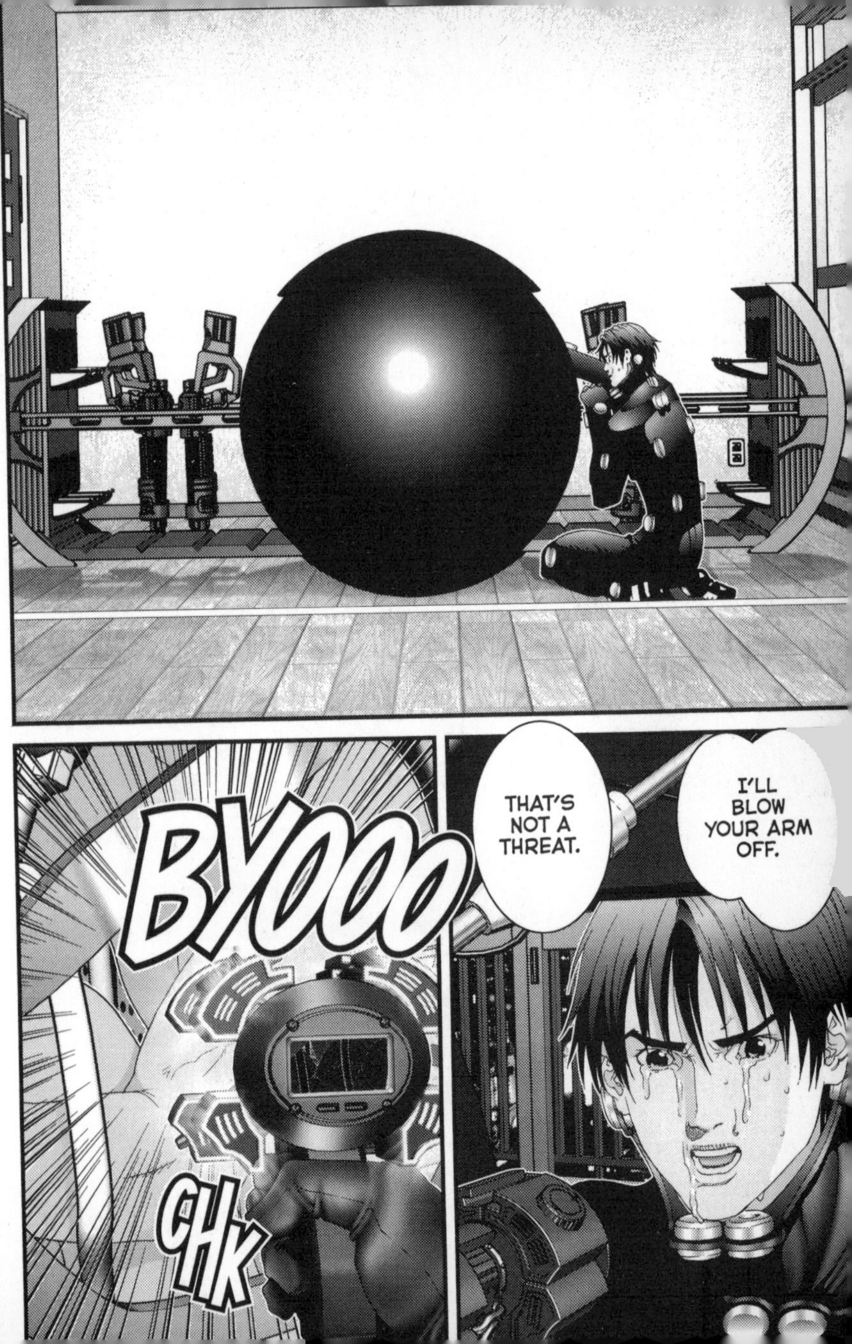
I'LL BLOW YOUR ARM OFF.
THAT'S NOT A THREAT.
BYOOO
CHK

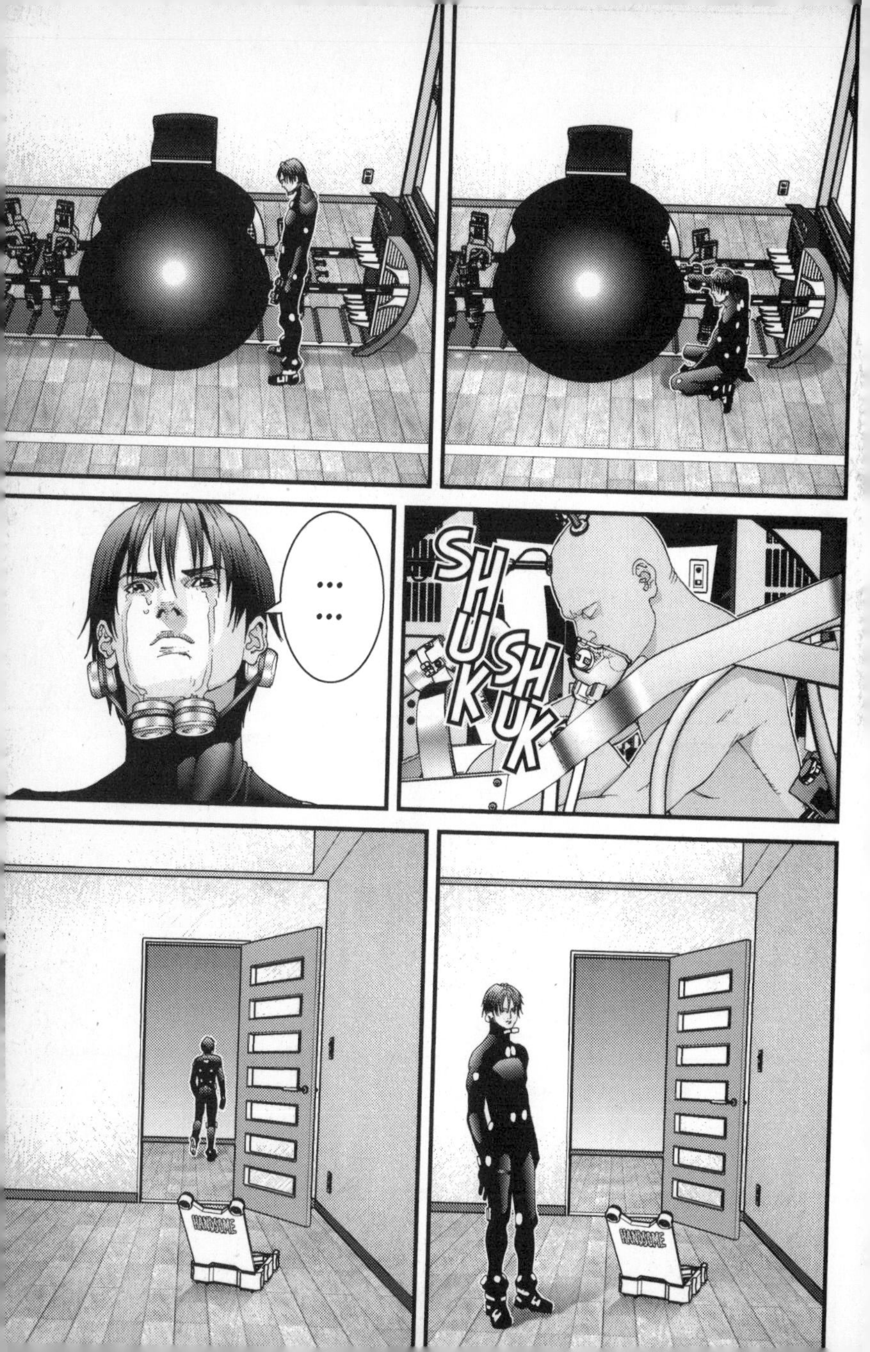
...
...
SHUSHUSH
KUKUK
HANDSOME
HANDSOME

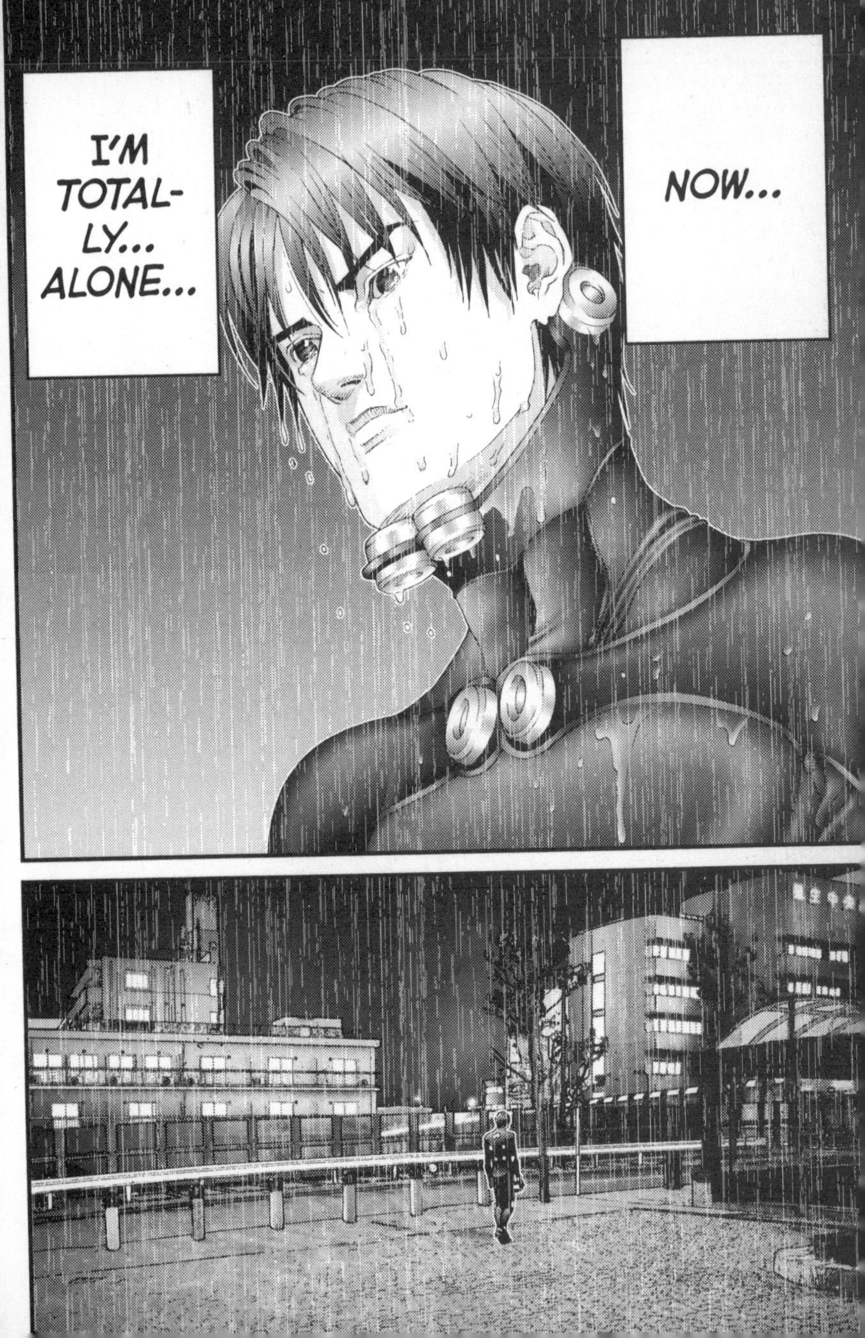
NOW...
I'M TOTAL-LY... ALONE...

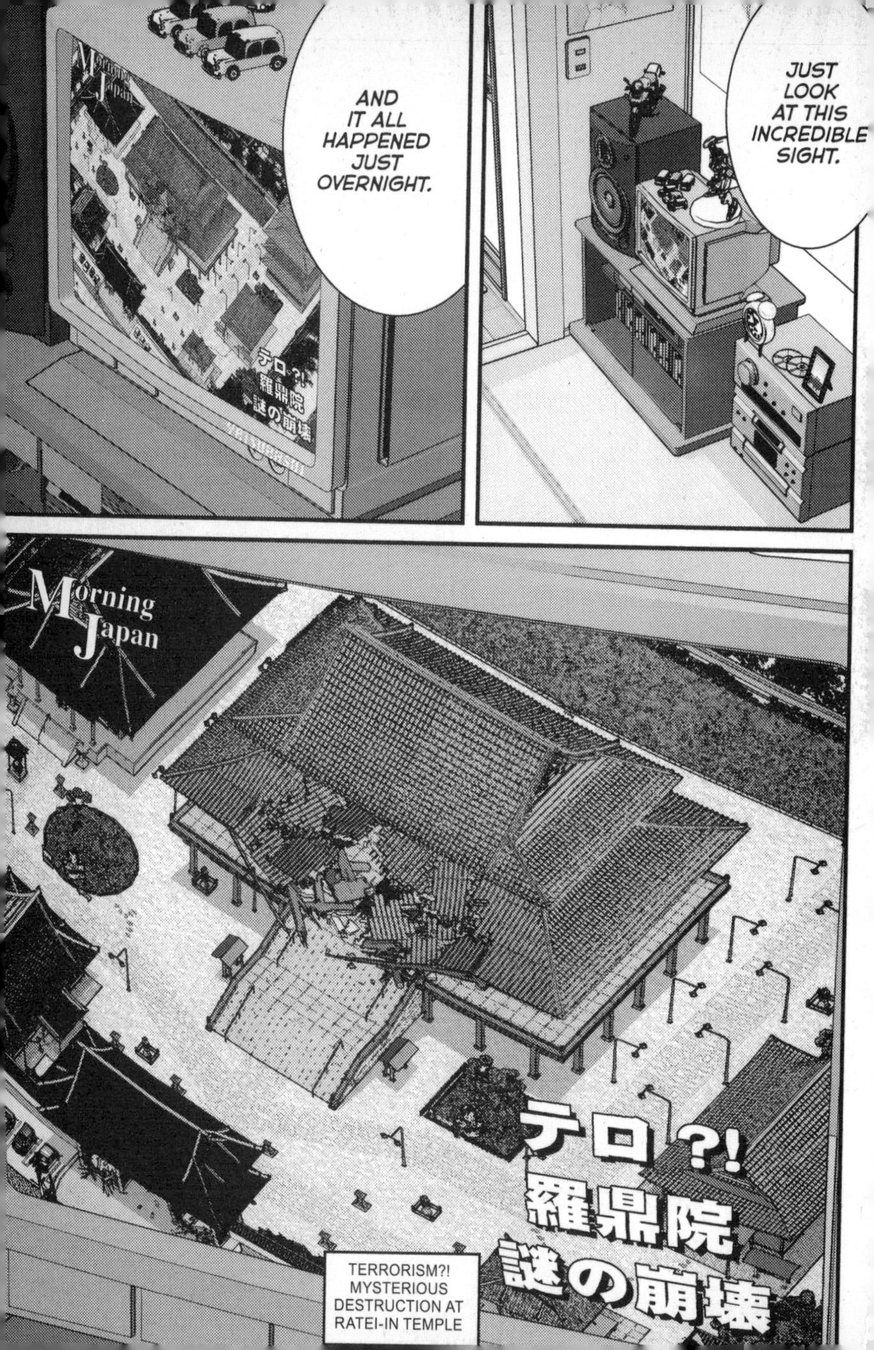
JUST LOOK AT THIS INCREDIBLE SIGHT.
AND IT ALL HAPPENED JUST OVERNIGHT.
Morning Japan
テロ?!
羅鼎院
謎の崩壊
TERRORISM?! MYSTERIOUS DESTRUCTION AT RATEI-IN TEMPLE

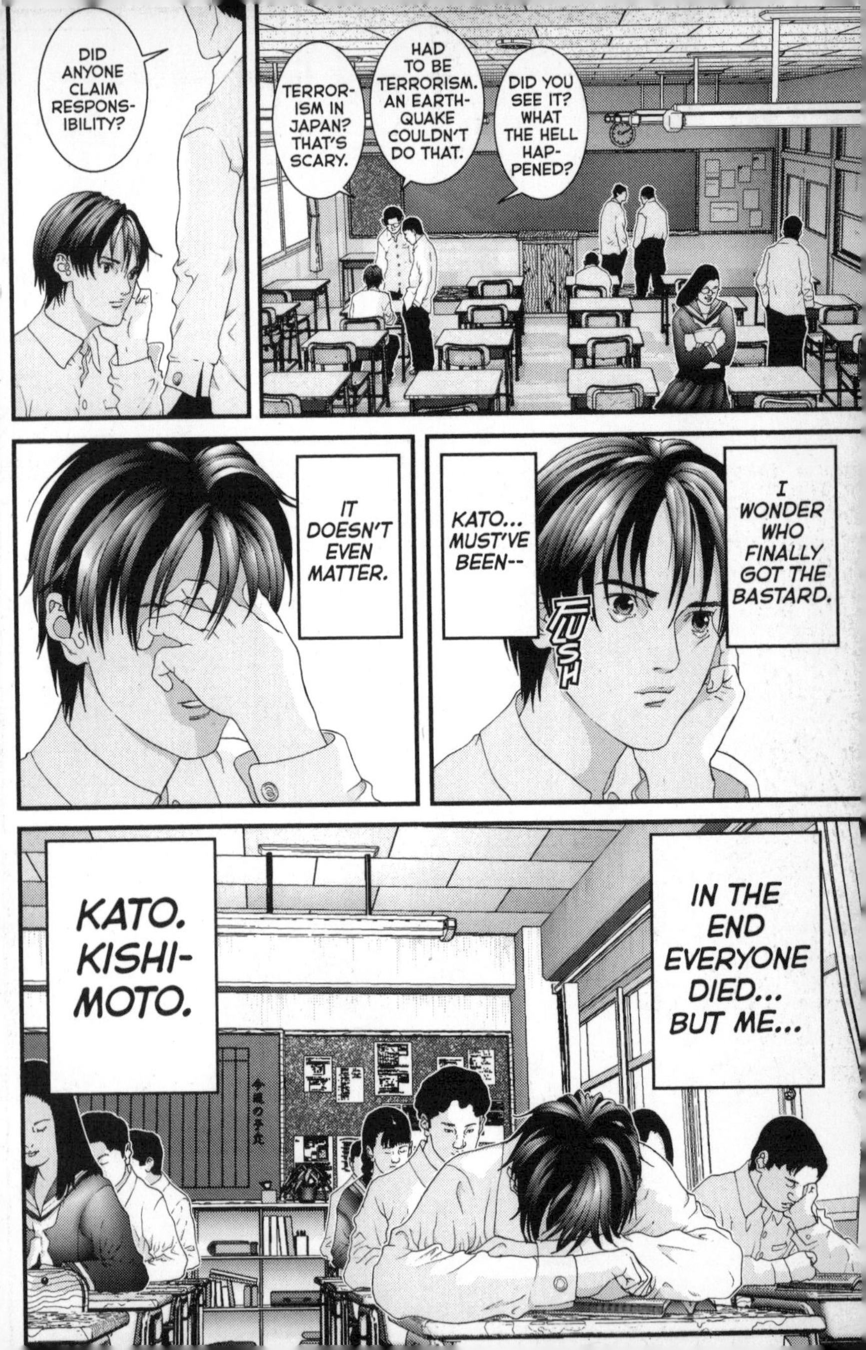
DID YOU SEE IT? WHAT THE HELL HAPPENED?
HAD TO BE TERRORISM. AN EARTHQUAKE COULDN'T DO THAT.
TERRORISM IN JAPAN? THAT'S SCARY.
DID ANYONE CLAIM RESPONSIBILITY?
I WONDER WHO FINALLY GOT THE BASTARD.
FLUSH
KATO... MUST'VE BEEN--
IT DOESN'T EVEN MATTER.
IN THE END EVERYONE DIED... BUT ME...
KATO. KISHIMOTO.

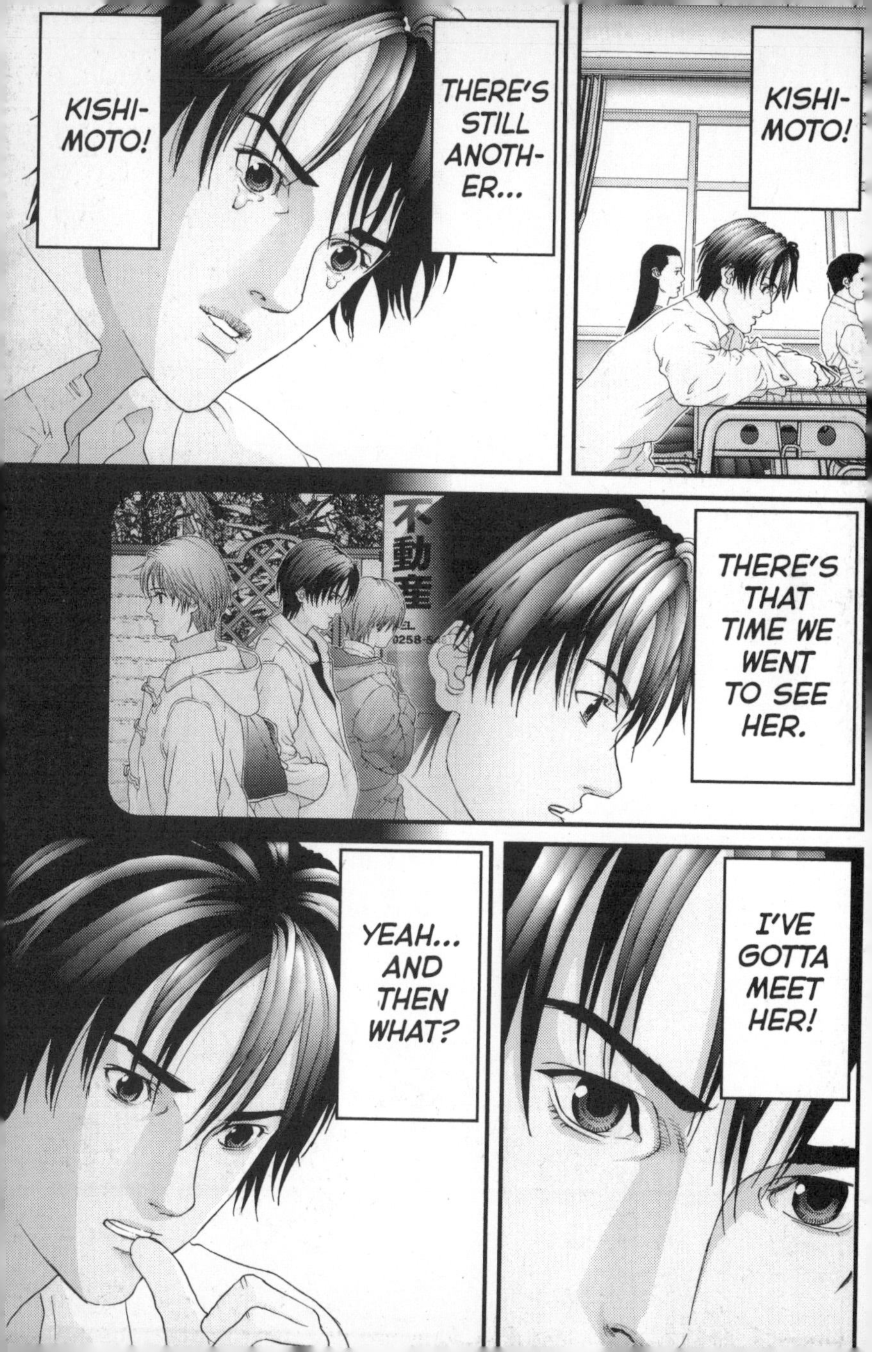
KISHI-MOTO!
THERE'S STILL ANOTH-ER...
KISHI-MOTO!
THERE'S THAT TIME WE WENT TO SEE HER.
不動産
I'VE GOTTA MEET HER!
YEAH... AND THEN WHAT?

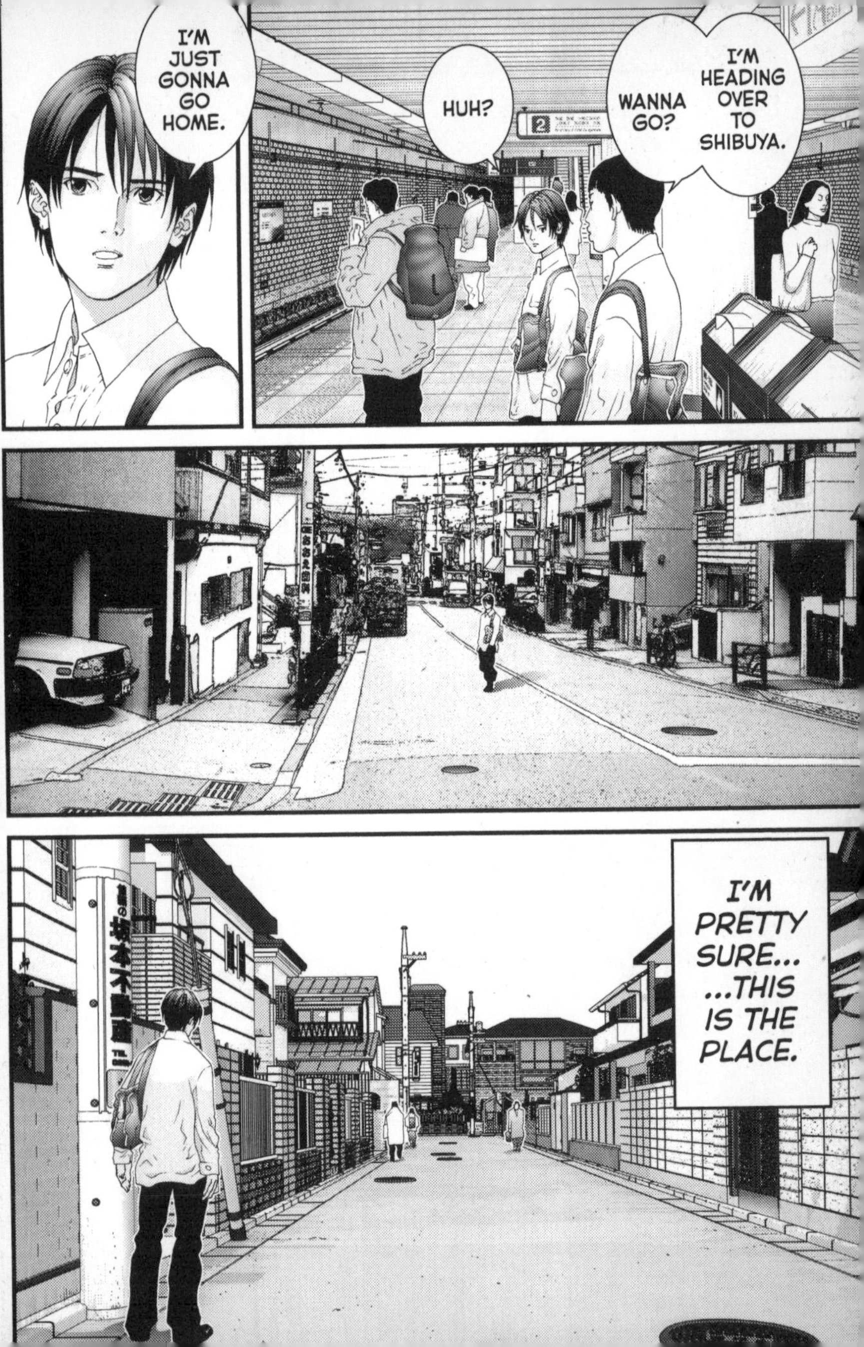
I'M HEADING OVER TO SHIBUYA.
WANNA GO?
HUH?
I'M JUST GONNA GO HOME.
I'M PRETTY SURE... ...THIS IS THE PLACE.

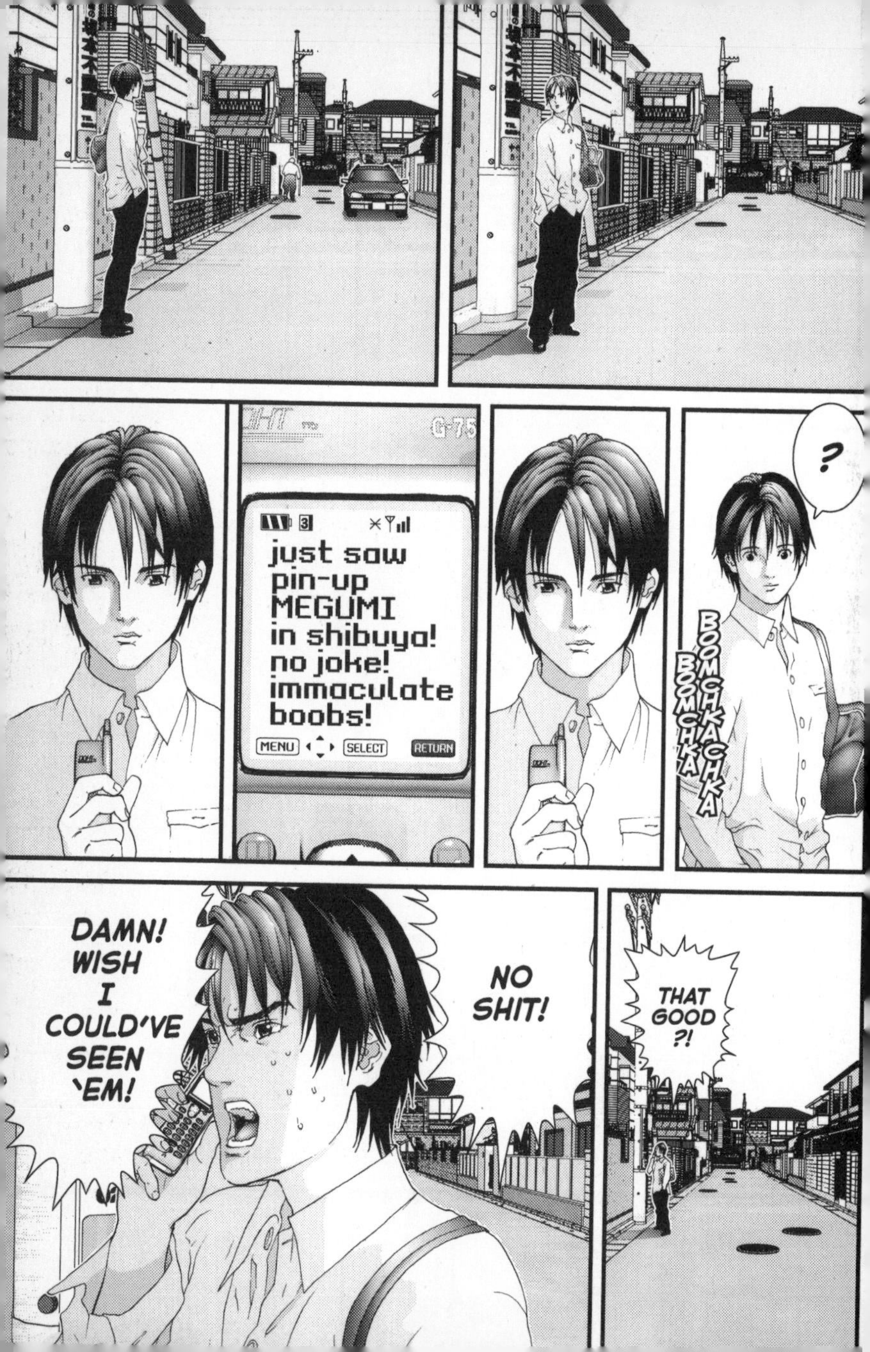
?
BOOMCHKACHKA
BOOMCHKA
just saw pin-up MEGUMI in shibuya! no joke! immaculate boobs!
MENU
SELECT
RETURN
THAT GOOD?!
NO SHIT!
DAMN! WISH I COULD'VE SEEN 'EM!

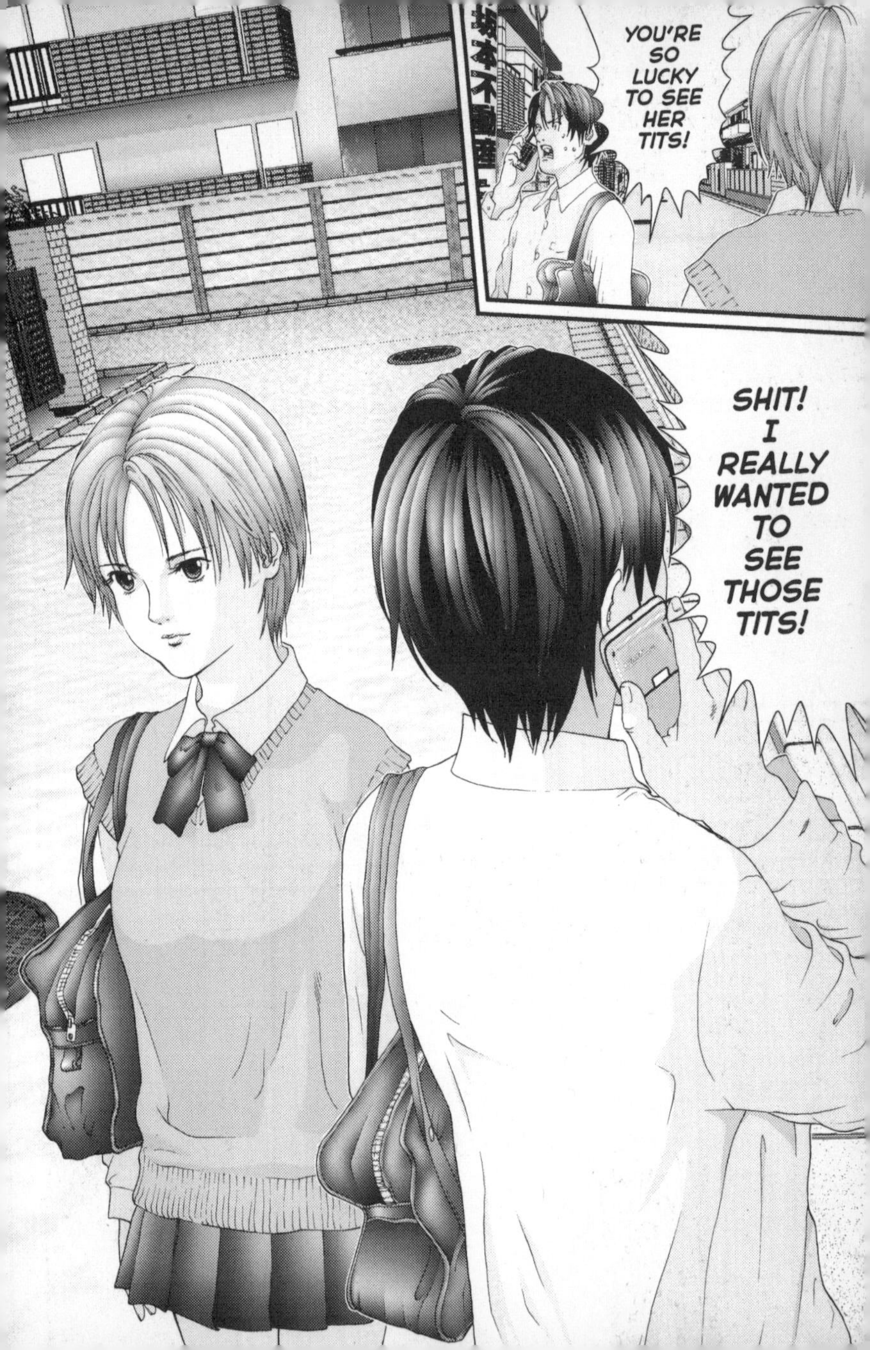
坂本不動産
YOU'RE SO LUCKY TO SEE HER TITS!
SHIT! I REALLY WANTED TO SEE THOSE TITS!

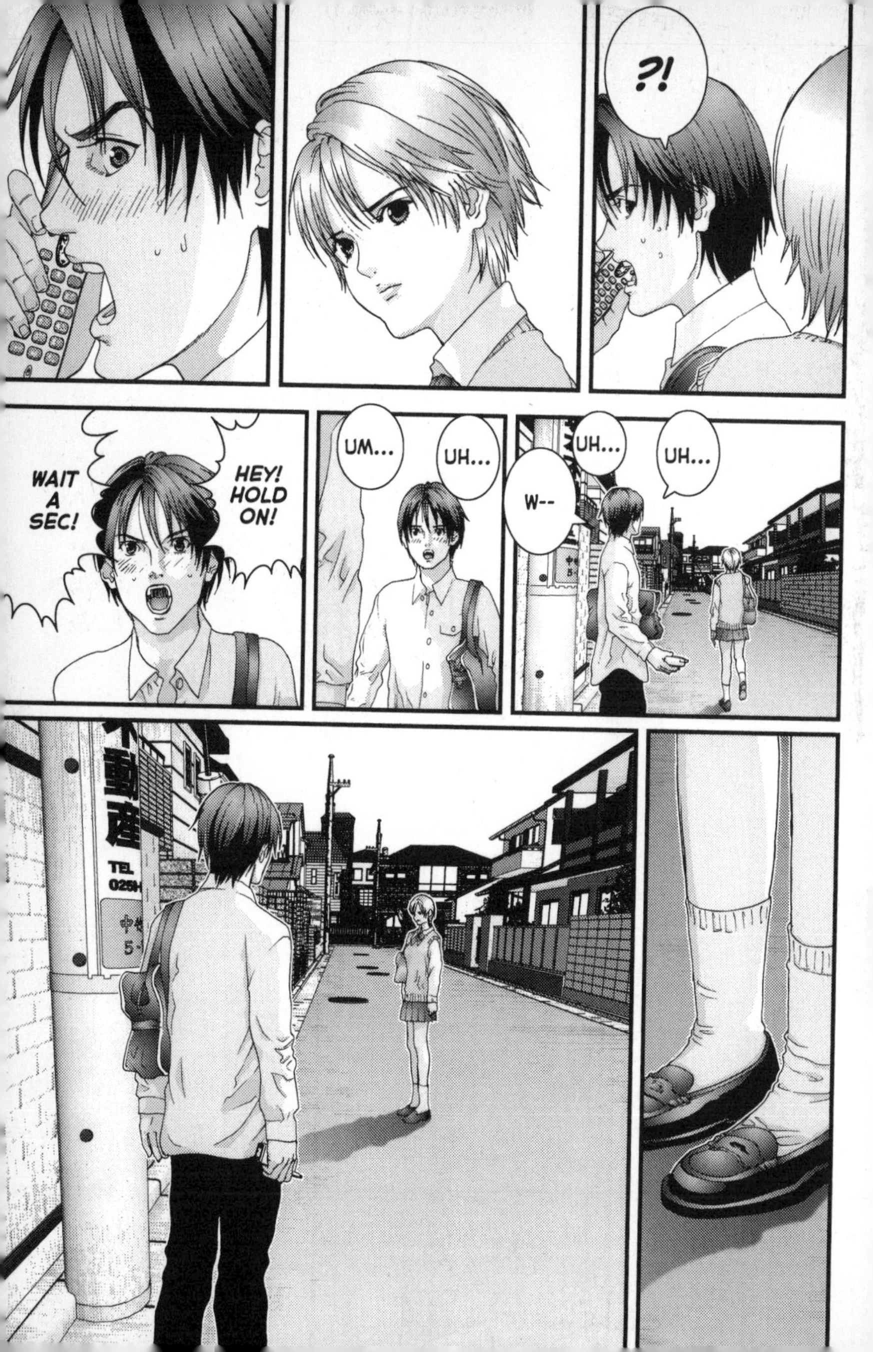
?!
UH...
UH...
W--
UH...
UM...
HEY! HOLD ON!
WAIT A SEC!
動産
TEL

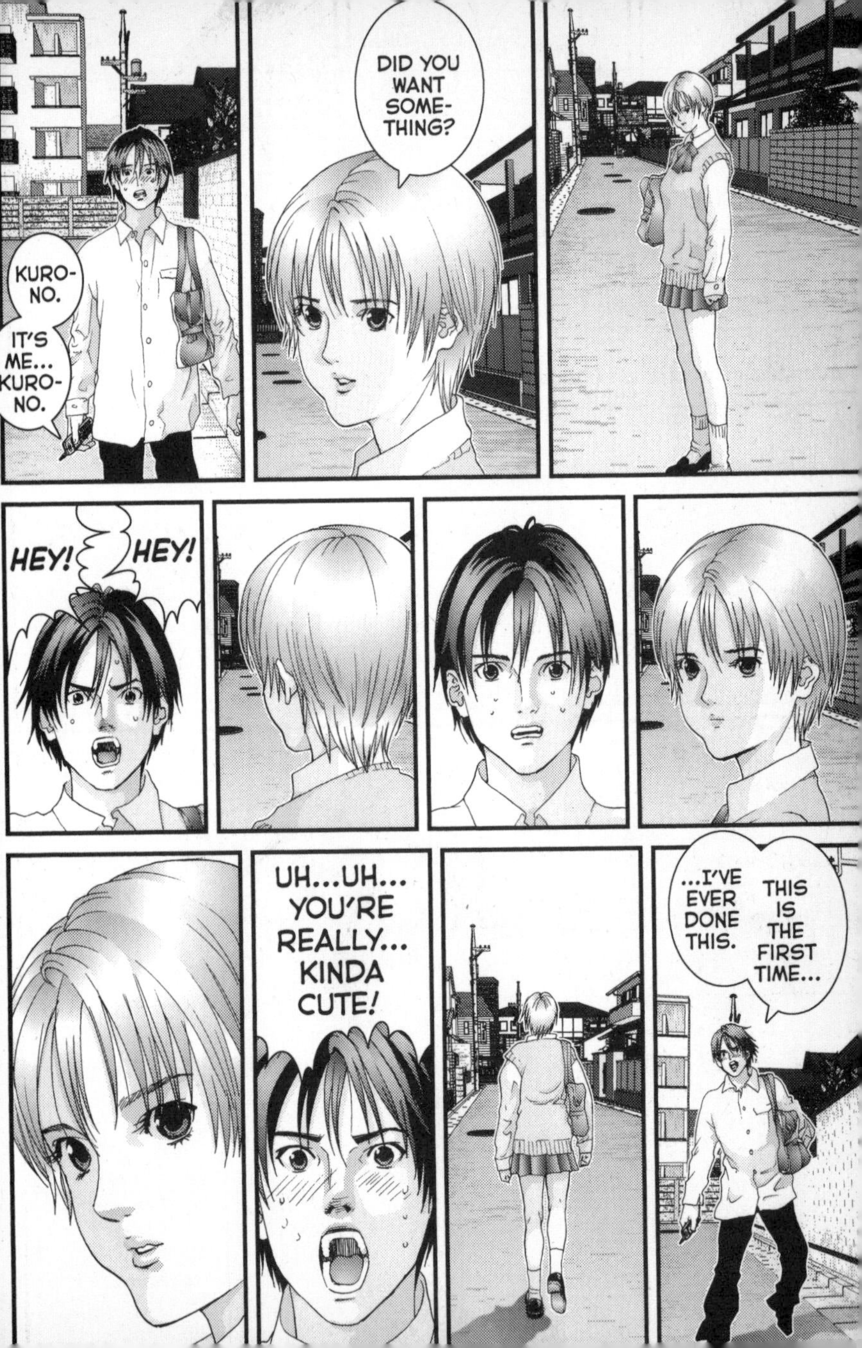
KURO-NO.
IT'S ME... KURO-NO.
DID YOU WANT SOME-THING?
HEY! HEY!
UH...UH... YOU'RE REALLY... KINDA CUTE!
THIS IS THE FIRST TIME...
...I'VE EVER DONE THIS.

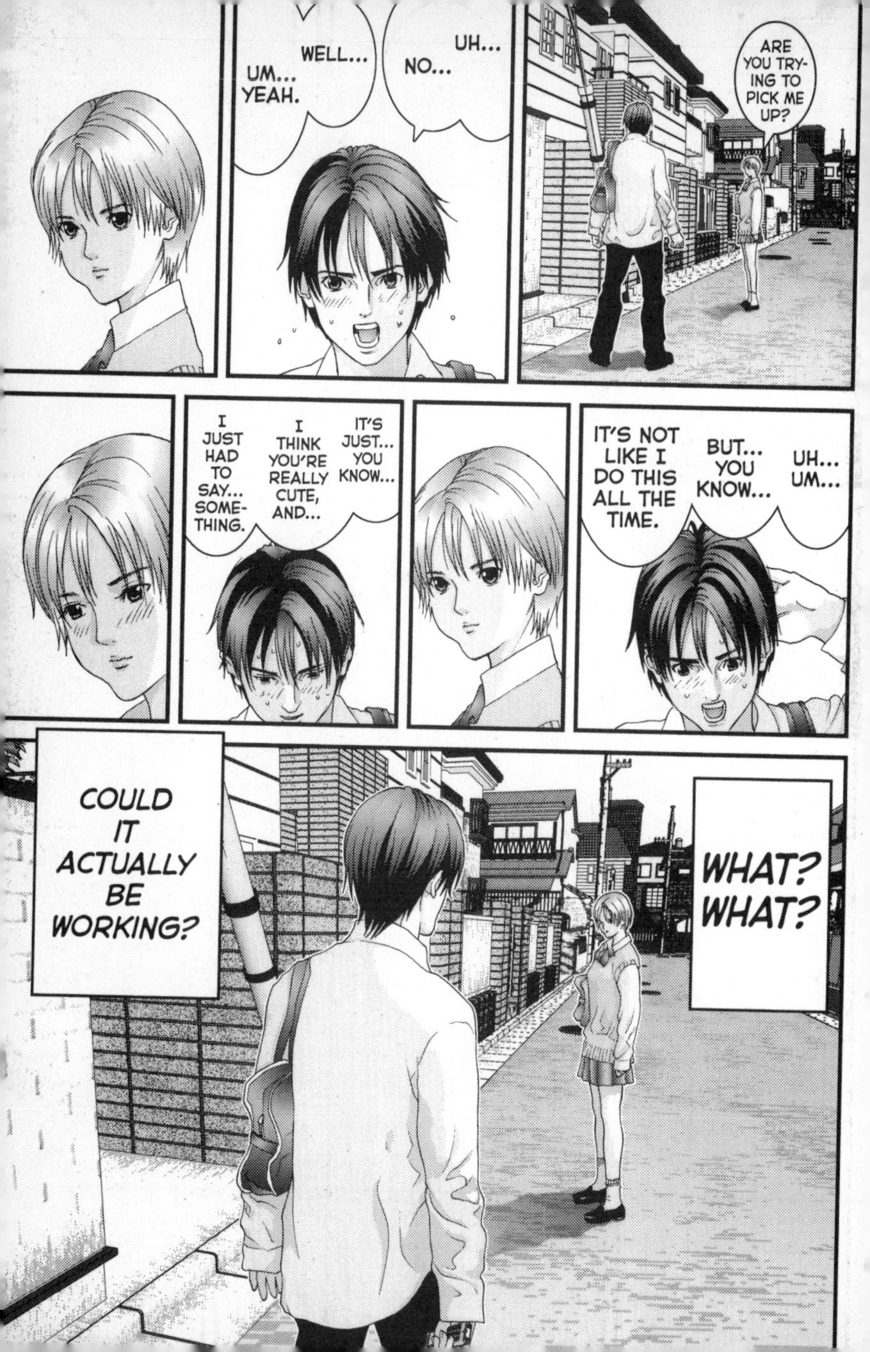

ARE YOU TRYING TO PICK ME UP?
UH... NO...
WELL... UM... YEAH.
UH... UM...
BUT... YOU KNOW...
IT'S NOT LIKE I DO THIS ALL THE TIME.
IT'S JUST... YOU KNOW...
I THINK YOU'RE REALLY CUTE, AND...
I JUST HAD TO SAY... SOMETHING.
WHAT? WHAT?
COULD IT ACTUALLY BE WORKING?

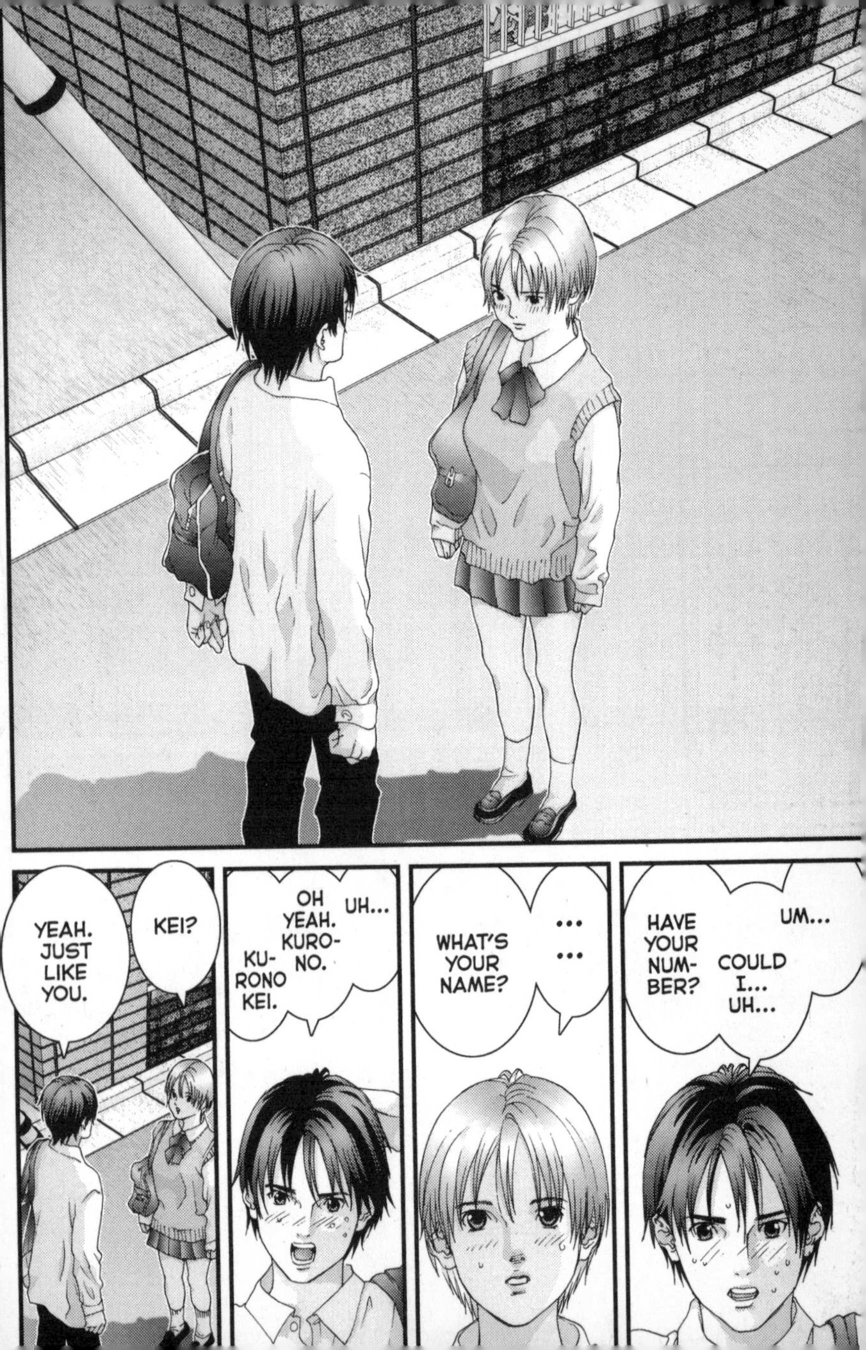
UM...
COULD I... UH...
HAVE YOUR NUMBER?
... ...
WHAT'S YOUR NAME?
UH...
OH YEAH. KURONO.
KURONO KEI.
KEI?
YEAH. JUST LIKE YOU.

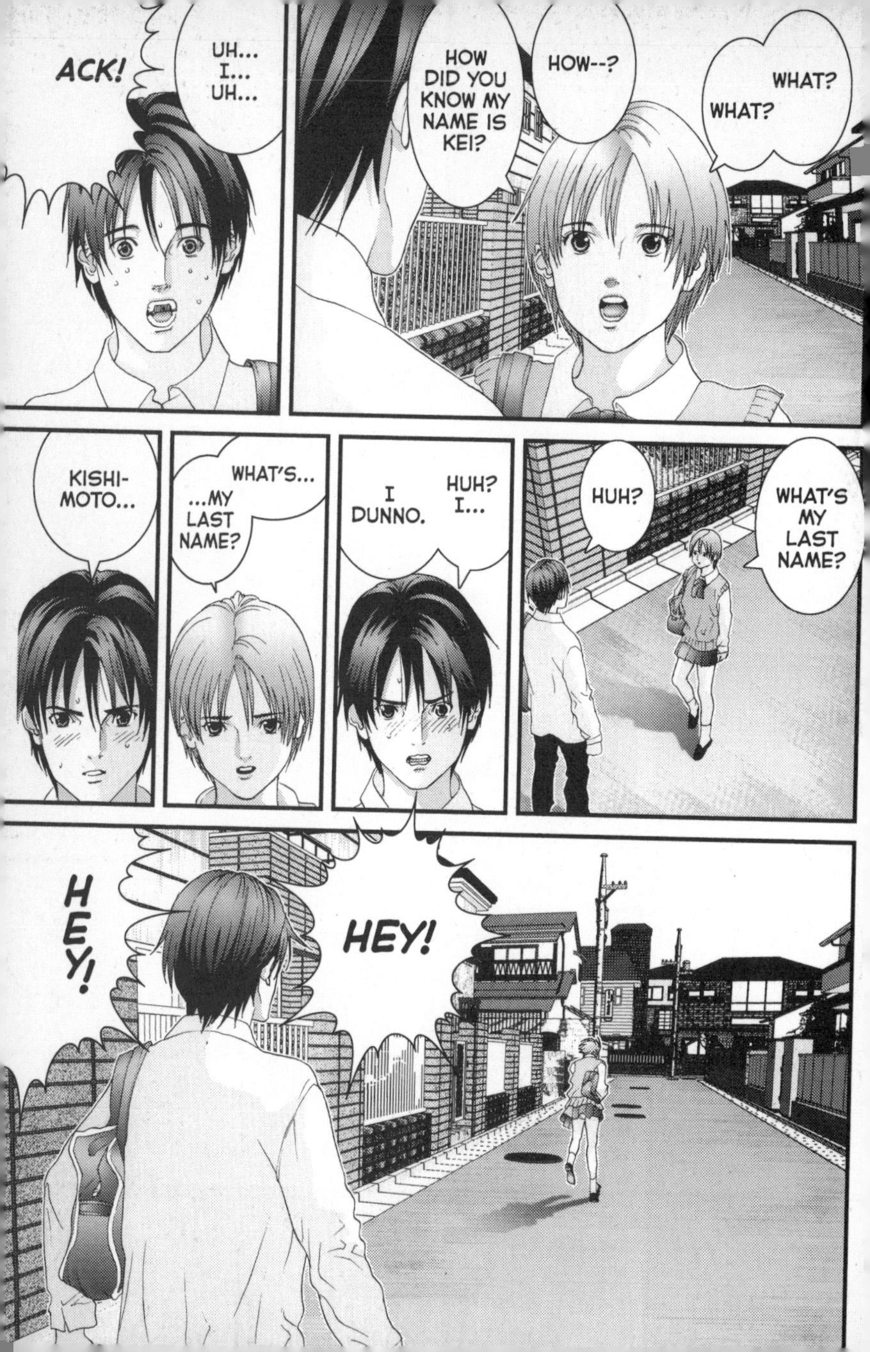

WHAT? WHAT?
HOW--?
HOW DID YOU KNOW MY NAME IS KEI?
UH... I... UH...
ACK!
WHAT'S MY LAST NAME?
HUH?
HUH? I...
I DUNNO.
WHAT'S... ...MY LAST NAME?
KISHI-MOTO...
HEY!
HEY!

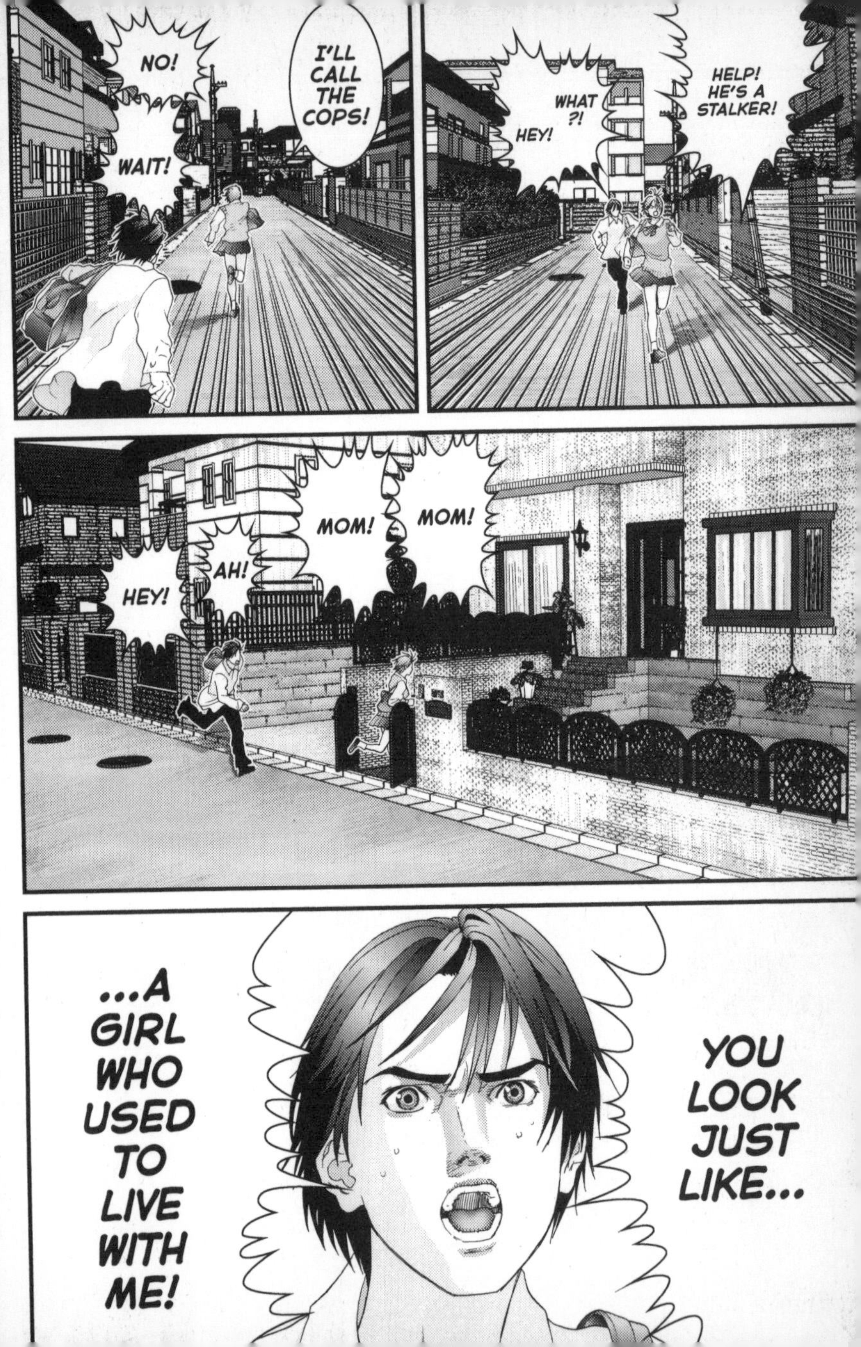
NO!
I'LL CALL THE COPS!
WAIT!
HELP! HE'S A STALKER!
WHAT?!
HEY!
MOM!
MOM!
AH!
HEY!
...A GIRL WHO USED TO LIVE WITH ME!
YOU LOOK JUST LIKE...

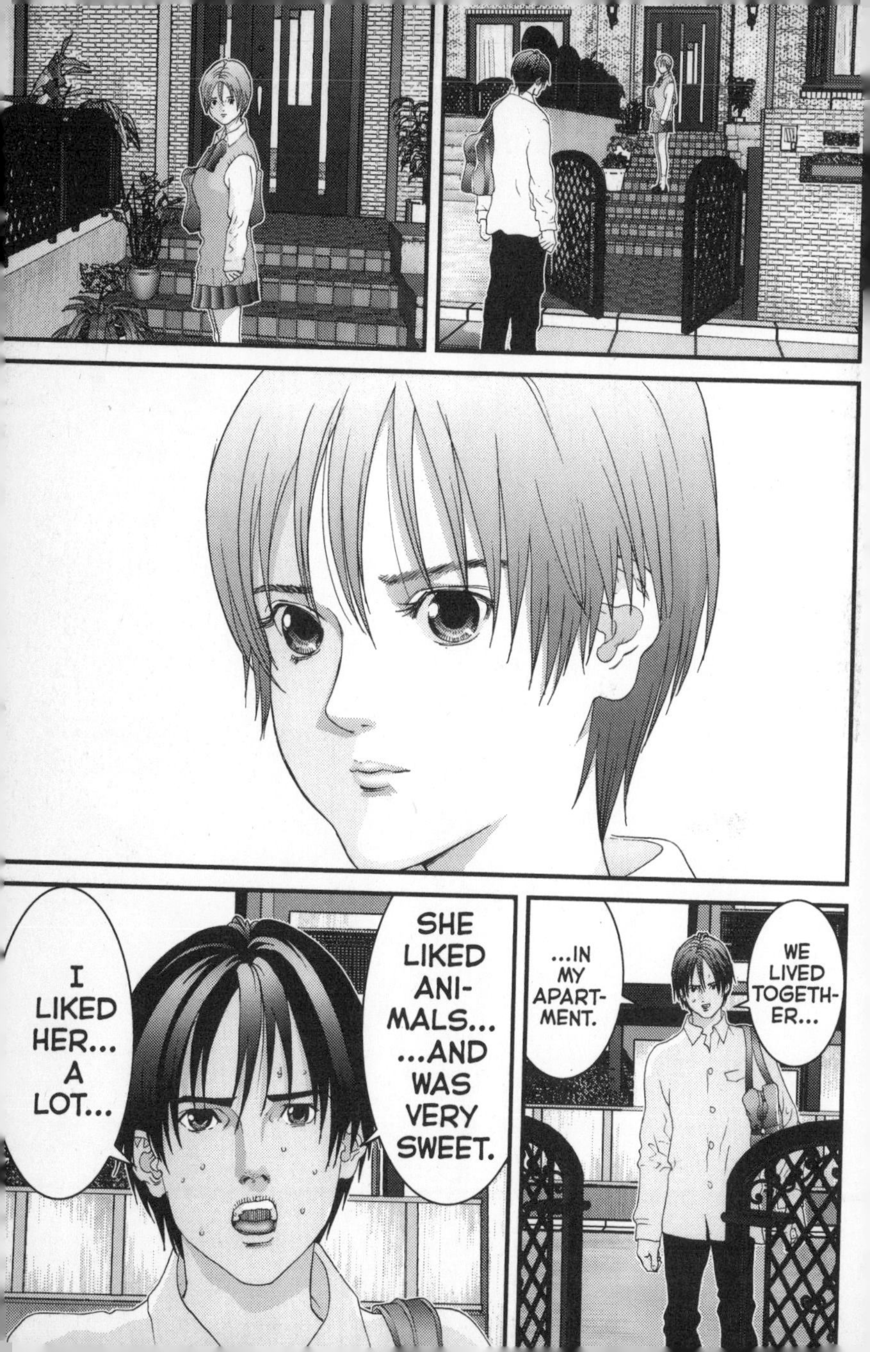
WE LIVED TOGETH- ER...
...IN MY APART- MENT.
SHE LIKED ANI- MALS... ...AND WAS VERY SWEET.
I LIKED HER... A LOT...

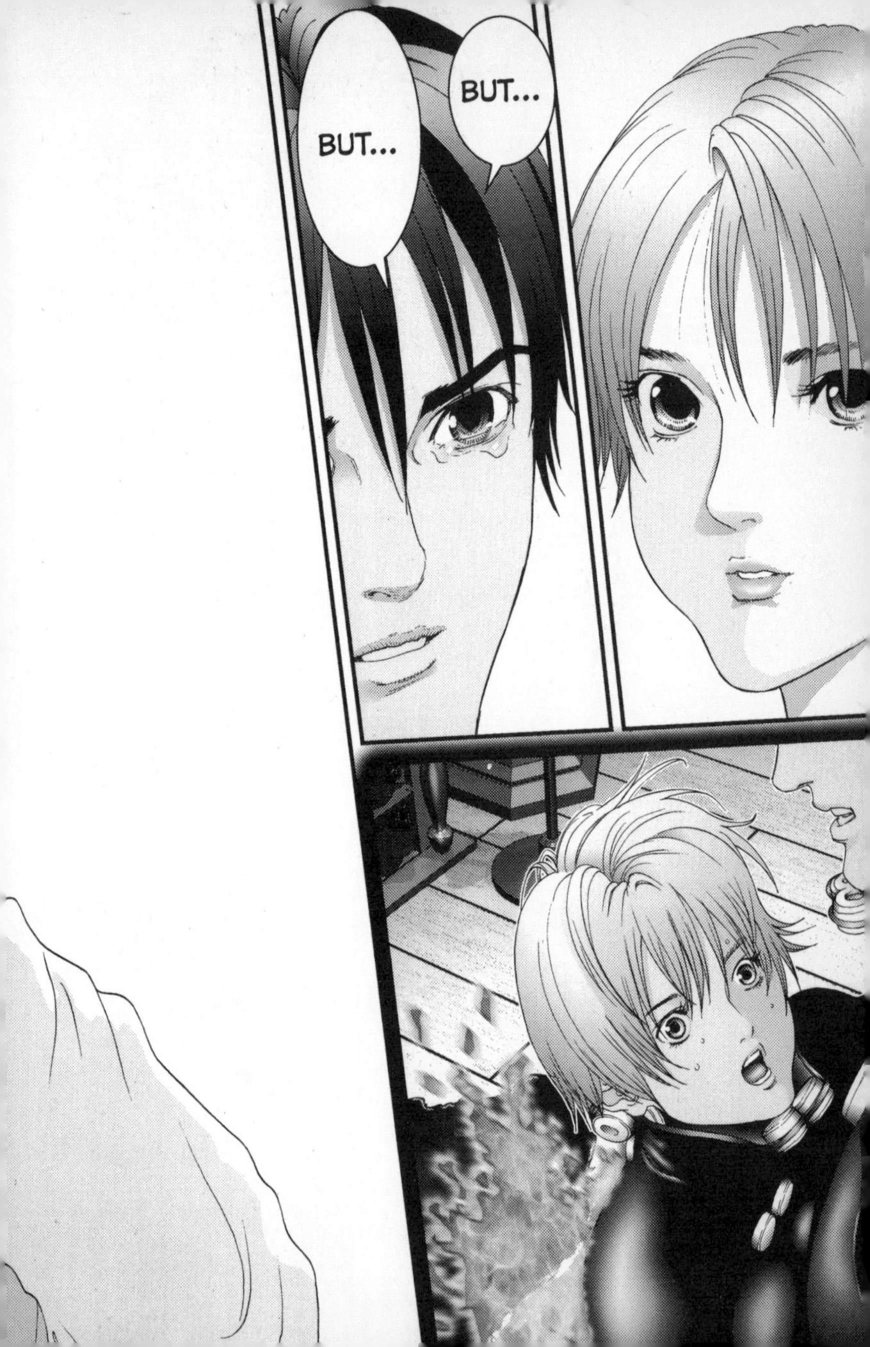
BUT...
BUT...

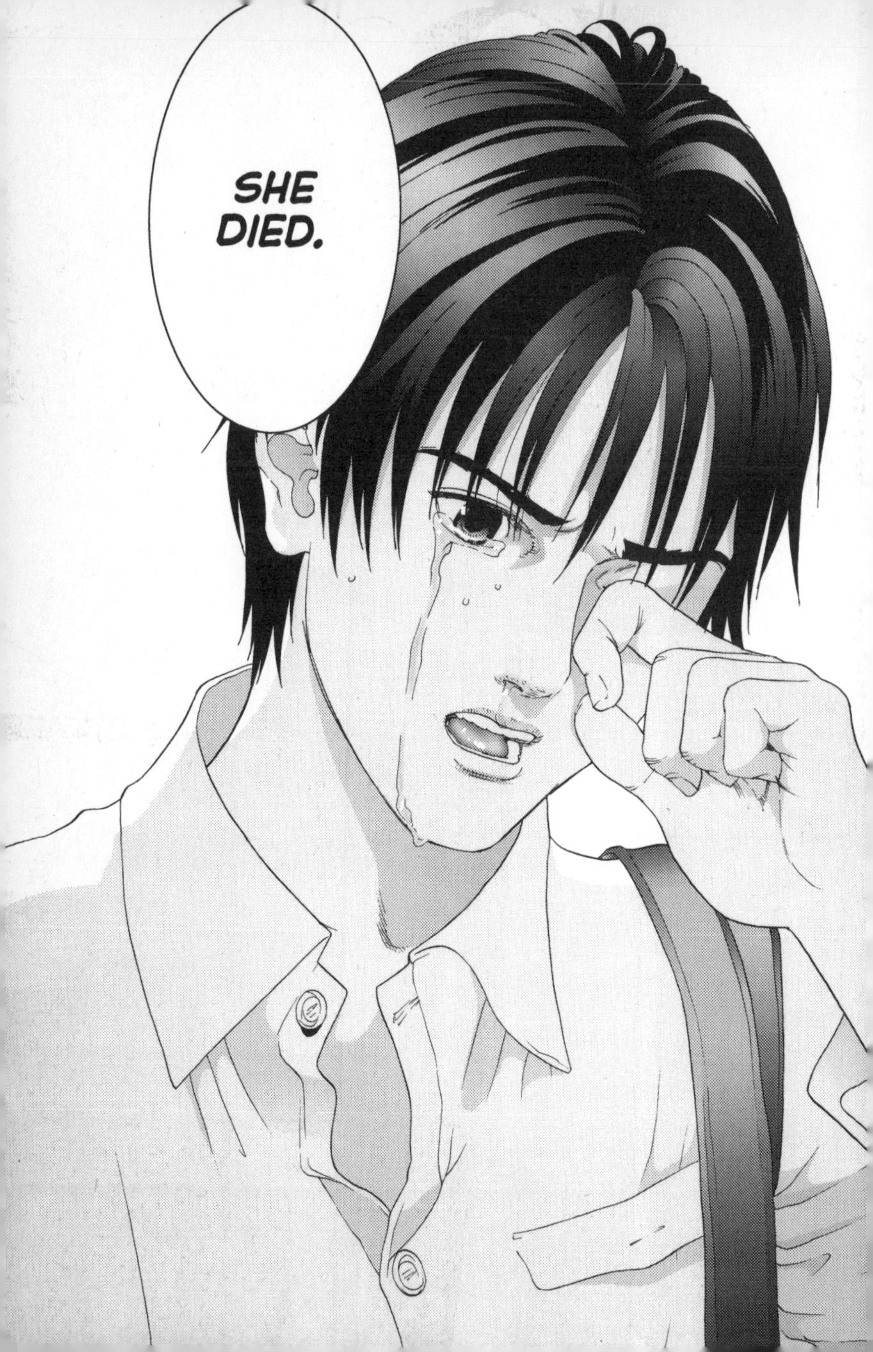
SHE DIED.

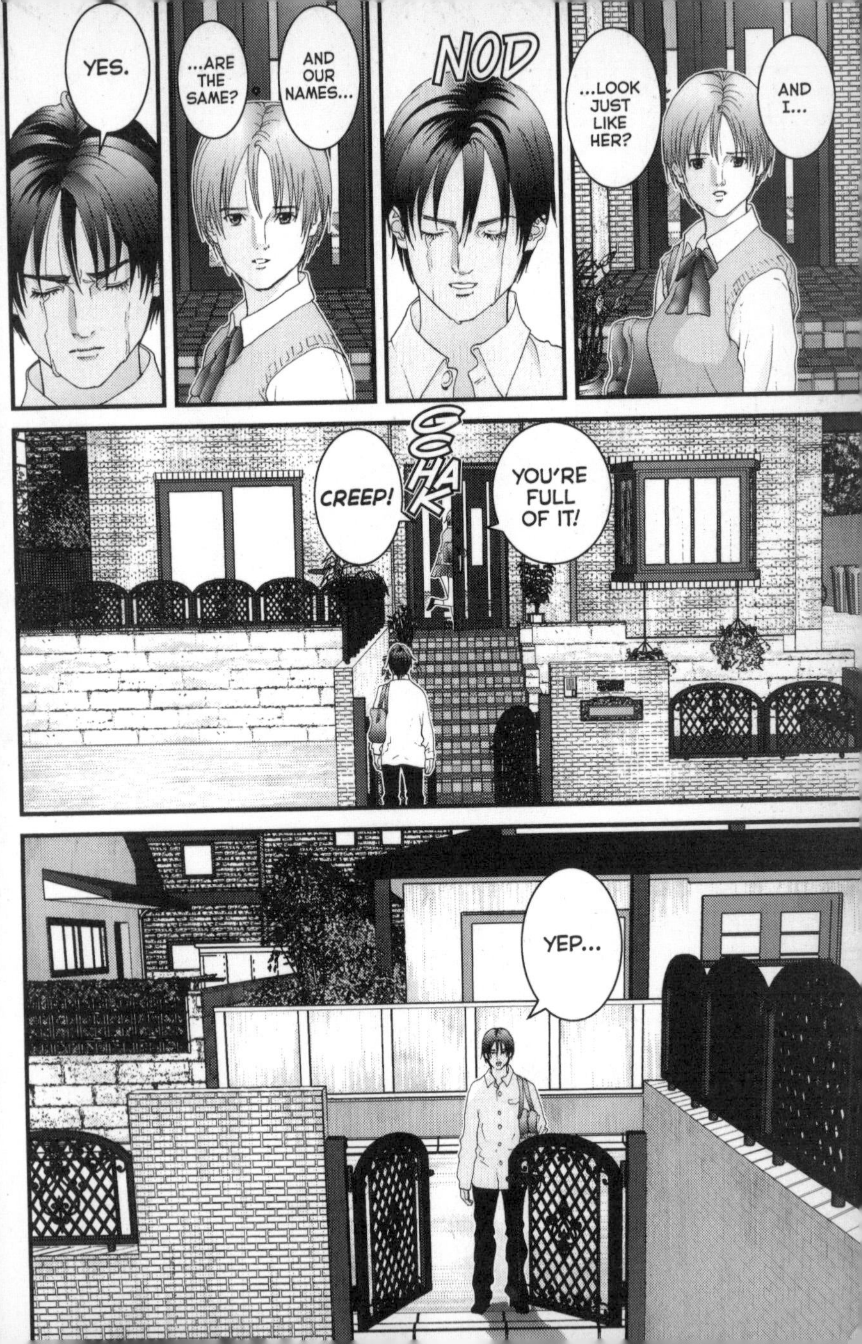
AND I...
...LOOK JUST LIKE HER?
NOD
AND OUR NAMES...
...ARE THE SAME?
YES.
YOU'RE FULL OF IT!
GCHAK
CREEP!
YEP...

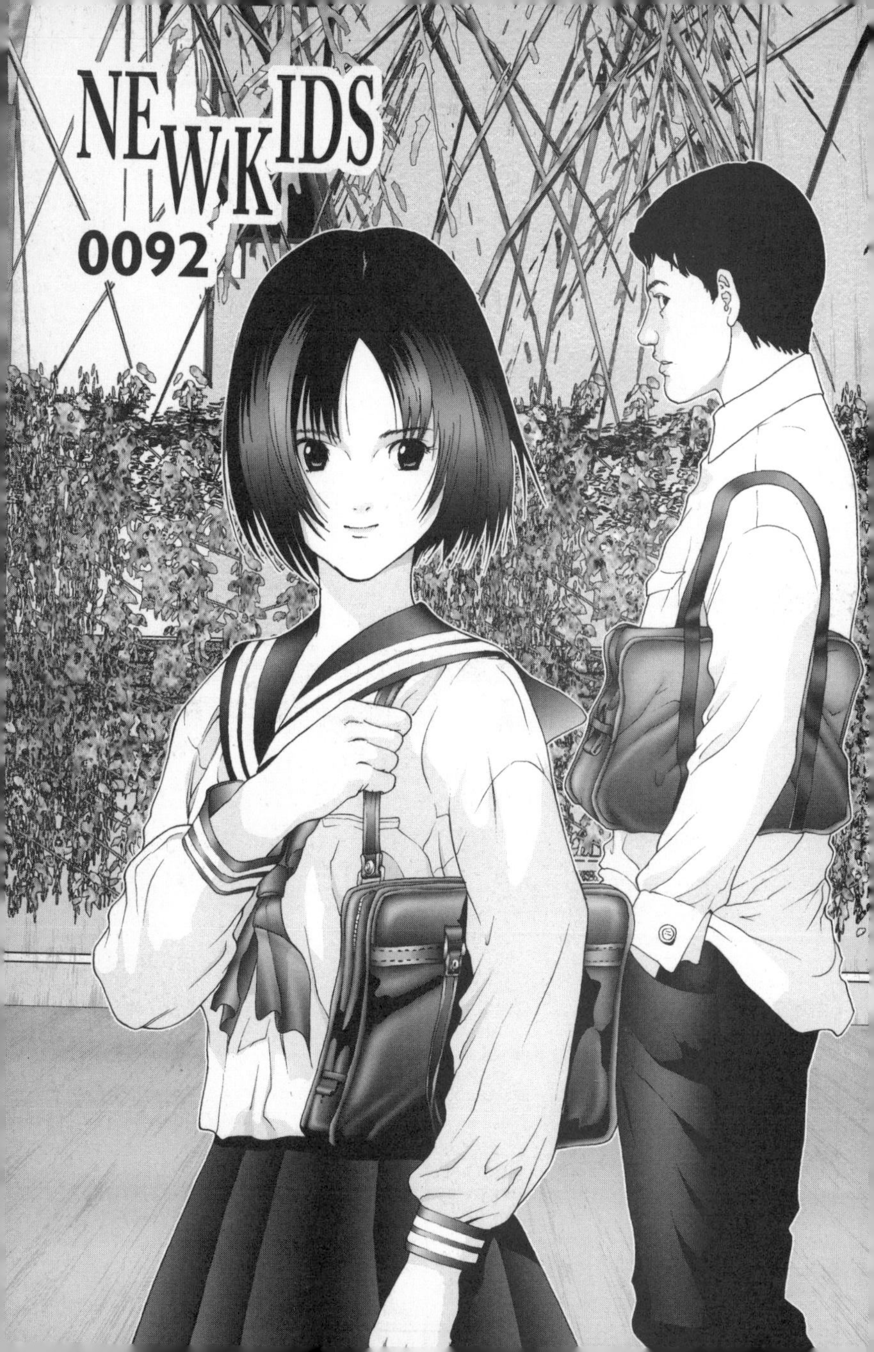
NEW KIDS
0092

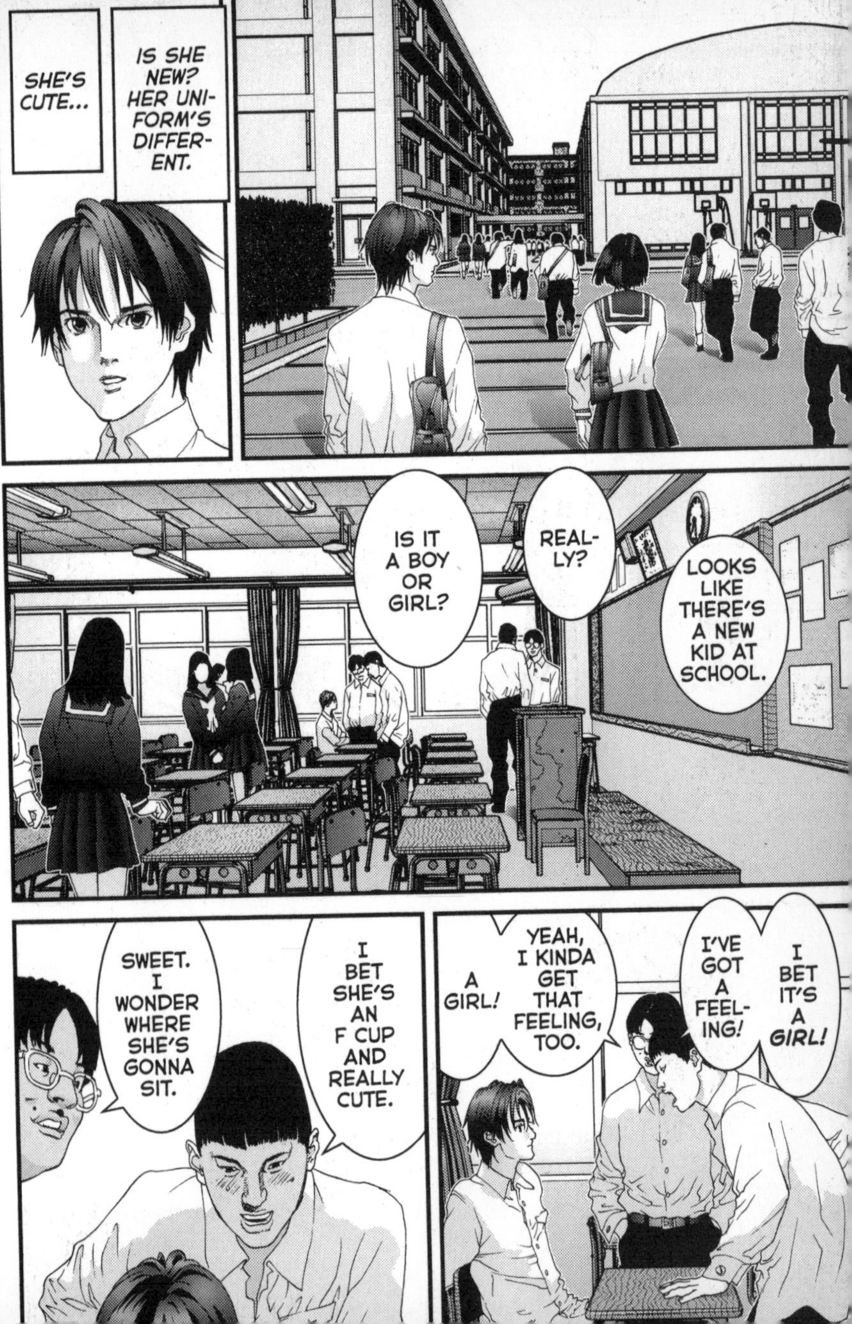
IS SHE NEW? HER UNIFORM'S DIFFERENT.
SHE'S CUTE...
LOOKS LIKE THERE'S A NEW KID AT SCHOOL.
REALLY?
IS IT A BOY OR GIRL?
I BET IT'S A *GIRL!*
I'VE GOT A FEELING!
YEAH, I KINDA GET THAT FEELING, TOO.
A GIRL!
I BET SHE'S AN F CUP AND REALLY CUTE.
SWEET. I WONDER WHERE SHE'S GONNA SIT.

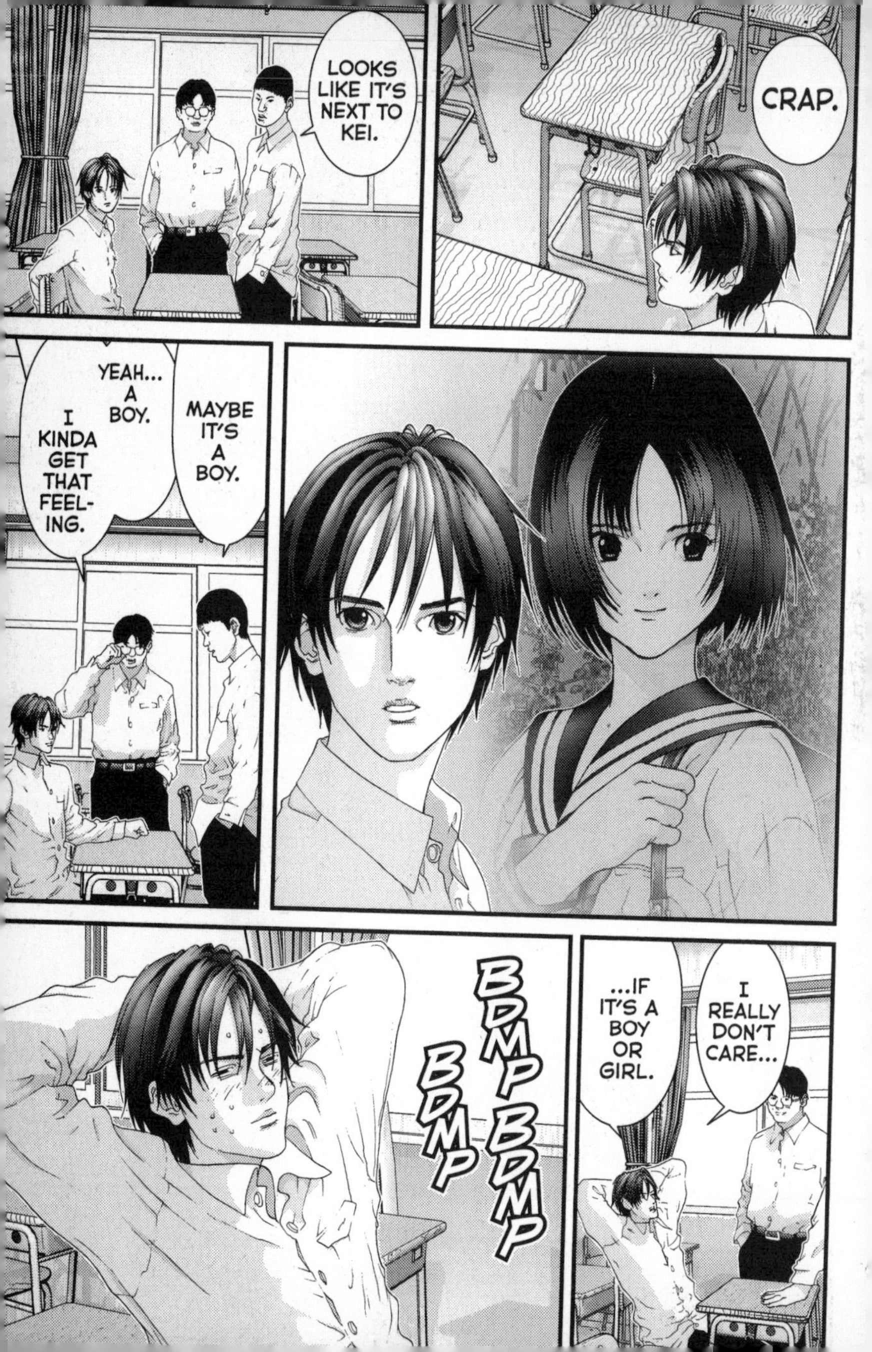
CRAP.
LOOKS LIKE IT'S NEXT TO KEI.
MAYBE IT'S A BOY.
YEAH... A BOY.
I KINDA GET THAT FEELING.
I REALLY DON'T CARE...
...IF IT'S A BOY OR GIRL.
BDMP BDMP
BDMP BDMP

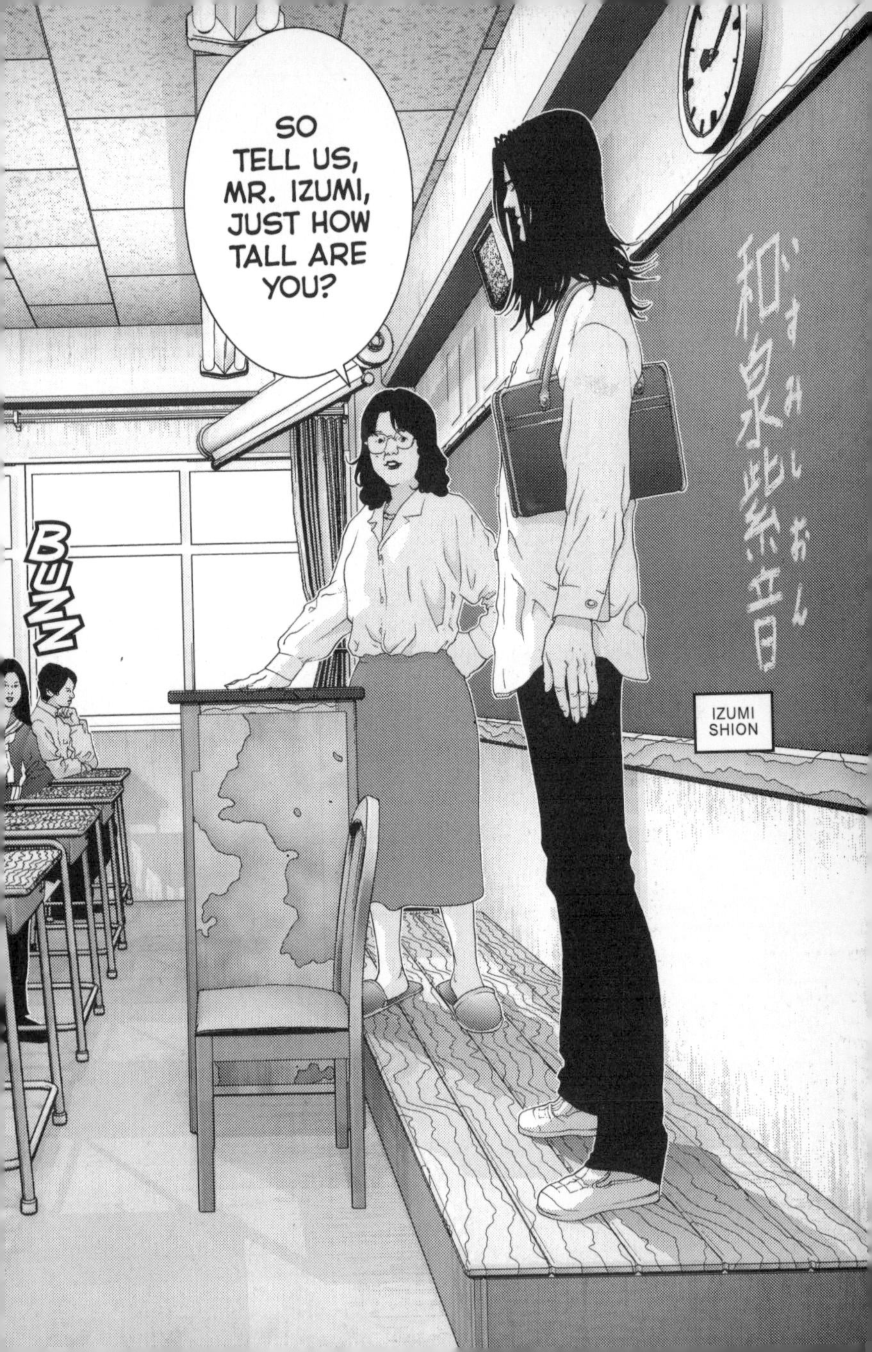
SO TELL US, MR. IZUMI, JUST HOW TALL ARE YOU?
BUZZ
和泉紫音
いずみしおん
IZUMI SHION

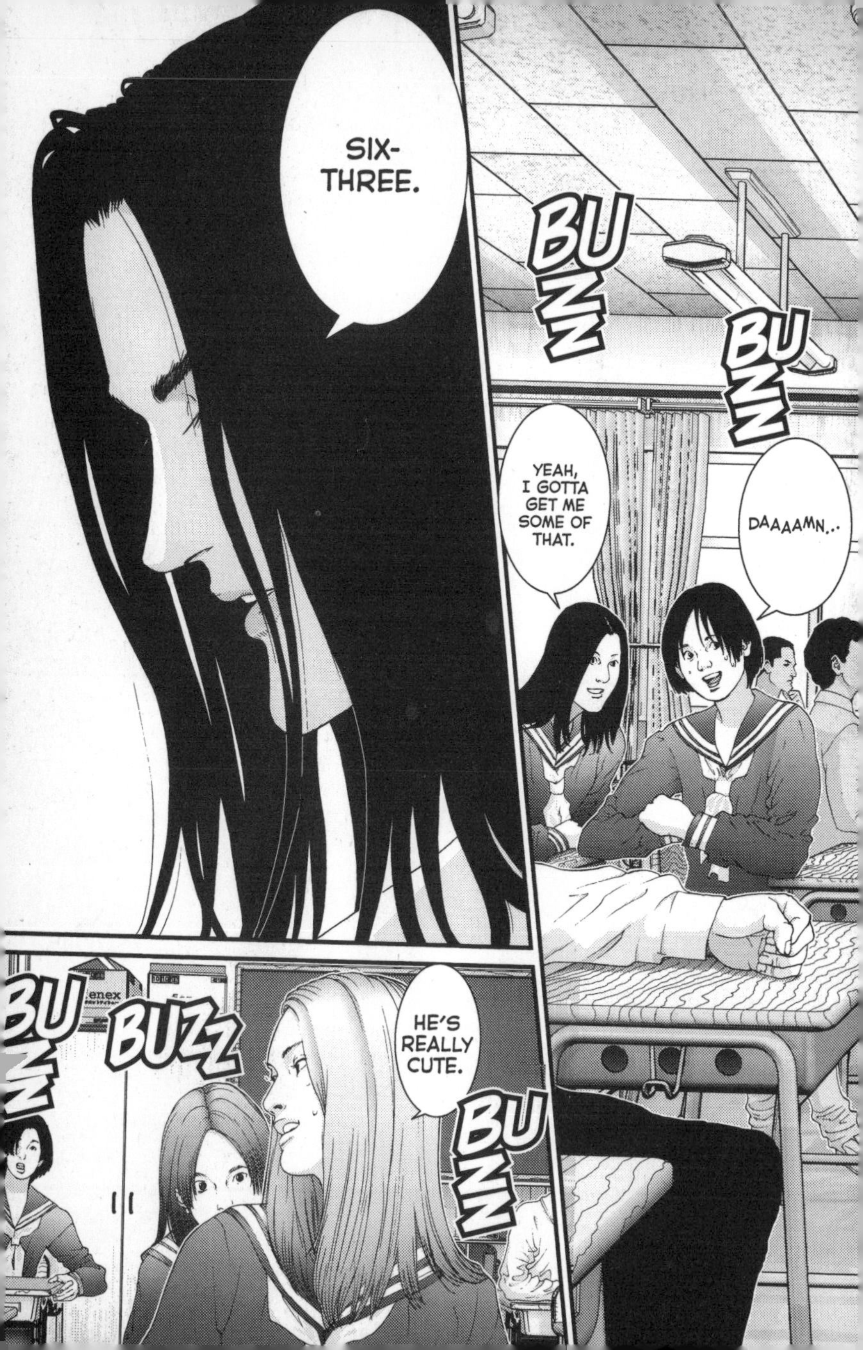
BUZZ
BUZZ
DAAAAMN...
YEAH, I GOTTA GET ME SOME OF THAT.
SIX-THREE.
BUZZ
HE'S REALLY CUTE.
BUZZ
BUZZ

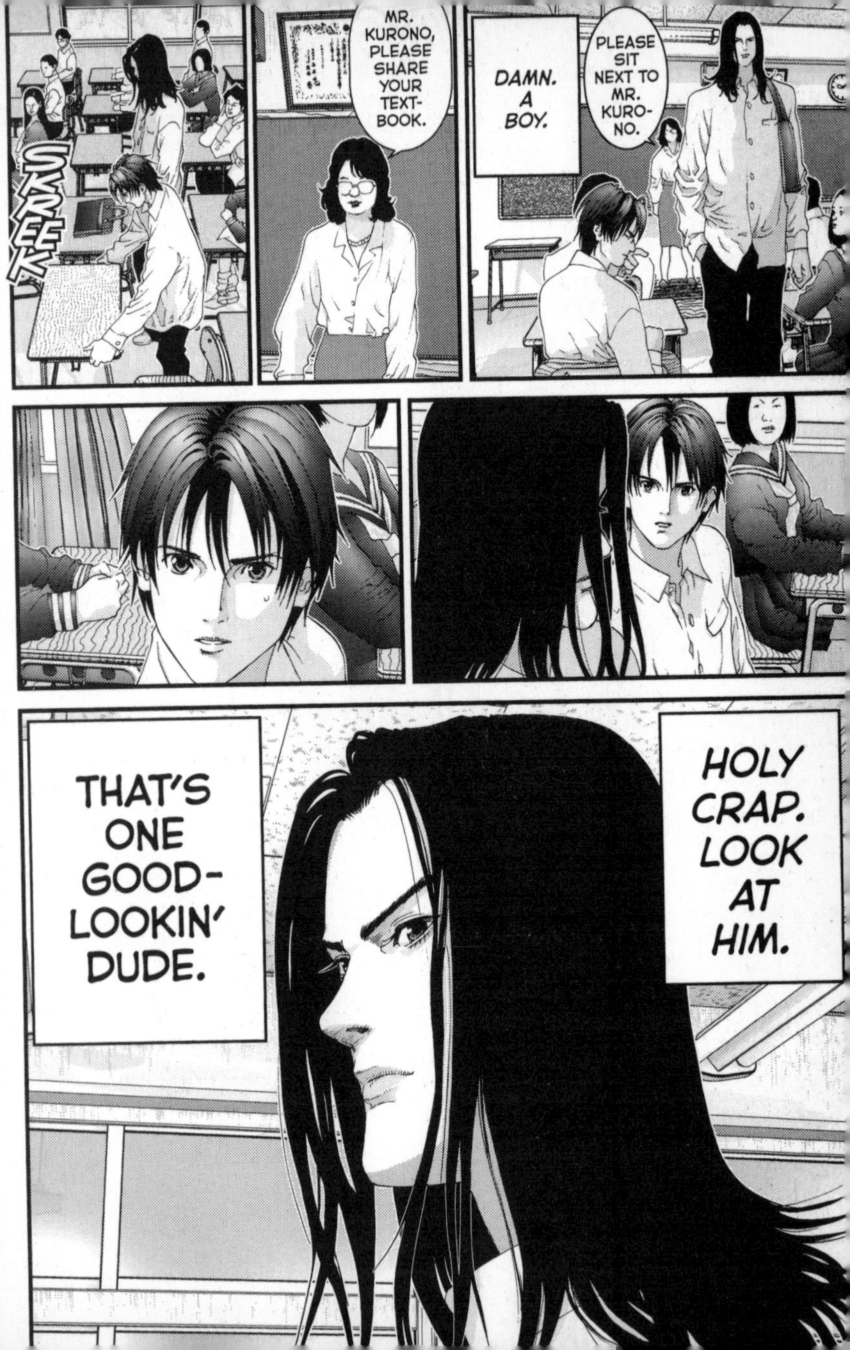
PLEASE SIT NEXT TO MR. KURONO.
DAMN. A BOY.
MR. KURONO, PLEASE SHARE YOUR TEXTBOOK.
SKREEK
HOLY CRAP. LOOK AT HIM.
THAT'S ONE GOOD-LOOKIN' DUDE.

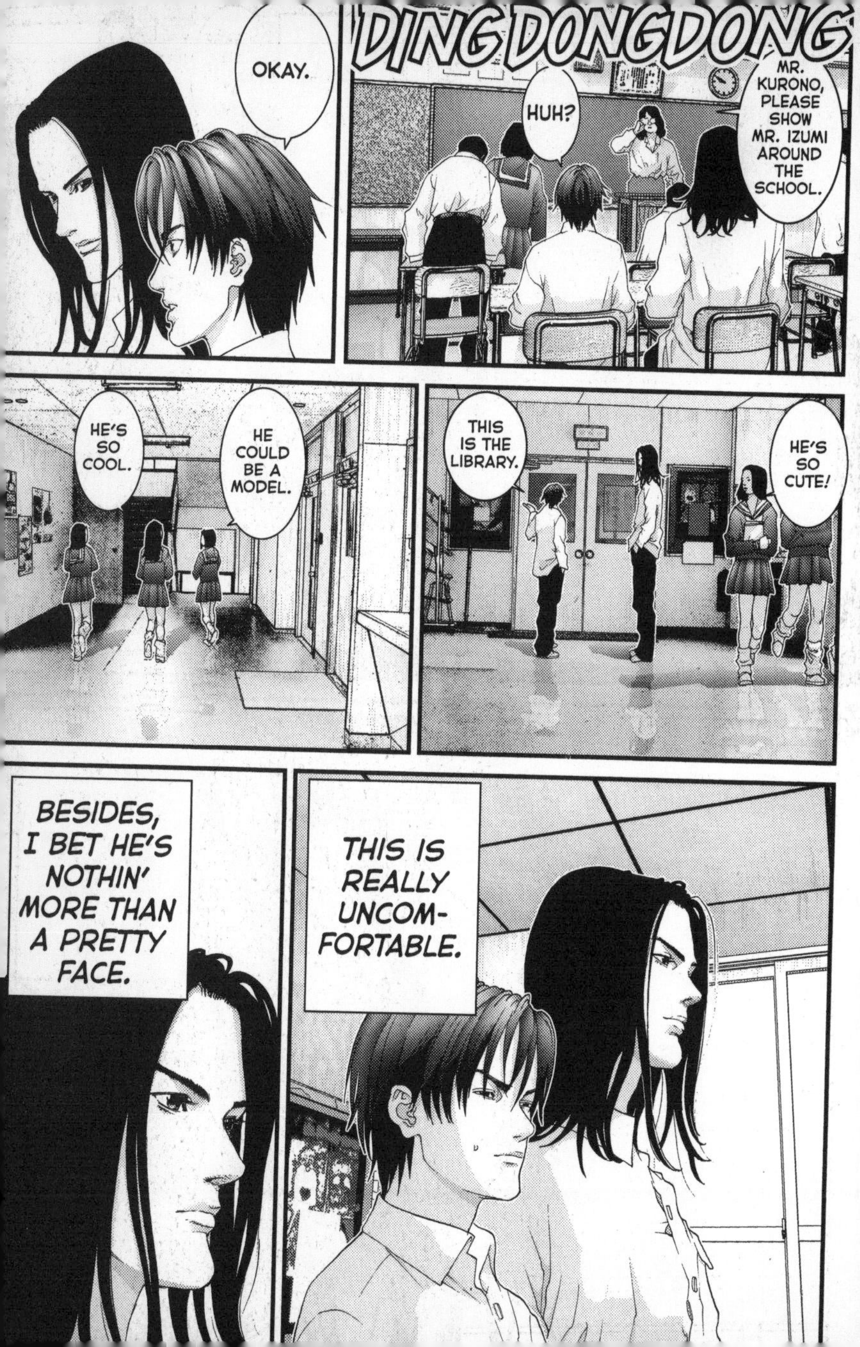
DING DONG DONG
MR. KURONO, PLEASE SHOW MR. IZUMI AROUND THE SCHOOL.
HUH?
OKAY.
HE'S SO CUTE!
THIS IS THE LIBRARY.
HE COULD BE A MODEL.
HE'S SO COOL.
THIS IS REALLY UNCOM-FORTABLE.
BESIDES, I BET HE'S NOTHIN' MORE THAN A PRETTY FACE.

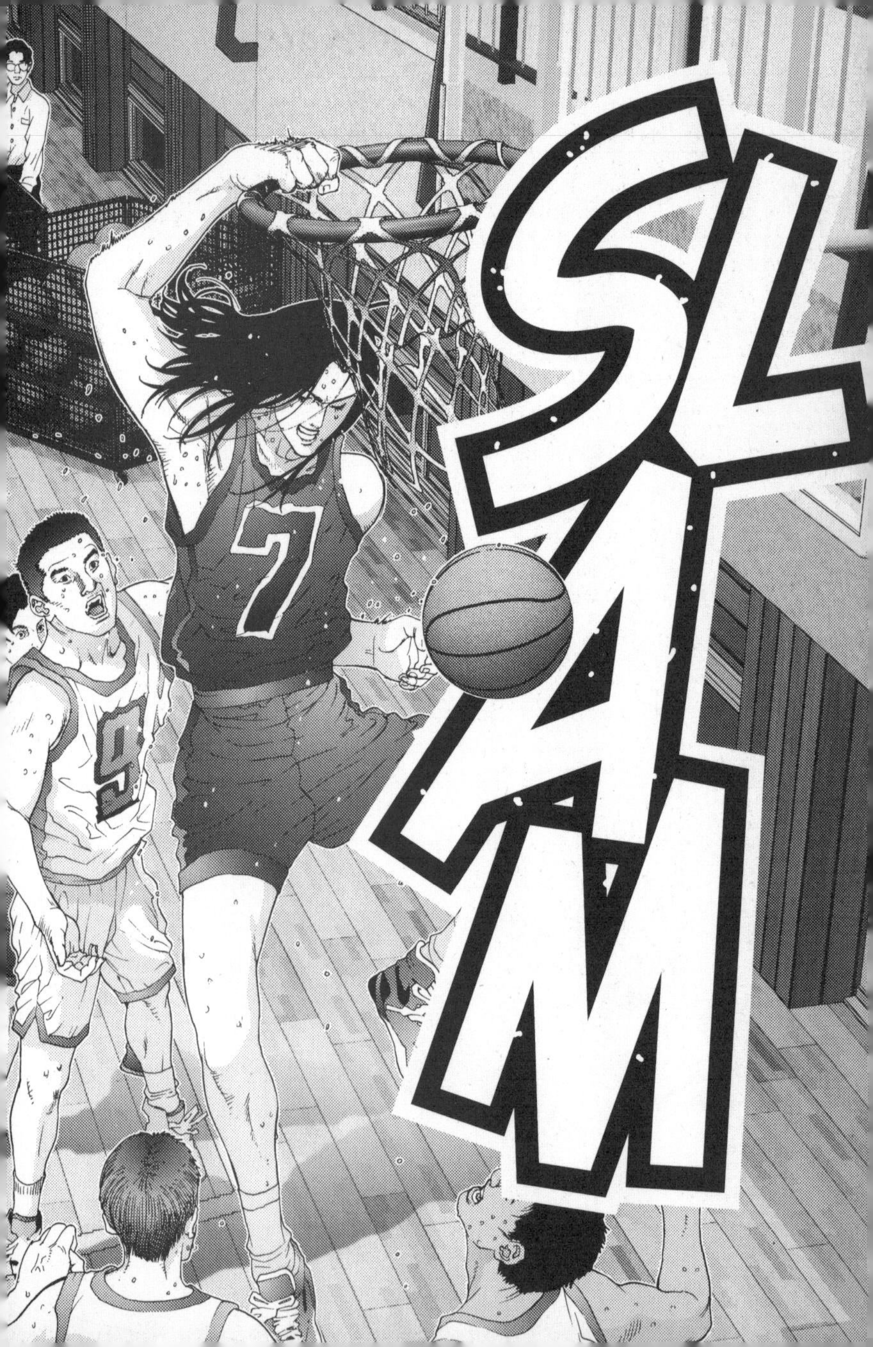
SLAM

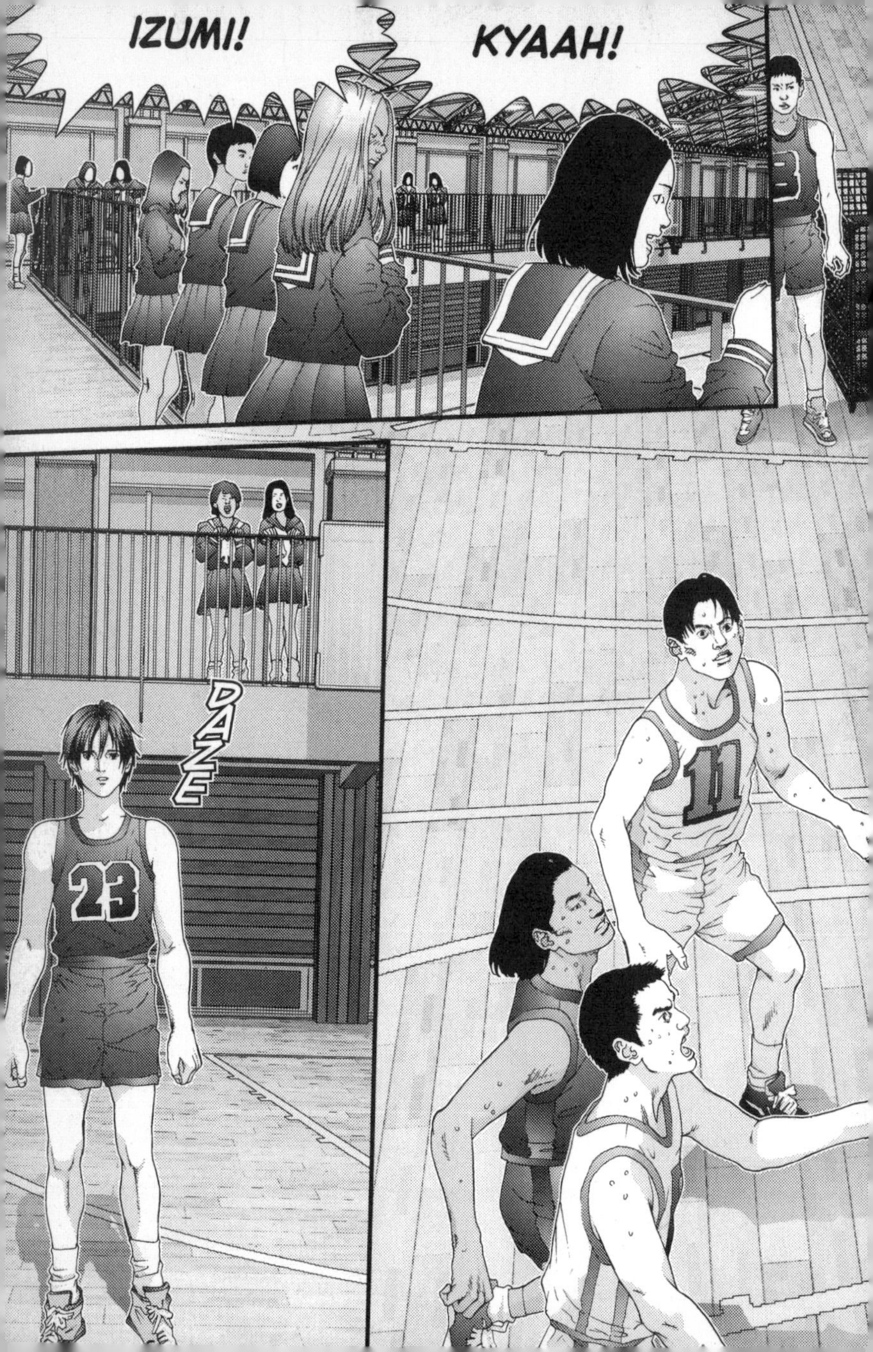
KYAAH!
IZUMI!
DAZE

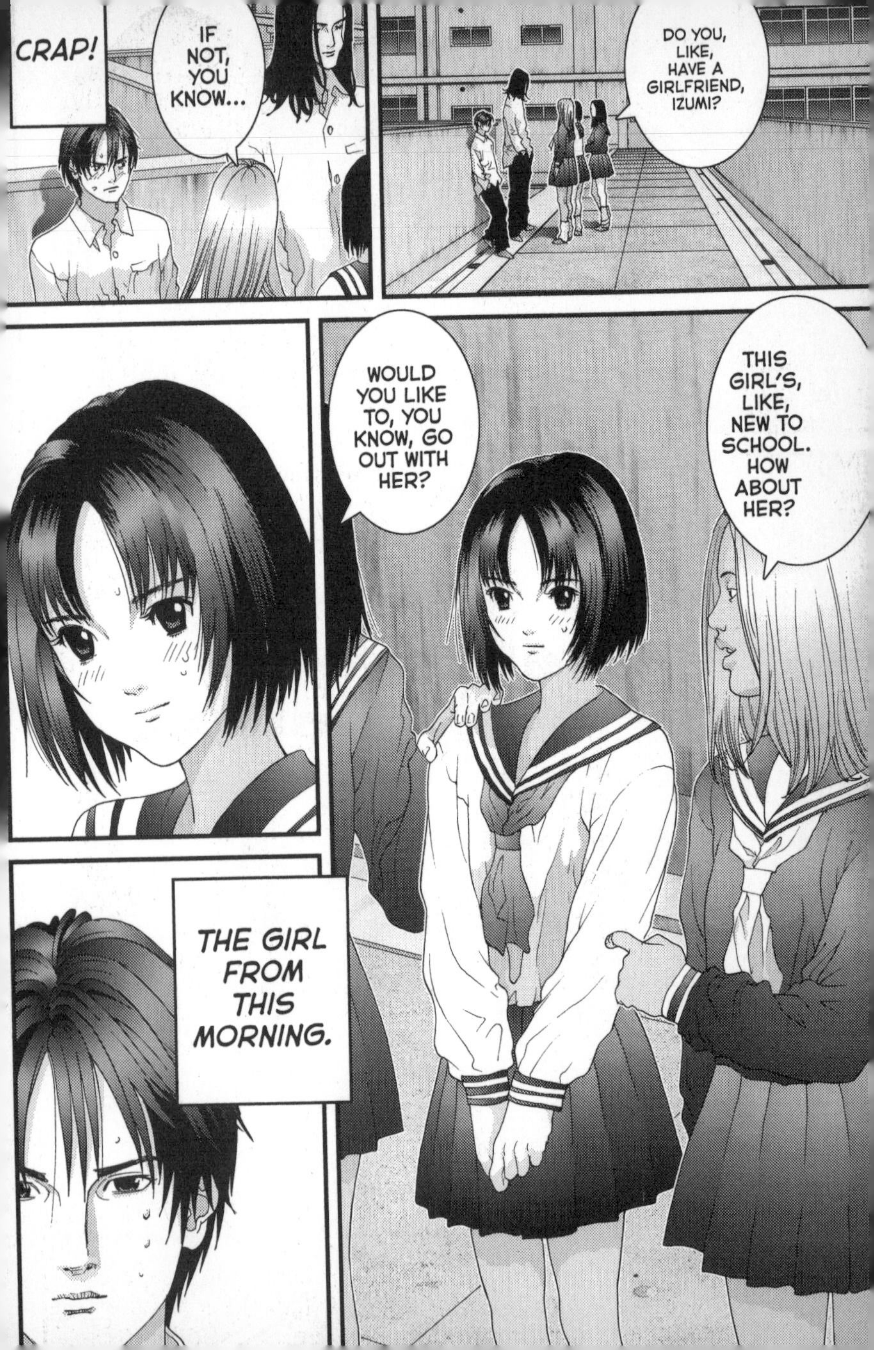
DO YOU, LIKE, HAVE A GIRLFRIEND, IZUMI?
IF NOT, YOU KNOW...
CRAP!
THIS GIRL'S, LIKE, NEW TO SCHOOL. HOW ABOUT HER?
WOULD YOU LIKE TO, YOU KNOW, GO OUT WITH HER?
THE GIRL FROM THIS MORNING.

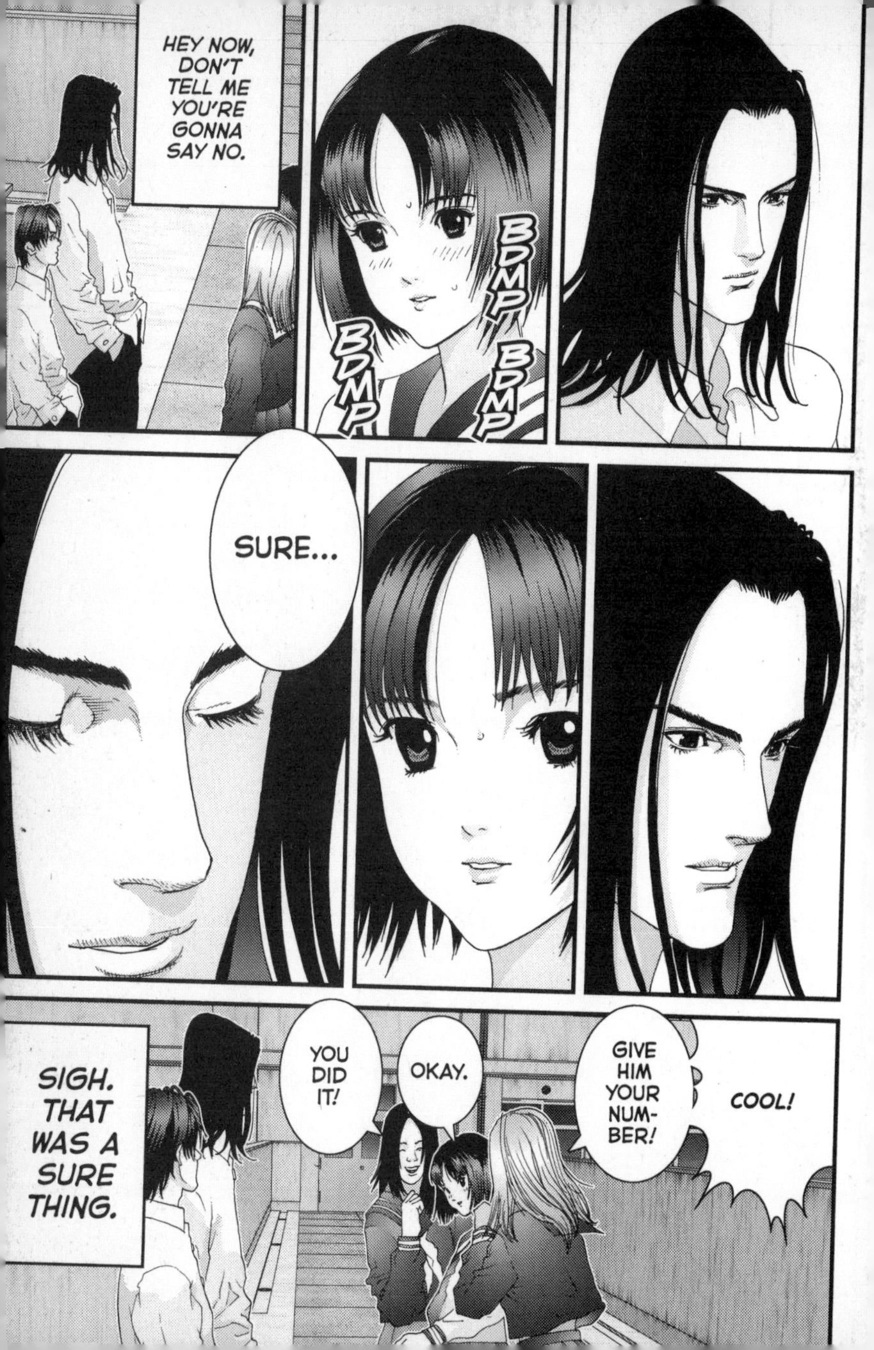

HEY NOW, DON'T TELL ME YOU'RE GONNA SAY NO.
BDMP
BDMP
BDMP
SURE...
SIGH. THAT WAS A SURE THING.
YOU DID IT!
OKAY.
GIVE HIM YOUR NUM-BER!
COOL!

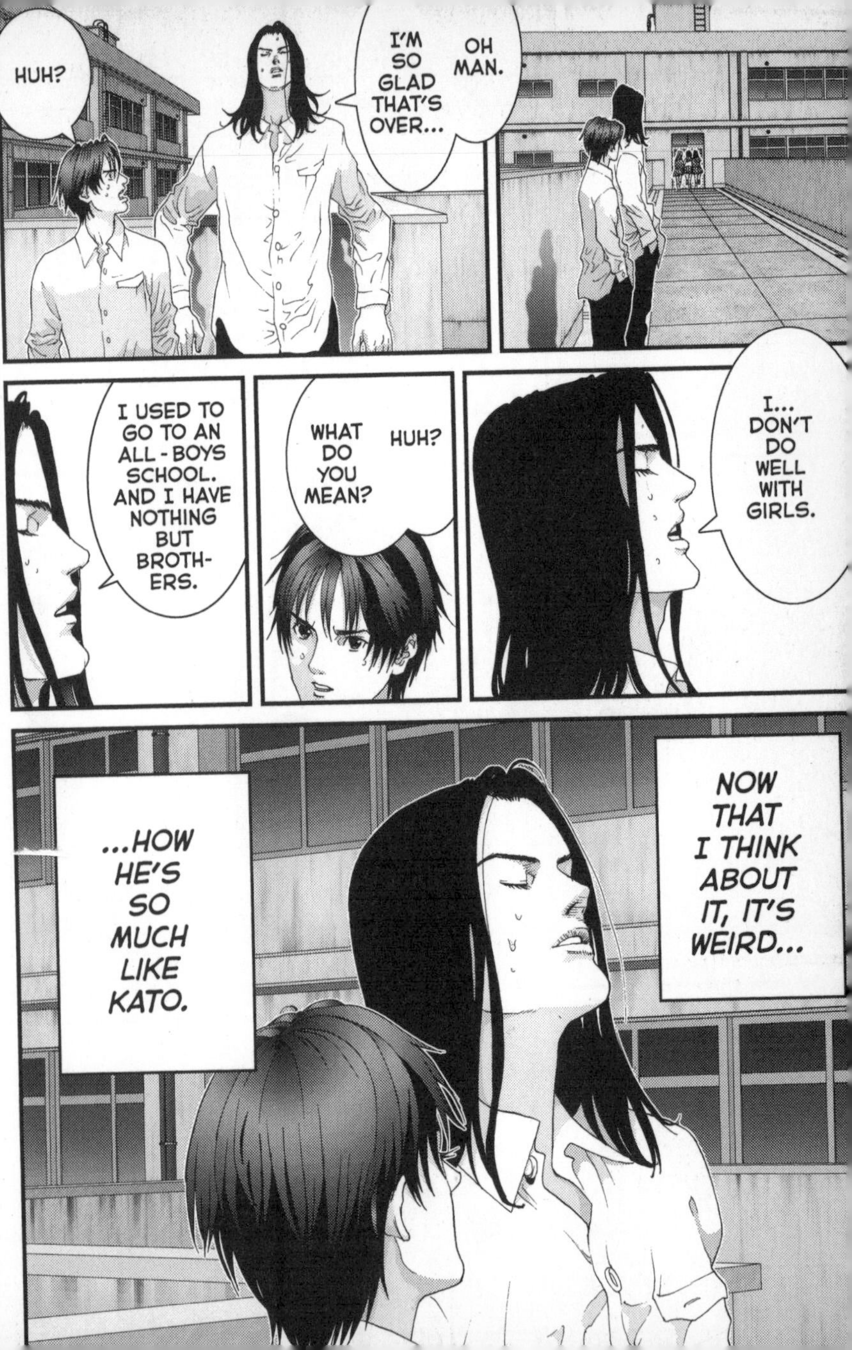
OH MAN.
I'M SO GLAD THAT'S OVER...
HUH?
I... DON'T DO WELL WITH GIRLS.
HUH?
WHAT DO YOU MEAN?
I USED TO GO TO AN ALL-BOYS SCHOOL. AND I HAVE NOTHING BUT BROTHERS.
NOW THAT I THINK ABOUT IT, IT'S WEIRD...
...HOW HE'S SO MUCH LIKE KATO.

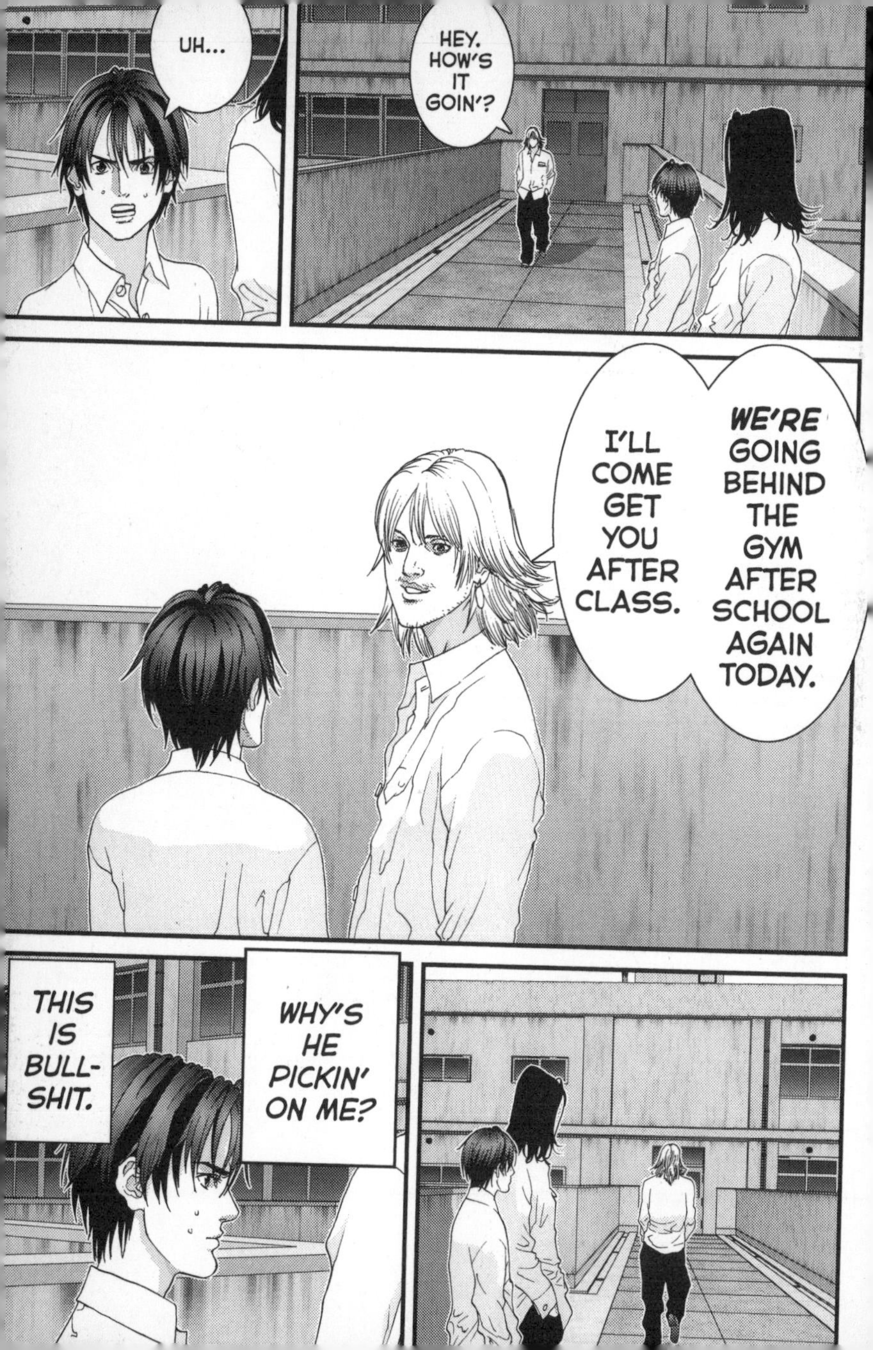
HEY. HOW'S IT GOIN'?
UH...
WE'RE GOING BEHIND THE GYM AFTER SCHOOL AGAIN TODAY.
I'LL COME GET YOU AFTER CLASS.
WHY'S HE PICKIN' ON ME?
THIS IS BULL-SHIT.

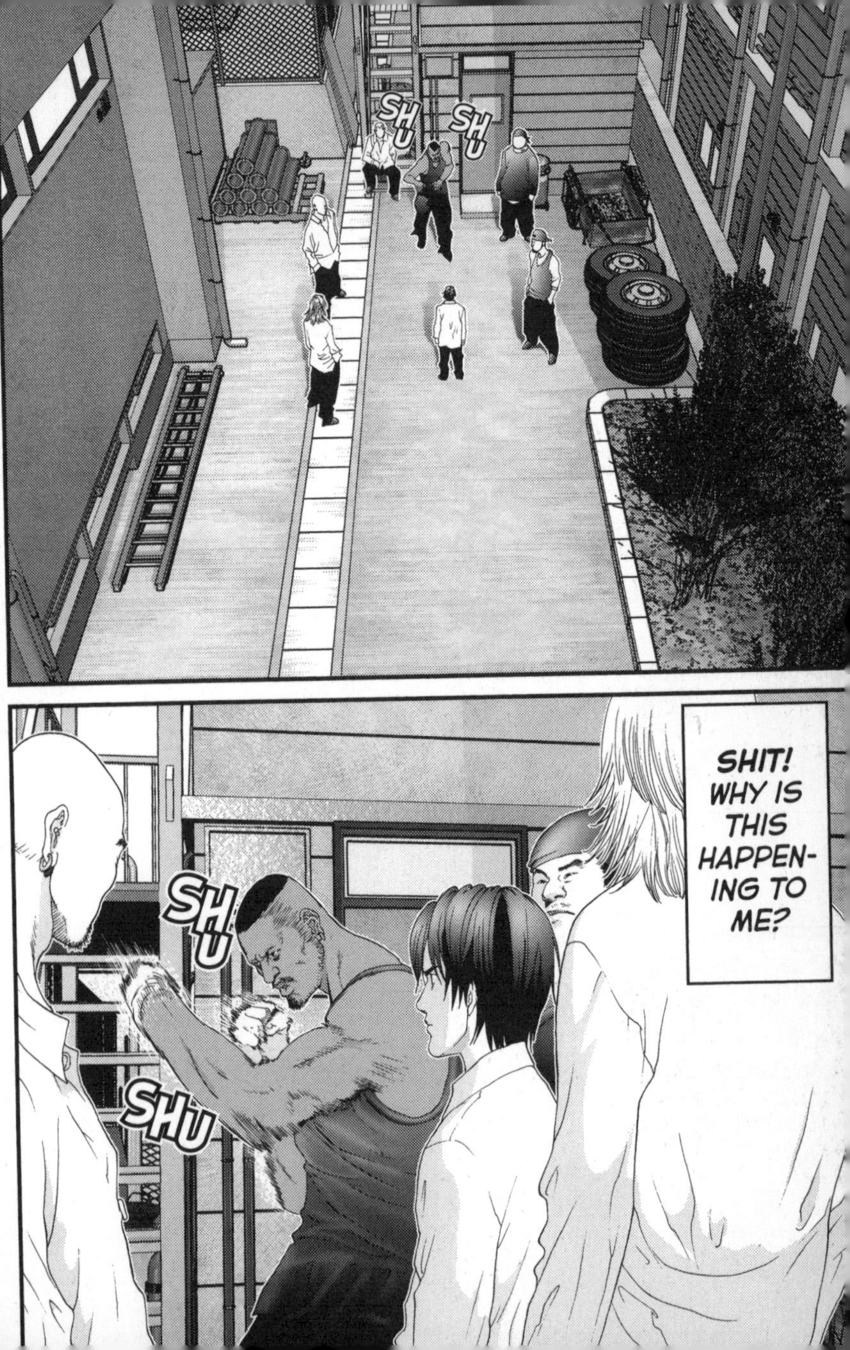
SHU
SHU
SHIT! WHY IS THIS HAPPEN-ING TO ME?
SHU
SHU

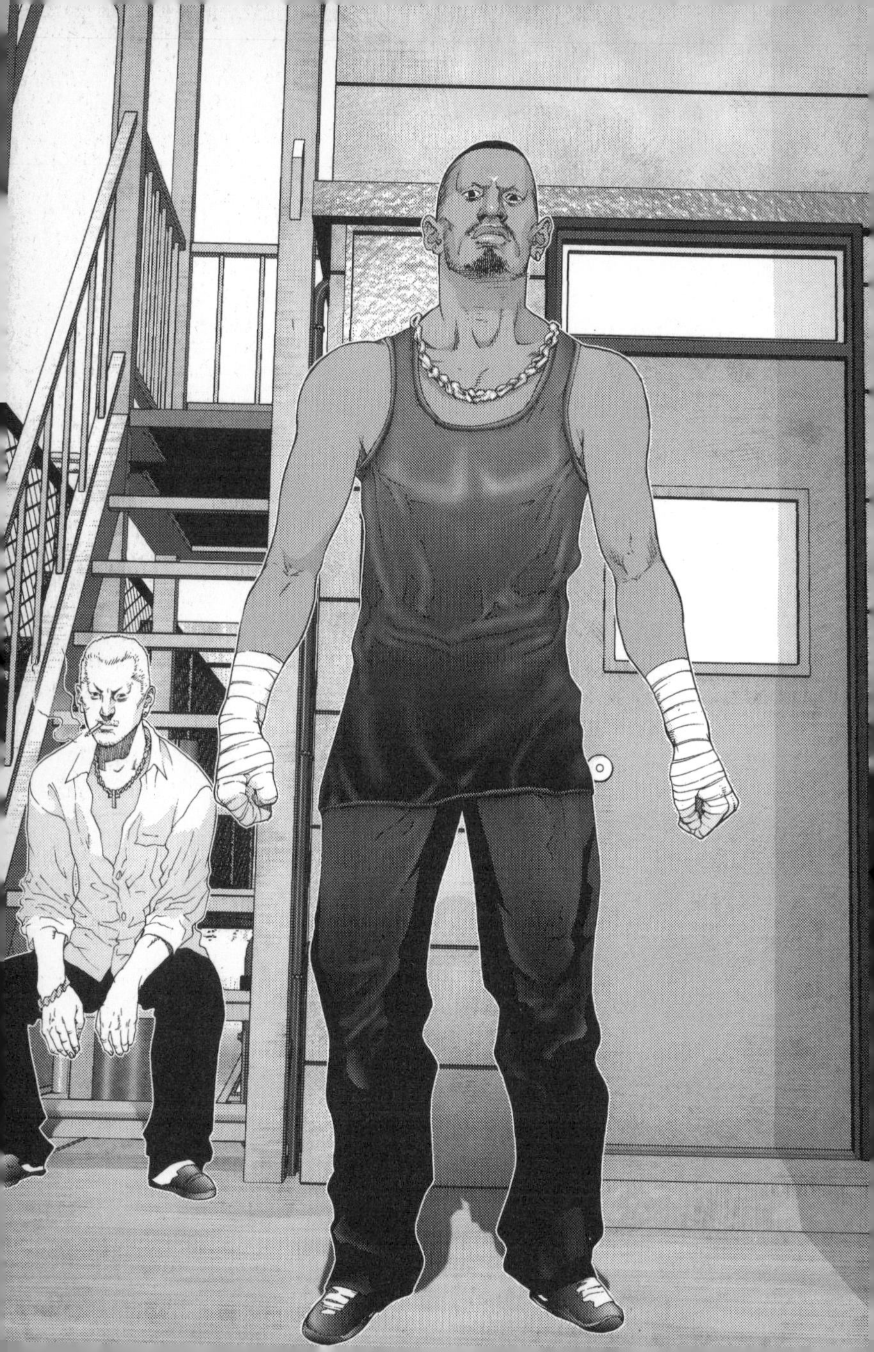

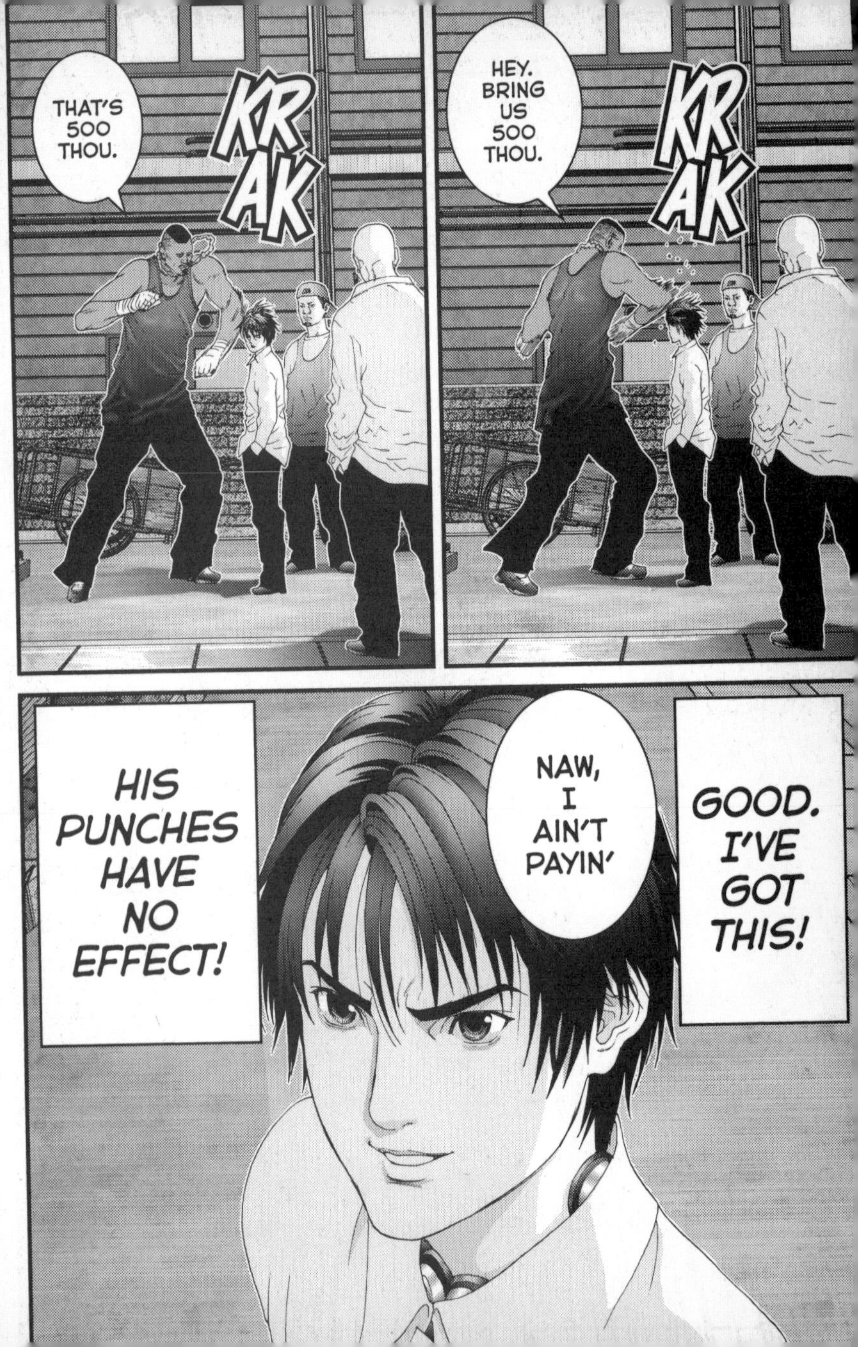
HEY. BRING US 500 THOU.
KRAK
THAT'S 500 THOU.
KRAK
GOOD. I'VE GOT THIS!
NAW, I AIN'T PAYIN'
HIS PUNCHES HAVE NO EFFECT!

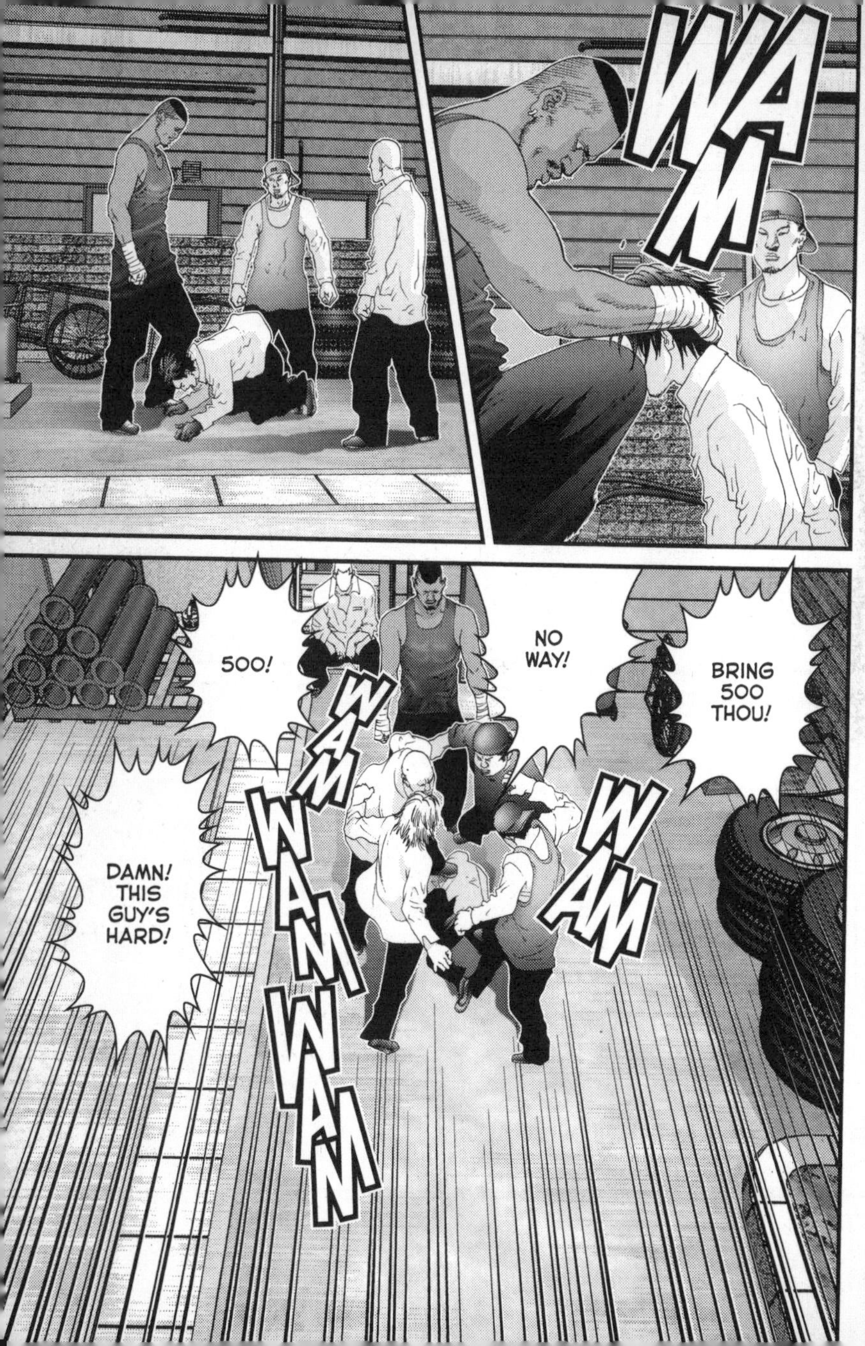
WAM
BRING 500 THOU!
NO WAY!
500!
WAM
WAM
WAM
WAM
WAM
DAMN! THIS GUY'S HARD!

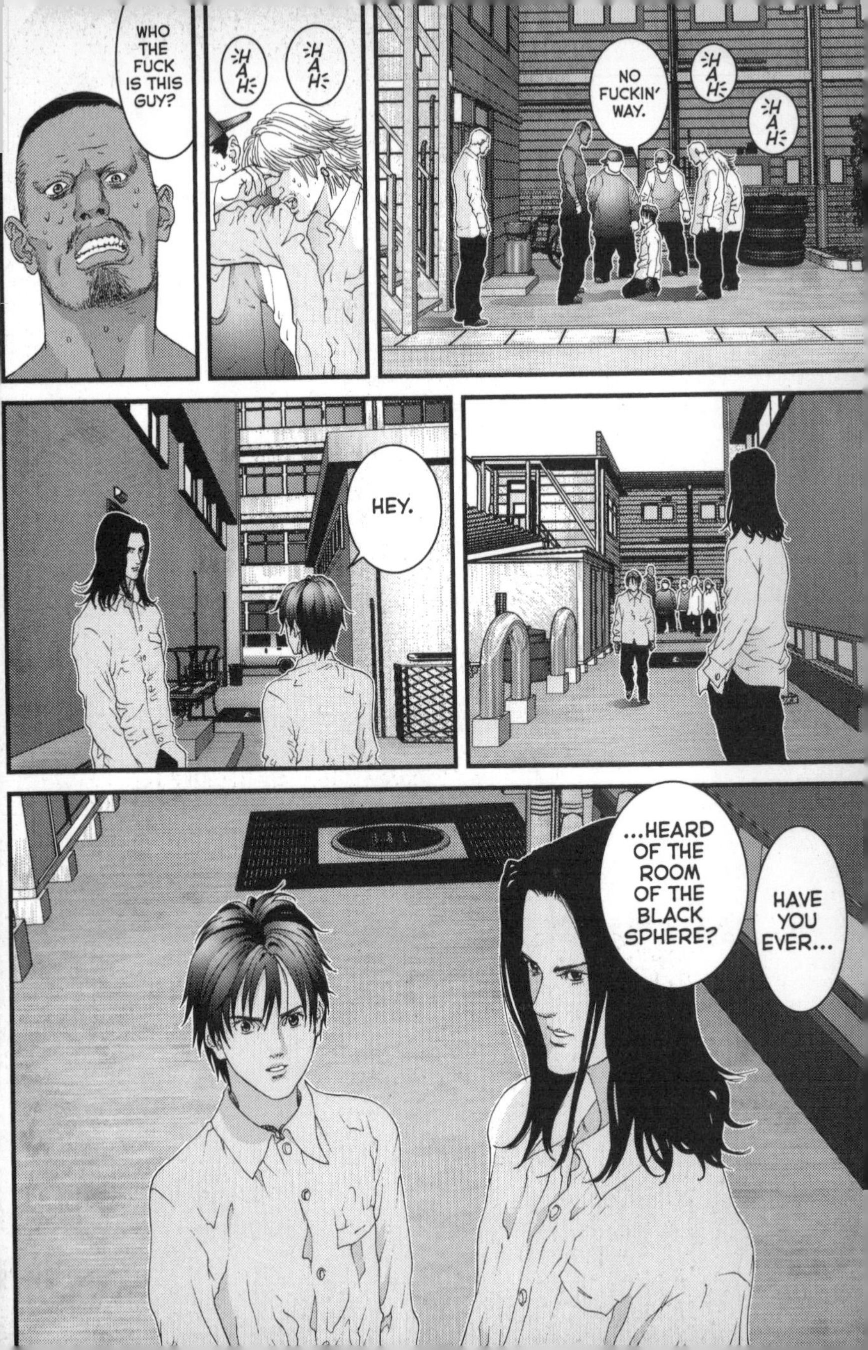
HAH
HAH
NO FUCKIN' WAY.
HAH
HAH
WHO THE FUCK IS THIS GUY?
HEY.
HAVE YOU EVER...
...HEARD OF THE ROOM OF THE BLACK SPHERE?

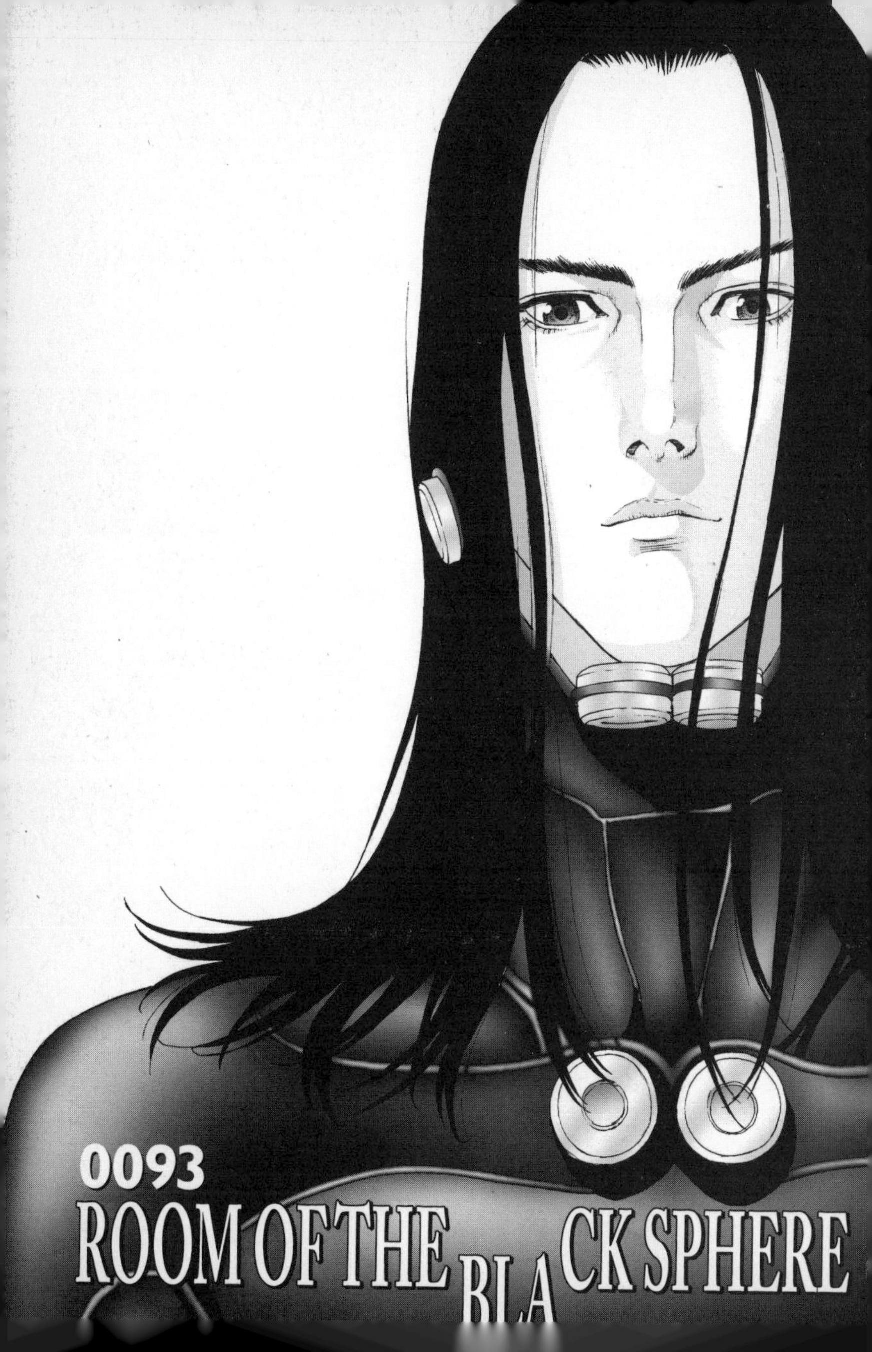

0093 ROOM OF THE BLACK SPHERE

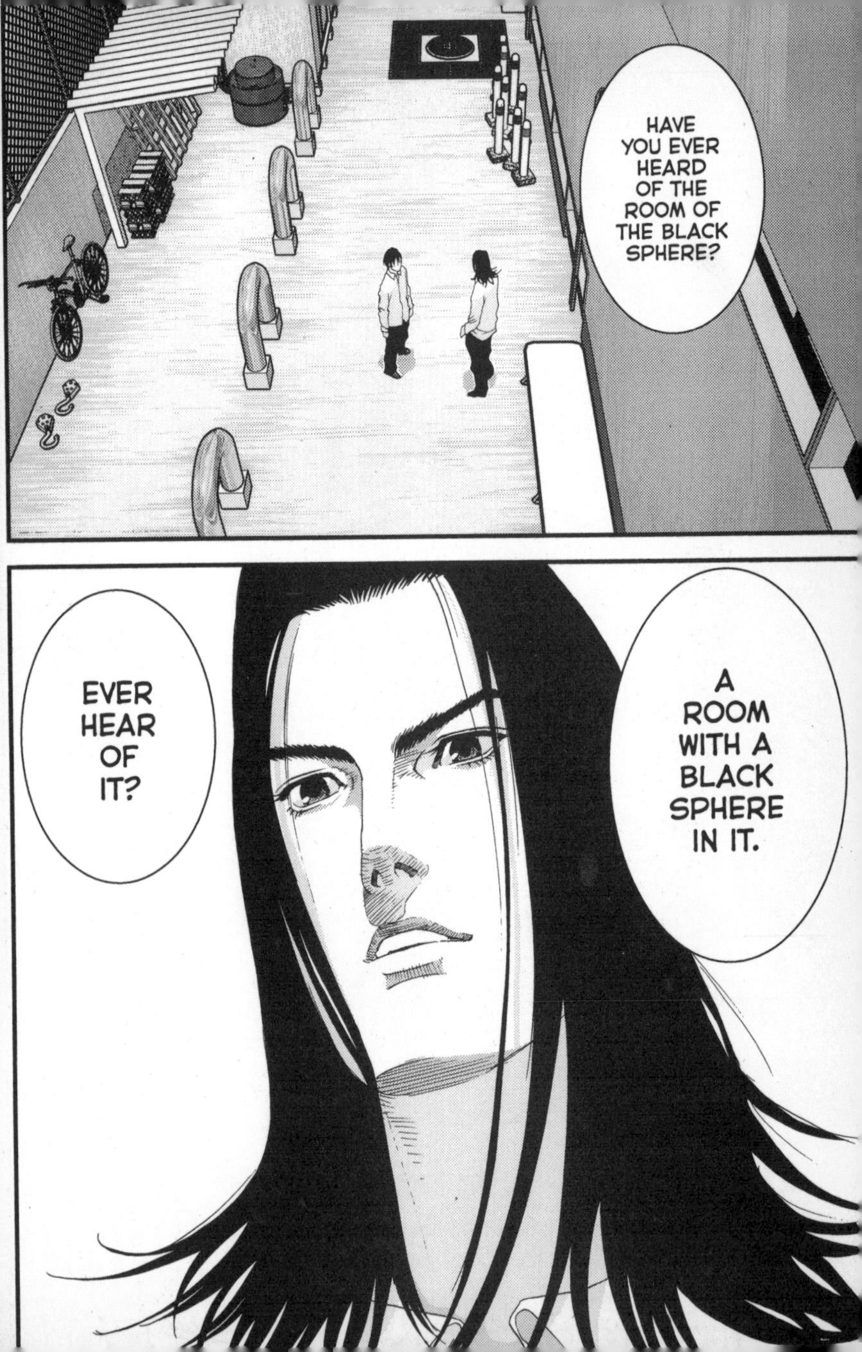
HAVE YOU EVER HEARD OF THE ROOM OF THE BLACK SPHERE?
A ROOM WITH A BLACK SPHERE IN IT.
EVER HEAR OF IT?

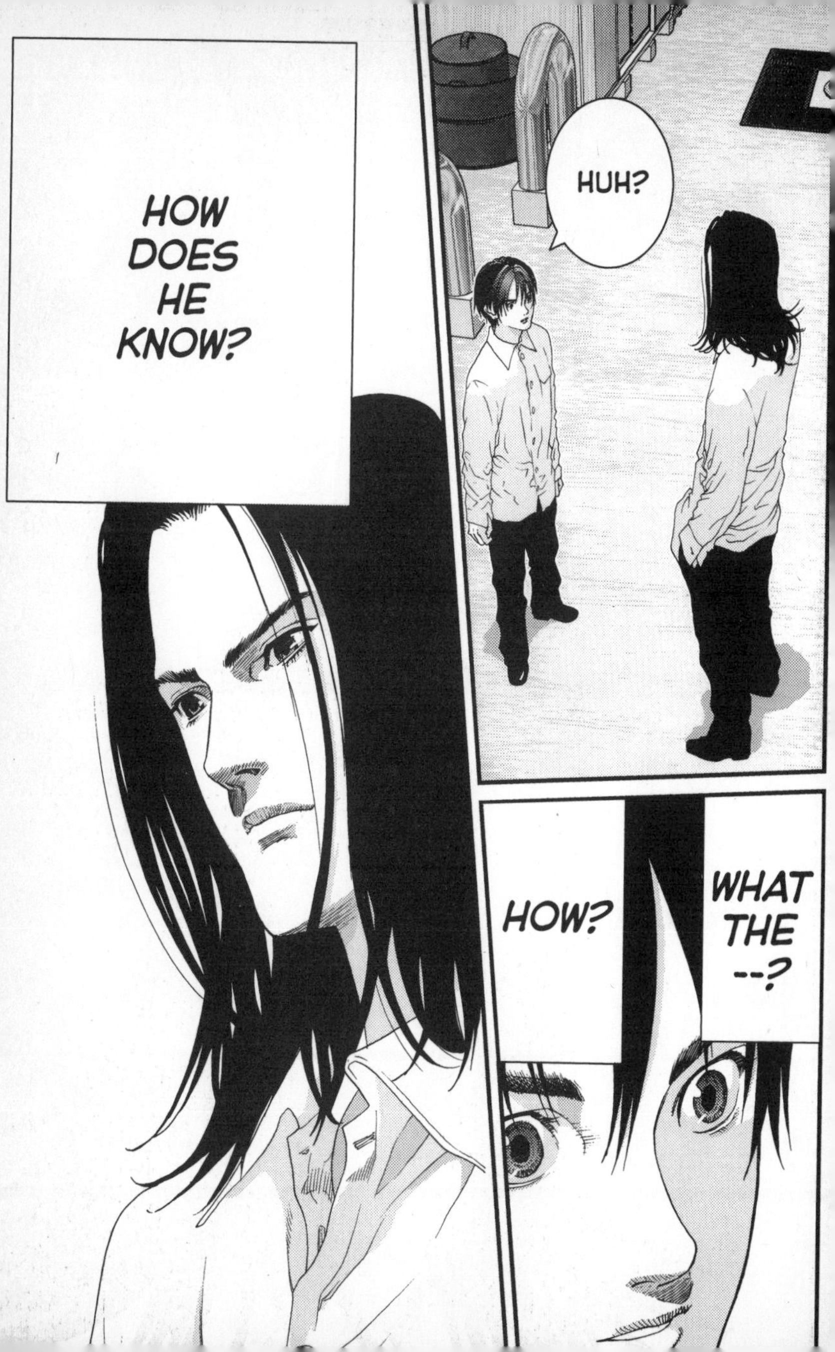
HUH?
HOW DOES HE KNOW?
WHAT THE --?
HOW?

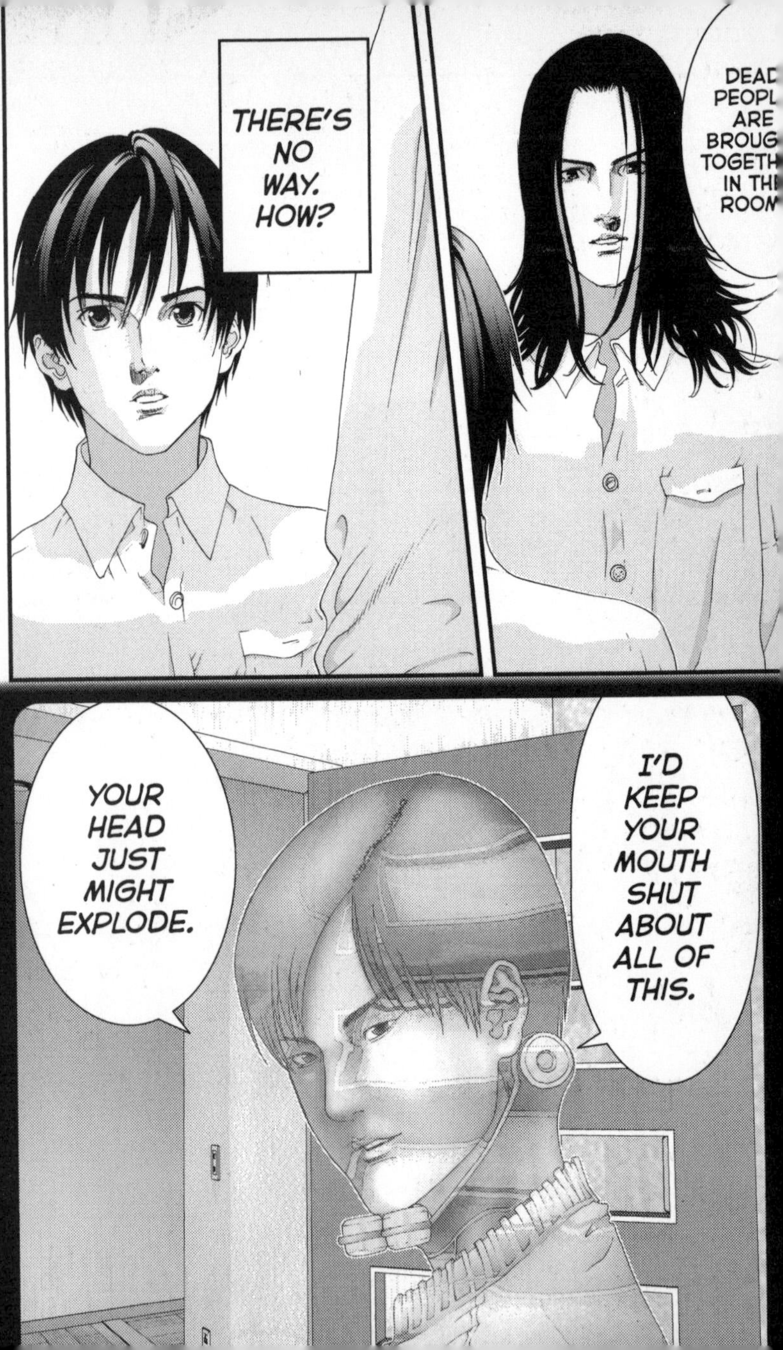
DEAD PEOPL ARE BROUG TOGETH IN THI ROOM
THERE'S NO WAY. HOW?
I'D KEEP YOUR MOUTH SHUT ABOUT ALL OF THIS.
YOUR HEAD JUST MIGHT EXPLODE.

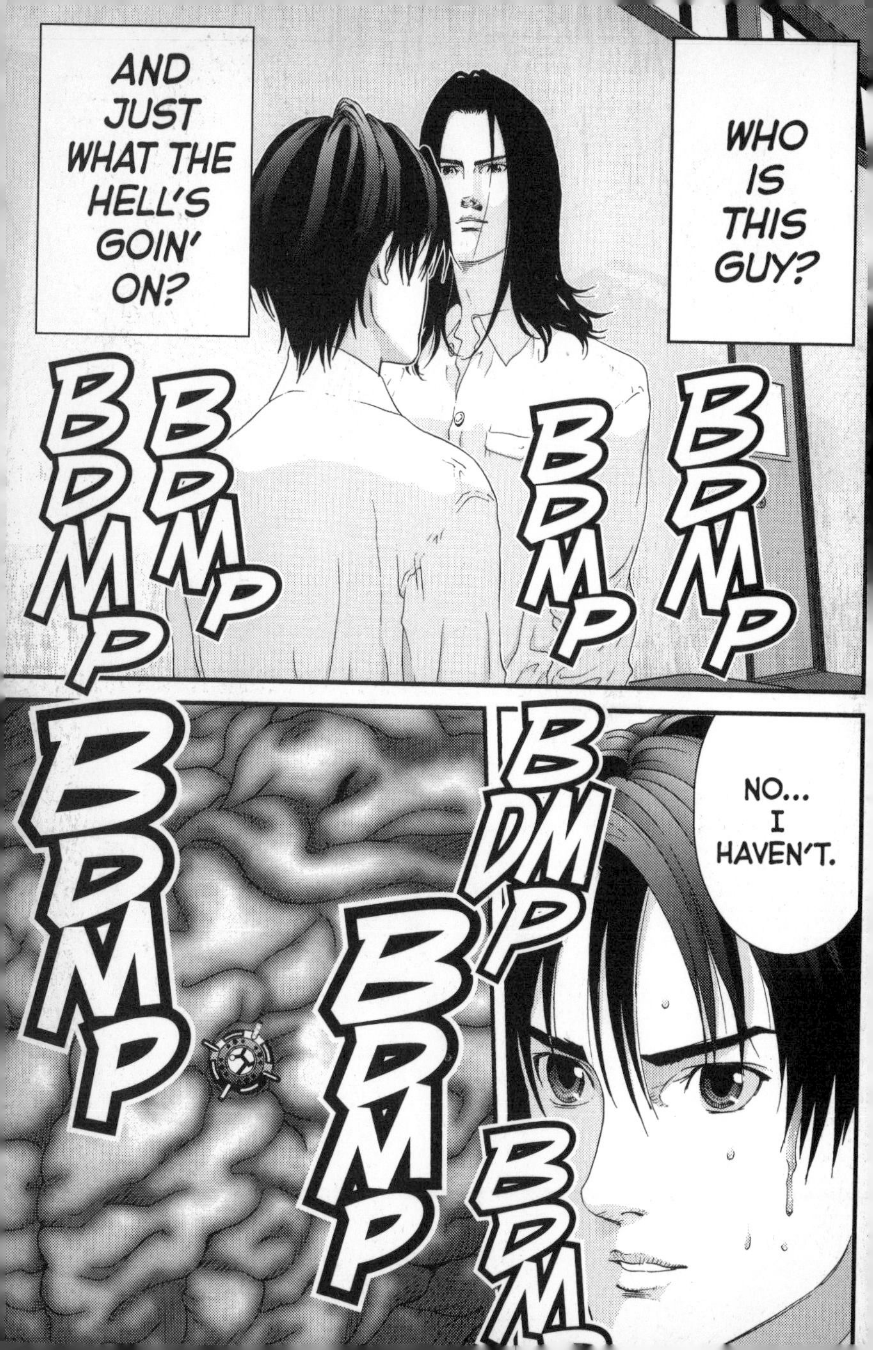
WHO IS THIS GUY?
AND JUST WHAT THE HELL'S GOIN' ON?
BDMP
BDMP
BDMP
BDMP
NO... I HAVEN'T.
BDMP
BDMP
BDMP
BDM

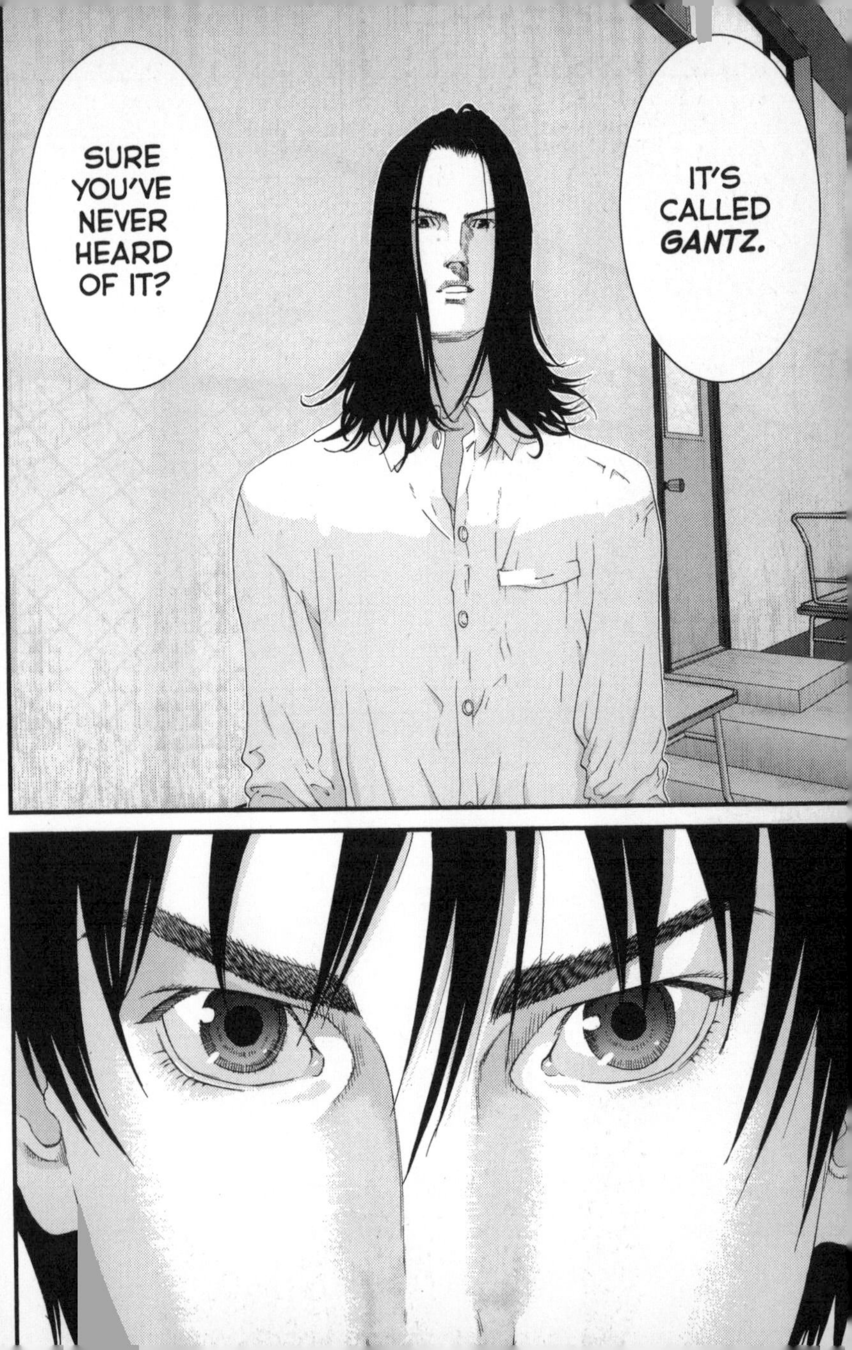
IT'S CALLED GANTZ.
SURE YOU'VE NEVER HEARD OF IT?

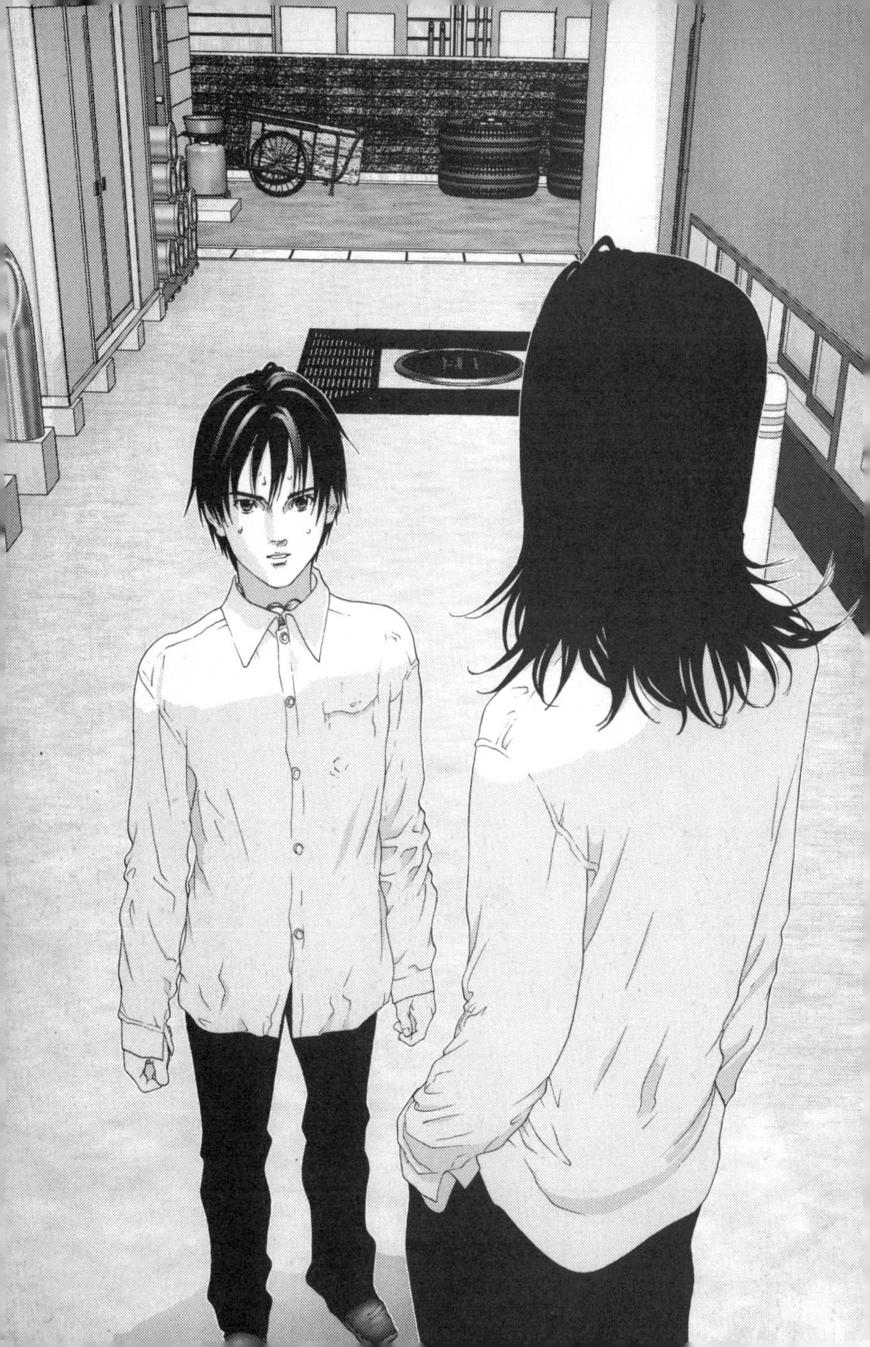

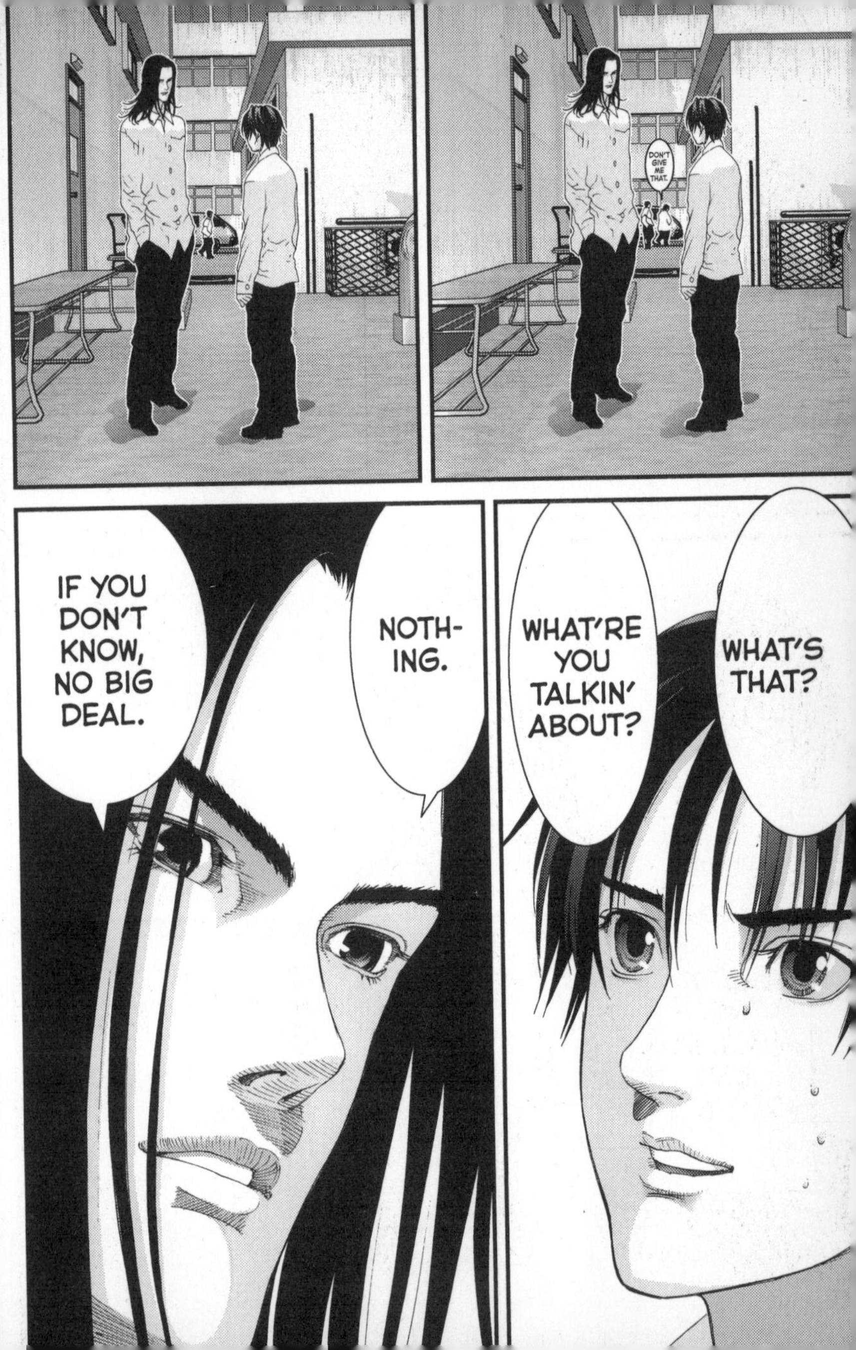
DON'T GIVE ME THAT.
WHAT'S THAT?
WHAT'RE YOU TALKIN' ABOUT?
NOTH-ING.
IF YOU DON'T KNOW, NO BIG DEAL.

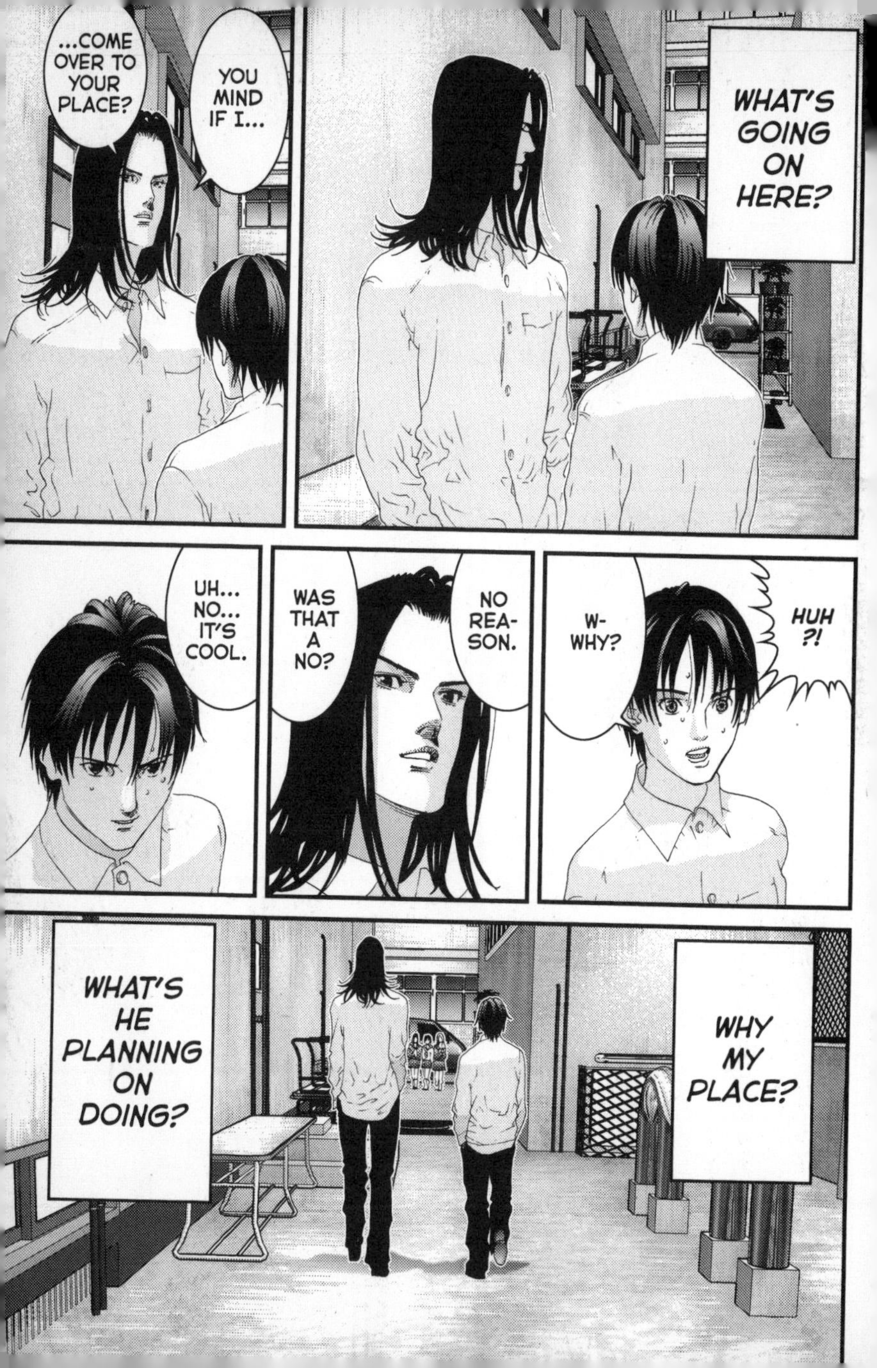
WHAT'S GOING ON HERE?
YOU MIND IF I...
...COME OVER TO YOUR PLACE?
HUH ?!
W- WHY?
NO REA- SON.
WAS THAT A NO?
UH... NO... IT'S COOL.
WHY MY PLACE?
WHAT'S HE PLANNING ON DOING?

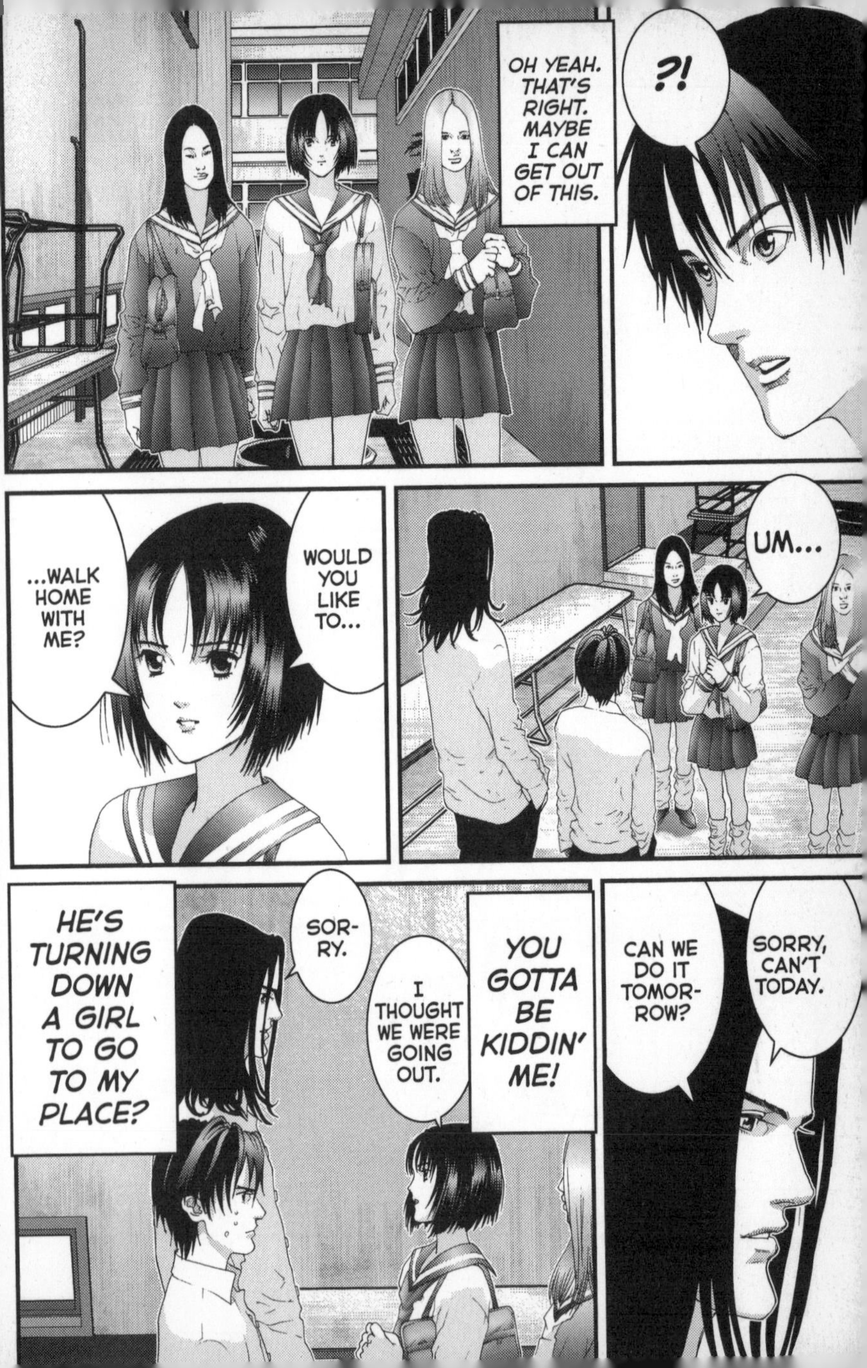
?!
OH YEAH. THAT'S RIGHT. MAYBE I CAN GET OUT OF THIS.
UM...
WOULD YOU LIKE TO...
...WALK HOME WITH ME?
SORRY, CAN'T TODAY.
CAN WE DO IT TOMORROW?
YOU GOTTA BE KIDDIN' ME!
I THOUGHT WE WERE GOING OUT.
SOR-RY.
HE'S TURNING DOWN A GIRL TO GO TO MY PLACE?

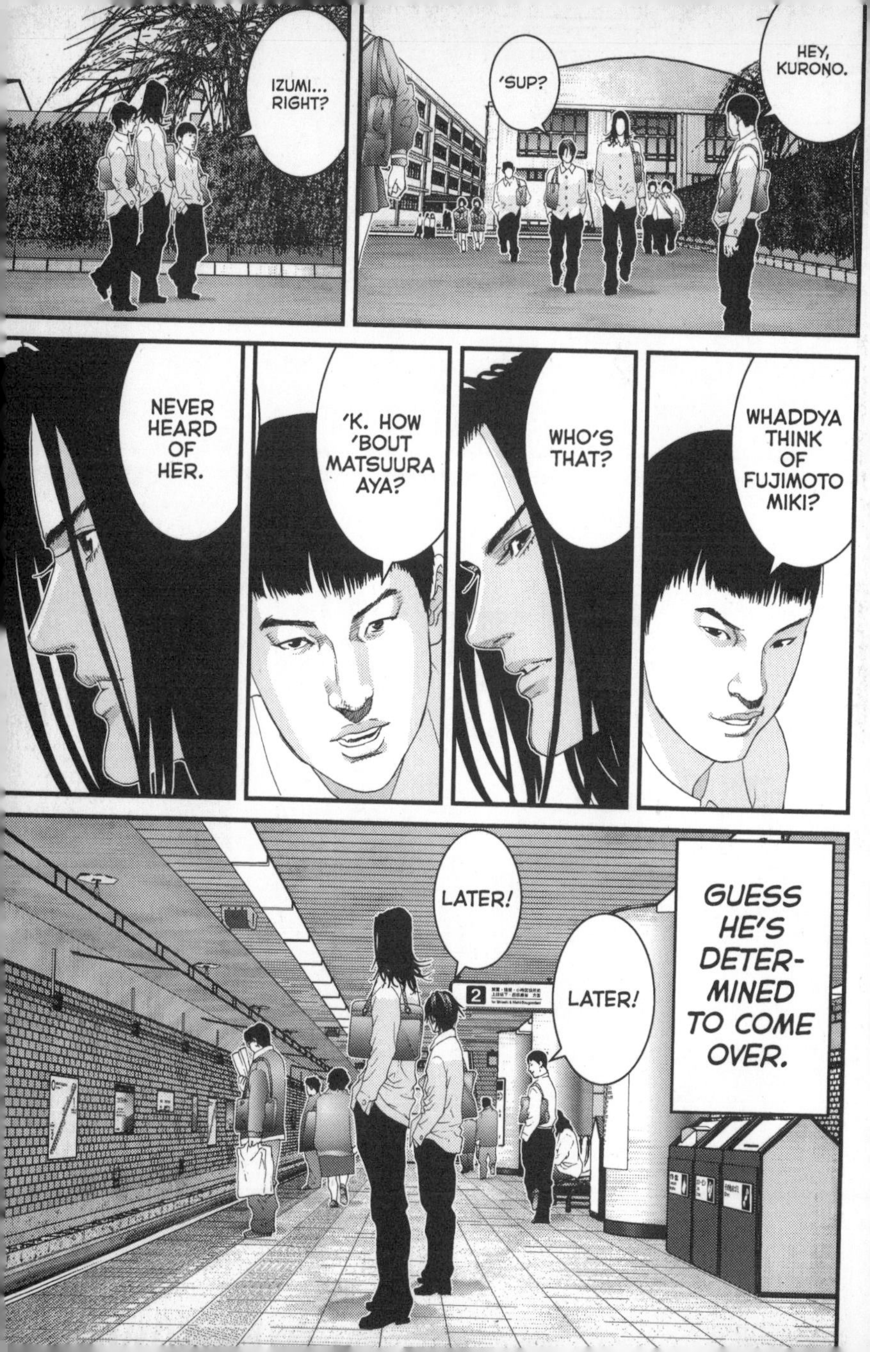
HEY, KURONO.
'SUP?
IZUMI... RIGHT?
WHADDYA THINK OF FUJIMOTO MIKI?
WHO'S THAT?
'K. HOW 'BOUT MATSUURA AYA?
NEVER HEARD OF HER.
GUESS HE'S DETER-MINED TO COME OVER.
LATER!
LATER!

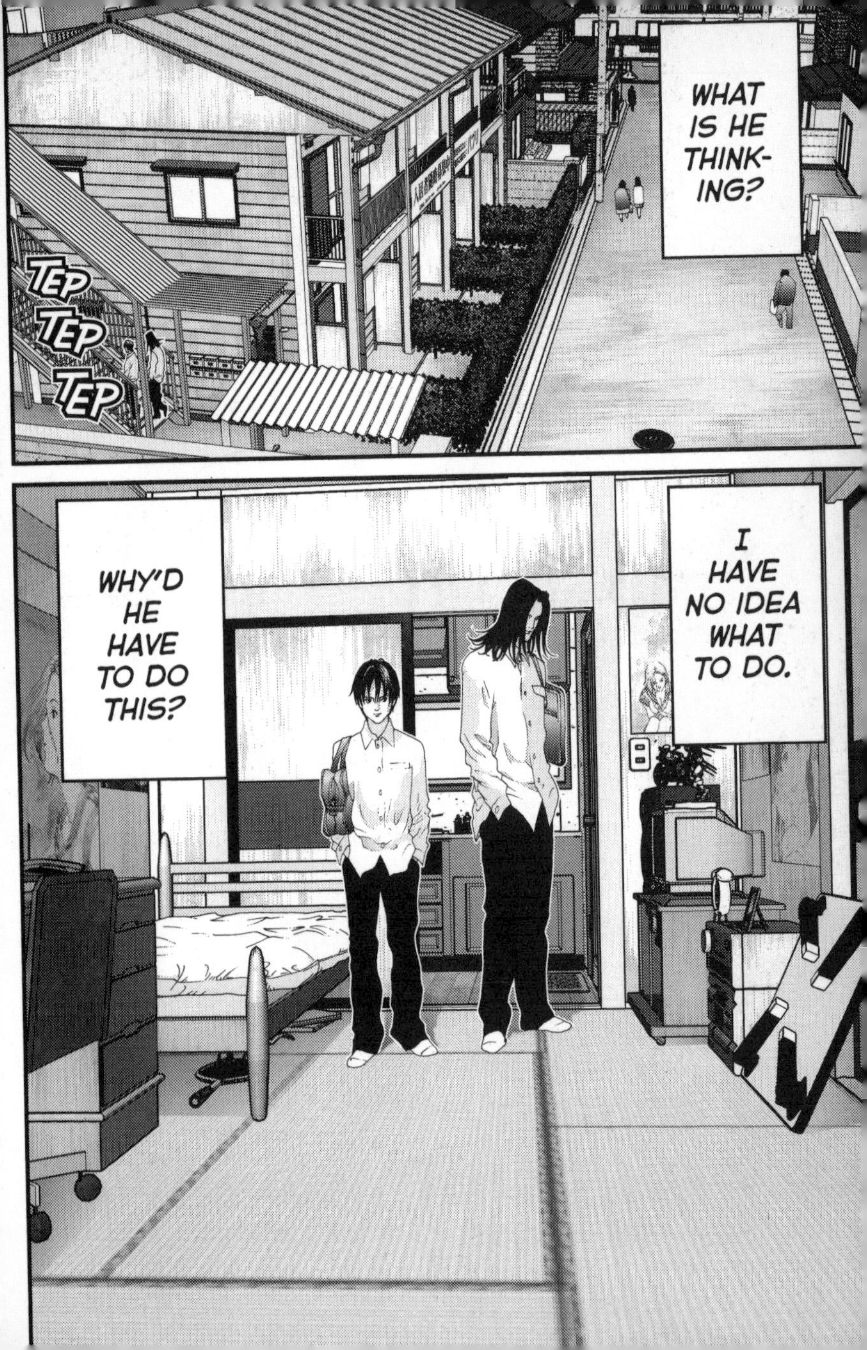
WHAT IS HE THINKING?
TEP TEP TEP
I HAVE NO IDEA WHAT TO DO.
WHY'D HE HAVE TO DO THIS?

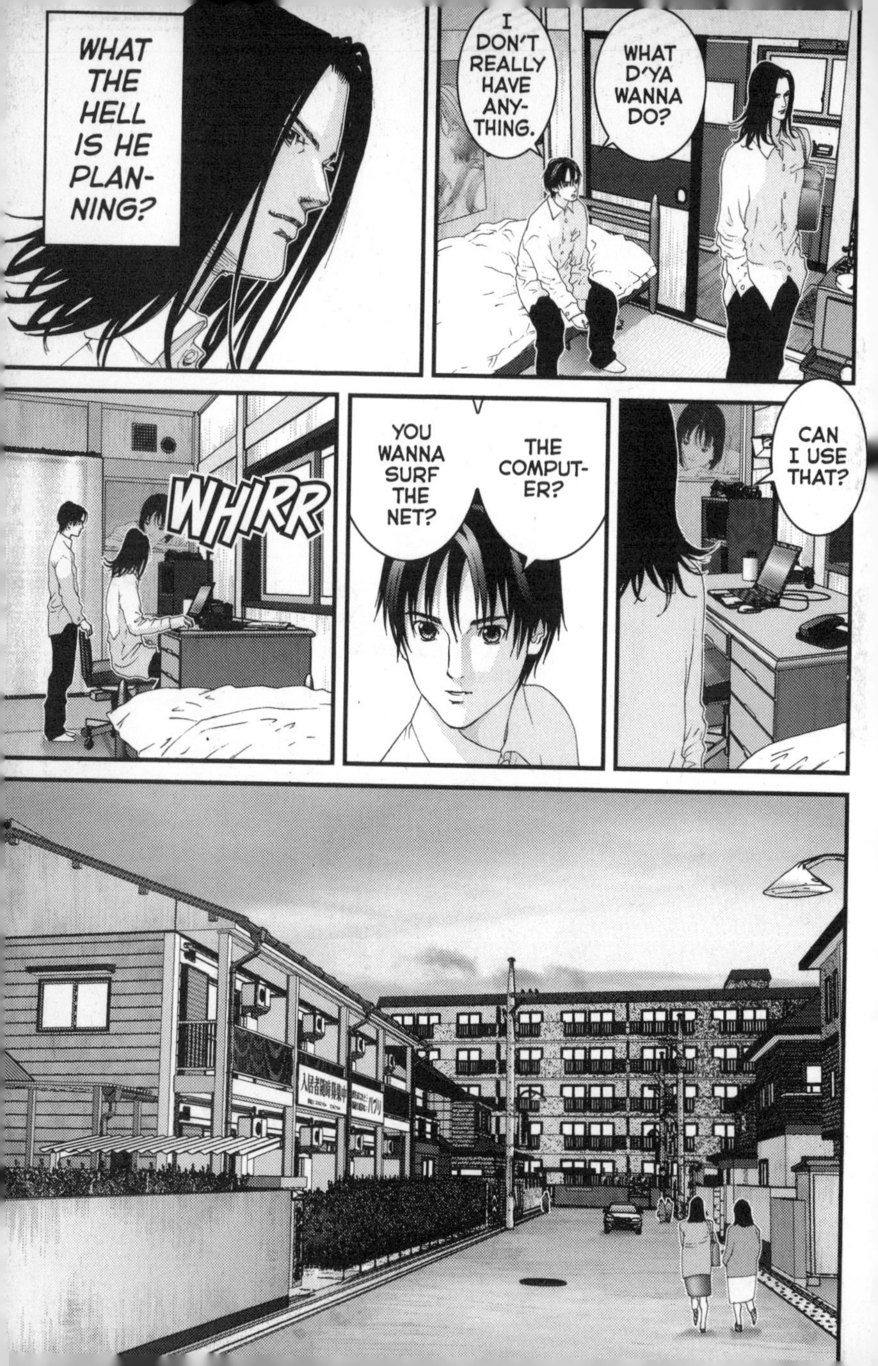
WHAT D'YA WANNA DO?
I DON'T REALLY HAVE ANY-THING.
WHAT THE HELL IS HE PLAN-NING?
CAN I USE THAT?
THE COMPUT-ER?
YOU WANNA SURF THE NET?
WHIRR

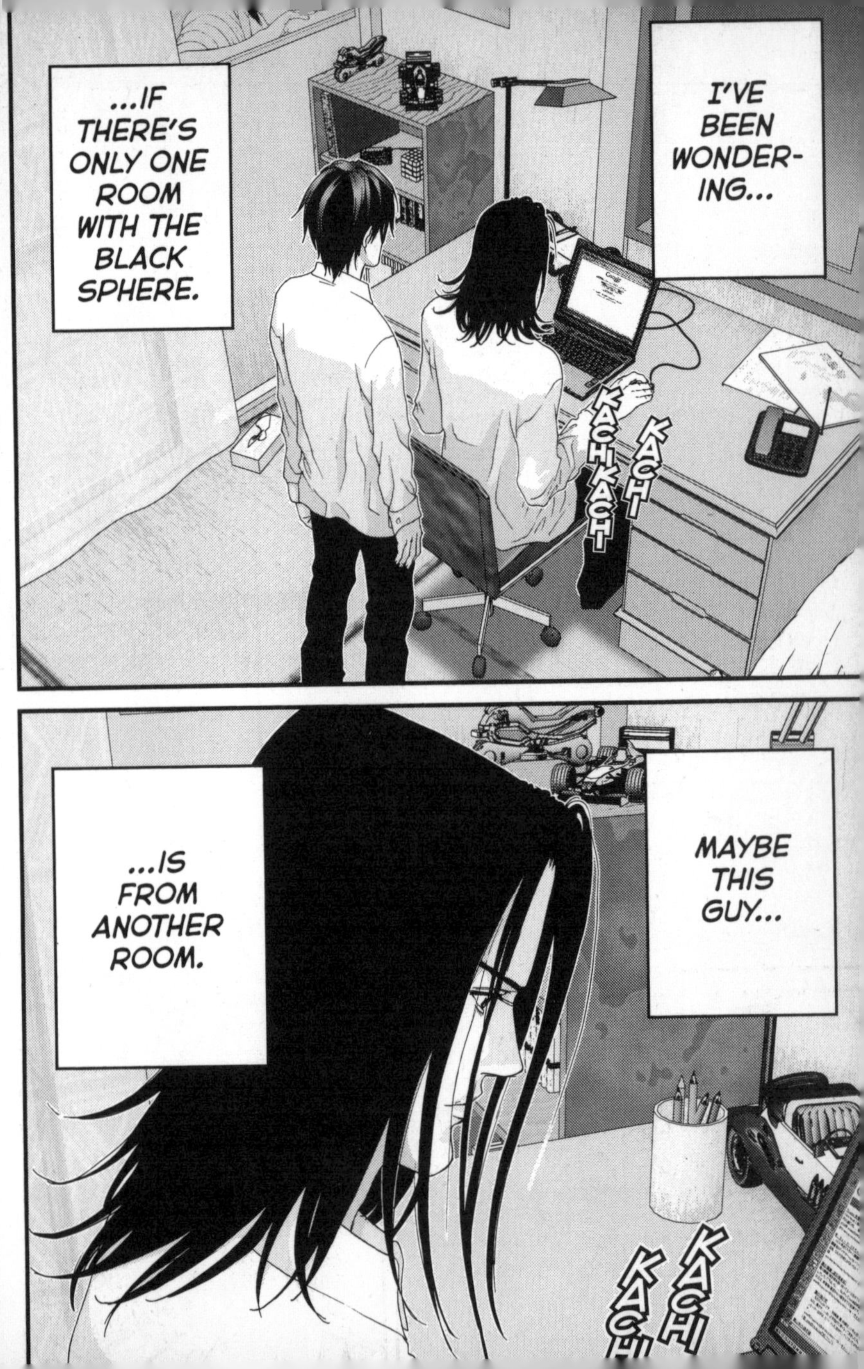
I'VE BEEN WONDERING...
...IF THERE'S ONLY ONE ROOM WITH THE BLACK SPHERE.
KACHI
KACHIKACHI
MAYBE THIS GUY...
...IS FROM ANOTHER ROOM.
KACHI

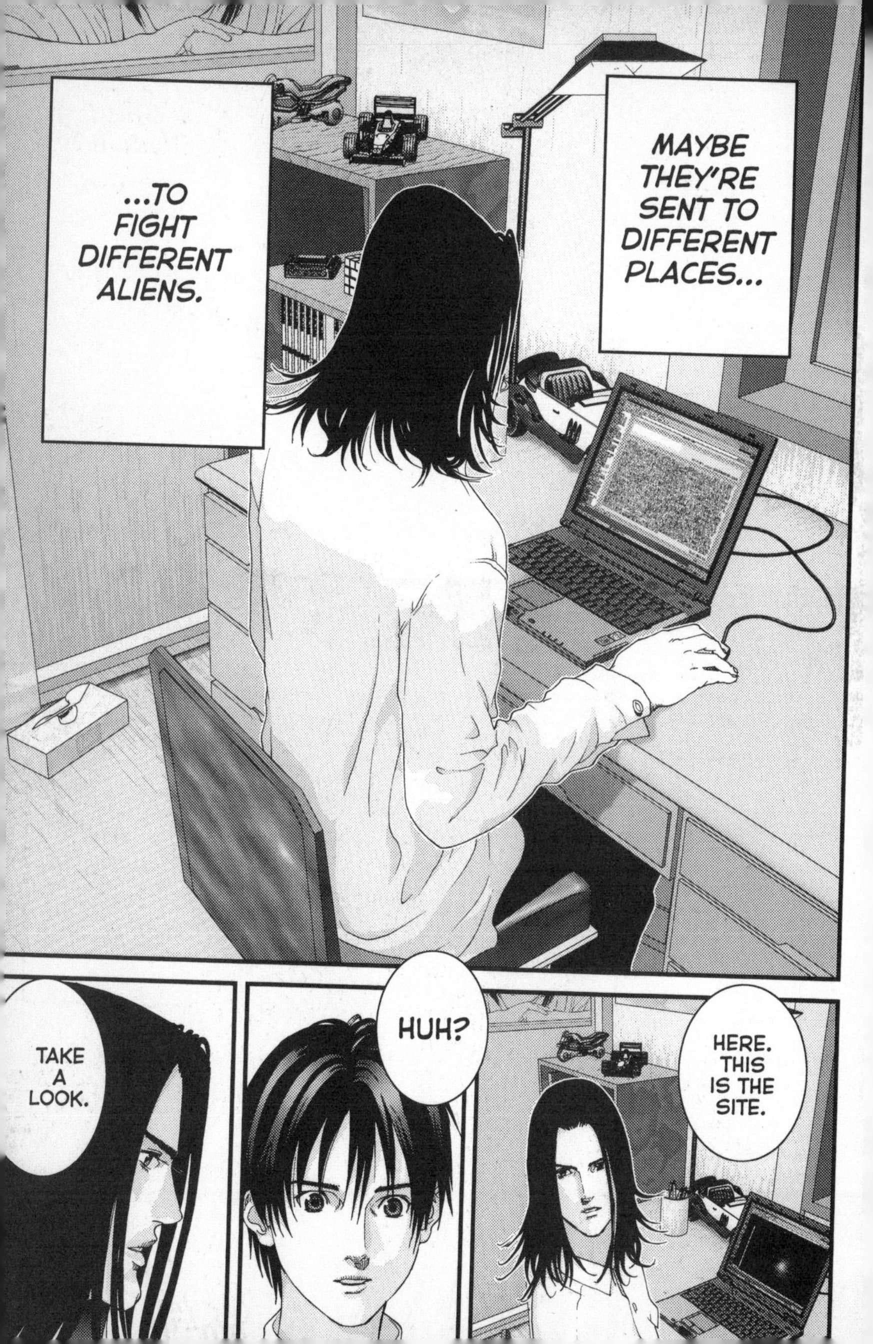
...TO FIGHT DIFFERENT ALIENS.
MAYBE THEY'RE SENT TO DIFFERENT PLACES...
TAKE A LOOK.
HUH?
HERE. THIS IS THE SITE.

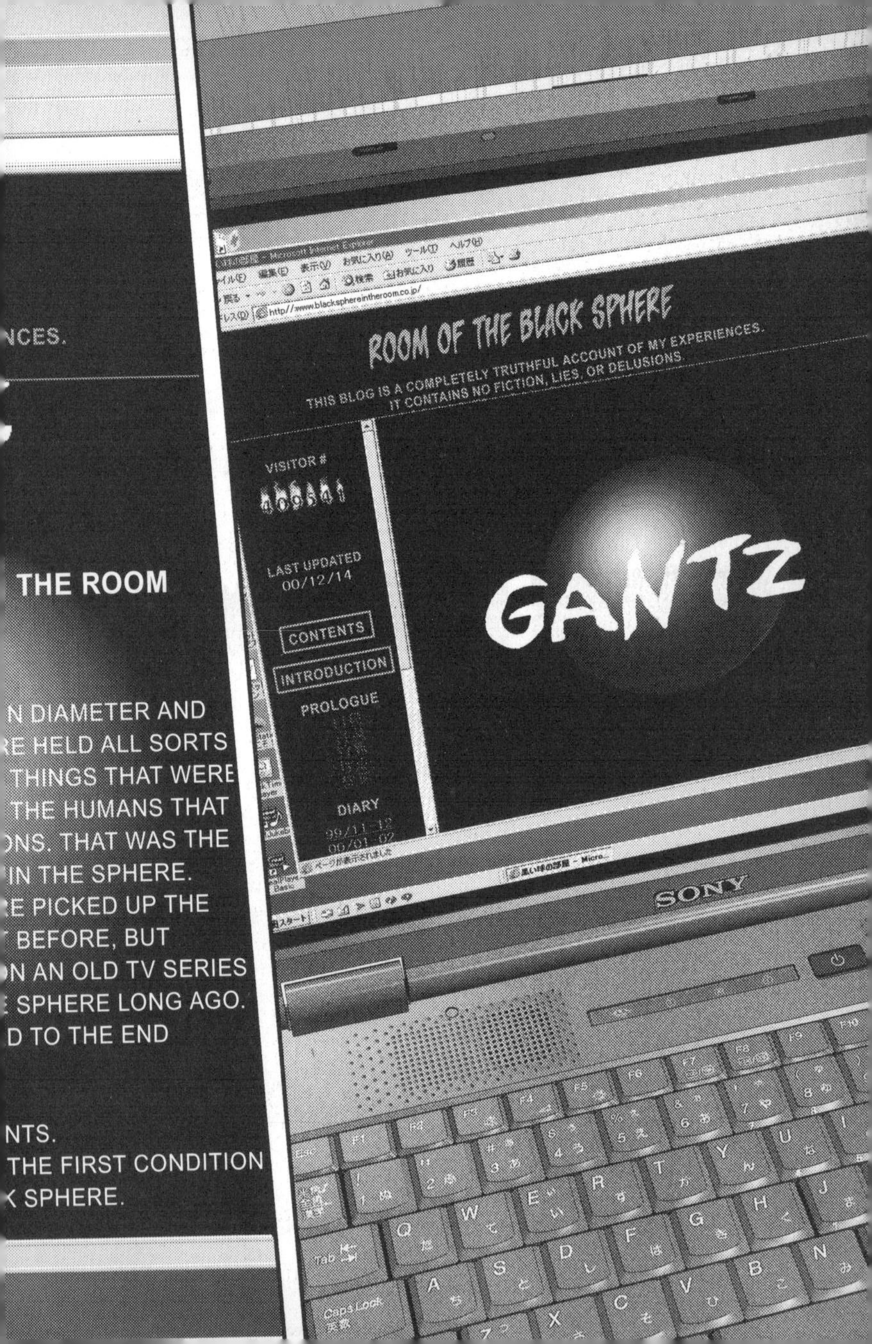

NCES.
THE ROOM
N DIAMETER AND
RE HELD ALL SORTS
THINGS THAT WERE
THE HUMANS THAT
ONS. THAT WAS THE
IN THE SPHERE.
E PICKED UP THE
BEFORE, BUT
N AN OLD TV SERIES
SPHERE LONG AGO.
D TO THE END
NTS.
THE FIRST CONDITION
K SPHERE.
http://www.blacksphereintheroom.co.jp/
ROOM OF THE BLACK SPHERE
THIS BLOG IS A COMPLETELY TRUTHFUL ACCOUNT OF MY EXPERIENCES.
IT CONTAINS NO FICTION, LIES, OR DELUSIONS.
VISITOR #
LAST UPDATED
00/12/14
CONTENTS
INTRODUCTION
PROLOGUE
DIARY
GANTZ
SONY

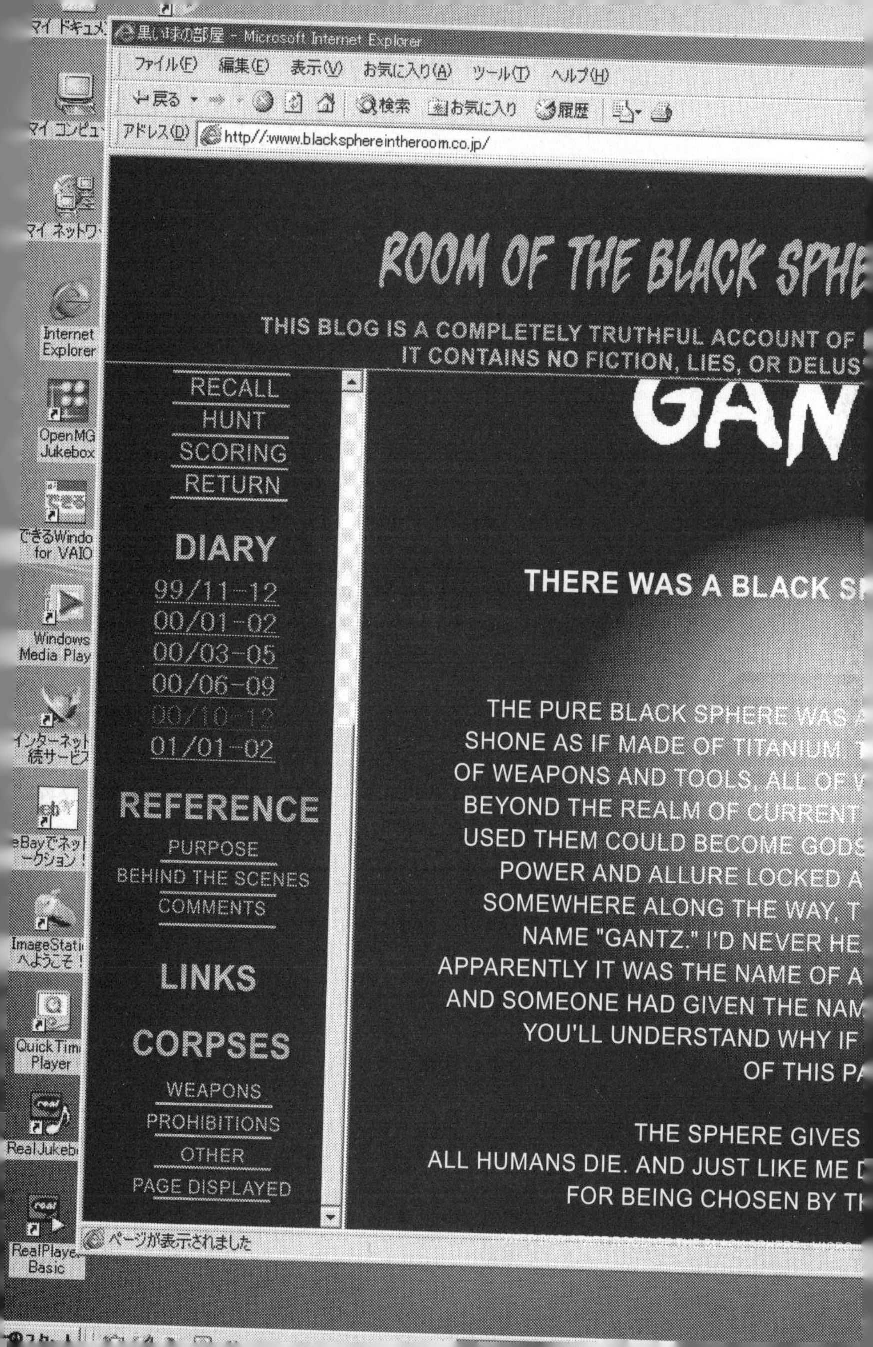

黒い球の部屋 - Microsoft Internet Explorer
ファイル(F) 編集(E) 表示(V) お気に入り(A) ツール(T) ヘルプ(H)
戻る 検索 お気に入り 履歴
アドレス(D) http//:www.blacksphereintheroom.co.jp/
ROOM OF THE BLACK SPHE
THIS BLOG IS A COMPLETELY TRUTHFUL ACCOUNT OF
IT CONTAINS NO FICTION, LIES, OR DELUS
RECALL
HUNT
SCORING
RETURN
DIARY
99/11-12
00/01-02
00/03-05
00/06-09
00/10-12
01/01-02
REFERENCE
PURPOSE
BEHIND THE SCENES
COMMENTS
LINKS
CORPSES
WEAPONS
PROHIBITIONS
OTHER
PAGE DISPLAYED
GAN
THERE WAS A BLACK S
THE PURE BLACK SPHERE WAS
SHONE AS IF MADE OF TITANIUM.
OF WEAPONS AND TOOLS, ALL OF
BEYOND THE REALM OF CURRENT
USED THEM COULD BECOME GODS
POWER AND ALLURE LOCKED A
SOMEWHERE ALONG THE WAY, T
NAME "GANTZ." I'D NEVER HE
APPARENTLY IT WAS THE NAME OF A
AND SOMEONE HAD GIVEN THE NAM
YOU'LL UNDERSTAND WHY IF
OF THIS PA
THE SPHERE GIVES
ALL HUMANS DIE. AND JUST LIKE ME D
FOR BEING CHOSEN BY TH
ページが表示されました
マイ ドキュメ
マイ コンピュー
マイ ネットワ
Internet Explorer
OpenMG Jukebox
できるWindo for VAIO
Windows Media Play
インターネット 続サービス
eBayでネット ークション
ImageStati へようこそ！
QuickTim Player
RealJukeb
RealPlaye Basic

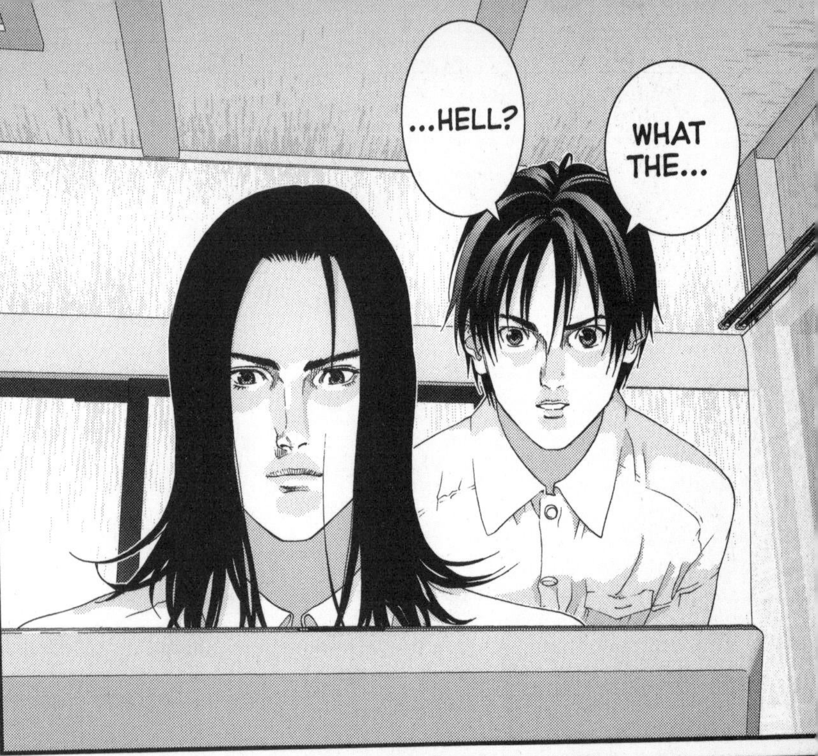
WHAT THE...
...HELL?
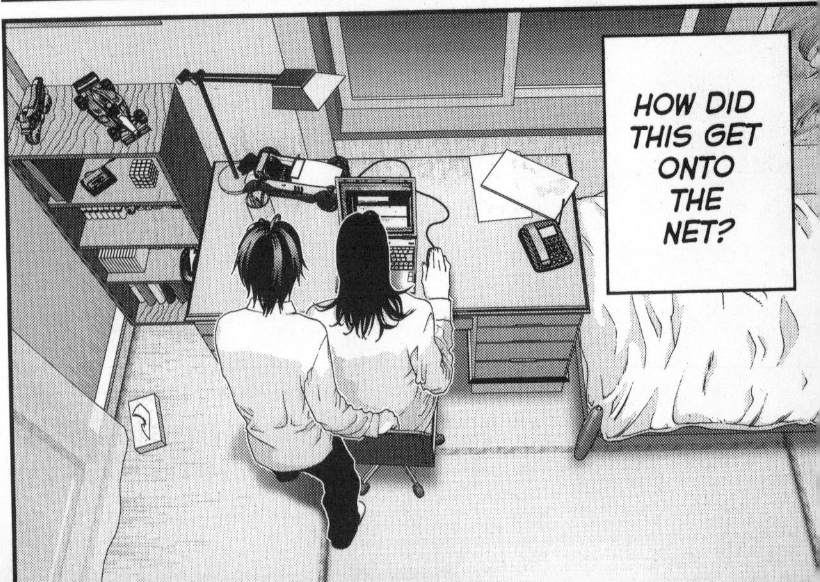
HOW DID THIS GET ONTO THE NET?

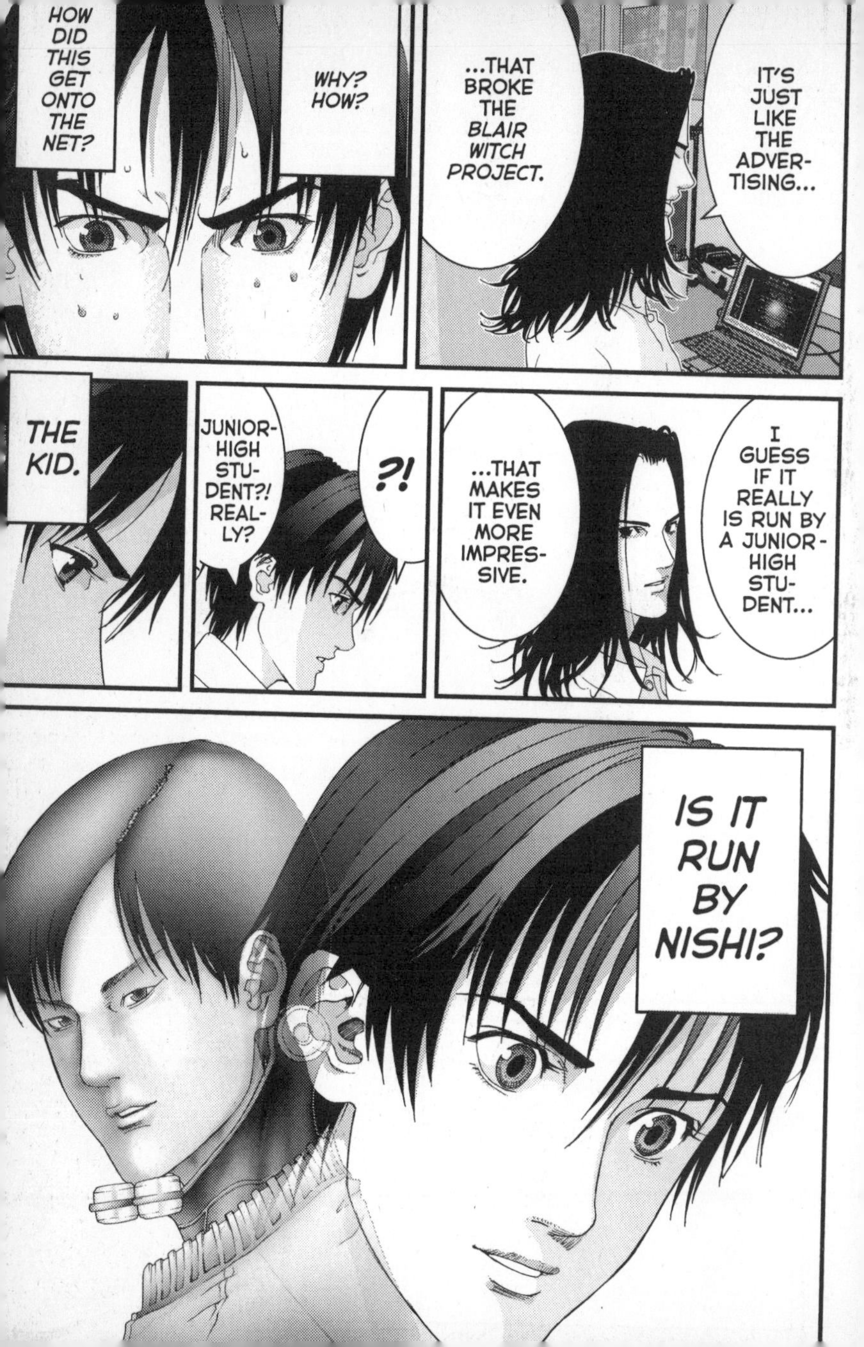
IT'S JUST LIKE THE ADVERTISING...
...THAT BROKE THE BLAIR WITCH PROJECT.
WHY? HOW?
HOW DID THIS GET ONTO THE NET?
I GUESS IF IT REALLY IS RUN BY A JUNIOR-HIGH STUDENT...
...THAT MAKES IT EVEN MORE IMPRESSIVE.
?!
JUNIOR-HIGH STUDENT?! REALLY?
THE KID.
IS IT RUN BY NISHI?

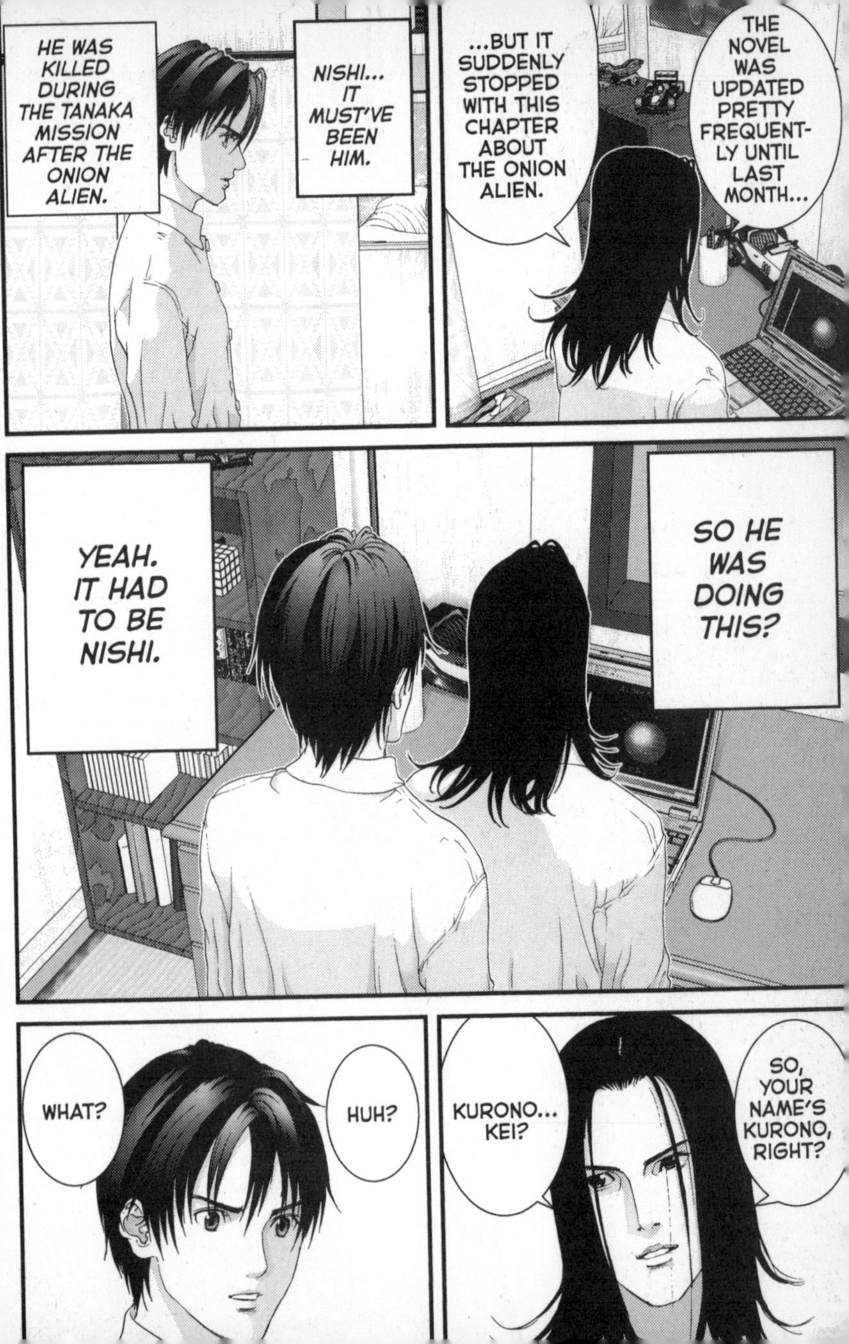
THE NOVEL WAS UPDATED PRETTY FREQUENT-LY UNTIL LAST MONTH...
...BUT IT SUDDENLY STOPPED WITH THIS CHAPTER ABOUT THE ONION ALIEN.
NISHI... IT MUST'VE BEEN HIM.
HE WAS KILLED DURING THE TANAKA MISSION AFTER THE ONION ALIEN.
SO HE WAS DOING THIS?
YEAH. IT HAD TO BE NISHI.
SO, YOUR NAME'S KURONO, RIGHT?
KURONO... KEI?
HUH?
WHAT?

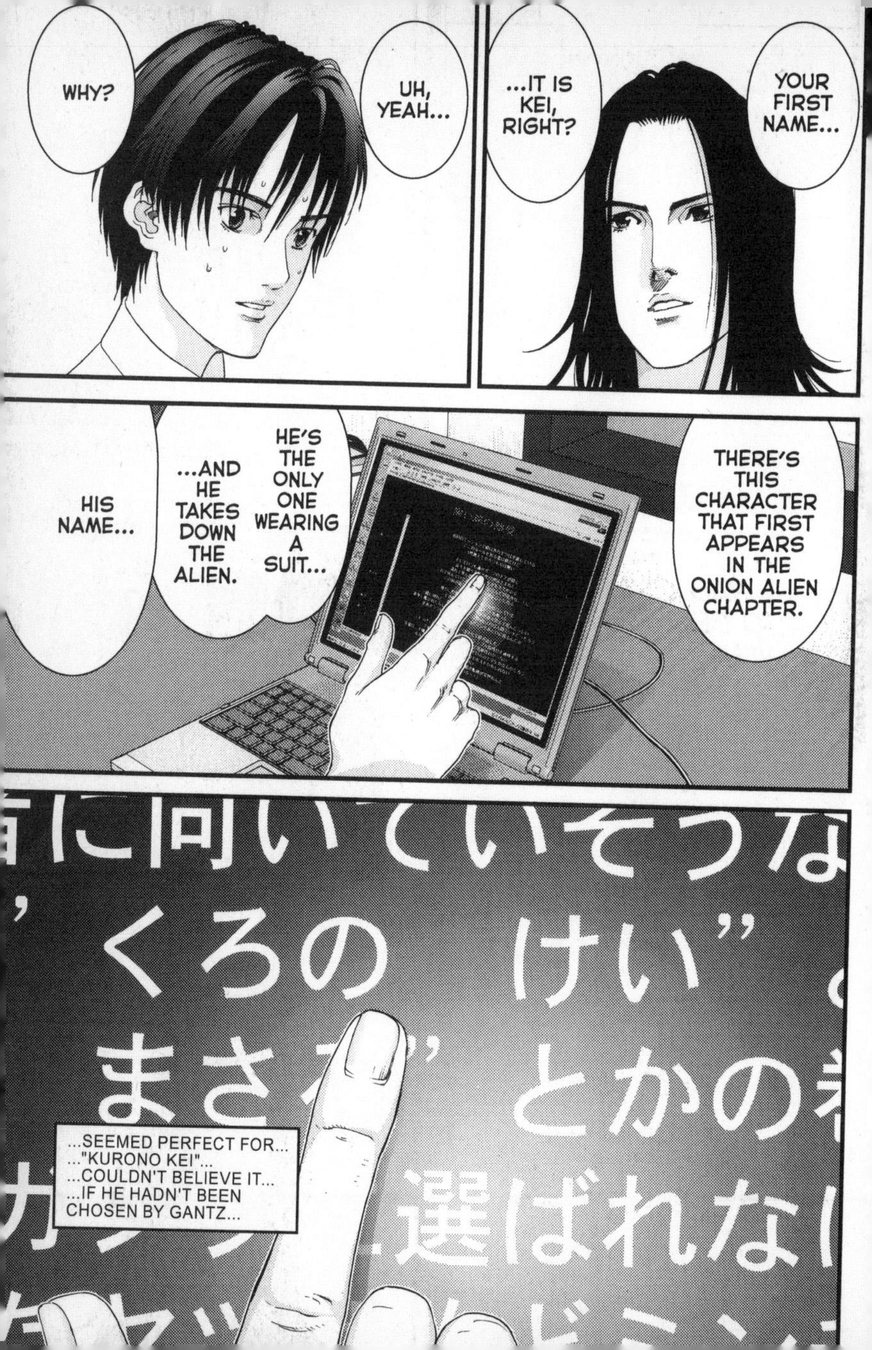
YOUR FIRST NAME...
...IT IS KEI, RIGHT?
UH, YEAH...
WHY?
THERE'S THIS CHARACTER THAT FIRST APPEARS IN THE ONION ALIEN CHAPTER.
HE'S THE ONLY ONE WEARING A SUIT...
...AND HE TAKES DOWN THE ALIEN.
HIS NAME...
に向いていそうな
くろの　けい”
とかの
選ばれな
...SEEMED PERFECT FOR...
..."KURONO KEI"...
...COULDN'T BELIEVE IT...
...IF HE HADN'T BEEN CHOSEN BY GANTZ...

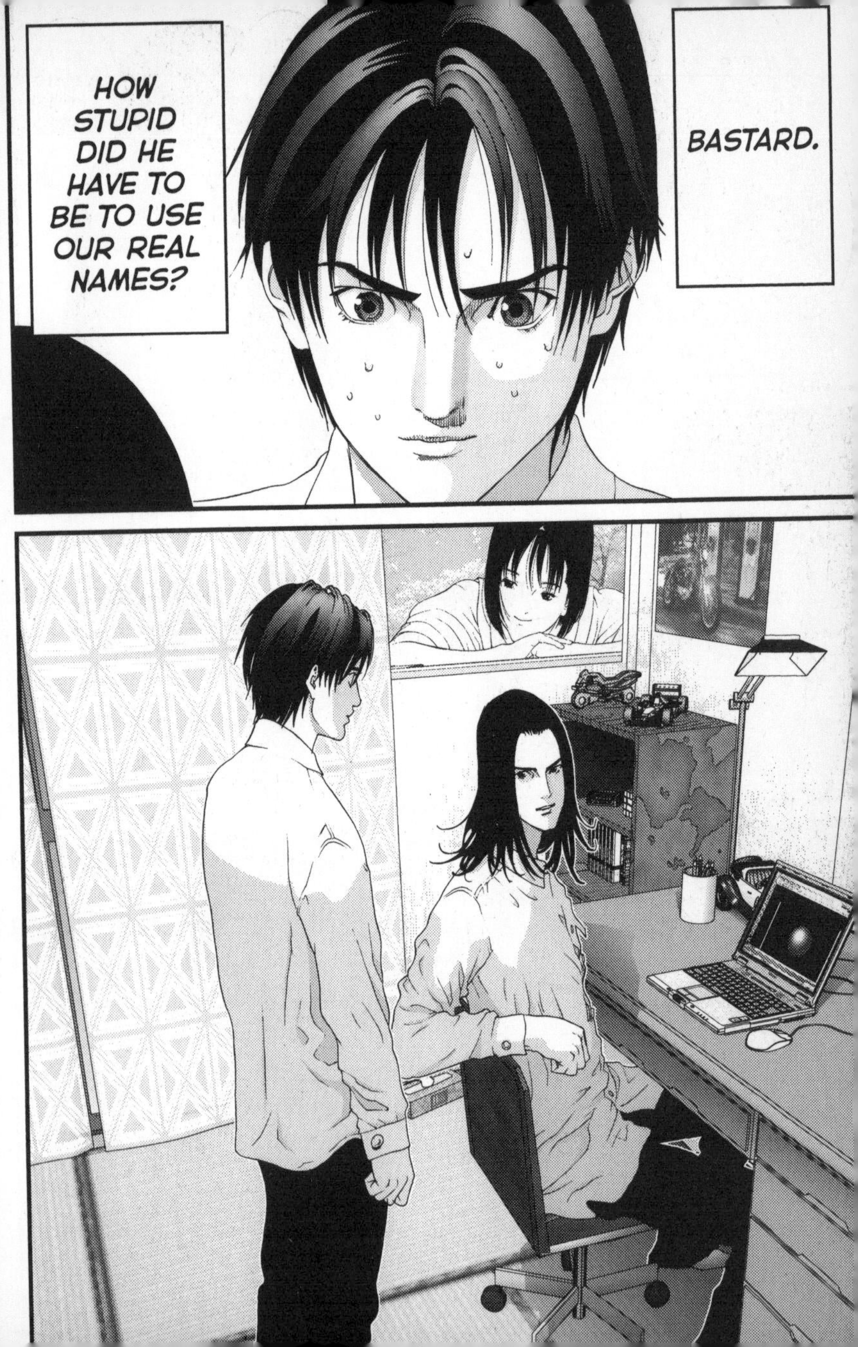
BASTARD.
HOW STUPID DID HE HAVE TO BE TO USE OUR REAL NAMES?

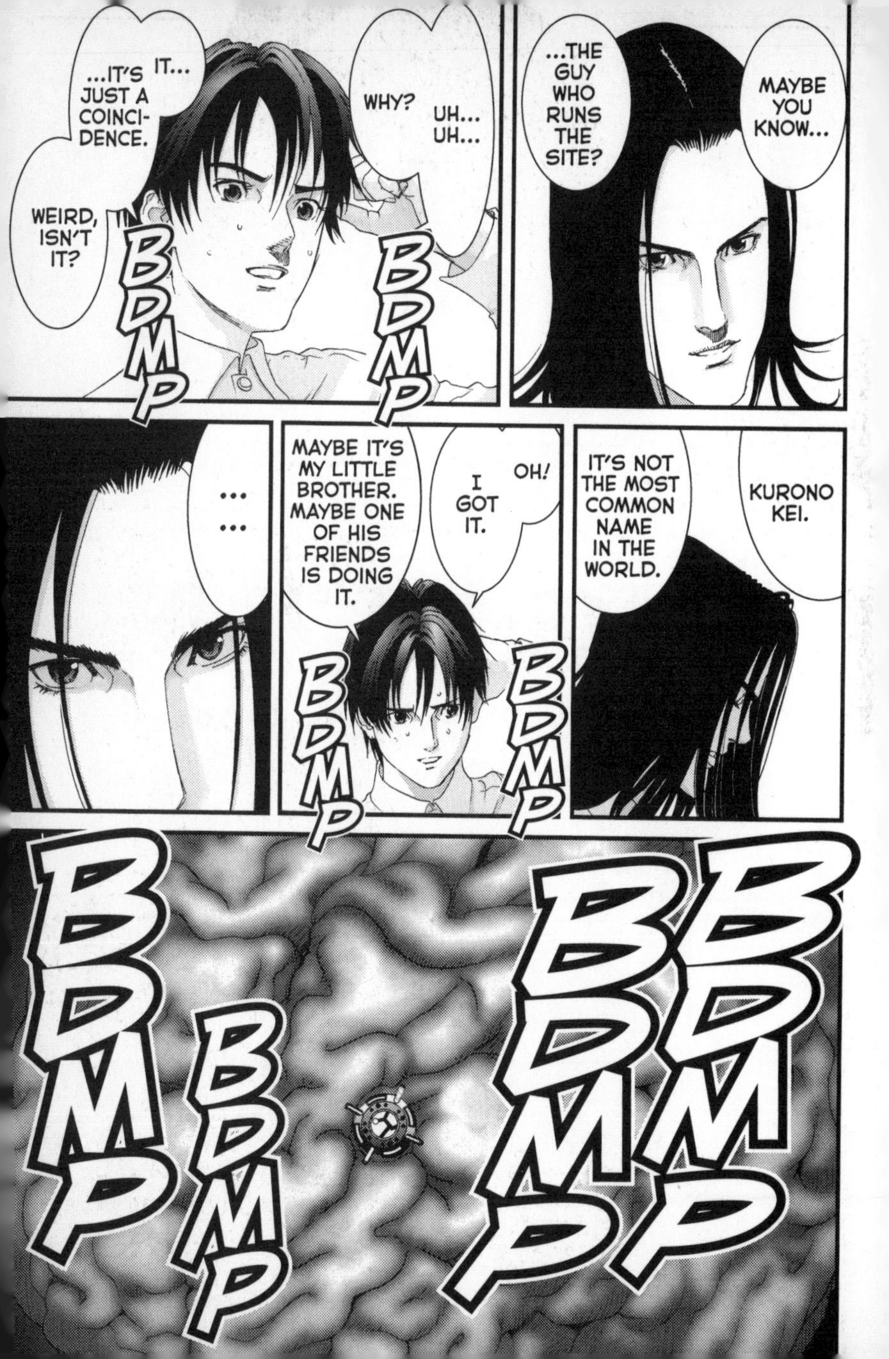
MAYBE YOU KNOW...
...THE GUY WHO RUNS THE SITE?
UH... UH...
WHY?
BDMP
IT...
...IT'S JUST A COINCIDENCE.
WEIRD, ISN'T IT?
BDMP
KURONO KEI.
IT'S NOT THE MOST COMMON NAME IN THE WORLD.
OH!
I GOT IT.
MAYBE IT'S MY LITTLE BROTHER. MAYBE ONE OF HIS FRIENDS IS DOING IT.
BDMP
BDMP
... ...
BDMP
BDMP
BDMP
BDMP

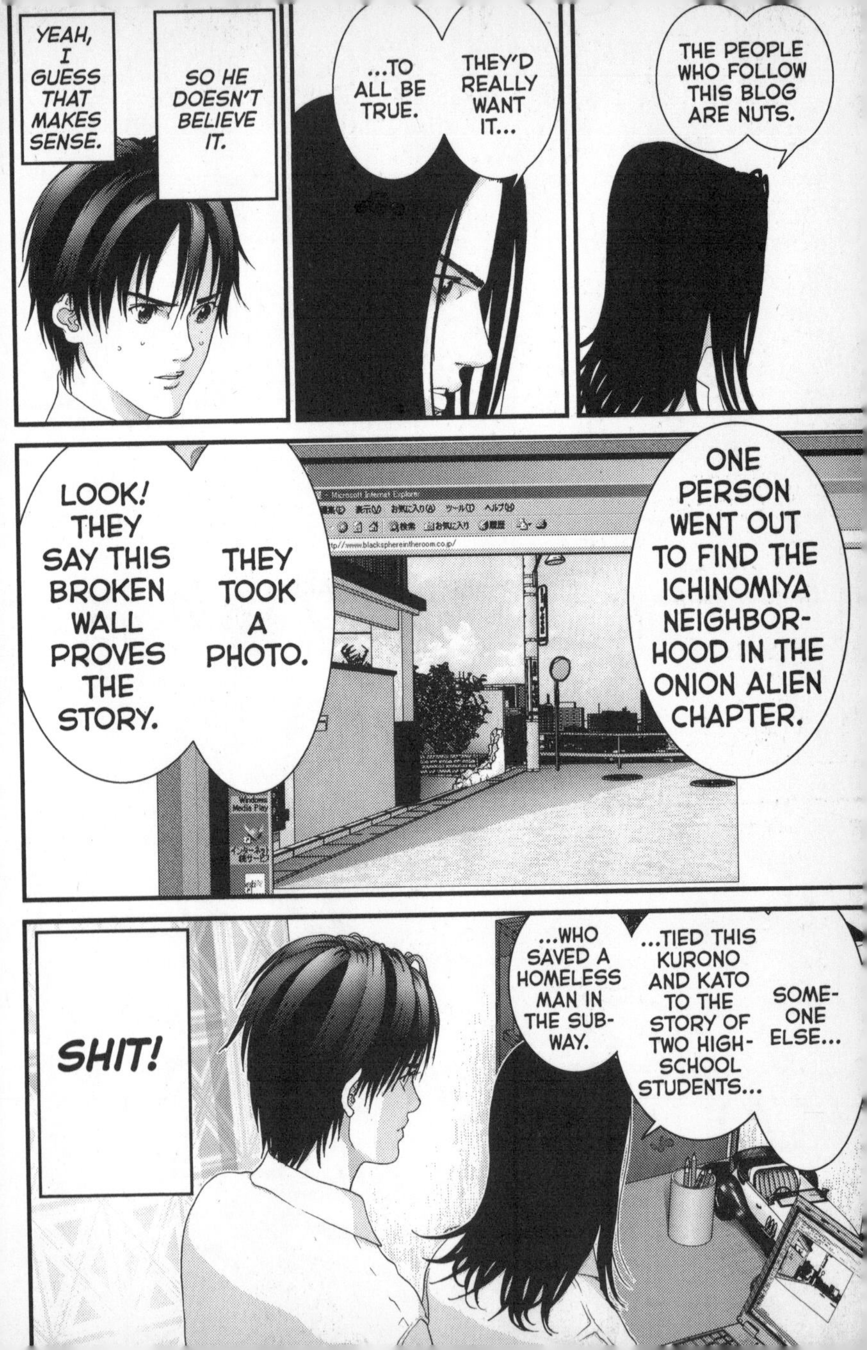

THE PEOPLE WHO FOLLOW THIS BLOG ARE NUTS.
THEY'D REALLY WANT IT...
...TO ALL BE TRUE.
SO HE DOESN'T BELIEVE IT.
YEAH, I GUESS THAT MAKES SENSE.
ONE PERSON WENT OUT TO FIND THE ICHINOMIYA NEIGHBOR-HOOD IN THE ONION ALIEN CHAPTER.
THEY TOOK A PHOTO.
LOOK! THEY SAY THIS BROKEN WALL PROVES THE STORY.
SOME-ONE ELSE...
...TIED THIS KURONO AND KATO TO THE STORY OF TWO HIGH-SCHOOL STUDENTS...
...WHO SAVED A HOMELESS MAN IN THE SUB-WAY.
SHIT!

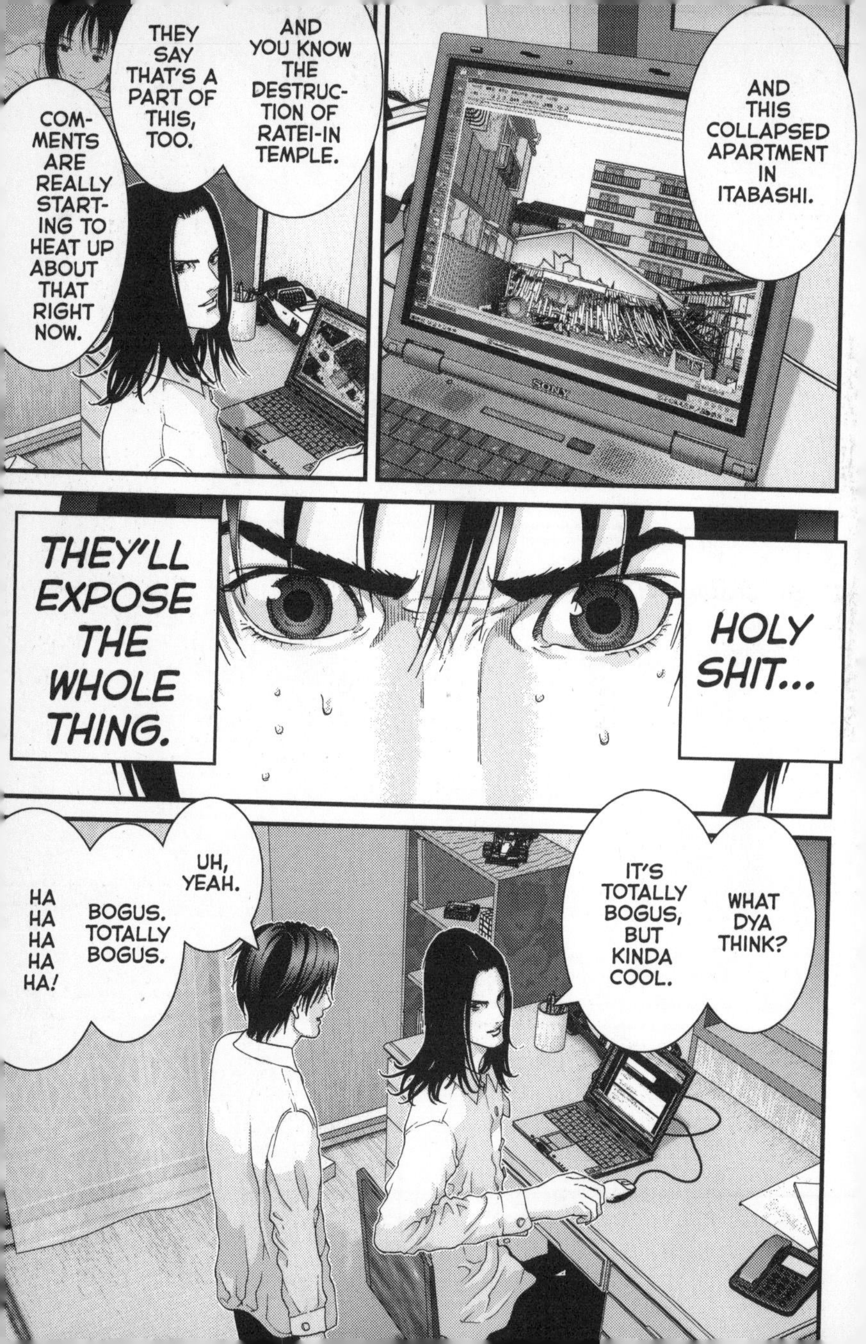
AND THIS COLLAPSED APARTMENT IN ITABASHI.
AND YOU KNOW THE DESTRUCTION OF RATEI-IN TEMPLE.
THEY SAY THAT'S A PART OF THIS, TOO.
COMMENTS ARE REALLY STARTING TO HEAT UP ABOUT THAT RIGHT NOW.
HOLY SHIT...
THEY'LL EXPOSE THE WHOLE THING.
WHAT DYA THINK?
IT'S TOTALLY BOGUS, BUT KINDA COOL.
UH, YEAH.
BOGUS. TOTALLY BOGUS.
HA HA HA HA HA HA!

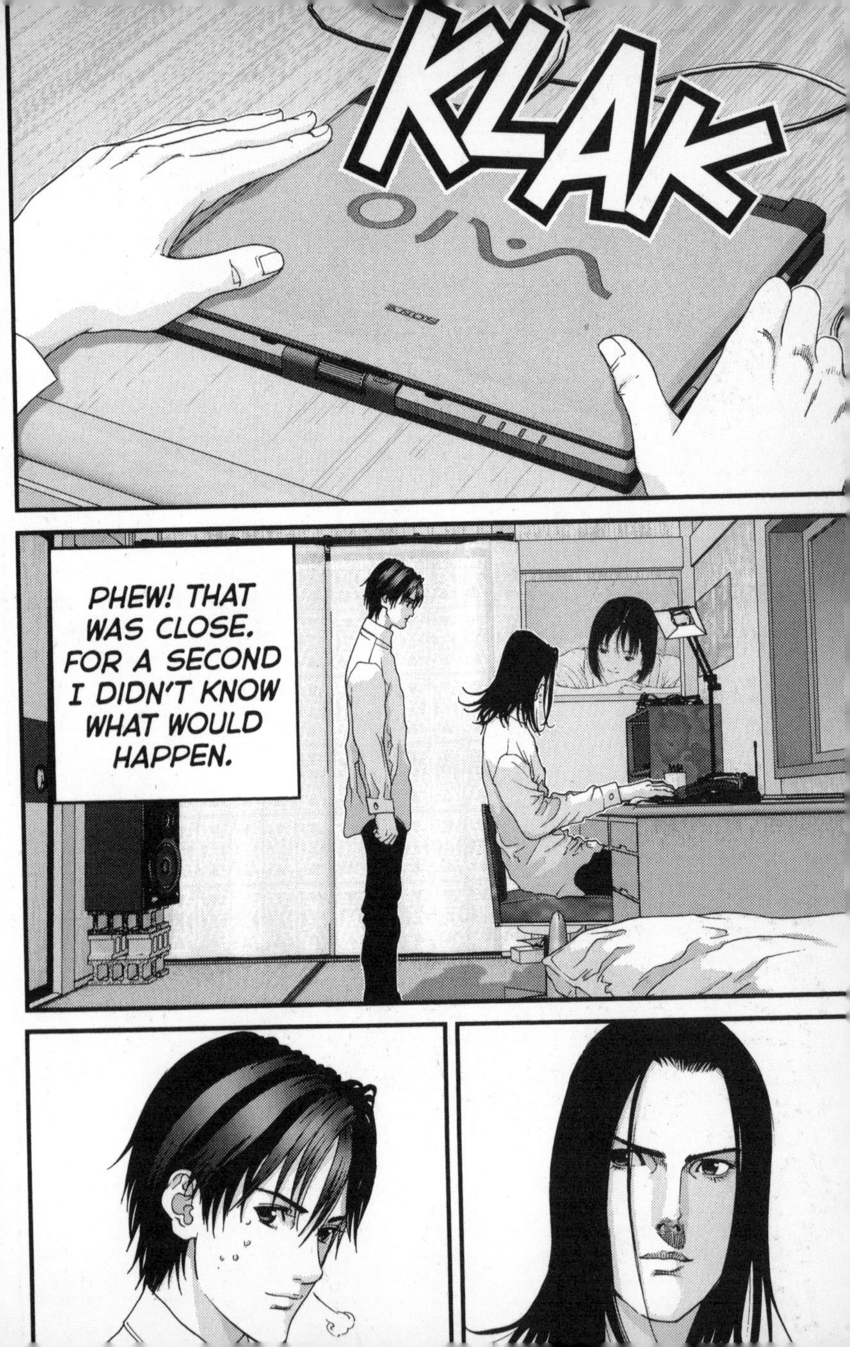
KLAK
PHEW! THAT WAS CLOSE. FOR A SECOND I DIDN'T KNOW WHAT WOULD HAPPEN.

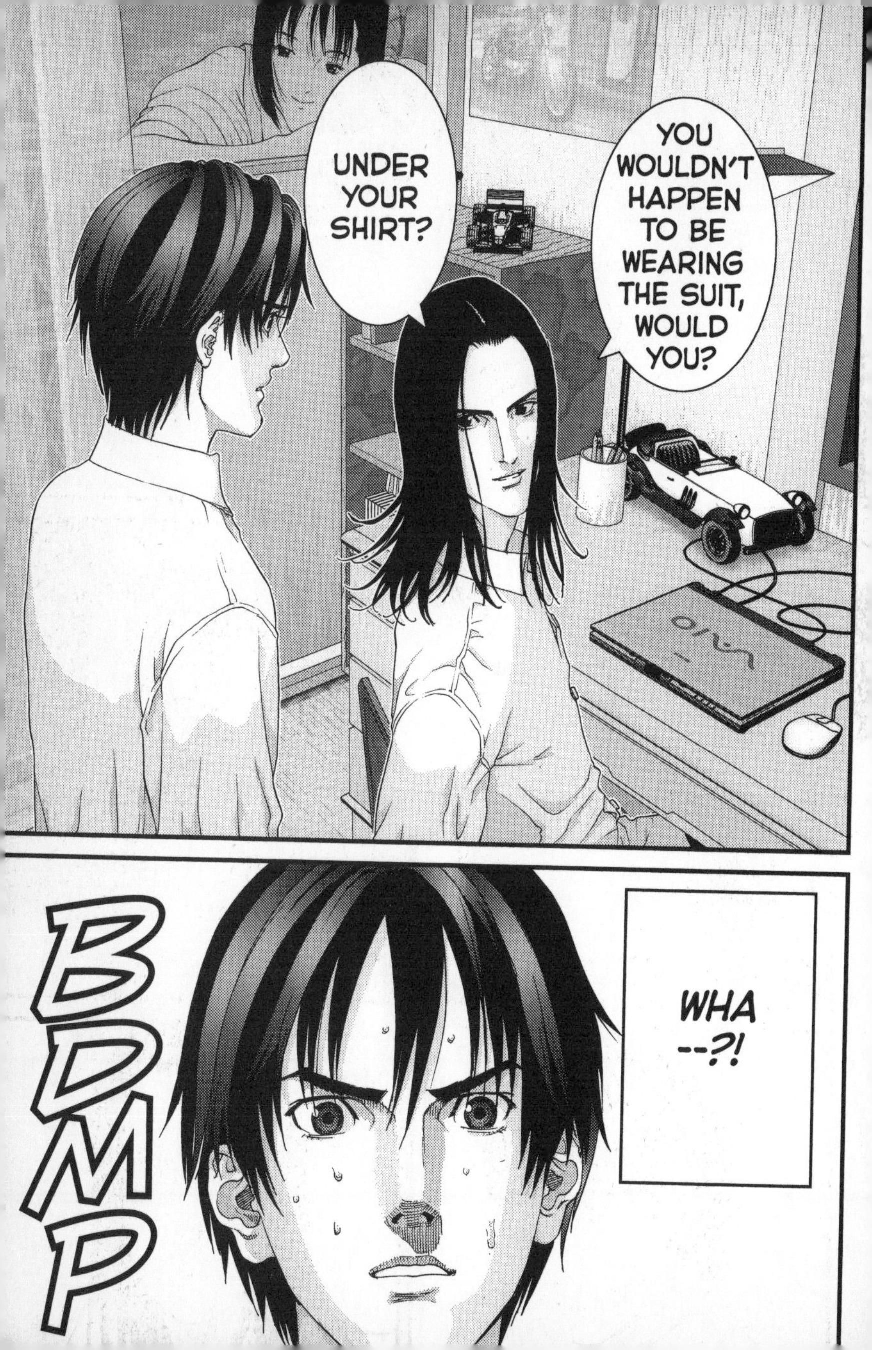
YOU WOULDN'T HAPPEN TO BE WEARING THE SUIT, WOULD YOU?
UNDER YOUR SHIRT?
WHA --?!
BDMP

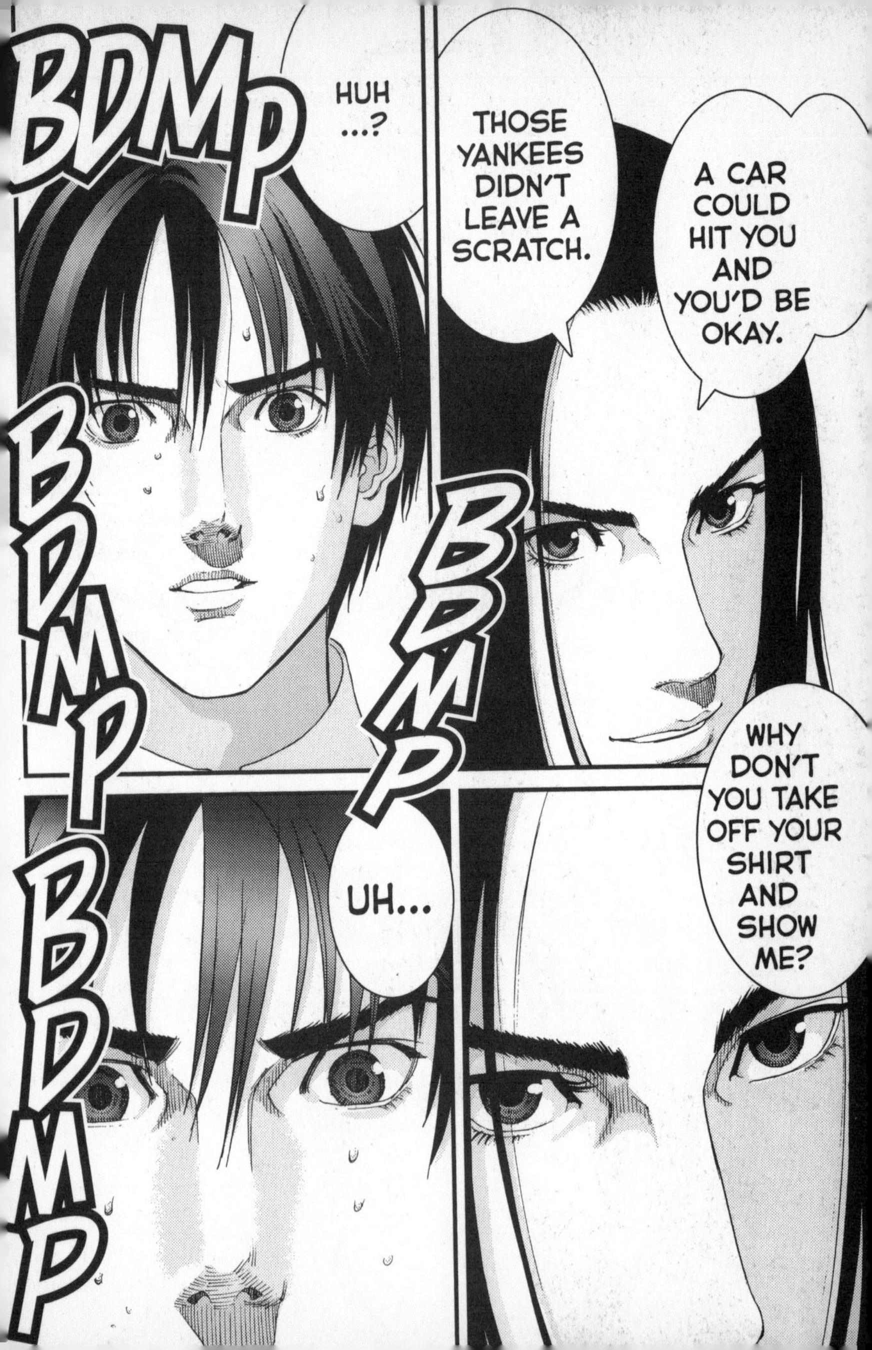
THOSE YANKEES DIDN'T LEAVE A SCRATCH.
A CAR COULD HIT YOU AND YOU'D BE OKAY.
BDMP
HUH ...?
BDMP
WHY DON'T YOU TAKE OFF YOUR SHIRT AND SHOW ME?
UH...
BDMP
BDMP

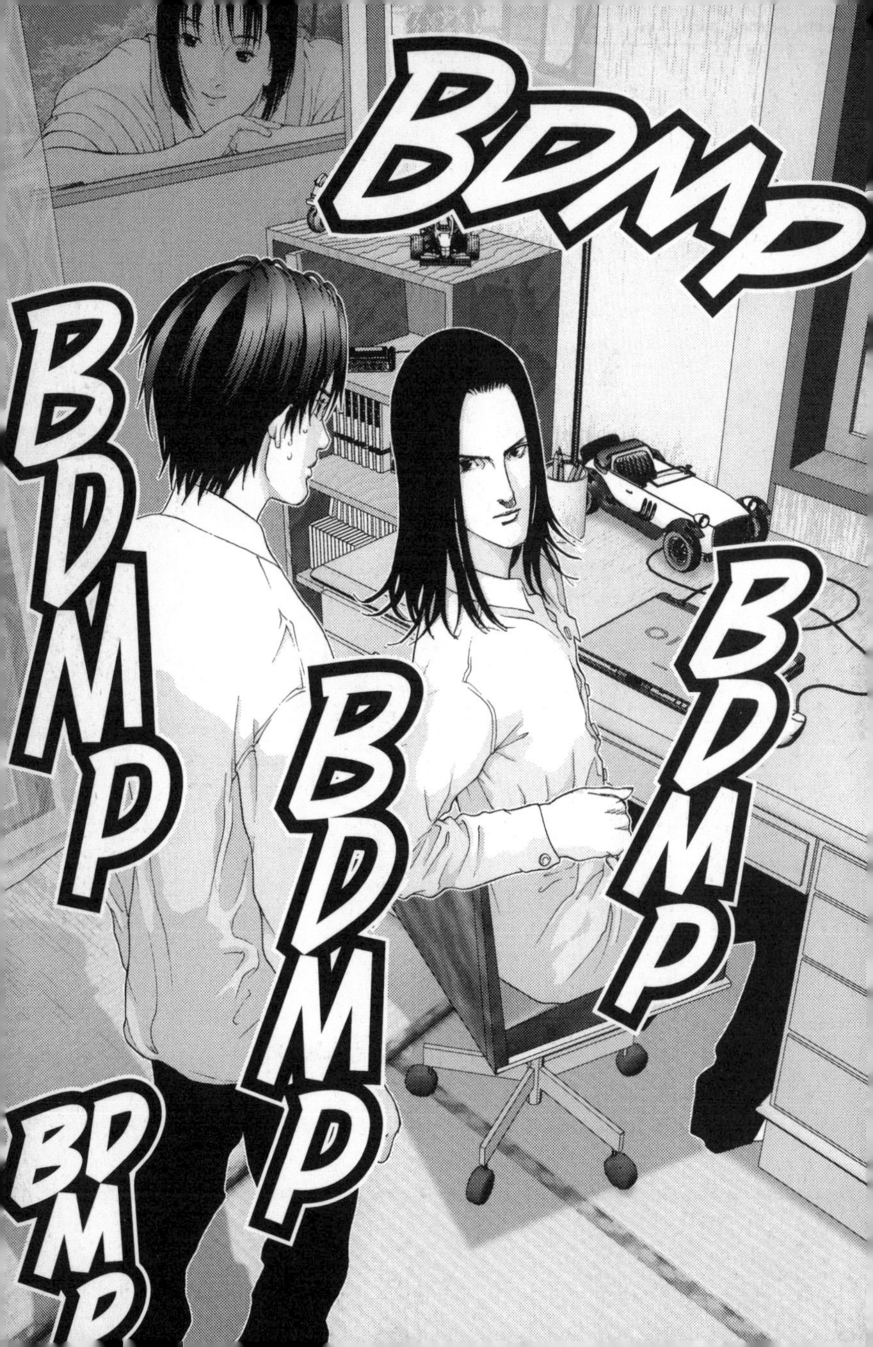
BDMP
BDMP
BDMP
BDMP
BDMP

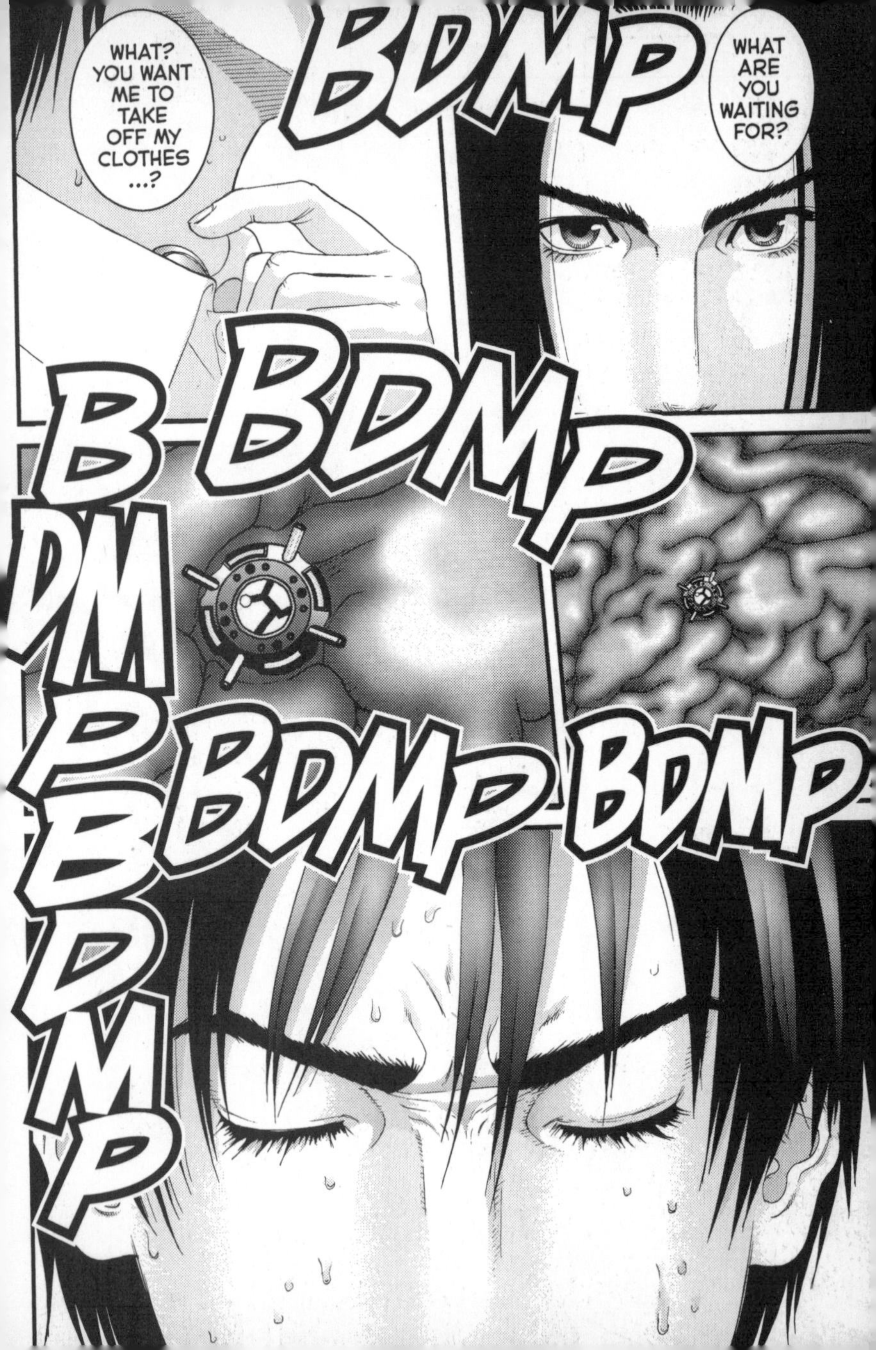
WHAT ARE YOU WAITING FOR?
BDMP
WHAT? YOU WANT ME TO TAKE OFF MY CLOTHES ...?
B-BDMP
BDMP BDMP
BDMP
BDMP BDMP

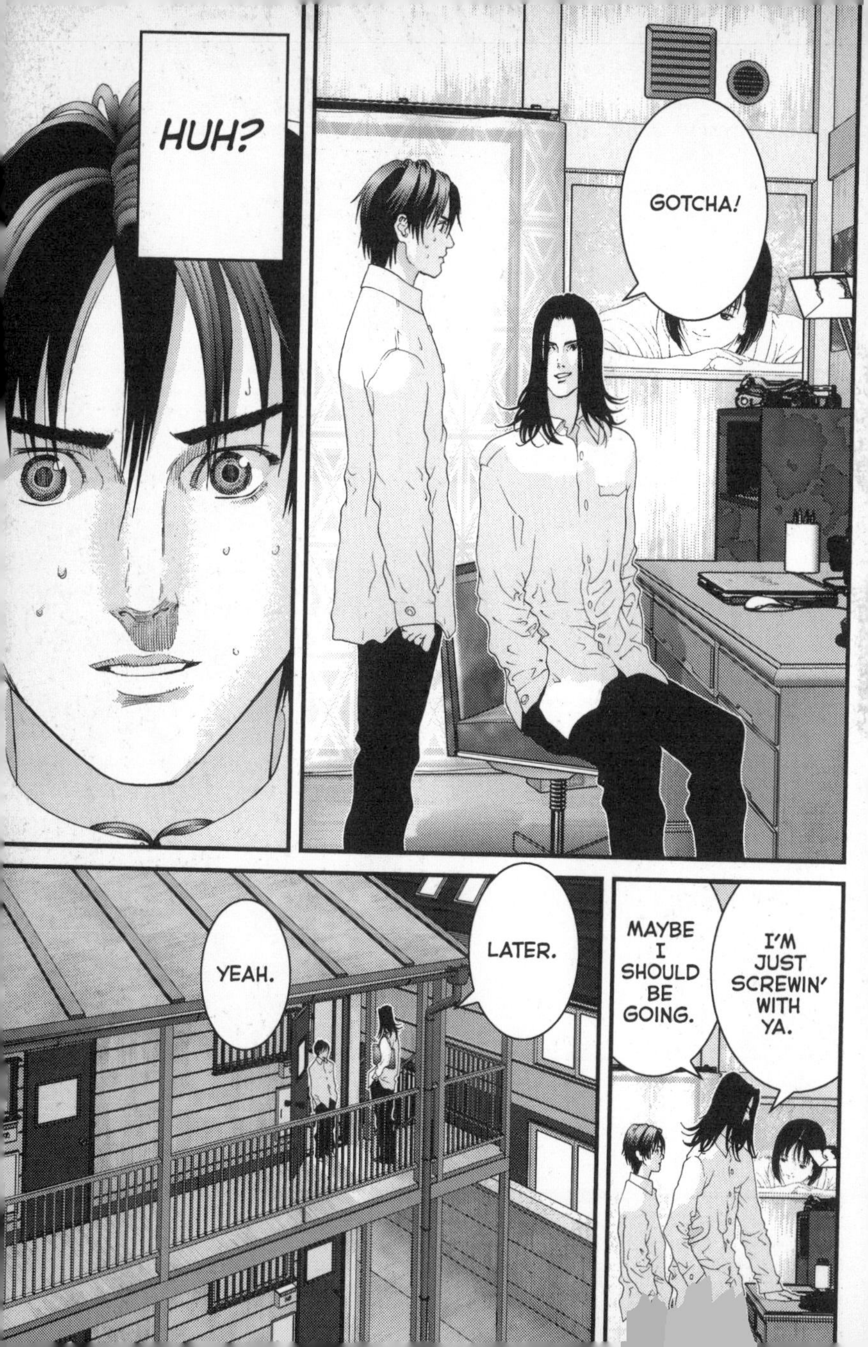
GOTCHA!
HUH?
I'M JUST SCREWIN' WITH YA.
MAYBE I SHOULD BE GOING.
LATER.
YEAH.

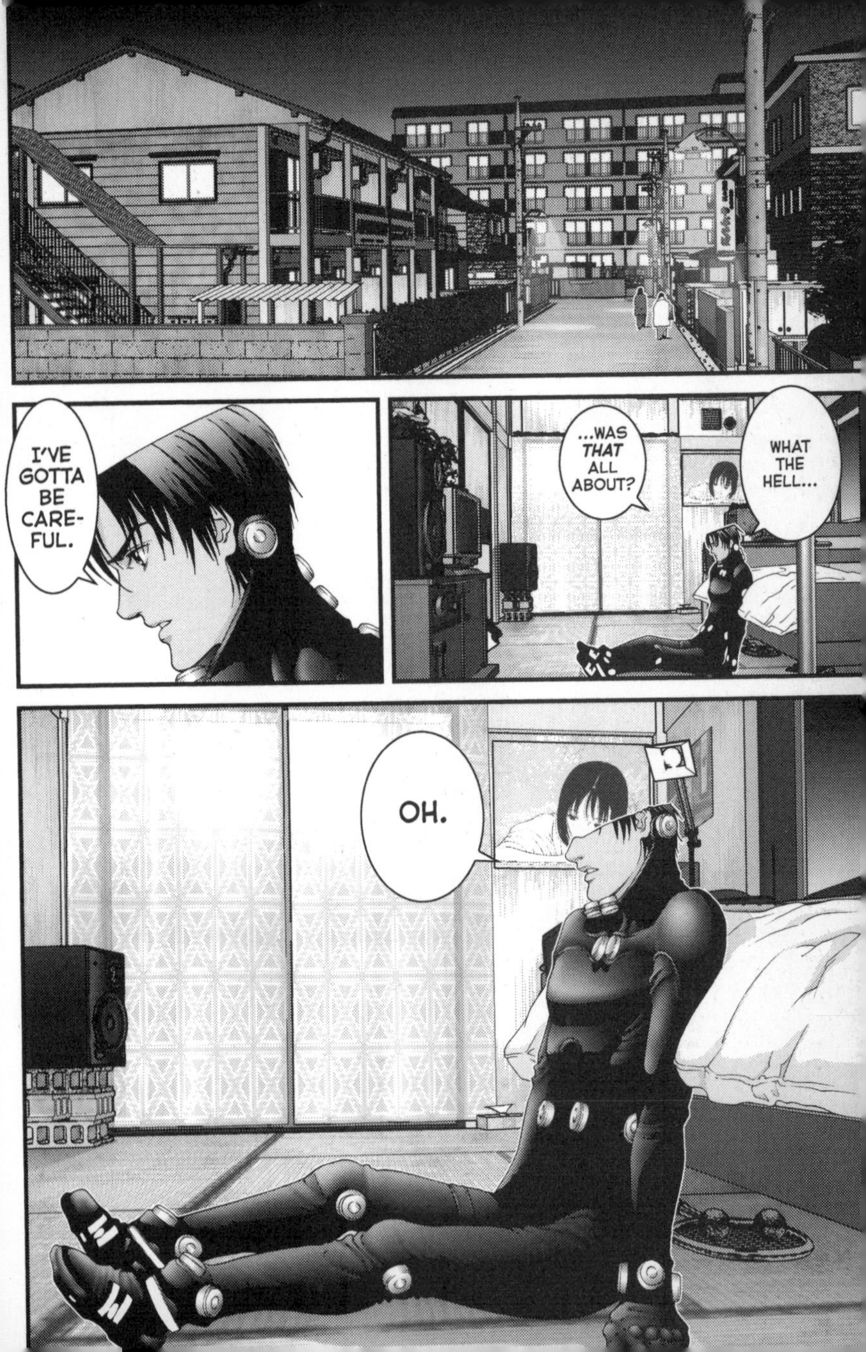
WHAT THE HELL...
...WAS THAT ALL ABOUT?
I'VE GOTTA BE CARE-FUL.
OH.

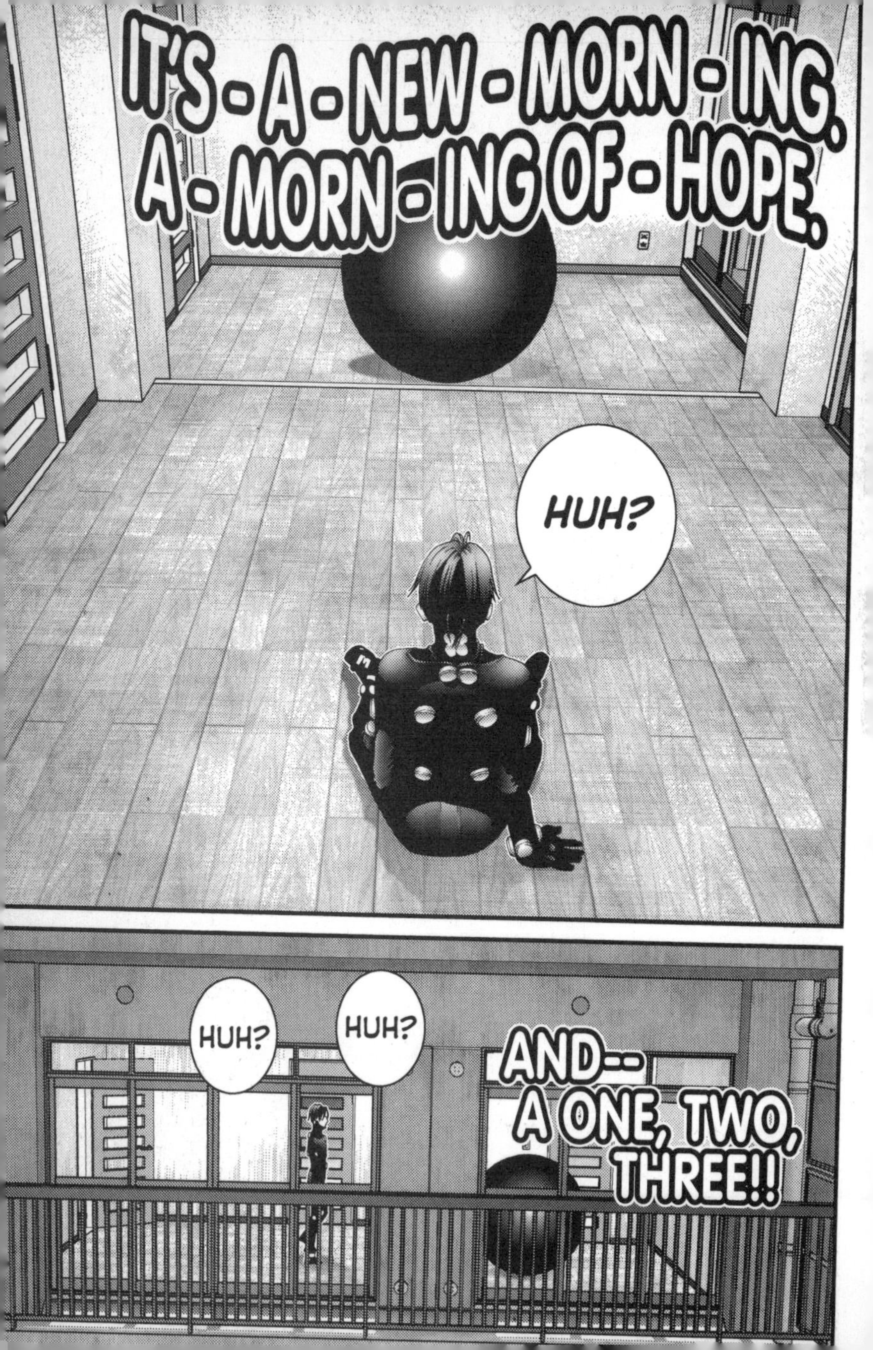
IT'S - A - NEW - MORN - ING.
A - MORN - ING OF - HOPE.
HUH?
HUH?
HUH?
AND--
A ONE, TWO, THREE!!

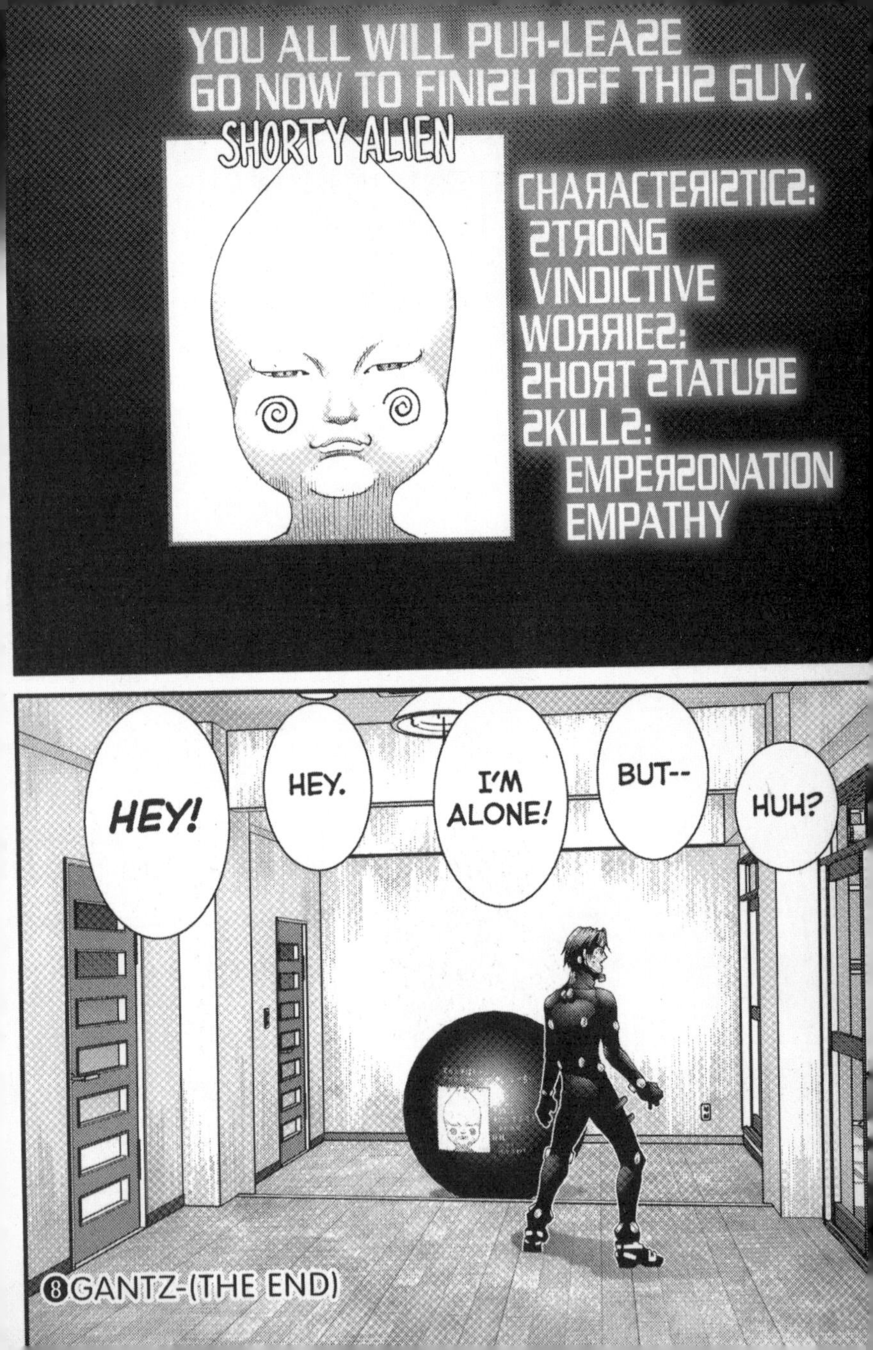
YOU ALL WILL PUH-LEASE
GO NOW TO FINISH OFF THIS GUY.
SHORTY ALIEN
CHARACTERISTICS:
STRONG
VINDICTIVE
WORRIES:
SHORT STATURE
SKILLS:
EMPERSONATION
EMPATHY
HUH?
BUT--
I'M ALONE!
HEY.
HEY!
8 GANTZ-(THE END)

Oku made it clear in the special digest issue of *Gantz* that went on sale in December that he doesn't like "cat ears."*

"I don't like the shape or the idea behind them and I have a thing against those who say things like 'cat-ear moe' and women who wear them for cosplay." Obviously, this anti-cat-ear sentiment runs pretty deep (even if there's no real reason for it). He even came up with an idea to put them on an alien that gets killed right away (although this ended up being just silly talk while drinking). That gave us the idea of putting a drawing of a cat-ear character in front of him and giving him two minutes to come up with this cat-ear alien. So, in a way, here's *Gantz*'s newest character—your first look at this mythical alien!

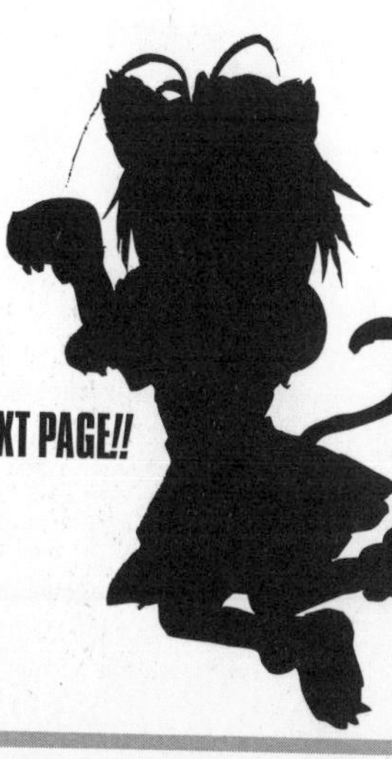

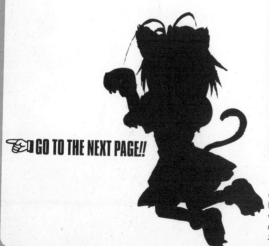

GO TO THE NEXT PAGE!!

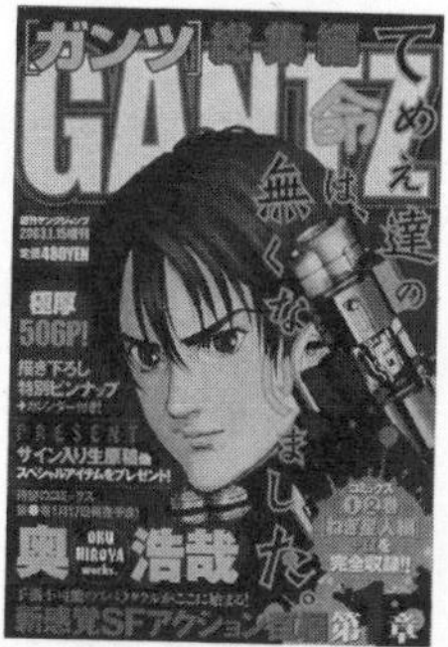

ガンツ
GANTZ
奥 浩哉
OKU HIROYA

Everyone's bought it by now, right?
GANTZ SPECIAL DIGEST ISSUE!

*Cat ears . . . we're not talking about the actual ears on a cat. It's the cat version of the women with bunny ears. Said to originate in Oshima Yumiko's *The Star of Cottonland*.

WILL YOU PLEASE ALL GO NOW AND SLAUGHTER THIS GUY.

CHARACTERISTICS

COMES IN A SET WITH CAT HANDS AND CAT FEET MOE . . .

LIKES

TORANOANA

(TRANSLATOR'S NOTE: A FAMOUS MANGA STORE)

CATCH PHRASE

MEEEOW

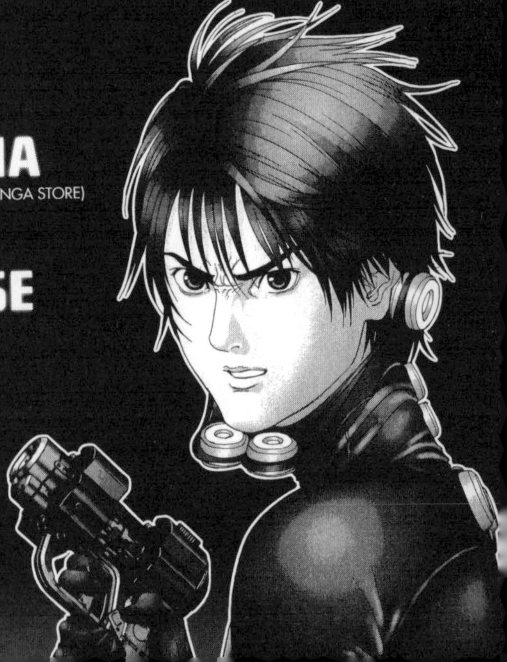

A WEEK AT OKU HIROYA'S STUDIO 奥浩哉スタジオの一週間

日 SUNDAY	Think of names
月 MONDAY	Create names, create backgrounds on computer
火 TUESDAY	Create backgrounds on computer
水 WEDNESDAY	Rough drafts, pen drawings
木 THURSDAY	Rough drafts, pen drawings
金 FRIDAY	Combine pen drawings of characters with backgrounds
土 SATURDAY	Complete! Satisfaction of job well done

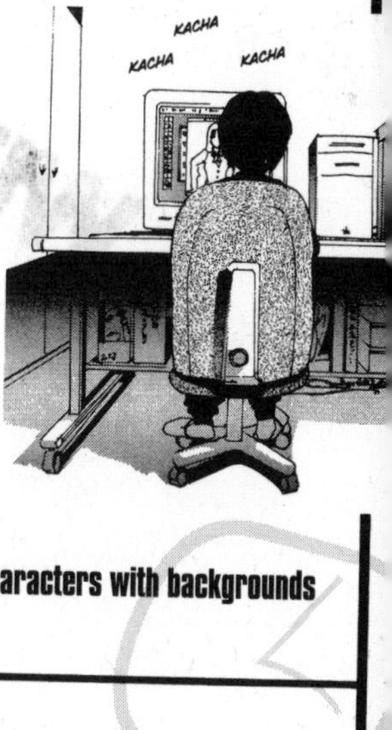
KACHA
KACHA
KACHA

The week is filled with routine work like this. Plus, before any new plots are hatched, 3-D CG of a temple or school have to be created, and if anything bogs the work down, it won't make it on time to get published that week. It's not like I'm goofing off or anything . . .

translation MATTHEW JOHNSON

lettering and retouch STUDIO CUTIE

publisher MIKE RICHARDSON

editor TIM ERVIN

book design SCOTT COOK

Published by Dark Horse Comics, Inc., in association with Shueisha, Inc.

Dark Horse Manga
A division of Dark Horse Comics, Inc.
10956 SE Main Street
Milwaukie, OR

First Dark Horse edition: September 2009
ISBN 978-1-59582-383-0

1 3 5 7 9 10 8 6 4 2

Printed in Canada

GANTZ

[ガンツ]

8

To find a comics 266-4226.

MIKE RICHARDSON P   A WEDDLE Chief
Financial Officer • RANDY STRADLEY Vice President of   sident of Business
Development • ANITA NELSON Vice President of Marketing, Sales, and Licensing • DAVID SCROGGY Vice President of Product Development • DALE LAFOUNTAIN Vice President of Information Technology • DARLENE VOGEL Director of Purchasing • KEN LIZZI General Counsel • DAVEY ESTRADA Editorial Director • SCOTT ALLIE Senior Managing Editor • CHRIS WARNER Senior Books Editor • DIANA SCHUTZ Executive Editor • CARY GRAZZINI Director of Design and Production • LIA RIBACCHI Art Director • CARA NIECE Director of Scheduling